THE ARCHITECTURE OF BALTIMORE

EDITED BY

MARY ELLEN HAYWARD AND
FRANK R. SHIVERS, JR.

THE ARCHITECTURE OF BALTIMORE

AN ILLUSTRATED HISTORY

WITH A FOREWORD BY Richard Hubbard Howland

CONTRIBUTIONS FROM
Robert L. Alexander
Robert J. Brugger
John Dorsey
Charles B. Duff, Jr.
Edward Gunts
Herbert H. Harwood, Jr.
Phoebe B. Stanton
Christopher Weeks

Merry Christmas to Bob and Cynthia, from the family's newest published author.

Charlie

2004

THE JOHNS HOPKINS UNIVERSITY PRESS | BALTIMORE AND LONDON

In Association with the Baltimore Architecture Foundation and the Maryland Historical Society

With the Cooperation of the Baltimore Museum of Art, the Enoch Pratt Free Library, the Baltimore Museum of Industry, the B&O Railroad Museum, and the Jewish Museum of Maryland

*This book has been brought to publication with the generous
assistance of Furthermore, a program of the J. M. Kaplan Fund,
and the Mercantile-Safe Deposit and Trust Company.*

The Johns Hopkins University Press

2715 North Charles Street

Baltimore, Maryland 21218-4363

www.press.jhu.edu

Library of Congress Cataloging-in-Publication Data

The architecture of Baltimore : an illustrated history / edited by Mary Ellen Hayward and
Frank R. Shivers Jr. ; with a foreword by Richard Hubbard Howland and contributions
from Robert L. Alexander et al.

    p.   cm.

Includes bibliographical references and index.

ISBN 0-8018-7806-3 (hardcover : alk. paper)

1. Architecture—Maryland—Baltimore. 2. Architecture, Domestic—Maryland—
Baltimore. 3. Historic buildings—Maryland—Baltimore. 4. Baltimore (Md.)—Buildings,
structures, etc. I. Hayward, Mary Ellen. II. Shivers, Frank R., 1924–

NA735.B3A73 2003

920′.9752′6—DC21   2003006811

A catalog record for this book is available from the British Library.

CONTENTS

FOREWORD

IN THE EARLY 1950S, both Eleanor Spencer and I were transplanted to Baltimore from New England to similar teaching careers in the Departments of the History of Art, at Goucher College and the Johns Hopkins University, respectively. As new arrivals we soon became aware of Baltimore's architectural past and present, and in 1953 we published *The Architecture of Baltimore*. We were inspired not only by the remarkable character of the city and its buildings but also by what we had learned from earlier studies—we were guided by the work of John H. Scarff, Laurence Hall Fowler, and J. Gilman d'Arcy Paul—and helped by the research of our students, notably, Claire Eckels, Robert Alexander, and Bennard Perlman. We also relied upon the magnificent resources of the George Peabody Library, the Enoch Pratt Free Library, the Maryland Historical Society, and the Peale Museum.

In the preface Wilbur Harvey Hunter, then director of the Peale Museum, who was himself conducting pioneering work on Baltimore and its buildings, called our book a step taken toward a fuller understanding and appreciation of Baltimore's architectural heritage. Over the years a sizeable number of scholarly studies of Baltimore's architectural and urban heritage followed. This new book collects past and recent research and points the way toward further studies.

In *The Architecture of Baltimore* we recorded the architectural treasures and achievements in the area before World War I, but we hoped also to encourage the growth in Baltimore of the emerging movement known as historic preservation, which had begun with the work of the Pilgrim Society in Massachusetts, the Mount Vernon Ladies Association in Virginia, and similar local groups, along with projects the federal government sponsored in the 1930s and 1940s. In the cause of the history of Baltimore architecture, the Municipal Art Society and Douglas Huntley Gordon were prime movers.

In the fifty years since our book was published, historic preservation has been legally mandated at national, state, and local levels. We may be thankful for the change. Henry-Russell Hitchcock, the noted architectural historian, observed that the architectural integrity of our cities depends not only on the preservation of a few certified "masterpieces" but on the retention of the "general visual texture," a comment singularly applicable to Baltimore. He also perceived that Baltimore's interest in the city and its buildings was "pious and familial."

This new volume continues the work of our earlier study, focusing attention on a wider variety of architectural types and neighborhoods, a broader sweep of the history of Baltimore building and development, and on recent changes brought about by city planning and architectural design. It presents the latest research of both established scholars who are among the national authorities in their fields and younger architectural historians who, as they continue the tradition of "pious and familial" concern, have been conducting research into the history of previously unrecognized areas of Baltimore's architectural fabric.

RICHARD HUBBARD HOWLAND

INTRODUCTION

BALTIMOREANS LOVE THEIR CITY in large part because of its architecture—its built environment, as students of the subject say—and because so much of it recalls the city's history.

That story, of course, began with geography and economy, typifying American experience. Unlike European cities, many of which developed at places with an antecedent urban history that stretched back to Roman times and even beyond, American cities came into being in the eighteenth and early nineteenth centuries, acquiring their identities because of physical properties that encouraged trade or industry—a river, a port, or other natural resources—and because they served the economy of a larger geographical area. Baltimore had no discernible history before the growth of its harbor; the wealth of the city in money and people flowed directly from the expansion of commerce at the end of the eighteenth century and the sustained growth of related industry through the nineteenth. Workers and dwellings swelled the community; between the period of the Revolution and the outbreak of the Civil War, Baltimore grew from little more than a cluster of villages to a small town and then, suddenly, to one of the largest cities in the English-speaking world of the day.

As with all cities, Baltimore's shape, density, and physical form at various periods ultimately depended on how people could move about—how and where they made their living and bought or bartered for essentials. The increasing speed and efficiency of public transport, the impact of the automobile and the construction of highways—all products of the Industrial Revolution—caused cities to expand. Enhanced mobility meant that citizens who could escape crowded living conditions did so, and in time, inner cities tended (there being exceptions) to house the less prosperous. Cities that matured in the mobile world of public transport and the automobile—Detroit, Los Angeles, and Houston, for example—were, from the outset, geographically and physically bigger and thinner on the ground than, for example, Manhattan, whose character and density were thrust upon it by the limitation of its site. Older cities, like Baltimore, were destined to become one center among many where people lived, worked, and shopped. After two world wars and various economic shifts, Baltimore has gradually become part of an almost continuous urban community stretching from Northern Virginia through New York City.

Conceding that Americans always take lessons from European styles and examples, some historians find in Baltimore a conservative inclination, an attitude that has produced a subtle rather than a dramatic city. Baltimore by and large has been content to follow rather than set architectural taste. Its patrons of architecture have from time to time preferred cosmopolitan styles; rarely have they indulged in stylistic hyperbole, and the architects who served them have accommodated their taste.

Be that as it may, natives and many newcomers delight in the truth that, architecturally (except in it dullest twentieth-century portions), Baltimore is not a "typical American city." It has retained more home-grown character than many East Coast cities. Because it reflects reserved taste, one must seek out its architectural distinction. Many important buildings figure prominently in biographies of leading American architects, from Latrobe, Robert Mills, and Maximilien Godefroy to Richard Upjohn, Stanford White, and Ludwig Mies van der Rohe. Without the local work of these masters, the Baltimore architectural scene would lack accents. But the predominantly nineteenth-century texture of Baltimore owes even more to the achievements of Baltimore's own architects, not to speak of the anonymous craftsmen and builders who established and long maintained a distinguished tradition of what the English call terrace design for houses. Probably in few American cities could one so immediately locate oneself if led, blindfolded, into minor streets. Despite the devastation caused by fires and by haphazard twentieth-century redevelopment, Baltimore, in the mind's eye, can balance such a major international monument of neoclassicism as Latrobe's Roman Catholic cathedral with street after street of neat houses whose brick captures every possible shade of red. The way these rows bind themselves together—white cornices at the top and recurrent white marble steps, all once so immaculately scrubbed—is even more peculiarly Baltimorean. Tending to the practical and understated, Baltimore architecture rewards the close look.

Seeking to characterize the city and the buildings that have formed it, these essays make an effort to place Baltimore structures in context, to describe the contemporary styles and manners they illustrated. Contributors have also been mindful of the subdued singularity that has made and still makes buildings in this city elegantly expressive of Baltimore itself. That is, one must develop an appreciation of built Baltimore if one is to define and understand what makes the city such a treasure.

As the visual evidence in this book makes clear, much has been lost that was worth preserving—indeed, some unique buildings have come down during preparation of this study. To record is not to save, but it is easier to save what someone has sympathetically recorded. The editors and contributors earnestly hope that readers will finish these pages with an increased respect for what remains, that this book will make Baltimoreans more aware of their architectural heritage. This volume may also help to demonstrate that the architectural integrity of our cities does not depend on the preservation and maintenance of a few certified "masterpieces." The retention of the general visual texture of the city is equally important. The single pictorial whole, the large compositions that provide the charm of so many famous foreign cities, often seems lacking in the American urban landscape. In this respect, Baltimore has much to offer, both in its older residential districts—Fells Point, Federal Hill, Otterbein, and Mount Vernon Place, among others—and in those neighborhoods developed early in the twentieth century, such as Roland Park, Guilford, and Homeland. Characteristic and almost dateless residential types, frequently repeated over long periods of time, provide the neutral backdrop against which more highly individualized monuments stand out as works of art.

Needless to say, preservation and progress must ever seek the middle ground. Pious antiquarians can mistakenly appeal for preservation of even the relatively worthless, merely because of its age, at the expense of natural and healthy growth. Self-interested developers, on the other hand, can be too ready to sacrifice all that has come down from the past, even the finest individual monuments or groups of buildings, in the name of financial gain, just as architects can squander valuable buildings on behalf of their own ambitions. An informed public, stirred to examine its architectural surroundings, alone can provide the balanced view that supports the preservation of threatened monuments and the new building projects worthy of the local past.

Knowledge of a city's architectural past reveals how each successive period had something worthy to contribute to the whole and therefore helps to inspire the faith that our own may do so as well. Architectural histories such as this resemble autobiographies written, so often hopefully, in one's middle age; they assume that there will be additional chapters. This book should inspire the citizens of Baltimore to ensure that the architectural chapter they will write in the first quarter of the twenty-first century may be a fitting sequel to their city's distinguished eighteenth-, nineteenth-, and twentieth-century past.

| | |

Studies in architectural history to some extent require a special vocabulary and specialized background knowledge. Aiming to reach a wide readership as well as scholars, this volume attempts to make the arcane accessible by explaining architectural terms on first mention and by means of a glossary of frequently used terms. Where appropriate chronologically, architectural styles are discussed briefly so as to give lay readers a sense of their origins and sensibility. Textual treatments of structures focus on their concept and construction; notes of later events and dates of demolition appear in the margins.

Believing that readers should be able to view images of all or nearly all buildings discussed in the text, the editors soon realized that, in a book of manageable length, many illustrations would have to appear in fairly small format on the page. Even so, in order to provide the detail often necessary for a full appreciation of a structure and its form, or an elaborate interior, we have assembled a gallery of larger images—architects' drawings, contemporary engravings, lithographs, daguerreotypes, photographs—of signature monuments, some of Baltimore's most important or representative buildings, and a sample of the rooms within them.

THE ARCHITECTURE OF BALTIMORE

1

GEORGIAN BALTIMORE, 1752–1790

IN THE 1750S, when King George II sat on the British throne, his subjects along the coast of mainland America numbered about a third of the British population. At the time, only some three hundred colonists lived in a place known as Baltimore Town, a settlement on the northwest side of a basin formed by the Patapsco River when it reached tidewater while winding its way to the Chesapeake Bay.

These few residents, like other Maryland settlers, traced their roots to England and Ireland in the seventeenth century, when, in a time of political unrest and religious intolerance, King Charles I had granted his former counselor George Calvert, the openly Roman Catholic first Lord Baltimore, a land grant in the New World as a reward for faithful service. In 1632 Calvert's grant stretched from the south bank of the Potomac, bordering Virginia, north to a latitude that eventually cut through the city of Philadelphia. After Calvert's death the second Lord Baltimore, George's son Cecil, called his settlement Maryland, apparently after Queen Henrietta Maria. As proprietor, he hoped Maryland would prosper and furnish him fat rents and fees; he also made it a religious refuge, opening its shores to other Christian believers. Landing on the north bank of the Potomac River in 1634, the first group of settlers established St. Mary's City. By the second half of the seventeenth century, despite internal strife and the eventual establishment of the Anglican church, Marylanders had joined their neighbors to the south in adopting tobacco as a principal cash crop. Eyeing the colony's most precious and perishable commodity and leading source of revenue, the assembly in 1683 designated official tobacco-shipping ports, some of which, mere points on the map, never took hold. Others—Oxford and Chestertown on the Eastern Shore, Port Tobacco on the

Western Shore, among them—grew into modest villages. Small towns such as Upper Marlboro and Joppa became county seats.

Beginnings

Although it might seem inevitable that a bustling harbor and trading center would arise on the Chesapeake Bay, the largest estuary on the continent, Baltimore Town actually came into being much later than other Chesapeake communities. In 1729, when the assembly looked for a place to build a warehouse for tobacco storage on the upper Patapsco, the largest local landowner, Charles Carroll of Annapolis, and eight other citizens of Baltimore County signed a petition "praying that a bill may be brought in for the building of a Town, on the North side of Patapsco River, upon land supposed to belong to Messrs. Charles and Daniel Carroll." The governor's council granted the petition, and in December of that year the Carroll brothers agreed to subdivide sixty acres and sell lots, each about one acre, at forty shillings. Charles Carroll chose for himself a prime waterfront lot on the eastern foot of the street he named Calvert, for the fifth lord proprietor, Charles Calvert. Waterside lots sold well, but interior land went much more slowly. By the terms of sale new owners had to erect a substantial dwelling within eighteen months of the date of purchase of the lot; a number of lots returned to Carroll because first owners failed to make improvements.[1] Shaped like an arrowhead pointing west, the original plat for Baltimore Town contained just one east-west thoroughfare, Long (later Market, then Baltimore) Street, and two perpendicular

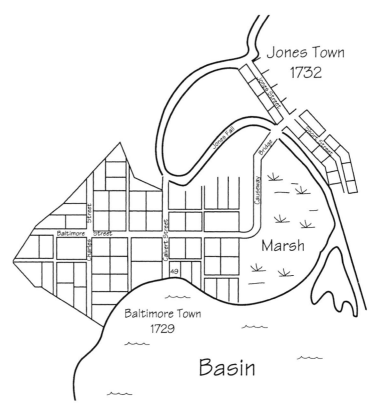

Baltimore Town, 1729, and Jones Town, 1732. From "Parceling Out Land in Baltimore, 1632–1796," pt. 1, Maryland Historical Magazine 87, no. 4 (1992). Courtesy of Garrett Power

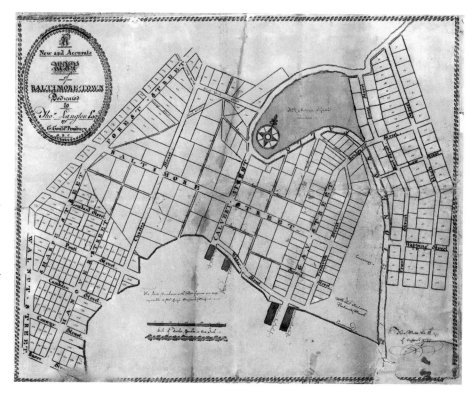

A New and Accurate Map of Baltimore Town, *by G. Gould Presbury, 1780, shows the additions made to the original town of 1729: Jones Town (1745 and 1750), east of Jones Falls; the Gay Street area (1747); and lots west of the basin along Sharp and Hanover Streets (1753 and 1765). Maryland Historical Society.*

streets. Parallel to Calvert, which ran north from the first wharf, Carroll charted Forest (later Charles) Street, four lots west.

A fast-flowing stream formed the eastern limit of the new town, entering the harbor basin from high ground to the north and west and periodically flooding its lower reaches (a marshy horseshoe bend just north of Baltimore Town at first discouraged land purchases there). The stream took its name from an early settler, David Jones, who, in 1661, had claimed 380 acres to its east. In 1732, foreseeing development on both sides of the falls, the assembly created Jones Town on its right bank and authorized commissioners to sell lots in a ten-acre parcel. A jury had to decide conflicting original claims, but by 1741 all the Jones Town lots had been sold, and an eastern, dog-leg extension of Baltimore Street crossed a causeway to this neighboring village, commonly known as Old Town. Four years later the assembly agreed to fold it into Baltimore.

Meanwhile a third settlement, farther east of the falls, grew vigorously. It owed its origins to the enterprising efforts of Edward Fell and his brother William, natives of Lancashire, England, and members of the Society of Friends. In several cases they sought to secure land at a two-thirds discount by claiming that it had reverted to the proprietor because unused or faulty in title (Edward Fell's new store in 1725, on land east of the falls which Carroll believed was his, accounted for the "supposed to belong" language in the Baltimore Town petition of 1729). By 1737, William Fell and his brother had purchased land in Old Town as well as Carroll's claim to Fells Point (then known as Island Point), thereby controlling about one hundred eighty-five acres east of the falls. Fells Point jutted into deep water, making it suitable for ship landings. Fell's lots sold briskly, and Fells Point flourished, rivaling

Baltimore Town in 1752. *The original John Moale drawing. Maryland Historical Society*

Baltimore in 1752, From a Sketch then made by John Moale Esq. Deceased, corrected by the late Daniel Bowley Esq. *Aquatint engraving by William Strickland, 1817. Maryland Historical Society*

Baltimore Town until, in 1773, it too became a part of Baltimore. The earliest buildings, undoubtedly of wood, received mention in a 1726 survey ordered by Edward Fell; they consisted of three houses, a mill, and some tobacco-storage buildings, along with an orchard on land "one-half cleared and of middling quality."[2]

In 1752 John Moale, a landowner with artistic bent, sat down on the northern slope of a high hill on the south side of the basin and sketched Baltimore Town, thus providing posterity with a unique portrait of an American city in its infancy. As later redrawn and printed, the image shows three streets running along the north side of the basin and two along the west. Not surprisingly, most of the houses appear to be simple wooden structures, one to one and a half stories high and two bays (or window/door openings) wide. The Anglican

Old City Post Office, Front near Exeter Street, Jones Town. Enoch Pratt Free Library

TOP, RIGHT:

The earliest houses in Fells Point included pairs of one-room-deep, story-and-a-half frame buildings like these in the 600 block of South Wolfe Street, photographed in the 1930s. Peale Collection, Maryland Historical Society

BOTTOM:

Adam Boss house, Bond Street, near Eastern Avenue, Fells Point. Photograph ca.1880. Enoch Pratt Free Library

church graces the crest of a prominent hill, a tobacco-inspection warehouse stands close to the water on the west side of the basin, and taverns hug the edge of the harbor.

A fair sampling of mid-eighteenth-century wooden structures remained in use long enough to enter the age of photography, their images complementing the Moale view and supplying a closer glimpse of what much of early Baltimore looked like. The simplest structures were only one and a half stories high and two bays wide, with gable roofs and dormer windows, like the building that served as the city's first post office, in Old Town on Front near Exeter Street. Similar houses still stand in the 600 block of South Wolfe Street in Fells Point. Only one room deep, with a garret for sleeping above, such houses were among the most modest structures built in the early city. More common were three- or four-bay-wide versions, with tall gambrel (broken-pitch) roofs with dormers. Many such houses appear in the 1752 Moale view; one, built somewhat later, known as the Adam Boss house, stood on South Bond Street, near Eastern Avenue, in Fells Point. Built of overlapping horizontal wooden boards (weatherboarding), the most common covering for frame houses, the taller, gambrel roof allowed for much more sleeping space upstairs. Common in the southeast of

England during the first half of the eighteenth century, such buildings were well known at the time from New York to Virginia.

Georgian Taste

Amidst the jumble of small frame structures in mid-eighteenth-century Baltimore, John Moale also carefully sketched three prominent private dwellings, each two stories high and built of brick. These more assuming structures adhered to formal design principles, carried stylish decorative elements, and resembled the substantial brick dwellings then being built in Annapolis, since 1694 the seat of Maryland's colonial government. The site of town houses built by rich tobacco merchants, many of whom served in the legislature, Annapolis provided much work for carpenters, stonemasons, bricklayers, carvers, and plasterers, many of them transplanted from Britain, and the men who called themselves master builders or architects—skilled craftsmen who offered clients designs copied from the most fashionable English architectural publications or from the raft of shorter and simpler builders' guides. Wealthy and educated colonials had easy familiarity with such books, which could be found in many a gentleman's library; such gentlefolk also had opportunities to travel to England and acquaint themselves with the latest tastes. At the time the style of choice followed the design principles established by the late-sixteenth-century Italian architect Andrea Palladio. Replacing the English Baroque style of Sir Christopher Wren, Palladian taste—later called the Georgian style, after contemporary British kings—altered the proportions and the character of English architecture.

Palladio, a student of Vitruvius, the noted Roman commentator on architecture, championed the principles of design inherent in ancient Roman temple forms and adapted these to both domestic and public architecture. His buildings featured steadfastly symmetrical designs, high basements and raised first floors, projecting central pavilions with columned entryways, and the further decoration of the façade with classical embellishments like pilasters, pediments, and full entablatures. Palladio's ideal composition consisted of a five-part block: a two- or three-story main building, often with temple front, and, on either side, a one-story hyphen (smaller connecting structure), which provided an indoor passageway to the two outlying buildings, or dependencies. These housed the kitchen, other work or service areas, and additional bedrooms. A distinctive Palladian window design followed Venetian models—a central arched portion flanked by two smaller side windows—and frequently appeared above the doorway of the building's main entrance.

In addition—and important for what was to follow—Palladio introduced a conviction that beauty resided not only within architectural massing, decorative features, and details but also in what his followers, after close study of his designs, described as "harmony in the proportions." More than his adaptation of the temple form, these proportions endowed eighteenth-century Georgian buildings with singular grace. Inevitably some Palladio-inspired buildings were larger and finer than others, but careful attention to harmonious proportions made them distinctive. This belief in a system of proportions as the source of excellence in design filtered down to even the smallest and most modest of buildings.

One of the most important architectural publications of the period, Colen Campbell's

Vitruvius Brittannicus (London, 1715–17), which illustrated Palladian-inspired British buildings, registered the change in taste. Later in the century, workmanlike books provided plates illustrating the classical orders (Tuscan, Doric, Ionic, Corinthian, and Composite), showing designs for columns, their bases and capitals (tops), as well as the entablatures supported by the columns, consisting of a lower architrave, a deep frieze area above, and, finally, the crowning cornice. The pattern books demonstrated ways for Georgian builders to adapt Pal-

Edwin Fotterall house. Detail from William Strickland's aquatint engraving based on Moale's early sketch of Baltimore. Maryland Historical Society

ladian designs for façades (building fronts), decorative elements, and floor plans, offering models for doorway and window enframements, projecting pavilions, porches, engaged columns (half-column projections from walls), pilasters (flattened columns projecting only slightly from the wall), and pediments (flat or triangular forms crowning entrance porticos, doorways, and projecting pavilions). Pattern books also illustrated interior features—fireplace mantels,

overmantel designs, and door and window casings. The craftsmen who used these books may or may not have troubled themselves with the theory behind Palladian proportions, but they recognized their distinction and appeal and applied them gladly.

In 1741, near the corner of what became Calvert and Fayette Streets, just down the hill from the Anglican church, the Irish-born merchant Edwin Fotterall built a brick dwelling that seems to have been the first major residence constructed in Baltimore, and it typified Georgian attention to symmetry and solid dignity. Five bays wide, it had a high gable roof. A slightly projecting central pavilion capped by a triangular pediment announced its prominence and stylishness, as did the stone quoins on the corners of the house. Closer to the harbor stood two other, somewhat more modest three-story brick houses, each lot surrounded by a fence. Only three bays wide, one had a prominent, pedimented doorway; the other a small pediment set in the center of the roof.

The brick, Palladian-style Fotterall house set the example for many dwellings that followed in Baltimore Town, which by 1774 had evolved from a village of twenty-five buildings to a town of some five hundred sixty houses and nearly six thousand people. Robert Long built his own brick house in Fells Point, where Edward Fell had laid out lots on part of the acreage he had inherited from his father. Following established custom, the Fell family leased the lots and imposed building requirements, in this case calling on the leaseholder within two years to erect on the premises "a good and Sufficient Stone or brick House to Cover Four Hundred Square feet covered with Jointed Cypress Shingles."[4] A young merchant from Pennsylvania who had arrived in Baltimore with capital and the aim of multiplying it, Long established a warehouse and dock on Thames Street and then leased two lots from Fell across the street from his business. In about 1765 workmen began building a home for him in the middle of the lots, reserving land for gardens on either side.

Two and a half stories high, the three-bay-wide structure rested on a tall "English" basement (much of it above street level), which originally had its own entrance under the high

A later chronicler of early Baltimore, Thomas Griffith, recalled that Fotterall's house had been "pulled down" and, along "with the rest of his property confiscated and sold, because he returned to Ireland at the time of the Revolution."[3]

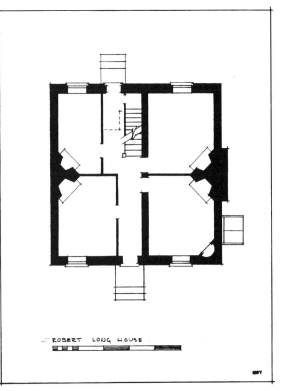

Robert Long house exterior as it appeared in the late twentieth century. Photograph by Michael F. Trostel

RIGHT:

First floor plan, Robert Long house. Drawing by Michael F. Trostel

The Robert Long house survives at 812 South Ann Street, maintained by the Preservation Society of Fells Point and Federal Hill.

front stoop (when the street level rose in the nineteenth century, the house lost much of its basement and the high stoop). Long's bricklayers laid the façade wall in the Flemish bond typical of the eighteenth century (with stretcher and header bricks alternating); here the glazed (burnt brick) headers made a stylish architectural statement. Georgian features included the strict symmetry of the façade design; the steeply pitched gable roof with dormer windows; the broad proportions of the windows set in heavily molded wooden frames, with their small, multipaned sash (twelve-over-twelve lights on the first floor, twelve-over-eight lights on the second);[5] and the molded brick water table, marking the break between basement and first floor. The pent roof (shedlike, deflecting rain from the house) running across the façade above the first floor level is a design feature Long brought with him from his native Pennsylvania, one that was rarely repeated in Baltimore.

The floor plan followed a traditional Georgian center-hall scheme. The narrow entrance passage widened to the rear to allow for the staircase. Two rooms opened off the hall to either side and all had corner fireplaces—to the front, a parlor and dining room; to the rear, an office and a bedchamber. The interior walls were plastered, but the partition walls between front and back rooms were constructed of vertical planking. In all likelihood detached buildings provided the original kitchen, smokehouse, necessary, and stable.

Brick houses less imposing than the Long house went up in revolutionary-era Baltimore. One, a two-and-a-half-story house on the north side of Shakespeare Street in Fells Point, built of Flemish bond and with Georgian proportions, featured a belt course (a row or two of slightly projecting bricks) marking the division between the first and second floors, multipaned windows, and a simple wooden cornice. Nevertheless, most new houses were

The brick building on Shake-speare Street eventually formed part of the 1600 block. In the oldest sections of the city about a dozen frame buildings survived into the early twenty-first century: in Fells Point, two groups of two-and-a-half-story houses in the 500 and 700 blocks of South Ann Street; a two-story, three-bay-wide house in the 500 block of South Bethel Street; a two-and-a-half-story, two-bay-wide, one-room-deep house in the 700 block of South Register Street; and in Federal Hill, a two-story, three-bay-wide dwelling at 130 East Montgomery Street.

wooden. By the 1760s and 1770s gambrel roofs had fallen out of favor and most frame houses were a full two stories in height, with gable roof, with or without dormers. The three-bay-wide Sulzebacher house stood in what became the 900 block of West Baltimore Street. Its large ground-floor window pointed to its use at one time as both residence and shop—a combination by no means exceptional. Other frame houses once may have sported the bright hues that visitors and local writers later made a subject of comment—red, green, and yellow.[6] Smaller homes nestled along the narrow streets or alleys dividing each block. Early records identified one-story houses set on high basements as "tenements," meaning rental units. Typically only one room deep with a high basement and tall attic lit by a dormer window, these houses measured less than twelve feet wide and only twelve feet deep. A tightly winding staircase occupied the rear corner of the room.

Revolutionary-period residents retained vivid memories of the city's villagelike character. Robert Gilmor Jr., who in 1778 arrived in Baltimore as a child of four, recalled breweries at the northwest corner of Gay and Water Streets (belonging to James Sterret, an early settler from Lancaster County, Pennsylvania) and on the banks of the Jones Falls near Old Town; Samuel Purviance's distillery, built in 1763, on Commerce Street, south of Water and west of Gay; and a row of warehouses just opposite, "built on the bank of the basin, from the lower stories of which next the water, tobacco was rolled into scows." As a boy, Gilmor explored the "sandy shores" of the basin, just south of Water Street, crabbing "with a forked

TOP, LEFT:
An early two-and-a-half-story brick house in the 1600 block of Shake-speare Street, Fells Point, as it appeared during the Works Progress Administration survey of Baltimore in the 1930s. Peale Collection, Maryland Historical Society
TOP, RIGHT:
Sulzebacher house, 900 block of West Baltimore Street, as it appeared ca. 1850. Enoch Pratt Free Library
BOTTOM, LEFT:
By 1860 or so this house and shop, which stood at the corner of West Saratoga and North Eutaw Streets, had become the Old Curiosity Shop. Enoch Pratt Free Library
BOTTOM, RIGHT:
A photograph probably dating from the late nineteenth century captured an assortment of early structures; the one on the corner (the northwest corner of German, later Redwood, and Liberty Streets) was known as the Old Carpet Loom building. Enoch Pratt Free Library

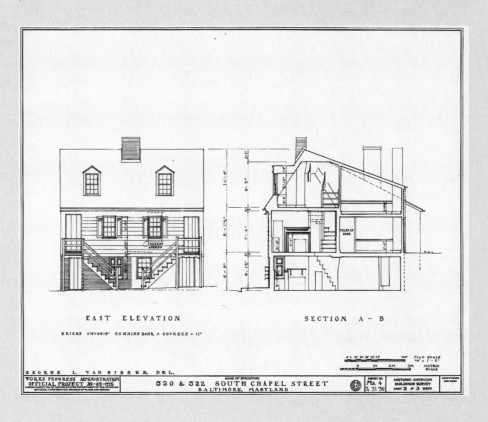

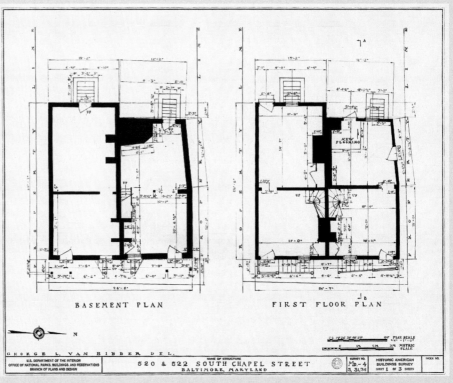

East elevation and cross section and floor plans for adjoining one-room-deep, one-and-a-half-story brick houses at 520–522 South Chapel Street, Fells Point. The Historic American Buildings Survey documented them in 1936, before their demolition, noting that Chapel Street, originally called Star Alley, had at one time been "a lane leading into the open country" and that the houses "were never more than the dwellings of the humblest people." The kitchen was located in the tall basement; at some later date, the rear roof was raised to extend over a one-room-deep addition. From John H. Scarff, Notes on 520–522 South Chapel Street, 4 Baltimore 13, Historic American Buildings Survey, Maryland, Library of Congress

The Robert Shields house, as captured in a late-nineteenth-century photograph. Wilson Collection, Maryland Historical Society

stick" from the foot of Gay Street to the head of the basin at Light Street. Beyond St. Paul's church on Charles Street almost nothing had been built, "fine trees" covering the hills to the north.[7]

Up Light Street, on the heights, wooden houses overlooked the basin. Gilmor described a wide marsh encircled by the loop of the Jones Falls, where he had "shot many a snipe and blackbird." In Fells Point, then "the residence of the principal shipping merchants," he noted "the sparse situation of the houses at the Point and the cornfields and trees" that lay between that place and Baltimore Town. Along Gay Street he remembered "few other than wooden houses as far as Market Street" and east on Market to Frederick Street. Many frame buildings also fronted on Charles Street. A row of one-story hipped-roof wooden houses graced the lower part of Charles Street—French town, as the natives called the area, which French refugees from Nova Scotia had settled after a British victory in 1756. The brick houses he described were mainly two stories high; a three-story brick house at Charles and Market Streets he saluted as "one of the best finished houses in the town." No streets in the town were paved until 1782.[8]

In the era of revolution, war, and wartime profits, prosperous merchants began putting up substantial brick houses. The house that Robert Shields built on the south side of Market Street near Calvert in 1772 typified the Georgian town-house format as adopted by prosperous Baltimoreans. As the town grew and land became more expensive, lots grew smaller, and builders began putting up houses with narrower street frontages—often twenty feet or less—and side-hall plans. London and Philadelphia houses provided architectural inspiration. Itself closely resembling the town houses of well-to-do Philadelphians, the Shields house—eighteen feet wide and three and a half stories tall—displayed all the design features associated with the Georgian style: Flemish-bond brickwork, belt courses separating the floors, a molded brick water table, a deep wooden cornice, and a steeply pitched gable roof with dormer windows. As at the Long house, broad wooden moldings framed the amply proportioned windows with their square, multipaned sash (twelve-over-twelve lights on the first floor, twelve-over-eight lights on the second and third floors). The house and its neighbors were built tight to the property lines, their street façades aligned. Such houses were two rooms deep and usually had a narrower back building for the kitchen, servants' quarters, and extra bedrooms. A native of the city later commented on these "magnificent mansions of brick," their "windows like multiplication tables and great wastes of wall between the stories, with occasionally courtyards before them."[9]

Early Country Houses

In his "Recollections" of 1844 Robert Gilmor Jr. noted that Chatsworth had "since been cut up into lots, and laid out in streets, and can scarcely now be recognized." A part of the old house was "still visible near the Reister's Town Road" as were some of the locust trees "which formed the grand alley in the garden."[10]

Colonial Baltimoreans of means maintained houses and property in the countryside, where, in warm weather, they enjoyed fresh air and tended their often-elaborate gardens. William Lux, a prosperous merchant and one of the largest landowners in Baltimore, seems to have built the first such mansion soon after his marriage in 1752, about a half mile northwest of town. Called Chatsworth, the house stood on 950 acres, property that had belonged to his father-in-law, Dr. George Walker, who served as one of the original town commissioners. Two stories high and four bays wide, with a hipped roof and wide porch facing the extensive gardens, Chatsworth cut quite a figure. John Adams enjoyed being a guest there when he attended sessions of the Continental Congress in Baltimore during the winter of 1776–77. Chatsworth, he wrote, featured a "large garden enclosed in lime [trees] and before the yard two fine rows of large cherry trees which lead out to the public road. There is a fine prospect about it." Mr. Lux, he concluded, "lives like a prince."[11] After the Revolution Chatsworth became a commercial pleasure garden known as Gray's Gardens, open to the public, offering refreshments and, in the summer months, musical entertainment; as the city expanded, the southern edge of the property ran along Saratoga Street between Pine and Greene Streets.[12]

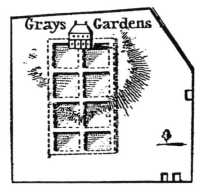

Gray's Gardens (originally Chatsworth), from Warner & Hanna's Plan of the City and Environs of Baltimore, *1801. Courtesy of Barbara Wells Sarudy*

Just to the south of Gray's Gardens, Jean Charles Marie Louis Felix Pascault, another

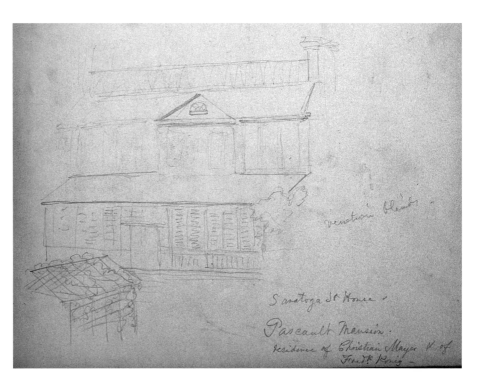

The Pascault house, as depicted in a sketch made by Maryland artist Frank Mayer between 1845 and 1850. Maryland State Law Library

Parnassus, *by Charles Willson
Peale, ca. 1769. Watercolor on ivory;
the reverse of a miniature portrait
of Dr. Henry Stevenson. Note the
rising terraces and avenue of trees,
making the approach to the house
as grand as possible. Maryland
Historical Society*

French-born refugee from Saint Domingue, who arrived in Baltimore in 1780, built his own magnificent country house. With a hipped roof, the six-bay-wide house stood two stories high on an English basement. On the south front the house displayed six bays, the central two forming a slightly projecting pavilion, with triangular pediment, much like that of the Fotterall house. A small semicircular window (lunette) decorated the pediment, and a wooden balustrade, or low railing, ran along the edge of the roof between its wide end chimneys. A long piazza (covered porch, or veranda) graced the garden front. A later observer described the Pascault home—with the "beautiful iron gates" Pascault had ordered from France—as "the oldest house in Baltimore," its interior imparting "an air of refinement" the young man had not seen outside of France.[13]

To the north and east of Chatsworth stood Parnassus, which Dr. Henry Stevenson built in 1763–69 on the east bank of the Jones Falls above Jones Town. Dr. Stevenson's brother John may have been the first of many wheat exporters in Baltimore; the doctor himself pioneered the use of smallpox vaccine in the colonies. In 1769 one wing of Parnassus became a hospital, where Stevenson inoculated Marylanders as well as people from adjacent colonies.

A classic Georgian five-part house with a main block and dependencies, Parnassus consisted of a two-story, five-bay-wide central section with hipped roof and central pediment, with one-story hyphens connecting the central block to the service wings. Visitors ascended graceful, curving steps to enter the house. Stevenson's terraced gardens were some of the earliest in the city.

At about the same time that Stevenson built Parnassus, Mount Clare rose as a country seat on the shores of the Patapsco, a mile or so west of Baltimore Town. Dr. Charles Carroll originally owned the site. He held extensive stock in the Baltimore Iron Company, which organized to exploit the rich iron-ore deposits in the region and helped to attract interest in the new town of Baltimore. One of Carroll's sons, John Henry, seems to have built a modest "bachelor's house" there. After his death in 1754 and the death of Dr. Carroll, Charles, the eldest son, inherited the plantation as well as nearby ironworks, mills, and shipyards.

In 1763 Charles Carroll (then known as the Barrister) married Margaret Tilghman and in 1767–68 began construction of a larger house at Mount Clare, using his brother's cottage as shelter. Carroll, whose principal residence remained in Annapolis, followed Palladian precedent when he added to the entrance front a projecting central pavilion, with columned portico, and dramatic Palladian (or "Venetian") window above. Carroll had the columns for the new portico brought from England, along with nails, locks, hinges, lead for the roof, and glass. He built an office wing to match the existing wing, later a kitchen, and gave both of them—connected to the main block by one-story hyphens—polygonal fronts. The clever

TOP:

Mount Clare as it appeared on the back of a painted settee, showing the main entrance, ca. 1804. The sketch of the house is probably the work of Francis Guy; the furniture was made by John and Hugh Finlay. Baltimore Museum of Art: Gift of Lydia Howard de Roth and Nancy H. DeFord Venable, in memory of their mother, Lydia Howard DeFord; and Purchase Fund BMA 1966.26.11

BOTTOM:

The garden façade of Mount Clare, showing the original main block of 1756–60 and the hyphens and wings added by Charles Carroll, Barrister, 1767–68. Drawing by Michael F. Trostel

curvilinear roofs of the hyphens had stairways connecting to the second story of the main block. On the garden side, overlooking the river, Mount Clare featured full-height brick pilasters marking each end of the house and supporting a central pediment, with ocular window. These polychromatic pilasters, with lighter bricks running down their centers, imitated the effect of quoins.

Inside, the plan was unusual for Baltimore. The small entrance hall led to a stair hall on the left and a study on the right. Beyond, the two main rooms faced the garden. Like walls in some other grand Maryland houses, those of the downstairs rooms were plastered but finished to give the effect of wood paneling.

The grounds at Mount Clare received the attention of Carroll and his wife alike. Managing the greenhouse, Margaret Tilghman Carroll once sent twenty pots of lemon and orange trees, along with other specially grown plants, down the bay to George Washington. Visitors approaching the house noticed a semicircular white picket fence that ran from the dependencies to a central point in front of the main entrance, where statues of lions rested on stone piers, marking the walkway to the entrance. A Virginia woman, paying a call in 1770, described the entrance's "Handsome Court Yard," but she reserved highest praise for the garden side. The house, she wrote, sat on a very high hill and commanded a fine view of the river. "You step out of the Door into the Bowlg Green from which the Garden Falls & when you stand on the Top of it there is such a Uniformity of Each side as the whole Plantn seems to be laid out like a Garden." "There is a most beautiful walk from the house down to the water," John Adams further testified in February 1777. "There is a descent not far from the house; you have a fine garden then you descend a few steps and have another fine garden; you go down a few more and have another."[14]

Yet another Georgian country house of the period testified to the eminence of William Gibson and his wife, Sarah Morris Gibson, Episcopal church members and friends of the Library Company and Benevolent Society. Their home, Rose Hill, was a lovely five-bay (44-foot) wide, two-story brick dwelling northwest of the city. It sat on a high basement, featured handsome stone window lintels, and welcomed visitors with wide stone steps and a pedimented garden entrance. Rose Hill's hipped roof, end chimneys, and roof-line pedi-

The dependencies and hyphens at Mount Clare suffered demolition in 1871; rebuilt in 1908, they did not conform exactly to Carroll's precedent. Thus modified, the building survives as a city-owned, privately restored and maintained landmark, with some original eighteenth-century Carroll furnishings, paintings, and other belongings.

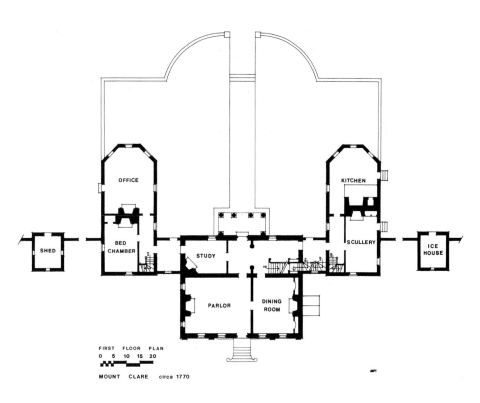

TOP:
First floor plan of Mount Clare, after the additions of the late 1760s. Drawing by Michael F. Trostel
BOTTOM:
Rose Hill, as depicted by Francis Guy on the crest rail of a painted chair made by John and Hugh Finlay, ca. 1804. Baltimore Museum of Art: Gift of Lydia Howard de Roth and Nancy H. DeFord Venable, in memory of their mother, Lydia Howard DeFord; and Purchase Fund BMA 1966.26.7

Standing in the path of the wide, tree-lined boulevard that designers envisioned for Eutaw Place, Rose Hill suffered demolition shortly after the laying out of the street development in 1854.

ment further illustrated the Georgian style. Poplar trees and a fancy picket fence framed the house as one approached its garden facade.[15]

Public Houses, Market, and Courthouse

Astride the postal road connecting Williamsburg and Philadelphia; with the deep water at Fells Point gathering a full complement of shipowners, captains, seamen, and other wayfarers; and serving as the export depot for wagonloads of grain being brought to town daily from the surrounding counties and Pennsylvania, Baltimore clearly called for meeting spaces and accommodations for travelers. Kaminsky's Tavern may have been the earliest such structure—a one-and-a-half-story frame building with gambrel roof, painted yellow in the later eighteenth century. It appeared in Moale's view of the fledgling town and survived on South Street until the late nineteenth century. In Fells Point the London Coffee House on South Bond Street, near the water, supplied a popular gathering place for sea captains and merchants. It followed the example of British coffeehouses, which posted the latest news and provided a space where shipowners and captains could meet to conduct business and keep up with the latest mercantile and political developments—away from the noisier and more raucous atmosphere of the taverns. Built of brick in 1771, the coffeehouse resembled a typical merchant's house of the period, with a steeply pitched gable roof and dormer windows, belt course, and water table. Elegant stone window lintels and sills set off the large multipaned windows. Inside, it had a large front public room; behind it and upstairs were rooms for private discussions.

For those travelers who could pay the extra fare, inns offered advantages over taverns, and colonial Baltimore had its share. Early in the War for Independence, from December 1776 to February 1777, the Continental Congress met at Jacob Feit's inn, a three-and-a-half-

The coffeehouse still stands at the northwest corner of Bond and Thames Streets and is undergoing renovation.

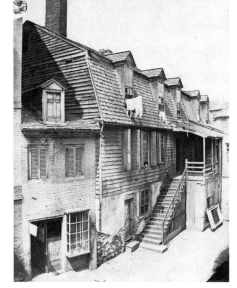

LEFT:
Kaminsky's Tavern as it appeared in the mid-nineteenth century, laundry hanging ingloriously from the upper windows. Originally a one-and-a-half-story building like the Boss house (and as it appeared in the Moale view), this later photograph shows it after the street grade was lowered. Enoch Pratt Free Library

RIGHT:
London Coffee House, Fells Point. Drawing by Michael F. Trostel and Peter Pearre

Congress Hall.
Enoch Pratt Free Library

story brick building on West Baltimore Street, later known as Congress Hall. With its hipped roof, dormer windows, belt courses, and windows with multipaned sash framed by wide wooden moldings, the large building (ten bays wide and five bays deep) typified the Georgian style. Early hostelries also included the Indian Queen on West Baltimore Street and Daniel Grant's Fountain Inn, also a three-and-a-half-story brick Georgian structure.

Completed in 1773, the Fountain Inn stood on a lot that extended 100 feet along the east side of upper Light Street and ran 180 feet to the alley behind it. The hotel itself occupied the entire frontage of the lot and stood 44 feet deep. According to a newspaper description of 1795 (when Grant put the inn up for sale), it had "excellent cellars," six parlors for meetings and meals—these interior spaces finished with mahogany—and twenty-four bedrooms. Servants lived in eight garret rooms. The façade boasted doors and windows with fashionable stone lintels with projecting keystones. At the rear, additional rooms, some possibly for guests, and various dependencies—three kitchens, laundry, springhouse, larder, icehouse, barber's shop, brick stables with eighty-four stalls, hostlers' room, granaries with lofts, coal house, and four offices—enclosed a paved and galleried interior courtyard, which strongly resembled the interior coach yard at the George Inn, Southwark, London. George Washington stayed at the Fountain Inn more than once; other notable guests included Jefferson, Lafayette, and various generals and diplomats.[16]

Late-eighteenth-century public improvements demonstrated that Baltimoreans aspired to a level of civility befitting a town rather than a collection of villages. For years local mar-

Congress Hall burned down in 1860; eventually its site became the home of the city's sports arena, erected in the 1960s. The Fountain Inn stood for nearly a century; its successor on the site, by then the northeast corner of Light and German Streets, the Carrollton Hotel, opened in 1872.

*The Fountain Inn, second from left,
in the mid-nineteenth century.
Peale Collection, Maryland
Historical Society*

*Interior courtyard of the Fountain
Inn. Enoch Pratt Free Library*

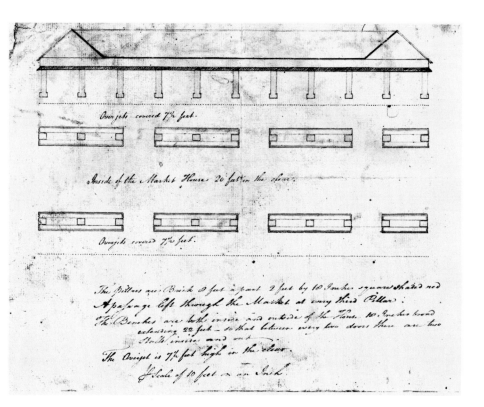

kets had been open street spaces, which, as in Europe, booths and carts occupied and then deserted at the close of market days. In 1784 authorities established three public markets—Central, or Marsh Market, at Market Place on the site of a drained marsh west of the Jones Falls and a few blocks north of the harbor; Hanover Market, at Camden and Hanover Streets, west of the basin; and the Fells Point Market, at the foot of Broadway—to provide space for merchants and to ensure some regularity of fresh foods. Plans in 1799 for an expanded Marsh Market called for a serviceable hall 100 feet long and 38 feet wide, open on the sides, with a roof supported by two rows of eighteen-by-twenty-four-inch brick pillars set eight feet apart. Passages through the market ran between every set of three pillars, which were outfitted with benches on both sides. The low-pitched roof extended seven and a half feet beyond the walls of the building, providing shelter for outdoor vendors.

In 1768 construction of a two-story brick courthouse and jail at the crest of a hill at the north end of Calvert Street, the widest thoroughfare in town, marked the decision of the General Assembly to name Baltimore, rather than Joppa Town, the seat of Baltimore County. Plain and practical, the barnlike courthouse did have a remarkable cupola, with the domed tower above the courthouse surmounted by a tall spire almost twice its height. By 1785 the city had developed northward beyond the courthouse building, which occupied the center of the road and blocked the further extension of Calvert Street. City fathers then contracted with Leonard Harbaugh, a Pennsylvania-born mason and agricultural-equipment inventor who had come to Baltimore in 1755, to excavate the ground around and beneath the building and construct a new, full-height stone basement with an arched carriageway wide enough for the passage of traffic. The project posed serious engineering challenges, which Harbaugh met successfully, and this eccentric structure stood for twenty years, known locally as "the courthouse on stilts." Staircases on either side led up to the courtrooms.

Churches

Although the Anglican church received state support in eighteenth-century Maryland, religious toleration generally prevailed as a principle. Roman Catholics practiced their faith privately. Many of Baltimore's leading citizens attended Presbyterian services; Baptists, Lutherans, and members of the Society of Friends also formed active congregations. After

St. Paul's Church, 1730. Detail from Baltimore in 1752, *William Strickland's aquatint engraving based on Moale's early sketch of Baltimore. Maryland Historical Society*

the Revolution other Protestant groups— German Reformed, Methodist, African Methodist Episcopal—made an appearance in the town. The churches these denominations built largely disappeared over the years, and few were architecturally distinctive.

St. Paul's parish, Anglican until the American Revolution and then Episcopalian, dated from 1692, when the parish covered much of Baltimore County. Two early

buildings served the parish until 1730, when the vestry decided to erect a third church (the first to be built in Baltimore) on Lot 19, an elevated position in the newly plotted community. Thomas Hartwell, one of the earliest builder-architects in the town, oversaw the construction work. His simple rectangular brick structure measured fifty by twenty-three feet and had a ceiling eighteen feet high. Following the usual orientation of Anglican churches, the altar stood at the east end. At the west end, surmounted by a window, Hartwell placed the main door; another one on the long south side, flanked by two windows, turned out to be more accessible from the town and more often used. Judging from Moale's drawing of 1752, the simple, gabled structure seems to have had pier buttresses and a simple belfry. St. Paul's resembled earlier and contemporary church buildings in Virginia and on both Maryland shores.

In 1780 the parish built a new St. Paul's, just south of the old building, which became a school. The much larger, two-story, six-bay-wide new church accommodated the growing congregation. The double story of windows brought in extra light; to the east, a large Pal-

The second St. Paul's Church, as captured in a detail of a painting by Thomas Ruckle, ca. 1810. The detached belfry standing in the churchyard came from the first St. Paul's. Peale Collection, Maryland Historical Society

RIGHT:

"Friends Meeting House," border detail from Thomas H. Poppleton's Plan of the City of Baltimore, *1823. Maryland State Archives*

The building, though no longer used as a Quaker meetinghouse, is the oldest house of worship still standing in Baltimore.

ladian window provided even more light to the altar. Reportedly, five aisles divided the main floor and a gallery surrounded three sides of the interior. As in the case of the old church, parishioners seldom used the western door; the builder placed two doors in the long south flank. Only one opened; the other, added to the exterior for the sake of symmetry (and a rarity in American eighteenth-century ecclesiastical architecture), was plastered over inside. Neither of these two early churches originally had a tower or steeple. A small belfry, an addition to the earlier church, went atop the later one in 1786.

Not so numerous as the parishioners of St. Paul's, members of the Society of Friends nevertheless prospered in the busy commercial city, and in 1781 they built a two-story meetinghouse in Jones Town at Fayette and Aisquith Streets. Built of brick with a gable roof, the austere and simple structure eschewed Georgian symmetry in favor of a functional design.

In 1784–85 the German Evangelical United Brethren hired master builder Jacob Small Sr. to build, and probably also to design, a fine church—a Georgian meetinghouse of generous proportions—at the corner of Conway and Sharp Streets. Soon known as the Otterbein Church after its first pastor, German-born Philip William Otterbein, this building measured forty-eight by sixty-five feet and stood two stories tall, with large, arch-headed windows. An elegant dentilled cornice extended across each side of the building and marked the two end gables. The two street elevations were laid in Flemish bond; the other two in common bond.

Its interior much modified (pulpit in the apse, gallery less in evidence), Otterbein still serves as a place of worship.

German Evangelical (Otterbein) Church, as it appeared in a late-nineteenth-century photograph. Maryland Historical Society

Employing proceeds from a state-sanctioned lottery (as did St. Paul's) and apparently inspired by illustrations of churches Wren and James Gibbs had executed in London, the congregation in 1789 added a two-level square brick tower articulated with corner pilasters and recessed circles, separated by a stringcourse; an octagonal belfry capped by a tall weathervane completed the composition. Originally, a door with an arched fanlight, set within a wooden casing topped by a flat entablature, permitted entry in the center of the Conway Street side. At some point in the nineteenth century, elders decided to move the entry one bay west toward Sharp Street and give it a vestibule. Inside, a gallery swept around three sides of the interior, and the pulpit rose on the north wall.

Exemplars: St. Paul's Rectory and Hampton Hall

St. Paul's Rectory, the oldest structure in central Baltimore, became the home of the Society for the Preservation of Maryland Antiquities (or Preservation Maryland) in September 1987.

Between 1789 and 1791, just northwest of the church on high ground donated by John Eager Howard, St. Paul's parish built an impressive and classically Palladian rectory, with an elegant central pavilion distinguished by a Palladian window and an elaborate pedimented doorway. Its unknown designer-builder gave the central building a width of five bays, or fifty-five feet, and a one-room depth of twenty feet. A semioctagonal projection at the rear of the house provided added room for a grand staircase, separated by a wide arch from the main floor. Entering the eighteen-foot-wide central hall, visitors turned left to a parlor or right to the dining room. From the dining room, a hyphen connected the house to a two-story brick kitchen wing. Many years later a room was added at the west, or parlor, end, thus balancing the façade. The upstairs housed bedrooms and a small porch. Above them dormer windows lighted an attic story, which supplied bedroom space for servants.

Exterior details displayed especially fine craftsmanship. The central projecting pavilion was capped by a triangular pediment with an ocular window. A crisply cut modillion cornice extended across the full façade. Beneath, a broad Palladian window, with pairs of Tuscan pilasters framing the sidelights and supporting, as at Mount Clare, a full entablature, called attention to the elegant doorway below. Four wide stone steps formed a base for the elaborate entryway, where Tuscan pilasters supported the modillioned triangular pediment set above a deep transom light. The excellent quality of the brickwork remains worthy of special notice. Above a fieldstone foundation, the front wall of carefully laid Flemish bond, with narrower-than-usual mortar joints, gives the front an especially even and uniform surface. The design includes a Flemish bond water table, beginning with a course of molded brick, and a three-course belt embellishing the second-floor level. Finely cut, splayed-brick lintels above the windows and limestone window sills exemplify the finest masonry workmanship.

Built about the same time as St. Paul's Rectory (between 1783 and 1790), though far from town, Hampton Hall, as it was first known, asserted the wealth and importance of Capt. Charles Ridgely, Baltimore County landholder, land speculator, and iron manufacturer. Ridgely made considerable gains during the Revolutionary War and further prospered dur-

TOP:

St Paul's Rectory, captured in a detail of a painting by Thomas Ruckle, ca. 1801. Maryland Historical Society

RIGHT:

St. Paul's Rectory, first-floor plan. Michael F. Trostel

BOTTOM:

Entrance hall, St. Paul's Rectory. Preservation Maryland

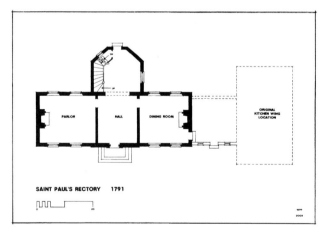

SAINT PAUL'S RECTORY 1791

Hampton the Seat of Genl.
Chas. Ridgley, Maryland. *The
Philadelphia artist William R.
Birch included this earliest-known
depiction of Hampton in his set of
engravings of American country
houses, published in 1808.
Maryland Historical Society*

ing the boom that followed. In 1783 he began work on an impressive country seat, properly
set on the crest of a hill, which followed the symmetrical, five-part Georgian plan, with two
hyphens connecting flanking wings to the central block. Hampton's importance lay less in
its design than its scale, which exceeded that of any dwelling in Baltimore or Annapolis.
Seventy-five feet deep, the house stretched 175 feet in length. As a space adequate to enter-
tain guests, Ridgely called for a large, first-floor center hall, 21 feet wide and running the full
depth of the house less front and rear porticos. Each of the floor's four rooms off of the center hall—music, drawing, dining, and sitting chambers—had a decorative overmantel with
molded picture reserve. Ceilings on the first and second floors were more than 13 feet high.
Walls and ceilings throughout bore signs of distinction and attention to detail: carved or
molded wood cornices, chair rails, and wainscoting. Sparing no expense, Ridgely paid his
master carpenter, Jehu Howell, for more than two thousand feet of modillion cornice and
about the same length of Doric entablature. He also ordered the finest oil colors (for prime
and many finish coats) for the walls of the great house—Prussian blue, vermillion, and
bright bluish green verdigris. Six commodious bedrooms filled the second floor. The third
floor provided ample space for storage and the servants' quarters, including eight bedrooms.

Outside, Hampton's two-story entrance portico emphatically stated the importance of
the house. Finials—in this case classical urns, in the Palladian manner—marked the corners
and apexes of the roof. The large, arched dormer windows of the third story bore decorative scrollwork and elegant muntins (the horizontal and vertical dividers among panes of
glass). On the chimneys, false windows with molded wooden frames and painted glazing
created a fashionable trompe l'oeil ("fooling of the eye"). Captain Ridgely covered the exterior stone masonry with a pinkish terra cotta stucco—its color probably owing to the iron-

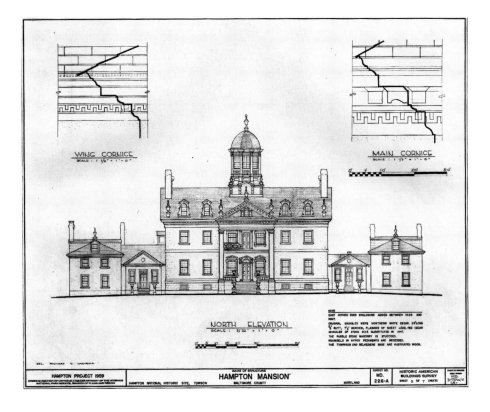

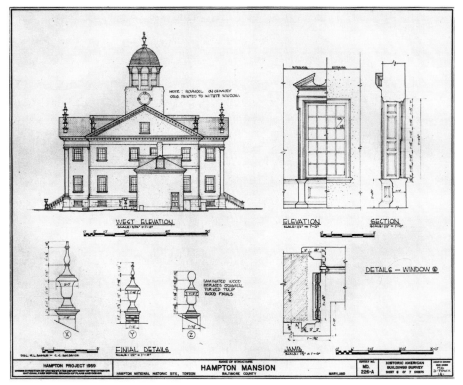

Hampton, elevation and section, as the Historic American Buildings Survey documented the mansion in the 1930s. Library of Congress

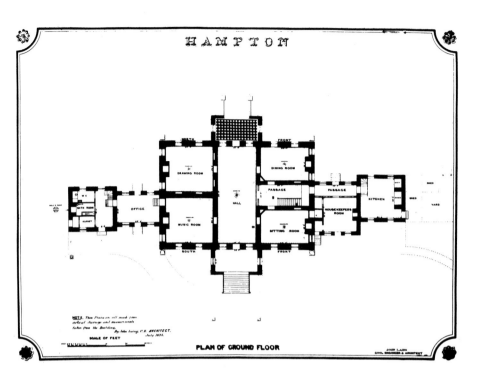

Descendants of Capt. Charles Ridgely lived at Hampton until 1945, when they conveyed the structure and then-surrounding grounds to a private foundation on behalf of the National Park Service. The Society for the Preservation of Maryland Antiquities assumed responsibility for maintaining the property and opening it to the public. In 1948, its authority expanded, the National Park Service formally acquired Hampton and designated it a National Historic Site —the first place in the country to receive federal protection on its architectural merit alone.

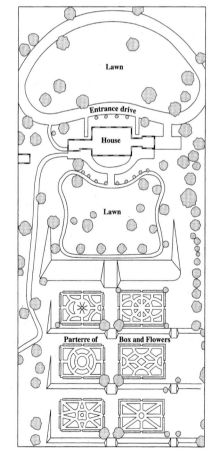

The gardens of Hampton in the late eighteenth century. Drawn from information provided by the Hampton Historic Site.

bearing content of the sand in its white lime-mortar—and had workmen lightly brush the stucco with white lines to give the exterior the look of rectangular cut stone, a practice characteristic of Palladian buildings. High above the center of the house, Ridgely called for a huge octagonal cupola with large sash windows (he ingeniously used them to ventilate the house below). This great crowning feature, unique to Hampton among American country houses, resembled the dome over Castle Howard in Yorkshire, which Ridgely, who cherished his Howard blood on his mother's side, may have emulated.[17] Ridgely died in 1790, the year of Hampton's completion.

Along with Mount Clare, St. Paul's Rectory and Hampton epitomized the Georgian style, which continued to engage and appeal to Baltimoreans for many generations.

2

FEDERAL DESIGNS, TOWN AND COUNTRY, 1789–1819

During the Revolutionary War Baltimore merchants began building fortunes as privateers licensed to seize British shipping and as providers of food and war materiel to the Continental cause. In the 1790s and early 1800s—when the United States fought an undeclared, or quasi war with France and Europeans embroiled themselves in Napoleonic conflicts—the city continued to prosper, furnishing combatants and their colonies with wheat, flour, cured meat, and other necessities (partly by means of trim and speedy Baltimore Clippers), returning with British manufactured goods, Mediterranean delicacies, and Caribbean rum, sugar, coffee, and fruit. Between 1790 and 1800 Baltimore enjoyed such unprecedented growth that its population doubled, from 13,000 to 26,000, making it the third largest city in the nation and eclipsing Annapolis as the business and financial center of the Chesapeake. Two maps, published nearly a decade apart, demonstrate this spurt. In A. P. Folie's 1792 map Baltimore and Old Town have grown together. Fells Point remains a separate settlement to the east, separated by marshes at the mouth of the Jones Falls and Harford Run.

Nine years later Warner & Hanna's lovely and detailed map of the city and its environs depicted considerable advances—a larger network of grid-pattern streets, partially filled-in marshes, and a causeway crossing the Jones Falls and connecting the city to Fells Point. Commissioners had authorized filling in the shallows of the basin along the original northern shore line at Water Street; by 1801, the water's edge lay at Pratt Street, where merchants extended long wharves into the harbor. Warner and Hanna showed that, to the west, the city had grown as far as Greene Street and settlement had begun south of the basin, in an area dominated by a large clay hill, which residents named Federal Hill

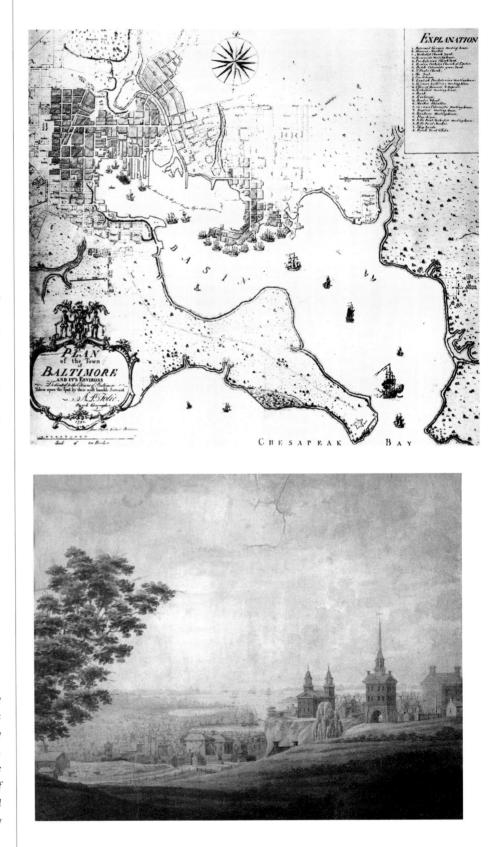

A. P. Folie, Plan of the Town of Baltimore and Its Environs, *1792. The Folie map demonstrated the merging of the original settlements of Baltimore, Old Town, and Fells Point. Federal Hill, south of the basin, shows signs of development. Maryland State Archives*

View of Baltimore, *watercolor by Francis Guy, ca. 1800. The "Court House on stilts" figures prominently in the right foreground of this view, which dramatically captures the original steep topography of the early town. Maryland Historical Society*

in honor of the ratification of the federal Constitution in 1788. Visitors remarked that the settlement was orderly and pretty. In 1791, French author and royalist the vicomte de Chateaubriand, noting the city's immigrant Acadians, called it "une jolie petite ville Catholique"—a pretty Catholic town—using two adjectives that no one would have used a decade earlier.[1] Building proceeded at a furious pace; the first Baltimore directory, in 1796, listed "house carpenter" as the most numerous single occupation, with masons not far behind. Several years before, an enterprising fellow who may or may not have directed any building in the city himself, advertised that he was available to teach courses in "Architecture—viz., Drawings of Ground-Plans and Elevations of Buildings, with the different orders and proportions."[2] In 1810 the census counted 46,555 people claiming Baltimore as home, including 10,971 in "the precincts"—the area immediately surrounding the city.

Through many and varied business connections, Baltimore merchants maintained their close ties to European culture and their acquaintance with the charms of the Orient. Families of means knew of fashionable preferences abroad (and elsewhere in America) and readily adopted cosmopolitan tastes. "Foreign" and "Imported" appeared often in eye-catching type in newspaper advertisements, which enumerated the latest goods to have arrived at the docks. Baltimoreans also commissioned in-town craftsmen (and the widow of one) to execute work, notably interiors and decorative-arts pieces, that both imitated European styles and expressed local preferences. Baltimore furniture, decorated with paint or fancy wood inlays, and beautifully detailed Baltimore silver of this period took their places in the forefront of American design. The merchant-craftsmen John and Hugh Finlay typified the trade; they advertised in 1803 that they had for sale, but also would "make to any pattern, all kinds of FANCY and JAPANNED FURNITURE." Their wares and shop skills ran to card, pier, tea, dressing, writing, and shaving tables; stands for candles and wash pans; bedsteads, along with bed and window cornices; cane-seat, rush-seat, and Windsor chairs; and fire-and candle-screens, "with or without views adjacent to the city."[3] In this flush time of European war and Baltimore profit, the wealthiest Baltimoreans could afford interiors, furnishings, and finery that spoke clearly of personal and family taste.

IN THE EARLY FEDERAL PERIOD, the finest examples of Baltimore architecture could be found in the country. The Warner & Hanna map depicted many hills surrounding the city, nearly all of them dotted with country retreats and formal gardens. The city remained small enough to permit easy travel between the town and residences in the adjacent countryside. Importantly, country houses enabled owners and their families to escape the summer's heat as well as the yellow fever epidemics that ravaged Baltimore after 1794. A visiting French nobleman, Moreau de Saint-Méry, noticed that the country north and west of the town was "everywhere interspersed with gentlemen's summer seats." A Baltimore newspaper with wide circulation declared in 1812 that these rural seats displayed "at the same time, elegant specimens of architectural taste, and the most improved state of cultivation."[4] Only a few of them survived the outward growth of the city, several disappearing as late as the mid-twentieth century, when students of taste and design recognized their character but before historians had fully recorded their features. Place names alone recall the houses or their owners—Belvidere, Bolton Hill, Mondawmin, Montebello, Druid Hill, O'Donnell Square, Patterson Park.

Many of the houses reflected a fashion known in Britain as Regency (for the regency of George IV) and in the United States as the Federal style. It had brought freshness to British design not long before Americans, having won independence and framed a stronger union of states, sought their own new approaches to building. Regency style grew out of the historical sensibility, books, and buildings of the avant-garde English architects Sir John Soane and Sir William Chambers and the Scottish-born architects Robert and James Adam. Like the Georgian style, that of the Adam brothers reflected the British preference for order and stability. It also reflected the mid-eighteenth-century fascination with new archaeological discoveries in Italy, at Pompeii, Herculaneum, and elsewhere. Taking new measurements and reconsidering the Georgian model, Robert Adam found the verticality and attenuated forms of classical exteriors appealing. His designs exhibited a fascination for thinness, along with a sense of fluidity. He announced that he wished to give a sense of "movement," which was "meant to express, the rise and fall, the advance and recess, with other diversity of form, in the different parts of a building, so as to add greatly to the picturesque of the composition."[5]

Adam thus challenged the formality, solidity, and authority that characterize Georgian style and its decoration. On the exterior, the Adam brothers freed themselves from geometric design. They introduced the concept of oval rooms and full-height curving or polygonal façade projections called bows, usually extending from the garden front. Enhancing the sense of verticality and graciousness, the bowed projections usually contained the "salon," meant for entertaining. With the introduction of oval and polygonal rooms, both in-

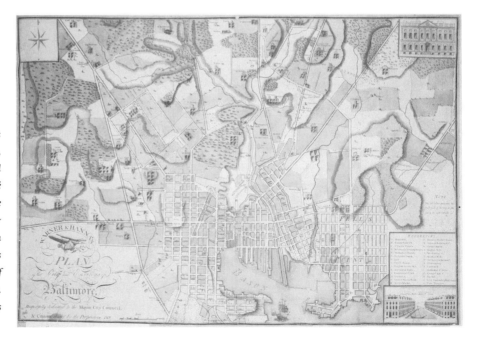

Warner & Hanna's Plan of the City and Environs of Baltimore, *1801. Originally drawn and published in 1799 by Charles Varlé and republished by the Baltimore printers and booksellers Warner & Hanna in 1801, this carefully drawn map notes the locations and owners of country seats, showing views of the houses and their gardens. Maryland State Archives

terior plans and the exterior form of the building that housed and reflected them became more complex.

Exterior and interior design details were adapted creatively from classical examples. Roofs became flatter and sometimes disappeared behind balustrades; Adamesque designs also muted or omitted the typically prominent Georgian dormers. The Adam brothers' exterior designs, further borrowing from recovered classical examples, introduced elliptical fanlights over doorways and plaques under windows. Exterior windows became narrower in proportion to height, and the glazing bars more delicate than in Georgian design. The elliptical superseded geometry; verticality triumphed over the horizontal. Inside, the Adams made use of molded plasterwork, which traced delicate foliage, urns, and decorative vines across oval ceiling medallions, decorative friezes, archways, "door caps," window cases, and fireplace mantels. Delighting in what they believed to be classical color schemes of delicate blues, greens, and pinks, they embraced the classical for its elegance, security, and patina of discipline. In the late eighteenth century the Adams' designs and theories defined what was fashionable in London, Bath, and Edinburgh and found expression in both English country and urban house design. Americans had neither the means nor the desire to build structures as grand as the Adams' English masterpieces, for example, Kedleston Hall, in Derbyshire. But the emphasis on scale and elegance of manner pleased them. When the new Adam fashion arrived in the United States in the pages of design folios and pattern books for builders, it rapidly won favor.

The Regency style also included a taste for the picturesque. Knowledge of foreign and historic design, and preoccupation with landscape design occasioned experiments with Chinese, Indian, Turkish, and Gothic styles—and even the aesthetic possibilities of the constructed ruin as a building form. The English were not alone in these developments. In France and Germany architects also took giant steps in the direction of definition of the aesthetic principles of design and the creation of a new style.

Craftsmen and Country Sites

Federal-period designs first appeared, as was common with the introduction of new architectural styles, in the form of interior decoration. As Baltimore overtook Annapolis, the widow of Charles Carroll, the Barrister, who had died in 1783, resolved to leave the family home in Annapolis and make the country seat, Mount Clare, her principal residence. The house was then thirty years old, and Mrs. Carroll decided to redo its interior in the fashionable Adam style. To handle the task she chose Joseph Kennedy, an Irish-born stucco workman, plasterer, and painter, who, in a later newspaper advertisement, claimed the Mount Clare interior as one of the best specimens of his work.[6]

The Kennedy mantels exemplified the early-Federal, high-style achievements of Baltimore craftsmen, whose growing number included John Rawlins, an English plasterer who had arrived in Annapolis in 1771. Rawlins there created the ceilings in Edward Lloyd's new house, perhaps the finest plasterwork in prerevolutionary Maryland. By the mid-1780s Rawlins had moved his business to Baltimore, where he received commissions to execute the stucco details at Perry Hall, the Baltimore County country house of Harry Dorsey

Salon ceiling medallion from Willow Brook, built ca. 1797. Baltimore Museum of Art
RIGHT:
"Old Wrought Iron Fanlight Grilles, Baltimore, Md., drawn by J. Appleton Wilson," 1898. Enoch Pratt Free Library

Gough, and the banquet room at Mount Vernon for George Washington. Rawlins's artistry became the epitome of Federal decoration in Baltimore, and after his death in 1788 his widow, Mary Rawlins, pledged to carry on his "Composition Work in all its Branches," specifying "Moulding, and Ornament for Doors, Windows, and for Wood Cornices, and particular Chimney Pieces."[7] Local craftsmen furnished customers with all sorts of molded landscape tablets, vases, flower festoons, sheaves of wheat, impressions of vines and ivy, and images of Apollo and Lyre; one boasted in 1797 of having composition ornaments "much superior to any imports, and much cheaper."[8] Artisans on the level of Kennedy and Rawlins might apply the stucco directly to the ceiling or cornice of a room and there mold it (strong beer apparently added moisture and promoted cohesion); more often plasterers poured the stucco into molds—available from manufacturers, although the more talented made their own—and then applied the dried pieces, masking the joints.[9] The "Carving and Gilding" partnership of James and George Smith seems to have adopted the more common method. In 1795 they advertised stuccowork executed in "the cheapest manner."[10]

Fanlights over main doorways, rooms painted in delicate hues, and fine plasterwork—distinctive marks of the Federal style—varied, of course, with the means of the owner, but suppliers increasingly included locals, who grew in number just as the skilled local artisans did. "House-Painting. In the newest European fashion," boasted one contractor, who also handled fancy pattern cloths for floors, blinds painted with flowers, and chimney screens decorated with rural scenes; rooms decorated "in an elegant manner," advertised a rival, the Fells Point painter and paperhanger Thomas Fletcher Dixon, in 1784.[11] They and their competitors used both oil and "distemper" (water-based) paints, sources normally being British or Dutch. Colors ran to various blues, pink, and pigments with natural names like *cream, pea-green, straw, stone,* and *slate* (presumably for flooring or detail work). After 1808 a firm of

Baltimore paint makers announced the availability of "PRUSSIAN BLUE of their own Manu-factures."[12] Paper hangings (later called wallpaper) and imitations of them became increas-ingly popular. "PAINTING in imitation of Paper-Hangings," one clever fellow announced in 1795. "By a mechanical process, which, from its facility, enables the operator to paint a room, staircase, &c, upon lower terms than it is possible to hang it with paper of equal beauty."[13] At first imported from London and Paris or purchased from Boston and Philadelphia, paper hangings and paper borders, too, became available from Baltimore suppliers in about 1801. Stenciled or block-printed, paper hangings at the time came not in rolls but in sheets, re-quiring much skill in the application.

Two grand country houses on the outskirts of Baltimore further introduced the new Federal style to the region. After returning from service in Washington's army, Col. John Eager Howard inherited land north of Baltimore Town. There (near the later intersection of Calvert and Chase Streets), between 1786 and 1794, he built Belvidere, an unusually large dwelling by American standards of the time. The central block was 63 feet wide by 40 feet deep, but when the two wings and hyphens completing a five-part plan were added, its length reached 150 feet. Kitchen and scullery occupied one of the wings. In 1798 Thomas Twining, founder of the English tea company, reported that Howard's mansion "was upon the plan of and possessed all the elegance of an English villa."[14]

Owing much to Georgian style, Belvidere nonetheless offered Adamesque novelty. The five-part plan, cubic form of the main block, hip roof with dormer windows (on the sides), molded water table, and belt course repeated older Georgian forms. But the door and win-dow proportions were taller and lighter than was typical of Georgian design, and slender, full-

height Doric pilasters framed the slightly projecting central pavilion, whose broken pediment was marked by a large lunette. Thin Doric pilasters also set off the tall second-floor central window. Belvidere illustrated another important feature of Adamesque design: a bow-shaped projection marking the garden front. The oval salon within, flanked by draw-ing and dining rooms to either side, over-looked and in this case opened onto the lawn and garden below. Twining wrote of taking breakfast in this "noble room." It afforded an "exquisite prospect," the grounds of Belvidere forming "a beautiful slant toward the Chesa-peake."[15]

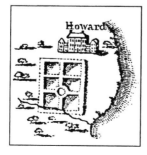

Belvidere, Governor Howard's estate, as pictured on Warner & Hanna's Plan of the City and Environs of Baltimore. *Courtesy of Barbara Wells Sarudy*

Within sight of Belvidere, on thirty-five acres north and west of it, the English-born import-export merchant George Grundy built Bolton in about 1786. Bolton took the more fashionable form of a freestanding villa without wings or hyphens and thus made a

Belvidere, entrance (north) front, from a photograph taken after the Civil War. Maryland Historical Society

Belvidere, garden front, as seen in an oil painting by Augustus Weidenbach, ca. 1841. Maryland Historical Society

Belvidere was demolished in 1875.

more assertive Adamesque statement than did Belvidere. The north-facing front of the house featured a projecting central pavilion, framed by a pedimented entrance portico; a two-story bow projected from the center of Bolton's south, or garden, front. The unknown designer achieved the verticality associated with the Federal style by placing full-height pilasters at each corner of the house and making door and window openings tall and narrow. Built of brick but painted off-white, Bolton rose two stories, had a hipped roof, and measured sixty-four feet wide by thirty-eight feet deep—slightly wider than, but not as deep as, the central block of Belvidere.[16] The wide entrance hall led to a library at the right, and, opposite, to the main stair. Beyond, the great hall ran back to the bow room and flanking drawing and dining rooms (each a spacious eighteen by twenty-two feet). In the absence of out-buildings, the house depended on its basement for kitchen, larder, scullery, housekeeper's room, and servants' bedrooms. Grundy eventually went bankrupt and lost Bolton.

An English-born landscape artist, Francis Guy, worked in Baltimore between 1798 and 1817, capturing many contemporary views of important buildings as well as painting house portraits on commission. His carefully rendered views of many of the stylish country houses of the day give a good picture of both their architecture and their garden surroundings. Guy also embellished a group of fancy chairs made by John and Hugh Finlay with images of grand Baltimore country estates.

Other Baltimore merchants soon adopted the fashionable Federal style for country estates, more than fifty of which were noted by federal direct-tax collectors in 1798 or appeared in Warner & Hanna's 1801 map. Willow Brook, the country house of Thoroughgood Smith, a prosperous merchant and Baltimore's second mayor, rose on twenty-six bucolic acres west of town (at what became Hollins and Mount Streets) in about 1797. It offered a classic example of a late Anglo-Palladian villa (originally derived from Palladio's farmhouse designs)—a relatively small house with a two-story central portion flanked by one-story wings. In both plan and elevation, Willow Brook's unknown designer demonstrated his familiarity with such English pattern books as Robert Morris's *Select Architect* (London, 1757). The Willow Brook property sloped away sharply to the east, and clearly both builder and patron sensed the potential of the site. Willow Brook's entrance portico, with a small porch, faced the northwest.

Visitors passed through a wide, rectangular hall to a polygonal bay at the rear of the house, which contained an elegant grand salon. Its twenty-two-foot-wide by twenty-five-foot-long elliptical shape, nearly fifteen-foot-high ceiling, and plaster details make it perhaps the finest Adamesque room ever built in Baltimore. The ceiling medallion is a particular triumph. From a center of elongated leaves radiates a circular pattern of ribs with shallow

Bolton, George Grundy's estate, as depicted on Warner & Hanna's Plan of the City and Environs of Baltimore, 1801. Courtesy of Barbara Wells Sarudy

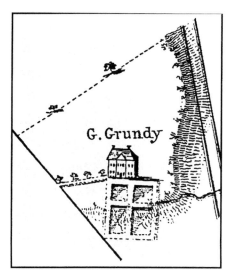

Bolton, entrance (north) front, as painted by Francis Guy on a chair's crest rail, ca. 1804. The Baltimore Museum of Art: Gift of Lydia Howard de Roth and Nancy H. DeFord Venable, in memory of their mother, Lydia Howard DeFord; and Purchase Fund BMA 1966.26.2

Bolton stood until 1900, when it
came down to make way for the
Fifth Regiment Armory.

Bolton, distant view from the south,
oil painting by Francis Guy, 1805.
Bolton's two-story bow overlooked
extensive gardens. In the lower
right-hand corner, owner George
Grundy proudly surveys the scene.
Maryland Historical Society

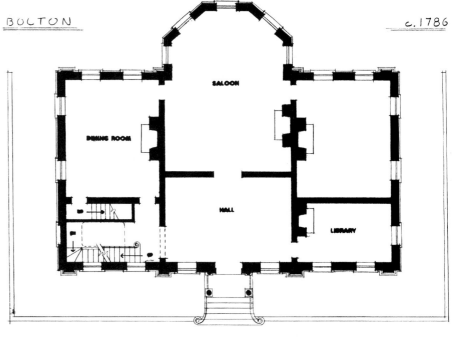

First-floor plan of Bolton.
Conjectural drawing by
Michael F. Trostel

Willow Brook. From a painted chair back by Francis Guy, ca. 1804. The Baltimore Museum of Art: Gift of Lydia Howard de Roth and Nancy H. DeFord Venable, in memory of their mother, Lydia Howard DeFord; and Purchase Fund BMA 1966.26.6

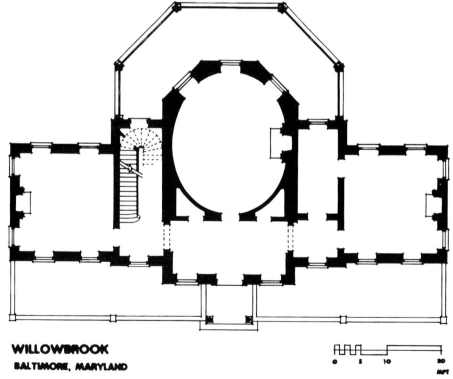

First-floor plan of Willow Brook. Drawing by Michael F. Trostel

WILLOWBROOK
BALTIMORE, MARYLAND

0   5   10   20
MFT

Upon the razing of Willow Brook in 1965, the Baltimore Museum of Art saved its entrance hall and oval salon, including its large, Adamesque ceiling medallion. The finely worked details, the scale and proportions of forms, and period furniture all produce a striking effect.

elliptical sections between. A circle of acanthus leaves frames the circle of ribs, while swags of bellflowers drip from the leaves against the flat ceiling. The composition ornament throughout the rest of the house also drew directly on the decorative vocabulary of the brothers Adam. The door case has pilasters decorated with composition acorns and oak leaves surmounted by a pineapple motif. Bellflowers and beading enrich the chair rail. Swags, urns, and foliate scrolls below a band of acanthus leaves decorate the plaster cornices in the entrance hall and parlor. The polygonal porch opening off the salon offered a spectacular vista of distant Baltimore and the Patapsco River.

As stylish as Willow Brook, but more original in design, Samuel Smith's country house, Montebello, stood on several hundred acres off Harford Road, two and a half miles north of Baltimore. Smith began building in 1799. At the time one of the wealthiest merchants in Baltimore, a Revolutionary War hero, and an incumbent congressman, he spared no expense on the summer residence he named after a French victory over the Austrians in 1800. Striking and beautiful, Montebello assembled all elements of the Adam style. Who designed it remains a mystery. Smith may have participated in its creation, and if so he may have been advised by William Birch of Philadelphia, also a painter and landscape designer. In any event, the elevations and plan of Montebello marked the house as a remarkable departure from buildings like Belvidere and Bolton. Delicate and full of curves, Montebello eschewed the four-square Georgian tradition altogether. The white-painted stucco exterior, the proportions and curving forms of the house, the flat and very low-pitched roofs hidden by balustrades, and the tall, narrow windows—all marked the height of Regency taste. The building related to the landscape in ways derived from early-nineteenth-century English books on gardening. It resembled the villas fashionable in England, where books with aquatint illustrations of designs of this kind had begun to appear. Nonetheless, it possessed an originality that was entirely American.

Montebello enjoyed a parklike setting, approached by a winding drive, with a level lawn in front. Very much intended as a villa, its stables and other outbuildings stood out of sight, away from the house. The design unusually combined one- and two-story elements. An elegant one-story entrance pavilion on the south side, with a colonnaded porch across the

front, housed the grand square saloon, or formal receiving room (twenty-five feet square and fifteen feet high), with its decorative plasterwork ceiling and circular skylight. Smaller square rooms opened to each side, enriched with Palladian windows set in arched recesses. The projecting colonnaded porch of the entryway stepped back toward the rooms on the east and west in graceful curves. The two-story main block sat to the rear, with bowed ends and a curved, central bay facing the garden. This contained an elegant oval dining room, which opened off of the grand saloon; the staircase and pantries occupied the west bowed wing; a drawing room, the eastern wing. Delicate balustrades, with very attenuated turn-

L.66—Montibello *[sic] the Seat of Gen. Smith. Maryland.* Etching Drawn, Engraved & Published by W. Birch Springland, 1808. 19 x 15 cm. Copy From Original Owned By The Maryland Historical Society. No Reproduction Without Permission.

Perspective view of Montibello, the Seat of Genl. S. Smith, Maryland, colored engraving by William R. Birch, published in his Country Seats, 1808. Maryland Historical Society

ings, ran around the flat roof of the one-story entry area and crowned the two-story sections as well, helping to hide the low-pitched roof and two chimneys while adding to the light, airy feeling of the villa. The second floor contained three bedrooms. The basement, which was fully exposed on the north side, housed service spaces; the kitchen was located directly beneath the dining room.

Another stylish villa, Druid Hill, was the work of owner Col. Nicholas Rogers, a prosperous flour merchant and self-described "gentleman-architect" who had served as a staff officer to Baron de Kalb during the Revolution. Shortly after the war, Rogers designed a country retreat, Druid Hill, on an estate northwest of Baltimore called Auchentorolie, which his wife had inherited. He took great care with the design both of the house and of the rolling land around it, choosing deciduous trees for their fall colors and mixing in evergreens. The house occupied a front of nearly sixty feet and was admired for its simplicity and elegance.

When this structure burned in 1796, Rogers promptly designed another house, completed it in 1798, and commissioned Francis Guy to paint its portrait soon thereafter. The second Rogers house was larger than the first and stylistically more adventurous. Crowning the hill, it sat on a high basement, was sixty-eight feet wide and fifty feet deep, and featured a stuccoed-brick exterior. Although it appeared to be a fashionable one-story villa, a second story was actually hidden behind a high balustrade, which ran around all sides of the house and extended out over the entrance portico. What appeared to be low attic windows belonged to a full second story (Thomas Jefferson adopted a similar scheme at Monticello). The entrance façade of Druid Hill presented the visitor with an imposing, deep, columned porch leading to a tall, arched entryway with sidelights. The slightly projecting central pavilion, rising above the roof line in stepped fashion, featured arched and oval second-floor windows and a top, rectangular panel decorated with carved swags.

A talented amateur architect with an impressive library of architectural books, Rogers prepared designs for a number of public and private buildings but never accepted a fee for his services. He drew on various sources for exterior design. The interplay of projecting and recessed panels above the entrance portico of Druid Hill reflected the influence of the British architect Sir John Soane (known through his published designs), as did the tripartite window designs on the side elevations. But the heavy English Baroque window frames at the basement level were old-fashioned and incompatible with the design of the windows above.

The lofty first floor, with thirteen-foot ceilings, had the characteristic plan of Baltimore country houses, accommodating saloon, drawing room, and dining room. These intercon-

Fallen into disrepair and an object of vandalism, the lovely Montebello came down in 1907. Its name survives in an area that serves as a city reservoir and the site of a hospital.

Montebello as it appeared in a late-nineteenth-century photograph. Peale Collection, Maryland Historical Society

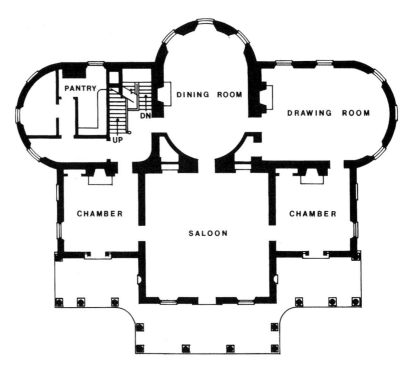

PANTRY

DINING ROOM

DRAWING ROOM

DN

UP

CHAMBER

SALOON

CHAMBER

FIRST FLOOR PLAN

0 5 10 15 20

First-floor plan of Montebello. Drawing by Michael F. Trostel

*View of Seat of Col. Rogers,
Near Baltimore (Druid Hill), oil
painting by Francis Guy, 1811.
Maryland Historical Society*

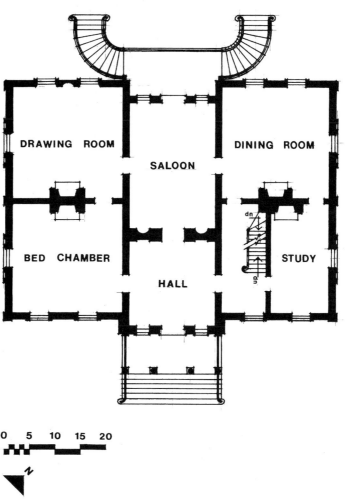

*First-floor plan of Druid Hill, ca.
1798. Drawing by Michael F. Trostel*

necting rooms provided the requisite three spaces for fashionable entertaining—a room for dancing, one for cards, and one for dining. To the left of the entrance was the principal bedroom; to the right, a stair hall and study. Although designed to be inconspicuous, the second story contained at least five bedrooms. Because the land dropped away to the north, the kitchen and other service spaces in the basement opened at ground level at the rear of the house.

Two early Baltimore country houses followed the path of Oriental fashion, which first appeared in England with publication of Sir William Chambers's *Designs of Chinese Building* in the mid-eighteenth century. Before taking up the study of architecture, Chambers had spent several years as a merchant seaman and made notes of the sights he had seen in the Far East. His work in the gardens of the royal retreat at Kew, completed in 1763, included a Chinese pagoda. Americans gradually chose those features of Chinese design that did not stray too far from the familiar; Jefferson's Monticello eventually drew upon Chinese angled-wood patterns in fancy exterior railings. Beech Hill, the summer house of the Scottish-born merchant Robert Gilmor, who had the house built on ten acres he purchased in 1797, seems also to have drawn inspiration from Chinese sources—and like Monticello, these appeared in details rather than structure. Lying on the first range of hills west of the town (just beyond what became Franklin Square), the property adjoined Willow Brook. Gilmor's son described the site as one with "a beautiful and extensive prospect, commanding a view of the city, bay, river and surrounding country." Typifying the practice of country-house families, the Gilmors spent June through mid-September there. A "cottage sort of house," as Robert Gilmor Jr. recalled, Beech Hill stood one and a half stories high and measured forty-three by thirty feet, with a high basement and two detached wings connected to the house by arcades.[17] With Chinese-style wooden railings around the porch and roof details of an Oriental flavor, Beech Hill betrayed the occasional taste for the whimsical seen in some Baltimore country houses of the day.

On the eastern side of the city, John O'Donnell's Canton offered another example of exotic tastes. The name of the estate recalled Captain O'Donnell's voyage to that Chinese port in 1785, thereby opening Baltimore's trade with the East. The long, low house, with a deep

Because the city eventually acquired the Rogers estate for a park and a city reservoir, parts of Druid Hill survive as the core of the contemporary Mansion House. Park visitors can look across a spacious meadow to the house on its rise much as did the Rogers family in 1800.

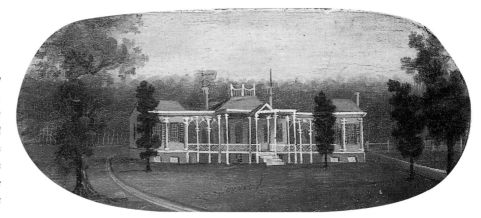

Beech Hill, as Francis Guy portrayed it on a chair back, ca. 1804. Baltimore Museum of Art: Gift of Lydia Howard de Roth and Nancy H. DeFord Venable, in memory of their mother, Lydia Howard DeFord; and Purchase Fund BMA 1966.26.5

View of the Bay from Near Mr. Gilmor's, *oil painting by Francis Guy, 1804. Maryland Historical Society*

veranda in front, had somewhat the appearance of a "pucka bungalow" (*pucka,* an Anglo-Indian word meaning genuine or good), thought the visitor Thomas Twining.[18] It was pleasantly situated among fields and woods, not far from the confluence of the Patapsco River and the Chesapeake.

The finest Federal-style villa to survive in Baltimore, Homewood House, derived solely from the Anglo-American world. The design has long been attributed to its owner, Charles Carroll of Homewood, whose celebrated father, Charles Carroll of Carrollton, in 1800 purchased 130 acres north of the city on which to build a country seat for his son and bride, Miss Harriet Chew, of Philadelphia, sister of Mrs. John Eager Howard, of Belvidere. If the new husband did design the house himself, he had the usual aids for such amateurs: design books from abroad, firsthand knowledge of other villas, and conversations with local carpenter-builders. Two brothers, Robert and William Edwards, acted as the contractors and Michael Keplinger supplied the bricks. The masonry of the exterior walls, well laid up, exhibits the narrow joints typical of the best Baltimore brickwork.

Adam exquisiteness dominated the taste of most country-house builders in Baltimore, but Homewood testified that affection for late Georgian architecture had not disappeared. One could describe the small house as a dainty anachronism, with its five-part Georgian plan clothed in delicate, Federal-style details. Carroll of Homewood chose a floor plan that harked back to older forms—a central block, hyphens, and dependencies—but ended up creating a fashionable, one-story, Adamesque villa. Its principal block contained a central hall that ran from front to back—southeast carriage entrance to northwest garden entrance—and contained four major rooms, two on each side of the hall. From the entrance portico, one could look to the city and harbor; through it, visitors entered the reception hall, off of which the drawing room on the right (east) and a dining room on the west opened directly. Two other rooms, roughly the same size as these, lay on either side of the rear por-

*Homewood House as it appeared in
a photograph taken ca. 1908 by
R. L. Harris. Maryland
Historical Society*

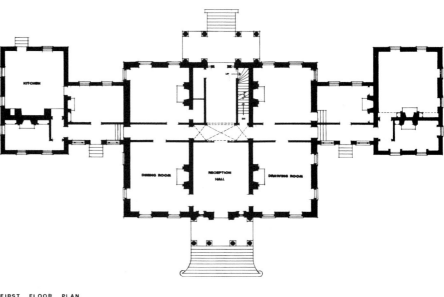

FIRST FLOOR PLAN

0   5   10   15   20

HOMEWOOD
BALTIMORE, MARYLAND

*First-floor plan, Homewood.
Drawing by Michael F. Trostel*

tion of the central hall. They may have been dedicated to family use, possibly a parlor or music room on the west and a major bedroom on the east. Corridors that divided the center block lengthwise ran off the central hall to connect the main block to the hyphens. A low-ceilinged second story, with dormer windows (one on either side of the main front), contained modest bedrooms for the children of the family. A simple staircase, hidden behind a wall, led to this floor and, like Jefferson's staircases at Monticello, was conspicuous by its understatement in the interior design. The basement contained storage spaces, including a wine cellar. Carroll placed the kitchen in the western wing; that on the east may have served as the master bedroom.

Homewood did not exhibit the polygonal bays and oval rooms that had begun to appear in other fashionable houses of the same date in Baltimore, but its well-hidden second story, attenuated windows, delicate exterior ornament, and interior decorations nonetheless embraced the new Adamesque style. A full-height, freestanding portico, with a broad sweep of steps, very slender Corinthian columns, and classical pediment, marked by a shield-shaped window decorated with swags and foliate motifs in high relief, dominated the façade. Interior details, equally Adamesque, exceeded even the delicacy of Willow Brook. A subtle shift toward a more refined style had occurred both in the taste of patrons and in the work of American craftsmen. Carroll's plasterers borrowed from pattern books but freely departed from them. Flattened oval pilasters framed the window and door cases. Plaster groin vaults graced the ceiling of the entrance and rear halls. Bellflowers accented the angles where the planes of the vaulting met, an oval medallion with radiating leaves marking the center. Four wooden columns in the corners of this section of the corridor appeared to support the plaster vaults; in reality, the vaulting springs from the corners of the walls.

Homewood reflected the younger Charles Carroll's taste, his insistence on the finest materials, and the skill of the builders and craftsmen he employed. Construction began in 1801 and went on for three years. The senior Carroll had budgeted $10,000 for the house. By 1804, to his surprise and considerable annoyance, costs approached $40,000.[19]

After the completion of Homewood, country-house building proceeded apace, with im-

Main doorway, interior view, and ceiling medallion of Homewood. Photographs by James T. van Rensselaer, Homewood House Museum, The Johns Hopkins University

migrant French architects offering Baltimoreans further examples of refined taste. This French influence arrived in Baltimore from a number of sources. Some soldiers stayed in town after service with the Marquis de Lafayette. Later, in July 1791, fleeing French revolutionary terror, a party of priests, servants, and candidates for the priesthood from the community of Saint Sulpice arrived from Paris. Not long afterward, many white residents of the French colony of Saint Domingue (later Haiti)—fifteen hundred people in fifty-three ships—fled to Baltimore to escape the wrath of former slave Toussaint L'Ouverture and his followers. This highly educated and cultured group of refugees made a distinctive mark on the young city, filling such professions as medicine, teaching, and shipbuilding and serving as artists, dancing masters, musicians, and craftsmen. In 1795 one of them, a copperplate engraver who had begun his career in Paris, J. J. Boudier, placed the public on notice that he could teach "Lessons on Architectural Drawing" and oversee construction.[20]

In 1810 Abraham Lerew (or Larue), evidently a French-born carpenter and architect, designed a summer house about five miles south of Ellicott City for Maryland legislator Charles Sterret Ridgely. Fully sympathetic to the work of the Adam brothers and Soane, Lerew's structure—Ridgely called the place Oakland—also reflected awareness of new directions in French design. A recessed central bay and windows framed by shallow, arched reveals stressed the flatness, the planarity, of the smooth outside walls, which Lerew stretched tightly between the horizontal course of masonry at the basement level and the broad cornice line. These horizontal accents unified the design, marked at its center by a dramatic entryway framed by attenuated Tuscan columns and set beneath a spectacular fanlight. A bold, tripartite window on the second floor level completed the composition.

Another French architect, Joseph Jacques Ramée, left Napoleonic Europe for New York in about 1812 and several years later moved to Baltimore, where he designed a curious country house for a banker, Dennis Smith, out the Frederick Road. Smith's Calverton featured a raised basement and a two-story portico with an arched ceiling, a peaked roof, and a second-story platform for ornamental statuary. The main block had a hipped roof and tall cupola. To either side, two-story bows contained circular rooms on the first floor, each twenty-six feet in diameter, which opened off the entry hall—a composition not unlike that used at Montebello. Its exterior was "rough cast of a straw color, the window sills and facings of marble and free stone." By 1823 Ramée had returned to France. He afterward published drawings of the house which suggested that flanking covered passageways may have led from the rear of the house to octagonal dependencies.[21]

Town Houses

Closer to the water, along Pratt and Water Streets and in Fells Point, merchants and ship captains built fashionable houses that owed equally to import-export profits and local craftsmen. Although much modest housing had heretofore been built of wood, brick remained the preferred material for those who could afford it. After 1799, however, all new buildings had to be of brick, to comply with a city ordinance aiming to reduce the danger of fire. Bricks

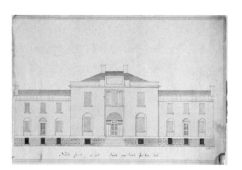

Oakland, north front, watercolored presentation drawing by Abraham Lerew, ca. 1810. Maryland Historical Society

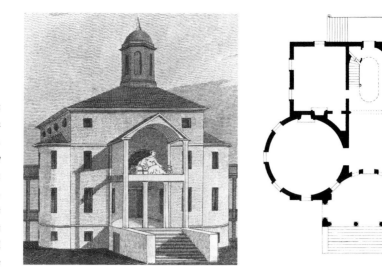

LEFT:
*Calverton, built in 1815, detail from
a nineteenth-century engraving.
Maryland Historical Society*
RIGHT:
*First-floor plan of Calverton.
Drawing based on exterior views
and contemporary descriptions
of interior, by Michael F. Trostel
and Peter Pearre*

Smith eventually went bankrupt
and lost Calverton, which
became the Hebrew Orphan
Asylum. It burned down
in 1873 or 1874.

signaled station and permanence; ample sources of clay in southwest Baltimore and else-where kept the price low, and active brickyards met the demand for locally made brick. "All the houses are of brick and built on the English plan," testified a French traveler in 1791; "that is to say, that they are narrow-fronted houses, not very high, and that they have consider-able depth." "This town is built chiefly of brick," agreed New York attorney James Kent in 1793; he marveled that so many houses stood side by side, apparently joined together. The Englishman Twining had only details to add to this large impression. "The houses here were larger and handsomer in general than in the lower streets," he wrote after walking about the heart of the city and along Baltimore Street one Sunday, "but all were nearly upon the same plan, being built of red brick, having two or three windows in front, and three ranges of rooms or stories in height, of which the lowest was generally occupied by the shop and the passage, and the two above by sitting-rooms and bedrooms."[22]

Between 1786 and 1788, on the north side of Water Street (opposite his docks and ware-houses), Robert Gilmor erected an imposing, five-bay-wide, three-and-a-half-story town house of this description. At this early date it stood alone and Twining described it as "a large, square, detached mansion, the handsomest I had yet observed in Baltimore."[23] On the second floor of the house, a thirty-foot drawing room stretched along the street side, a de-sign feature common to these dwellings, in which the merchant's counting rooms often oc-cupied parts of the ground floor.

Contemporary observers rightly commented on the comparative sameness and restraint of Baltimore town-house designs in this period—two and a half or three and a half stories high, three to five bays wide, simply framed windows symmetrically arranged, and dormer windows to provide light to the garret. Most lots for three-bay-wide houses ranged between eighteen and twenty-five feet wide; five-bay-wide houses usually occupied fifty-foot-wide, or larger, lots. The width of a house typically extended fully across the lot, and in areas of the city where there were no back alleys (as in early Fells Point), rear yards had to be reached via an arched opening between houses called a sally port. Behind the main house, a narrow "piazza," or "pantry," usually contained service stairs and formed a connection to the wider,

Detail from portrait of Robert Gilmor, by Charles Willson Peale, 1788, showing the view of the harbor and Federal Hill just outside his front window, on Water Street. Colonial Williamsburg Foundation

RIGHT:

The merchant Jesse Hollingsworth built this house at 931 Fell Street between 1782 and 1796, and in 1796 he sold it to John Steele, former ships' captain and now shipowner. Typical of stately town houses of the Federal period, the building was fully restored in the mid-twentieth century. Photograph by Jane Webb Smith

long back building, which housed kitchen, breakfast room, upstairs bedrooms, and possibly servants' quarters. Back buildings were always a few feet narrower than the main block of the house, so that light and air could reach rear rooms from the side yard. Baltimore builders adhered to a side-hall floor plan even then associated with Philadelphia. The entry hall led back to a set of stairs and opened into front and rear parlors, the latter often used as a dining room.

Insurance records, orders for materials, and auction announcements supply verbal descriptions of some of these town houses. In 1798, building not far from Robert Gilmor on Water Street, Samuel Smith, one of Baltimore's wealthiest merchants, began constructing a brick town house three and a half stories high and five bays wide, after his own design. He commissioned several craftsmen—John Scriggs, likely a carpenter; Robert Stewart, a stonecutter; and a brick mason, James Morris—to construct the massive pile, some fifty-three feet wide and forty-five feet deep. The house had a fashionable octagonal projection at the rear, along with an attached back building, which sheltered pantries, kitchen, extra bedrooms, and other service spaces. A separate two-story building contained a springhouse and a smokehouse, while a one-and-a-half-story (nineteen- by thirty-one-foot) stable and a coach house faced the alley running behind the property. The elegance of Smith's interior can be inferred from his orders, in the fall of 1796, to his agents in Leghorn, Italy, requesting various marble chimney pieces "after the English Fashion as elegant as can be made for 130 Guineas & carefully packed"; one set of elegant pink and white marble ornaments for the "chimney mantel piece"; and another set of variegated marble, along with candles, Parmesan cheeses, and cases of the "best Florence wine in flasks."[24]

Not all merchants succeeded, of course, and in 1800, when Adrian Valck abruptly offered his three-story brick residence for sale, his misfortune inadvertently supplied another detailed inventory and a picture of the scale and comfort merchants demanded of builders. The published sale notice described the recently built house as "new, commodious and elegant." It stretched about thirty-seven feet along Pratt Street and was eighty-five feet deep. An entry room, parlor, dining, and housekeeper's rooms occupied the ground floor, piazza and pantry connecting to "a spacious brick kitchen with a bake oven, smokehouse, etc. and lodging rooms for servants over it." A salon with two fireplaces occupied the entire front of the house on the second floor, with two more rooms in the rear. Four chambers occupied the third floor. "All the apartments have fireplaces, are distributed conveniently, finished well and with taste, some with wainscoting, closets, recesses, cornices, stuccoed ceilings, chimney pieces of Italian marble fully carved in a superior style of workmanship etc.," the advertisement declared. "Under the whole house and kitchen are excellent cellars. On a back lot and adjoining, fronting a nine foot alley, is erected a brick stable for 4 horses, coach house and office."[25]

"Baltimore Room." The second-floor front parlor from the house at 913 East Pratt Street, built ca. 1810 for merchant Henry Craig. The Metropolitan Museum of Art, Rogers Fund, 1918 (18.101–4). Photograph by Richard Cheek. Copyright The Metropolitan Museum of Art

Of all these period Baltimore mansions, few received more studied attention than the house Dr. Joseph Allender built for his bride, Mary Biays, in 1800. Mary's father, Joseph Biays, an established Fells Point merchant, supplied the land—a portion of a double lot, some sixty feet wide, on what was then Fell Street (later the segment of Thames Street between Broadway and Bond Street). Facing the street, the property ran back to the water. Biays's own house stood on its western portion.

The Allenders' three-and-a-half-story house measured a bit more than thirty-six feet wide, an arched front door and a sally port to the rear service yard nicely balancing the façade. Flemish-bond brickwork, traditional symmetry, and finely detailed dormer windows lent elegance to the conservatively styled exterior. Inside, the Allender house illustrated the two-room-deep, side-hall plan so common in Baltimore town houses of the period. Behind the main house, the piazza connected to a three-story, two-room-deep back building (the kitchen was located in the basement, at the rear). The first floor consisted of entrance hall, parlor (or reception room), and dining room. Graceful stairs led to a grand drawing (and dancing) room running the entire width of the second-floor front. Curved niches, ornamented with decorative plasterwork, flanked the fireplaces in both the dining and drawing rooms. Adamesque touches—classical swags, *paterae* (oval decorative forms), and elongated columns—also appeared in the plaster cornices of the house, the doorway enframements, and the chair rails.

Beginning in 1810, on a high and highly desirable city lot (on the south side of Pleasant Street between Charles and St. Paul Streets), the recently widowed Judith Riddell and a carpenter-builder whom she hired, John Donaldson, created another well-documented town house in the Federal style. A brick building twenty-eight feet wide, it stood two and a half stories high, with a back building along its western side. Brick masons laid the façade in Flemish bond, and Riddell called for two marble courses to mark the façade at the first- and second-story levels. With a wide marble stoop and iron railings as ornate as any in the city at the time (and identical to those at Homewood), the entrance was the focus of the façade. Rather than having a projecting portico, the frontispiece was recessed the depth of the front

NORTH ELEVATION

1621 THAMES STREET
FELL'S POINT   BALTIMORE   MARYLAND

North elevation, 1621 Thames Street, the Joseph Allender house. Historic American Buildings Survey, Library of Congress

The Allender house stood at 1621 Thames Street until 1937. Before its demolition, the Historic American Buildings Survey took photographs of interior spaces and produced measured drawings of the structure. "It has been a prey to neglect, antique hunters, fire, vandalism and now the elements," wrote the Baltimore architect who measured the building. "But enough remains to suggest its original elegance. Rooms that once knew the manifold activities of family life hear now only the rain dripping from floor to floor and the hollow echoes of the ship noises in the nearby harbor."[27] A few of the elaborate door cases and other details, including one of the several marble mantels that enriched the major rooms, survive at Olney, a country house in Harford County, Maryland.

wall and had broad sidelights; slim columns flanked the double door, and an arched, leaded fanlight extended over the whole. The fanlight was the work of John Martin, identified in city directories as an "ornamental sash maker." Panels with raised octagons decorated the doors and appeared under the sidelights, on the imposts to either side, and in the soffit of the arch overhead.[26]

While the floor plans generally followed common side-hall design, Riddell, who eventually married a member of the Carroll family, spared no expense on interior details, especially on the first and second floors. She ordered cloudy-marble mantels, slabs, and hearths for the drawing and dining rooms, where Donaldson installed the richest woodwork: wainscoting, a deep cornice, interior shutters for the two windows in each room, and elegant door enframements consisting of pilaster-like posts supporting a deep lintel ornamented with Federal-style oval designs and corner blocks with circular designs. Fancy wallpaper embellished the drawing and dining rooms. The stair railing and wainscoting along the stairway were mahogany; the balusters, curled maple. Paneled wainscoting ran along both sides of the front entrance hallway. An elliptical arch, supported by pairs of attenuated, fluted Doric columns, separated the front from the rear stair hall. A similar arch, set just inside the front door, formed a vestibule. Both the front and rear windows of the main house boasted panes slightly larger than the norm; they had been ordered from Boston.

Riddell's house thus exceeded typical specifications and costs, but it also illustrated the height of fashion—and the advance of technology. Fireplaces in the four major rooms made use of the innovations of Benjamin Thompson, Count Rumford, who had found that lower,

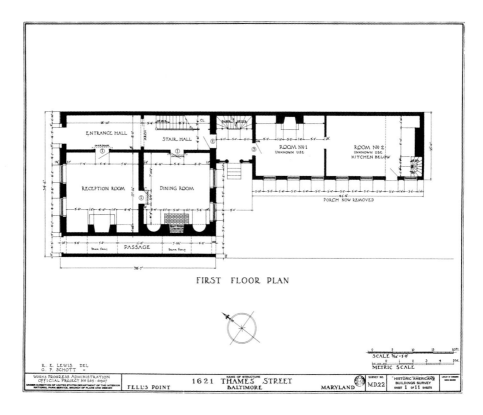

FIRST FLOOR PLAN

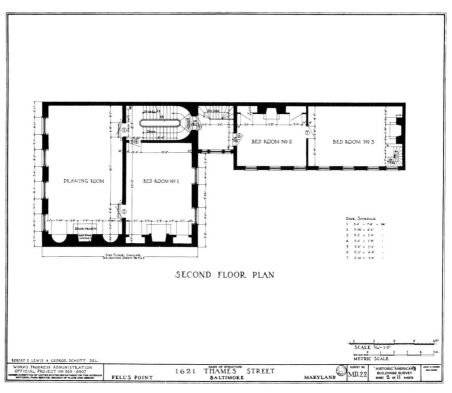

SECOND FLOOR PLAN

First- and second-floor plans, 1621 Thames Street. Historic American Buildings Survey, Library of Congress

Drawing room doorways, 1621
Thames Street. Photograph by
E. H. Pickering, 1936. Historic
American Buildings Survey,
Library of Congress

narrower, and shallower fireplaces, with side walls narrowing toward the top, or throat, of the firebox, gave off more heat and drew smoke better than did old-fashioned hearths. The Riddell house kitchen featured another Rumford design—a roasting oven set in the chimney above the firebox, a closed space that maximized heat transfer. Benefitting from pipes newly laid by the Baltimore Water Company, formed in 1804, the house had running water.

No less than country houses, stylish Baltimore town houses borrowed heavily from English and also, occasionally, Continental fashion. A French soldier who stayed in the United States after the Revolution, Paul Bentalou prospered as a Baltimore merchant, and between 1797 and 1799 he commissioned émigré architect and sculptor John Abraham Chevalier to build a double house immediately to the east of Samuel Smith's dwelling on Water Street. While his background and training remain unknown, Chevalier clearly knew of and appreciated prevailing French architectural taste. Intending the separate residences to appear as one (making the structure much larger in scale than nearby mansions), he created a three-and-a-half-

LEFT:
Riddell-Carroll house entrance,
11 East Pleasant Street, as
photographed in the 1930s,
shortly before demolition.
Enoch Pratt Free Library
RIGHT:
Reconstructed first- and second-
floor plans, Riddell-Carroll house.
Drawing by R. Anderson. From
Robert L. Alexander, "The Riddell-
Carroll House in Baltimore,"
Winterthur Portfolio
28 (1993): 124.

story structure that rested on a high basement and extended fifty-eight feet along the street. A French-style shallow-hipped roof with two dormer windows and end chimneys capped the building, whose six-bay-wide façade displayed unusual sophistication, the second and fifth bays projecting slightly from the façade to add dimension and interest. The houses had French casement windows, perhaps the first of their kind in Baltimore. To add further decorative effect to the façade, Chevalier placed recessed stone panels with carved garlands between the second- and third-floor openings. The portico of the Bentalou house, with its two arched entryways set between three engaged Ionic columns, carried a full entablature and cast-iron balcony. The wide stone steps, which curved out where they met the footway, further unified the composition and added to the impression that one viewed a single mansion.

Except for having two doors instead of three, the imposing entryway of the Bentalou house duplicated the projecting center section of the garden elevation of the house of Marquis de Voyer d'Argenson in Paris (the important neoclassical mansion, with interior decoration by Jean-Honoré Fragonard, had been completed in 1770). Robert Gilmor Jr. described the Bentalou pair as "the two handsome houses in the French style."[28]

Remaining in Baltimore, Chevalier in a newspaper notice years later described himself as a "sculptor and architect" whose skills enabled him to design "the exterior and interior of buildings, public or private and like-wise to execute them in marble, free-stone, plaster or wood." He referred prospective patrons to the "architecture and sculpture" of the Bentalou houses (which had by this time been sold to John Hollins and Cumberland Dugan). He also took credit for the front of General Smith's house on Water Street and for the "porticos and sculpture both exterior and interior" of another Gilmor town house on Water Street, this one on the south side, completed in 1810 for Robert Gilmor Jr.[29]

Another fine town house, the Caton-Carroll mansion at the corner of Front and East Lombard Streets (originally King George Street), showed some of the design features Chevalier employed in the Bentalou house, though in a less decorative form. Work on it probably began in 1808, when Henry Wilson purchased its site for $3,500; in 1812, he sold the land and the house on it for $12,000 to Christopher Deshon, a merchant who had come to Baltimore from Saint Domingue. In 1818 Richard Caton acquired the mansion from Deshon for $20,000. Caton's father-in-law, Charles Carroll of Carrollton, after 1826 the last living signer of the Declaration of Independence, spent his final winters with his daughter Mary Caton and her family in the residence and died there in 1832.

Restrained in its outward appearance, the three-and-a-half-story house originally had two entrances on Lombard Street. One, to the west, led to Caton's counting room; the other, set behind a columned entrance portico in the center of the house, opened into a grand stair hall, with elliptical staircase rising in open flight to the third floor. Five bays wide, with the center three projecting slightly forward, the house featured a stone stringcourse that divided first and second floors and recessed stone panels that marked the transition between second and third floors, as at the Bentalou house. The house had no back building; the basement providing kitchen space.

Inside, the boldly curving, cantilevered staircase supplied the most important architec-

The Riddell house came down in 1935. Some of its woodwork and its leaded fanlight survive at the Baltimore Museum of Art.

Bentalou (later Dugan-Hollins house), on Water Street, in a late-nineteenth-century photograph. Maryland Historical Society

The Bentalou house was demolished at the end of the nineteenth century.

*Caton-Carroll house exterior. Enoch
Pratt Free Library*

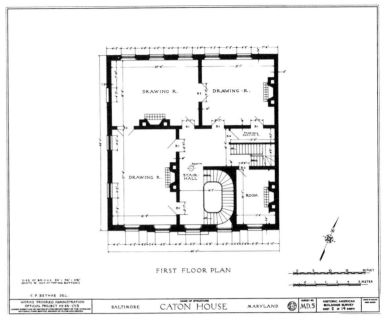

*First-floor plan of the Caton-Carroll
house. Historical American
Buildings Survey,
Library of Congress*

*The dining room, as furnished
when the Carroll Mansion was open
to the public as part of the Peale
Museum. Peale Collection,
Maryland Historical Society.
Photograph by Marion E. Warren*

Today, the City of Baltimore owns
the Caton Carroll house, which,
while largely preserved, is closed
to the public.

The Lorman house, as captured by Historic American Buildings Survey photographer E. H. Pickering, 1936. Maryland Historical Society

Third floor

11) South East Chamber
10) South West Chamber
9) North East Chamber
8) Front Chamber
7) North West Chamber
6) Dining Room
5) Drawing Room
4) Reception Room
3) Housekeeper's Room
2) Library
1) Breakfast Room

Second, or main, floor

N
▼

First, or ground, floor

Michael Trostel's conjectural floor plan, based on an insurance policy and estate inventory, of the house Robert Gilmor Jr. constructed in 1810. From Lance Humphries, "Robert Gilmor Jr. (1774–1848): Baltimore Collector and American Art Patron" (Ph.D. diss., University of Virginia, 1998).

tural element of the house. Contemporary records referred to so spectacular a feature as a "geometrical stair." Other Federal-period Baltimore houses—that of Robert Gilmor Jr. on the south side of Water Street for one—reportedly had similar staircases. The one at the Caton house rose from the entrance level to the second, principal floor above, with its major rooms for entertaining—a drawing room, dining room, and music room—and then in similar fashion to the third floor, with its bed chambers. Handsome carved wooden door cases on the second floor attested to the skill of the craftsmen employed. A contemporary observer with a keen eye credited Deshon with having built "the finest house in Old Town."[30]

In 1815 William Lorman, a wealthy merchant, ordered the construction of a house that represented new developments in architectural style. Three stories tall and three bays wide, the house, with its low, hipped roof, took on cubic form. It stood several blocks north of the old business district near Pratt and Water Streets, on the southeast corner of Lexington and Charles Streets, facing Lexington. The exterior recalled design features found on both the Bentalou and Caton-Carroll houses. As at the Carroll house, Doric columns framed the crisply cut main doorway, with its slightly projecting stone entablature. Articulating the simple shape of the brick cube, slightly advancing bays marked opposite corners of the house. First-floor windows on the Lexington Street façade rested on stone aprons decorated with ovals in relief; similar panels decorated the Charles Street façade between second- and third-floor windows. The French-style full-length windows, with classical pediments, opened onto wrought-iron balconies decorated with a pattern of interlocking ovals. A deep marble stringcourse ran around the house at the line of the principal floor, making a bolder statement than that at the Caton-Carroll house.

An architect who had charge of remodeling the building after Lorman's death recalled that one entered Lorman's business office through a "small and unpretentious doorway" on the Charles Street side. The first floor also housed a family dining or breakfast room, along with kitchen and pantries. A broad stairway led to the principal second story, which contained a reception room, a drawing room or salon, and a formal dining room. The architect noted that the second floor hall had "a very fine stucco cornice and a groined and vaulted ceiling of low elliptic arches with a depressed dome as a central feature," the trim being "in the usual minute and delicate mouldings of that period, painted white," with doors of "solid mahogany, polished." Five bedchambers occupied the third floor. In the rear of the dwelling, guests could exit from the dining-room balcony down a curved double flight of steps to a boxwood garden.[31]

Row Houses

The Federal period of architecture coincided with Baltimore's development into a city of row houses. In Georgian London, builders put up rows of uniform, connected dwellings in imposing groups, their compositions giving an entire streetscape a unified scheme. This concept flowered in the building of Queen Square (1729–36), the Circus (begun 1754), and the Royal Crescent (1767–75) in Bath; the creation of London squares in the eighteenth century; the work of the Adam brothers in both London and Edinburgh; and later the dramatic terraces of John Nash in London.

In Baltimore, the first grand rows were built by enterprising merchants who sought people like themselves as tenants. In 1796 two prominent flour merchants, Cumberland Dugan and Thomas McElderry, erected expensive and impressive three-and-a-half-story rows facing each other on their respective, neighboring wharves, which extended some sixteen hundred feet into the harbor. With London's Adelphi Terrace as a model, they leased commercial space at wharf level and rented commodious living quarters above. The group of houses merited enough attention to be included as one of the two architectural details

"View of the Market Space—Canal," inset detail from Warner & Hanna's Plan of the City and Environs of Baltimore, *1801, showcases the three-and-a-half-story row houses built by Thomas McElderry and Cumberland Dugan on their respective wharves.*
Maryland State Archives

LEFT:

A group of stylish three-bay-wide, two-and-a-half-story houses on South Charles Street. Computer-assisted drawing by Rosalie Fenwick, SMG Architects, Baltimore, based on a Historic American Buildings Survey photograph from ca. 1930

RIGHT:

Two-bay-wide, two-and-a-half-story houses in the 1600 block of Shakespeare Street, Fells Point, built in the 1790s. Computer-assisted drawing by Rosalie Fenwick, SMG Architects, Baltimore

Pascault Row

Pascault Row, built ca. 1819. Computer-assisted drawing by Rosalie Fenwick, SMG Architects, Baltimore, based on a depression-era Historic American Buildings Survey photograph

found on Warner & Hanna's contemporary map of the city. The same speculators also built two similar rows a block north of the harbor, facing Market Place, as did John O'Donnell of Canton, who put up two rows of six houses each facing Commerce Street. In 1802 Dr. James McHenry, who had served in Washington's cabinet and owned both a town and a country house, built a row of five three-and-a-half-story houses on Washington Square, later to be the site of the Battle Monument. At about the same time Richard Caton put up four stylish row houses at Albemarle and Front Streets in Old Town. Built as a unit under a single roof, with only partition walls between dwellings, row houses proved to be as popular among merchants and their families as the earlier detached town houses, and every bit as fashionable. At twenty or twenty-five feet wide and thirty-six or forty feet deep, they were also about as large. Like the detached Allender residence, most row houses also had long, narrower back buildings for kitchen, family dining room, and extra bedrooms.[32]

Meanwhile, the demand for living space in the rapidly growing port gave rise to additional rows, smaller but comfortable. Speculators were soon building pairs and small rows of two-and-a-half-story houses for the working men of the city, particularly in the maritime communities west of the harbor basin and in Fells Point and Federal Hill. The houses resembled larger and higher-style Federal rows in their proportions and detailing and were built in both two- or three-bay-wide versions. Three-bay-wide houses, two rooms deep and usually with a one-story back building housing the kitchen, had side-hall plans—a parlor and dining room on the first floor, bedrooms above, and a single room in the dormer story. Even smaller and more economical two-bay-wide, two-room-deep houses filled the streets in equal measure. Entering them, one walked directly into the parlor, with the tightly winding, narrow stairs set in the front corner of the dining room, between the partition wall and the fireplace.[33]

Baltimore became a city of brick row houses for several practical reasons besides the fire-prevention ordinance of 1799 and the low cost of local brick. The success of speculative row-house building in Baltimore (and Philadelphia) also derived from the ground-rent system, by which, in 1765, Edward Fell had leased land to Robert Long. A method of tenure derived from English practice and fostered by the lords proprietor of Pennsylvania and Maryland, ground rents allowed the original landowner to retain title to the land while renting the use of it (in the form of a renewable ninety-nine-year lease) to builders or, later, house buyers. Since a given tract of land could only produce ground rents for every house built, speculators naturally tried to pack as many ground-rent-producing dwellings on the land as possible. The system obviously benefitted landlords, but it also cut costs for builders and, eventually, home buyers, who, instead of having to buy the land outright, could instead pay a modest annual sum (typically 6 percent of the value of the land) for its use.

Large landowners like Fell and John Eager Howard squeezed as many row-house building lots as they could into the blocks they laid out. They then leased the lots to builders under building clauses requiring that houses of certain dimensions be erected within three years. In addition, because they wanted the ground-rent-producing houses to be up as soon as possible, they were often willing to advance builders some of the cost of construction. When houses sold, the new owners began paying ground rents to Fell, Howard, or the many other landowners responsible for developing the early town. As the nineteenth century progressed, modest row houses filled the blocks of the growing city, especially in waterfront areas. Early rows were small, three or four houses only, but by the 1830s some developers had amassed enough capital to put up rows of eight to ten houses at one time. Each row house had its own back yard, with privy; expensive rows also had rear service buildings or stables, which opened onto an alleyway.

Baltimore builders favored the aesthetically pleasing exterior combination of red brick trimmed with the white marble from the quarries north of Baltimore, near Cockeysville. The skill of masons in building vernacular brick residences became proverbial. Their hands and eyes shaped houses, sometimes with the help of pattern books and builder's guides, and, by extension, entire blocks. The "rectilinear openings" of each house pierced the faces of the buildings "sharply and with absolute regularity, having stone sills and lintels that perform structurally and provide a minimal ornamental touch," wrote a later student of the row house aesthetic. "The whole front has the functional rhythm of a work song."[34]

The majority of Federal-style row houses in Baltimore were two and a half stories high and two or three bays wide. After the early years of the century, few speculators tried their hand at large, fashionable, expensive rows. One noteworthy exception was Louis Pascault, the builder of the fine country house south of Gray's Gardens. In about 1819, on the southern portion of his land (near the Lexington Market, which the city had established in 1782), this proud "gentleman of the old regime" financed the building of eight large, three-and-a-half-story brick row houses—the last major, large Federal-style houses to be built in the city. The speculative venture seemed to have promise; the row went up only a few blocks north of the newly opened Medical College of the University of Maryland. Each house was twenty-eight feet wide and had a three-story back building, bringing the total depth of the structure to ninety-three feet and six inches. Intended to attract well-to-do buyers, the houses included fine design features resembling those of the Caton-Carroll and Lorman houses: doorways with engaged Roman Doric columns supporting a deep entablature and rectangular stone panels decorating the façades between the second- and third-floor levels. The fine brickwork was laid in Flemish bond; all window openings had stone lintels and sills.

The early city historian Thomas Griffith described the "eight commodious dwellings" as having been erected by Pascault, "M. Rezin Wight and others," and in fact, soon after completion Pascault deeded some of the dwellings to master builder Rezin Wight, with whom, along with other craftsmen and suppliers, he had probably entered into a construction partnership. But much to Pascault's embarrassment, the houses, however stylish, failed to attract residents, being located too far from the central city. In 1819 Griffith noted that the enterprise had been a financial failure because, "being considered too distant for men of business, as most all of our citizens are," they would "not command rent nearly equal to common legal interest."[35]

Churches and Public Buildings

Upon leaving their homes, Baltimoreans of the period presented themselves in buildings erected for purposes religious, social, and civic which offered examples of rising sophistication. One noteworthy place of worship, the First Presbyterian Church, at the northwest corner of Fayette Street and Guilford Avenue, clearly announced the pre-eminence of enterprising Scots-Irish merchants, who, as early as the 1760s, had established the lucrative Baltimore wheat and flour trade with Europe and the Caribbean. After the Revolution, Presbyterians became the largest and wealthiest denomination in Baltimore. In 1789 the congregation hired carpenter John Dalrymple to design and probably supervise construction of a new and much larger structure, which, in 1796, one traveler described as "the handsomest building in town."[36] Dalrymple's mason, John Mosher, was a Roxbury, Massachusetts, native who settled in Baltimore after fighting with Washington's army. He went on to provide

Pescault Row survived until the 1980s, when the University of Maryland at Baltimore saved the houses from use as warehouses, shops, service buildings, and the like, by restoring and converting them to offices and student housing. While dutifully saving the structures, the university reconstructed the interior spaces and completely rebuilt the original back buildings.

First Presbyterian Church, from a daguerreotype of ca. 1855. Peale Collection, Maryland Historical Society

Interior of First Presbyterian, a view from the choir loft toward the altar. Watercolor by Edmund G. Lind, 1859, completed just before the building was razed. Peale Collection, Maryland Historical Society

the brickwork of many of the finest buildings in the city, including important residences. Mosher was also an engineer and a member of the Baltimore City Council; he surveyed and laid out streets and in his old age served as surveyor of the port.

Both the interior and the exterior of the First Presbyterian Church were dramatic. Its scale and design differed from anything that had come before. The exterior of the church featured a temple front supported by four full-height Roman Doric stone columns. On either side rose two tall towers marked by octagonal belfries whose distinctive ogee roofs could be seen from long distances, giving the church the nickname "Two Steeple Church." On the entry façade, beneath the porch, tall pilasters echoed the rhythm of the stone columns and framed the pedimented entrance doors. A deep Roman Doric entablature ran around the front and sides of the building. Inside, the church seated more than a thousand people in both box pews and in the galleries that filled three sides. Two levels of arched windows created a bright and airy space centering on a full-height, recessed arch framing the altar. Slender columns, based on those of the Tower of the Winds in Athens, supported the galleries with their vase-shaped balusters. The flat ceiling had a coved plaster cornice. When completed in 1795, the tall steeples of the church made it a landmark for sailors.

The church was razed in 1859, when the congregation moved north to Park and Madison Avenues.

Light Street Methodist Church, built 1797, as photographed by William Getz, ca. 1868, just prior to its demolition in about 1872. Peale Collection, Maryland Historical Society

In about 1795 the Methodists, a denomination that had organized in Baltimore in 1784 and afterward grown rapidly in the United States, built another imposing, Federal-style church. The Lovely Lane congregation hired George Wall and his brother Jacob to build the Light Street Methodist Church on the site of the original log meetinghouse, west of Light Street in Lovely Lane (later German, then Redwood Street) at Wine Alley, where their community had formed as the Mother Church of Methodism in America. The Walls designed a two-and-a-half-story brick building that adhered to the Methodists' desire to avoid ostentation. With a front-facing gable but without a tower, it employed tall, arched, multipaned windows that resembled those of the older Otterbein Church. A broad platform of steps led to three pedimented doorways, Doric pilasters supporting their full entablatures, the central entrance having a triangular pediment. An ocular window set in the gable end and squat roof finials further decorated the façade.

In 1796 the German Reformed congregation hired Ludwig Herring, a Lancaster, Pennsylvania–born builder, to erect a church on Redwood between South and Gay. Originally a simple brick, gable-roofed structure with arched windows, resembling the Methodists' Light Street building, the church gained prominence seven years later when the group commissioned another local builder, George Rohrback, to add a tall steeple. Rohrback seems to have drawn on three examples from Plate 29 in James Gibbs's *A Book of Architecture* (London, 1728) to create his four-tiered design, which featured a pilastered square base, an octagonal second tier with arched openings, an octagonal third tier with arcaded roof line, and a tall,

St. Peter's Protestant Episcopal Church, completed at Sharp and German Streets in 1803 and seen here in a late-nineteenth-century photograph, could easily have been the work of the Wall brothers, for it bore a strong similarity to the Light Street structure. Peale Collection, Maryland Historical Society

arcaded belfry with needlelike spire. This proud steeple housed a clock on its third tier, which, until 1866, served unofficially, but effectively, as the city's standard timepiece.

Growth and prosperity in late-eighteenth-century Baltimore, as well as a growing cosmopolitanism, created a desire for a place—so common in European cities—for social and civic gatherings. In 1797 the six-member board of the Dancing Assembly called for construction of a building for dancing, concerts, and various events too large for even the most commodious private residence. The board assigned one of its number, amateur architect Nicholas Rogers of Druid Hill, to design the hall. Rogers went to work, again consulting English architectural references from his library. His design for what became the Assembly Room resembled the buildings of contemporaries—the Boston architect Charles Bulfinch, William Thornton in the rude village of Washington, and "gentlemen architects" in Charleston, South Carolina. It also owed a debt to neoclassical styling in London, especially Sir William Chambers's Somerset House, which derived from the High Renaissance palace schemes of Raphael and others and defined the mode for institutional and government buildings.

Completed two years later, the Assembly Room, built of brick with light-colored stone trim, extended nine bays across East (later Fayette) Street, with a width of three bays running back along Holliday Street. It followed the Chambers formula in the proportions of its openings and the organization and decorative treatment of its other elements. The front featured a high English basement, first-floor windows set within shallow arched reveals, and a tall principal floor marked by a central temple-front design with an elegant cartouche in the

LEFT:
The First German Reformed Church, built 1796, steeple added 1803; border detail from View of Baltimore, *lithograph by E. Weber & Co., ca. 1848. Maryland Historical Society*

RIGHT:
The steeple of the First German Reformed Church as it appeared in a mid-nineteenth-century photograph. Peale Collection, Maryland Historical Society

"New Assembly Room," inset detail from Warner & Hanna's Plan of the City and Environs of Baltimore, *1801. Maryland State Archives*

Perspective view of the Assembly Room. From John H. B. Latrobe's Picture of Baltimore, Containing a Description of All Objects of Interest in the City; and Embellished with Views of the Principal Public Buildings *(Baltimore, 1832). Maryland Historical Society*

Later, a third story having replaced its pediment and balustrade, the Assembly Room housed the city high school, and then, after 1868, Baltimore City College. It burned to the ground in 1873 during the Holliday Street Theatre fire.

pediment. The emphatic stone belt course dividing first and principal floors and the richly balustraded cornice provided horizontal accents. The entrance, reached by a broad flight of steps, was framed by engaged Doric columns supporting a broken pediment, and it sported an elaborate fanlight. Brick pilasters, with bases and capitals of stone, defined the temple front and also marked the corners and bays facing Holliday Street. Blind, recessed panels of stone or stucco further articulated the façade above the windows of the principal floor and may have set the fashion later seen in the Caton-Carroll house, among others. The craftsmen-builders of the Assembly Room included, besides young Robert Cary Long Sr., John Donaldson, carpenter, and the stonecutters William Hessington and Alexander Lauder.

The structure registered a resounding success. The private Library Company occupied the first floor, while the principal floor was used as a ballroom and banquet hall. Chancellor James Kent described the building as "very long" with "a very elegant appearance in front."

The Baltimore Courthouse, as captured in a mid-nineteenth century carte de visite. Maryland Historical Society

He added that it was "the most elegant dancing Assembly Room in the United States." Although no interior plan survives, the English observer James Buckingham wrote that "the suite of dancing and refreshment rooms, in which the regular winter balls are held, are not surpassed in beauty by any in Europe. There are many such larger, but for richness, taste—and effective decoration, nothing can be more chastely beautiful than these."[37]

Meanwhile, the courthouse in the middle of Calvert Street—despite standing on high stilts—so obstructed traffic and further development of the street that city fathers in

1805 resolved to replace it. They must also have envisioned a building more in keeping with the city's growing size and dignity. The new courthouse stood on the northwest corner of Washington (later Monument) Square. Completed in 1809, it remained for generations the most important civic building in Baltimore. Irish-born George Milliman served as architect on the project; he, along with others, had begun his career as a carpenter and progressed to a more elevated profession. Although a "self-instructed architect," as a successor put it, Milliman was known as a "man of taste and judgment."[38]

Because the site sloped abruptly southward, the new building stood on a wide, stone terrace that contained fireproof vaults. In its dimensions and details it related more closely to the prevailing English manner than did the Assembly Rooms, for it was less formal and its elements less ponderous in their dimensions and materials. Sixty by 140 feet long and two stories tall, the building featured a domed cupola. Its front and side elevations differed. The front on Lexington Street may have seemed rather old-fashioned in 1809, with its slightly projecting, pedimented central pavilion, marked by a Baroque window decorated with garlands in the gable end. Other features, however, clearly bespoke the influence of the English Regency or late Federal style, especially on the Calvert Street façade. Here, the flattened decorative elements, the slender dimensions of the full-height Ionic pilasters, the first-floor windows set in arched, shallow reveals, and the tripartite windows all emphasized the smooth, cubic volume of the building. This volumetric quality was enhanced by the low roof and prominent cornice and central, stepped pediment. A Federal-style cupola marked the building's prominence.

Authorities tore down the second courthouse in 1895 to make way for a much larger Beaux-Arts-style replacement, which would occupy the entire block.

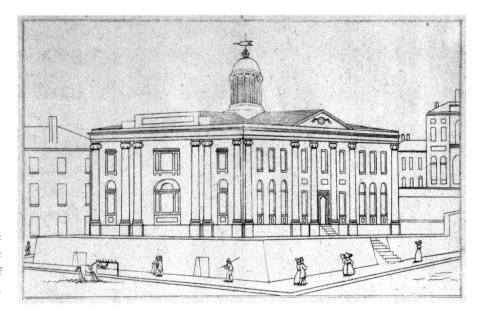

The Baltimore Courthouse, at Calvert and Lexington Streets, built 1806–9, from Latrobe, Picture of Baltimore.

3

MONUMENTAL BALTIMORE, 1806–1831

"Proud Baltimore that envi'd commerce draws," chanted an unknown poet in the *Newport* (Rhode Island) *Mercury* in 1790.

> Few are the years since there, at random plac'd
> Some wretched huts her happy port disgrac'd;
> Safe from all winds, and cover'd from the bay
> There, at his ease the lazy native lay—
> Now rich and great, no more a slave to sloth
> She claims importance from her hasty growth.[1]

Census figures, as well as the experience of Ellen Moale, confirmed this rapid growth. The first child born in Baltimore Town after the charter of 1752, Moale died in 1824, when Baltimore's population had reached some 70,000 (census reports put it at 62,738 in 1820). In 1830 that figure reached 80,620, placing the city behind only New York and Philadelphia among American cities.

Geography continued to play a major role in the unfolding drama. The new republic's north-south postal road passed through Baltimore; turnpikes reached out from the city to the north and west, and those pikes leading through Frederick and Hagerstown eventually connected to the National Road, which led to the Ohio country. Well inland from Philadelphia and New York, Baltimore on the Chesapeake beckoned the riches of the West.

"Jolly fellows of the Venetian stamp," John Pendleton Kennedy, a Baltimore attorney and novelist, wrote of the men of this era. They were "fiery and loud," he thought, "with stern glance of the eye and brisk turn of the head, the swashbuckler strut of defiance, like gamecocks."[2] Some of these men laid the cornerstone of America's first Roman Catholic cathedral in 1806 and established the University of Maryland College of Medicine in 1807. Other Baltimoreans were just as busy. In 1808 Elizabeth Anne Seton opened a female academy, forerunner of all American parochial schools, and later founded the Sisters of Charity, an order of Roman Catholic nuns. The Peale brothers in 1814 welcomed Baltimoreans to their museum of art and oddities on Holliday Street. Daniel Coker and other black leaders formed an independent African Methodist Episcopal Church in Baltimore. In the early nineteenth century the city gained the Maryland Institute, St. Paul's Episcopal charitable and educational programs, Quaker reform movements, and African-American schools. Elizabeth Lange established another Catholic order, the African-American Oblate Sisters of Providence.

Shrewd and aggressive, the merchant princes of Baltimore captured the attention of the British during the War of 1812 because so many of them had received congressional authority to prey on enemy merchant vessels. When, in September 1814, the king's army and navy followed the sacking of Washington with a coordinated attack on Baltimore, "that nest of pirates," as the British called the city, many of these same merchants organized the city's defense. After the peace of 1815 municipal leaders commissioned America's first public monuments, one to George Washington and the other to the Balti-

Plan of the City of Baltimore,
Thomas H. Poppleton, surveyor,
engraved by Joseph Cone, 1823.
Maryland State Archives

moreans who had lost their lives in the Battle of North Point, and they hired Rembrandt Peale to paint portraits of local war heroes.

The envy of the *Newport Mercury* poet extended, notably, to Baltimore's new urban look: "High in renown, her streets and domes arrang'd / A group of Cabins to a city chang'd."

In 1816 the General Assembly authorized Baltimore to annex adjacent tracts that tripled its acreage and to appoint commissioners who would oversee the laying out of new streets and public lots. The commissioners hired an engineer-surveyor, Thomas H. Poppleton, whose draft of a street plan the city published in 1823. Praising its "striking regularity," the commissioners noted that "the disjointed settlements which before made up the city are interwoven and connected together in a manner which, we flatter ourselves, could not be improved. The combination exhibits the metropolis of Maryland in an aspect of great beauty." For the first time, it appeared, "All is certainty."[3]

All may not have been so certain, but Poppleton's plan guided city growth for two generations, largely laying out a gridiron street pattern, defining the standard Baltimore block, and creating a durable hierarchy of main streets, side streets, and narrower alley streets running down the middle of many blocks. These thoroughfares developed an attendant social hierarchy.

Although Poppleton laid a grid that usually worked best in flat terrain like Philadelphia's, visitors continued to marvel at Baltimore's hilly topography—along with its dramatic effect and scenic possibilities. In the late eighteenth century Moreau de Saint-Méry had closed his complimentary description of the place by writing, "but what gives Baltimore a pleasant air, peculiar to itself, is the hill which dominates it on the north." He explained that John Eager Howard owned the tract and had built Belvidere and outbuildings on its northern side while leaving the southern expanse open and "beautified" as a park. "Its elevated situation; its groves of trees; the view from it, which bring back mem-

View of Baltimore, *drawn by William H. Bartlett and engraved by S. Fisher, London, 1839, known as the "Constantinople" view because of its romanticized image of the Monumental City. Baltimore Museum of Art*

ories of European scenes," Saint-Méry went on, his feelings rising to the challenge, "all these things together fill every true Frenchman with both pleasure and regret; his mind and heart alike rejoice in the vistas and the sensation they inspire."[4] In 1816 an English visitor, Adlard Welby, published his own impressions of what he had seen in the United States, including Baltimore. Sadly enough, his little book included no illustrations, but he did have much to say about the city, which then had begun to move into the phase Baltimoreans and others eventually called monumental. In Baltimore, he wrote,

> The view is fine from an eminence about half a mile from the town, nor are you disappointed on entering the city; though not so large, it is yet the most pleasing by far of the eastern ports we have visited: whether the beauty and taste, the variety to be considered, or the plan and situation—the whole is indeed strikingly interesting. A beautiful marble column is in part finished, a national monument to the memory of those who fell in the battle at North Point; not far from this is in progress a superb Catholic cathedral, and close to it stands a Unitarian church, an edifice not surpassed in beauty by any in the city. Besides there are a variety of churches and other public buildings: one of the most prominent the College of Physicians [Davidge Hall], a heavy combination, and not rendered the more pleasant by, we will hope, the inappropriate neighborhood of a burial ground [Old St. Paul's]. On the whole the traveler cannot but be pleased with a view of Baltimore and the State of which it is the chief town.[5]

RISING TO THE STATUS of major American city, its citizens triumphantly building major churches and monuments, Baltimore, for a magical moment and for the first time, connected with the most innovative and distinguished architects working in the country—Benjamin Henry Latrobe, Maximilien Godefroy, and Robert Mills.

These exceptional designers exemplified the taste and ideas at work in European architecture. Following upon the revolution in taste created by the Adam brothers in the 1770s, largely inspired by the recent excavations at Pompeii and Herculaneum—which had turned away from the reigning version of Palladianism and its domesticated variant, the Georgian—young neoclassical designers offered new, radically creative ideas. In France, Claude-Nicolas Ledoux in the late 1770s and 1780s introduced an entirely new vision, designing buildings that made use of crisp and rigid geometrical forms with flat-surfaced massing. In England, Sir John Soane, appointed architect of the Bank of England in 1788, created vaulted interiors that had the same radical, abstract quality as Ledoux's work and exteriors marked by smooth, planar surfaces and bold, simple massing. Soane's new form of classicism was very different from that of Robert Adam, which drew mainly on Roman prototypes. Now, Ledoux, Soane, and their followers turned to Greek forms and created a style of austere simplicity that relied for effect on the relationships of interlocked geometrical forms rather than the delicate and decorative effects of Adamesque classicism.

This version of the new classicism, preferring the severe and little ornamented, nonetheless proved fruitful in its employment of structural elements—columns, arches, domes, wall masses—and manner of relating them one to another. It exploited them in a manner for which there was no precedent in ancient architecture. Isolating and magnifying a part of an antique structure, neoclassicists sometimes made a whole building out of what had been a single element. They conceived of giant, freestanding columns much larger than anything built in classical antiquity. Architects of this movement experimented with building size, scale, and materials; they readdressed questions of volume and form in interior spaces. Pre-occupied with the expression of function in the form of buildings and the aesthetic power of architecture, neoclassicists challenged all that had preceded them as effectively as did po-litical revolution. Yet this revolutionary architectural manner, while it refreshed thought about architecture and theories of design, led to the rediscovery, reconsideration, and re-vived appreciation of historic styles.

The largest surviving collections of buildings in the neoclassical style are in cities that grew rapidly at the end of the eighteenth century and attracted aspiring architects—among them, besides Baltimore, St. Petersburg and Helsinki. Latrobe, Godefroy, and Mills gave the city on the Chesapeake vivid examples of European innovation. They came from elsewhere and stayed only briefly in Baltimore; no American city in this period was big enough to support a truly ambitious architect, so men of that calling were itinerant. Even so, they launched a kind of school in Baltimore and established high standards indeed.

Basilica and Chapel

Born in England of an American mother, Benjamin Henry Latrobe acquired formal train-ing in architecture from London architect Samuel Pepys Cockerell. He also studied engi-neering, thereby learning how to combine grandeur of composition with disciplined detail and how to solve problems of cubic relations, such as making walls flow smoothly into vaults and introducing light from overhead. He studied in the offices of successful practitioners at home and in Germany, then traveled on the Continent, where he gained a strong working knowledge of both old and new architectural forms. In 1796, after the death of his wife and his own financial ruin, Latrobe left for America, eager to see the New World and hoping to obtain eco-nomic relief from his mother's family. After landing at Norfolk, Virginia, he made his way via Richmond to Philadelphia. There he soon won a commission to design the Bank of Pennsylvania and the Water Works. In 1803 President Jefferson called Latrobe to Washington to design dry docks for the navy and work on the ris-ing federal capitol.

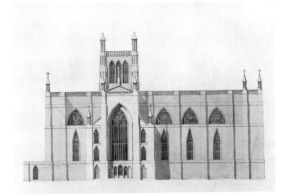

Benjamin Henry Latrobe's Gothic design for the Baltimore Cathedral. Watercolor on paper, 1805. Maryland Historical Society

The following year, the Roman Catholic bishop of Baltimore, John Carroll, asked La-trobe to examine plans for a new Roman Catholic cathedral in the city. The project had great significance. In 1789 the Vatican had directed all Catholic parishes in the United States to or-ganize into a diocese, acknowledging Carroll as the first bishop and establishing Baltimore as the episcopal see. The first Roman Catholic church in the city, St. Peter's, had gone up

Latrobe's sectional watercolor rendering of the cathedral as built, 1808. Basilica of the Assumption Historic Trust, Inc.

nearly twenty years earlier, the work of a skilled builder, John McNabb. The modest brick structure (twenty-five by thirty feet) stood on land donated by Charles Carroll of Carrollton just south of the hilltop site Bishop Carroll had secured for the cathedral. St. Peter's had undergone enlargement in 1784, and the addition was larger than the church itself, but Bishop Carroll wanted to build a cathedral. Latrobe offered to draw plans himself, free of charge.

In 1805 Latrobe sent Carroll two designs for a new building, one Gothic, one classical in style. Both sets of drawings, which remain in the church's archives, eclipsed the diluted-Georgian and Federal styles then prevalent and thus provide evidence of varied taste in American architecture at the time. Gothic Revival architecture had made sporadic appearances in England for nearly a half century, but no one before Latrobe had suggested this mode of building, based on a style lately thought barbarous, for a major structure in the United States. Latrobe evidently approved of its ecclesiastical tone. His classical scheme, on the other hand, offered a fresh version of the domed Roman Pantheon—a templelike portico, large areas of plain wall, reduced decoration, and a decidedly Latrobean interpretation of classical motifs.

Late in 1805 Bishop Carroll chose the classical design. Preceded by an Ionic portico, it followed the plan of a Latin cross supporting a broad dome. Portions of the side walls advanced and receded, marking off segments that corresponded with different treatments of the interior vaulting. To this simple plan, based on six variant drawings, Latrobe made many changes as work went forward. Earlier sketches suggested a smaller but higher dome resting on a lofty colonnaded drum, a rectangular rather than semicircular apse (east) end, and different treatment of the transepts.

Construction proceeded with annoying slowness—and worse. The cornerstone was laid in July 1806, but for a while the builder in charge, George Rohrback, willfully changed various details so that Latrobe—then busy in Washington—felt continually harassed. He said he would have resigned the commission had it not been for Bishop Carroll's intervention.

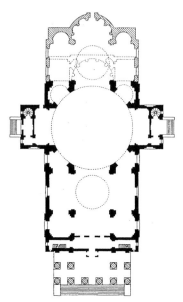

Interior of the Catholic
Cathedral, Baltimore, *drawn by
William Goodacre Jr., ca. 1825.
Basilica of the Assumption
Historic Trust, Inc.*
RIGHT:
*Floor plan showing the original
cathedral building and additions.
Archives of the Catholic
Archdiocese of Baltimore*

Rohrback became so confused at one point that he looked at Latrobe's drawing for the vaulted crypt upside down, supposing the section to show a foundation of inverted arches. Latrobe dismissed him. By 1811 the walls had been raised. Then came stoppage due to the war with Britain. Carroll died in 1817, when work had resumed on roof, dome, and interior; in 1821, even though towers and porch remained unfinished, lavish ceremonies dedicated the Cathedral of the Assumption of the Blessed Virgin Mary.

Latrobe's cathedral supplied one of the grandest interiors in the country. Strong wall planes carried a full entablature (cut through for windows without frames) and held recessed panels intended to be decorated with bas-reliefs of the life of Christ. Discontinuous nave vaulting, including both barrel and domical vaults, created a series of differing voids that mounted upward toward the crossing of nave and transept. The spacious interior, colored in pale grey, blue, and bright gold, culminated in the dome, which covered the crossing and extended across the aisles. Windows in the dome admitted indirect light, suffusing worshipers below.

The arched panels on the exterior of the walls and the handling of the domes revealed that Latrobe knew, admired, and had learned from the work of Soane, for whom similar arched forms were a personal design mannerism. But the plan of the interior of the basilica suggested that Latrobe developed his design not only through improvisations upon Soanean themes but also from an early and brilliant neoclassical work in the new style, the Church of St. Mary, East Lulworth, Dorset, England, where Bishop Carroll had been consecrated. Built in 1786 by an architect named John Tasker, St. Mary's served the Weld family, Catholic gentry, as a private chapel and was, to any observer, a striking early example of the new neoclassical style. Bishop Carroll, because of his association with Lulworth, could well have suggested that Latrobe adapt and repeat elements of its design. In any case, the cathedral, which for many years dominated the skyline and was the first thing mariners saw as they approached the city, stood among the major neoclassical structures built anywhere in the early nineteenth century.

For about ten years, Latrobe's work in Baltimore overlapped with that of Maximilien Godefroy, a Frenchman who had served as an officer in the French army until he fell out of favor with the revolutionary government and left for the United States. Godefroy arrived in Baltimore in 1805 to accept a professorship of civil and military architecture and the fine arts at St. Mary's College, a liberal arts school for boys closely associated with St. Mary's Roman Catholic Seminary on Paca Street, which the Sulpician order had opened under Bishop Carroll's direction in 1791. His position at the college marked him as the first professional teacher of architecture in Baltimore, possibly the first in the United States.

The story of Godefroy's early professional training in France remains murky, but he grew up in the Paris of Claude-Nicolas Ledoux and must have been aware of the customs-houses that Ledoux had built between 1785 and 1789, with their simplified classical details and emphasis on mass and proportion. He also shared the French interest in Egyptian architecture, dating from Napoleon's conquest of Egypt in 1798 and the publication in 1802 of Denon's *Voyage dans la Basse et la Haute Egypte*. Both stripped-down classicism and Egyptian

By 1832 an unknown architect had added the present onion-shaped domes to the towers of the Baltimore Cathedral, completely unlike Latrobe's original scheme for small, stepped domes matching the main dome. In the 1870s Latrobe's grandson, John H. B. Latrobe, oversaw the erection of the porch, modifying somewhat the original design. In 1890 church authorities extended the east end of Latrobe's cathedral forty feet. Pope Pius XI elevated the cathedral to basilica status in the fall of 1937. A historic trust established to protect and restore the basilica announced plans in December 2000 to build a visitors' center beneath the building, accessible from Charles Street via a sky-lighted walkway at crypt level, and to restore the building to Latrobe's fundamental design, including reopening the dome skylights and replacing stained glass with clear glass in the nave.

St. Mary's Chapel, watercolor elevation by Maximilien Godefroy, 1807. Maryland Historical Society

Interior of St. Mary's Chapel, mid-twentieth century. Peale Collection, Maryland Historical Society

Late-twentieth-century renovations gave St. Mary's Chapel an exterior of cleaned and repointed brick. During renovations the vestibule was eliminated and its volume thrown into the nave, so the original interior proportions are difficult to assess; now the nave seems long in relation to its width.

St. Patrick's Roman Catholic Church, Fells Point, built 1806. From John H. B. Latrobe's Picture of Baltimore, Containing a Description of All Objects of Interest in the City; and Embellished with Views of the Principal Public Buildings *(Baltimore, 1832). Maryland Historical Society*

forms of architecture appear in Godefroy's American work, together with excursions into the Gothic and the Tuscan of Renaissance Italy.

In 1806, when the Sulpicians decided to build a seminary chapel, they set Godefroy to work on the plans. He might have taken as his inspiration the home church of the order, St. Sulpice in Paris, an inventive mixture of late Baroque, sedate references to Roman architecture, and new cubic mass. Instead he decided to use Gothic, making St. Mary's one of the earliest attempts in the United States to borrow from Gothic examples. Godefroy could have known the literature on and illustrations of Gothic design that were appearing in England, but his chapel made little attempt to replicate medieval buildings, either in overall form or structure. Instead, it carried a pledge of interest in Gothic and a suggestion that the style should be linked to religious purposes. Like the inventive neoclassicism of Latrobe, it announced the advent of a new attitude, a conscious interest in forms other than the classical. The Sulpicians consecrated the chapel in 1808.

Godefroy called for an exterior of stucco, a treatment that related not to Gothic but to neoclassical practice. The front, inspired by French eighteenth-century illustrations of designs in the Gothic manner, was essentially flat. The buttresses—structurally unnecessary—support the freestanding portion of the façade, offering decorative and stylistic reminders of the Gothic. Except for their pointed windows, the side elevations were as simple and severe as those of the neoclassical contemporaries of the chapel. The ivory and gold interior, with its pointed arches and tall, bundled columns arranged close to one another, exhibited but slight reference to Gothic. Consisting of a nave flanked by narrow side aisles, the chapel plan could not have been simpler. A narthex, or vestibule, separated by a screen from the nave space, lay below the gallery. The apse, raised above the floor of the nave, was as broad as the nave, and rounded. Side chapels increased the dimension of the nave on either side. The gilt capitals, composed of classical elements and arranged in a manner with no ancient precedent, resembled designs published in eighteenth-century pattern books. Godefroy enlivened the ribs of the roof—like the exterior buttresses, decorative, not structural—with coral-painted ribbon designs, echoing rococo taste. Henry Russell Cleveland, an early-nineteenth-century American critic and one of the first to arrive at an understanding of aesthetic principles, described St. Mary's Chapel as "a little bijou."[6]

Much admired, St. Mary's Chapel was copied even before its completion. In 1806 a Catholic parish in Fells Point, St. Patrick's, built a church that one might describe as a

The German Lutheran Reformed church, built 1808, as it appeared on the border of Thomas H. Poppleton's Plan of the City of Baltimore, 1823. Maryland State Archives

When Zion Lutheran Church burned in 1840, the congregation rebuilt it, moving the tower forward of the body of the structure, which is how it appears today.

classical version of the chapel. In 1807–8 elders of the first German congregation in Baltimore, at the time half a century old, took measurements of the chapel while planning Zion Lutheran Church on North Gay Street and then hired two builders who had worked at St. Mary's, George Rohrback and Johann Machenheimer, to build it. Zion became a free and simplified "copy," resembling a large brick box with a short tower rising over its front entrance. Its doorways on North Gay and on the south side had round-arched openings, but windows were pointed in the Gothic manner. Although the window arrangement suggests a building of two stories, there was no gallery. The treatment of the wood cornice evoked the medieval practice of continuous small, arched brackets carrying a tilted surface to shed rain. A brick mason's traditional manner of working appears in the vertical and horizontal bands that articulated the façade. These thickened sections of brick gave strength, while the thinner, recessed walls cut expenses.

Forays

During the next few years Godefroy turned his hand to new forms of urban architecture. The Commercial and Farmers Bank at Howard Street and what became Redwood Street, completed in 1810, offered the architect latitude. Models for bank buildings were rare, as most banks of the day had typically begun operations at merchants' homes or in their counting rooms. Responding to this challenge, Godefroy created a solid structure with broad, unadorned wall planes and a dramatic, deep, corner entrance, topped by a wide, recessed, coffered dome. On either side of the dome, carved in the spandrels of the arch, allegorical figures—Mercury representing commerce and Ceres representing agriculture—celebrated the mainstays of the local economy. Godefroy evidently was a strong believer in adorning architecture with sculptural forms and for many of his local buildings made use of the talents of Italian-born sculptor Antonio Capellano.

At the northeast corner of Lexington and St. Paul Streets, Godefroy's Masonic Hall, begun in 1812–14, met the needs of the fraternal and benevolent organization that had flourished in America since the 1730s. The Masons had unusual standing in the community because Masonic ritual graced the cornerstone-laying for most public buildings and monuments. With its screen of four Greek Doric columns leading to a recessed vestibule, the rectangular, one-story façade of the hall made a strong architectural statement. As he had done at St. Mary's Chapel, Godefroy again combined the decorative motifs of arches and rectangular recessed panels. Construction stopped during the war with Britain; when it resumed in 1819, an assistant, Jacob Small Sr., added a story and a large central arch over the columned portico. Both Godefroy's bank and the completed Masonic Hall, with their strong cubic volumes and deeply recessed-arched entrances, reflected more French than English inspiration.

For a brief time Godefroy had a hand in the design of one of the city's most ambitious structures, the Baltimore Exchange and Custom House. In 1815 prominent city merchants organized a company and issued stock to provide funds for construction of an impressive maritime business center. Since many merchants still lived near the harbor, the Exchange

Used as a federal courthouse after 1822 (and as such the scene
of hearings that produced a
constitutional quarrel between
Chief Justice Roger B. Taney and
the Lincoln administration in
1861), the Masonic Hall was
demolished in 1895.

would stand far to the southeast of Latrobe's cathedral, its front on Gay Street stretching from Water to Lombard Streets, just a block north of the harbor basin. The call for plans drew entries from many hopefuls, among them Latrobe and Godefroy, working in partnership. Latrobe, in Washington, felt deserving and resented the need to enter a competition. "Yet we cannot avoid it," he wrote Godefroy, "for such is the deplorable state of the arts among the mushrooms of fortune upon whose vile patronage we depend."[7]

Aiming to make their design as appealing as possible, Latrobe executed a large perspective view that laymen could more easily understand than architectural plans, elevations, and sections. His watercolor shrewdly depicted the Exchange as seen from the front door of his friend and patron, the merchant Robert Goodloe Harper. Construction of the north-south wings would be delayed until officers of the Exchange had determined the number of tenants, so Latrobe obscured the length of the Gay Street wing with trees. His artistic ability served him well; he succeeded in achieving a picturesque naturalism by playing off the firm lines and geometric forms of the building and the light tonality of its stone against the dark-green, lacy foliage and wispy clouds. The commission went to Latrobe and Godefroy.

Latrobe had planned largely to oversee the work while Godefroy served as local representative. Godefroy's jealousy and concern for his own reputation, however, soon dissolved the partnership, forcing Latrobe to supervise construction by mail, with occasional visits to Baltimore. Finally, in late 1817, he moved to the city, where he lived for several months while directly involved in the construction. The principal builder on the project, Jacob Small Jr., a carpenter and self-trained architect, had served with distinction in the recent war with Britain.

Latrobe's H-shaped plan featured long, three-and-a-half-story buildings set on high basements facing Gay Street, on the east, and Commerce Street, on the west, with a large, domed Exchange Hall and flanking offices filling the crossbar. Although the western structure never materialized as Latrobe envisioned it (after 1871 a one-story post office filled the site), his eastern wing, facing Gay Street, testified to the grandeur of the overall plan. In his late style for public buildings, Latrobe avoided exterior columns, giving the wall planes more prominence. In the Exchange, true to form, he established a rhythm by the placement of windows and the use of shallow recesses. He divided the Gay Street building into five parts, the central and end pavilions advanced slightly forward of the intervening sections; groups of arched and rectangular windows at the second-floor level followed suit. As built, dark stone gave weight to the high basement. Three great arches at the entrance, along with stringcourses of colored stone, established the building's decorative pattern. Bands separating the stories and the bare cornice gave a predominantly horizontal accent. Additional dark

Gay Street façade, Baltimore Exchange. Watercolor by Benjamin Henry Latrobe, 1815. Maryland Historical Society

Sectional view of the Exchange, clearly showing the central rotunda and great dome. Watercolor by Benjamin Henry Latrobe, 1815. Maryland Historical Society

stone bands tied together groups of arched windows on the advanced pavilions, linking them at impost level (the bases of arches) and curving around each opening. Baltimore architects continued to use this so-called aqueduct motif to decorate façades for several decades. Latrobe flanked the entry with reliefs of the familiar Mercury and his winged staff, or caduceus; his design, if not the completed building, also included a sculpted female figure—an allegorical representation of Baltimore—set above the parapet capping the entrance façade. As usual, changes to the plan were made during construction; Latrobe also decided to raise the height of the dome to 115 feet by placing it on a higher drum.

The Exchange opened in 1820, though work continued until 1822, when federal customs officials and the Baltimore branch of the Bank of the United States occupied portions of the building. Visitors entered from Gay Street, climbed tall steps, and passed through a vaulted archway and a screen of Ionic columns into the central hall, above which rose the impressive dome. Stairs and passageways around the hall and along the wing led to the offices of merchants, attorneys, and brokers. An observation area in the dome, whose height came to symbolize Baltimore's position as a major shipping center, received signals from the observatory on Federal Hill, thus giving merchants the earliest possible notice that their vessels had arrived home.

The cathedral and the Exchange supplied sophisticated and powerful examples of public architecture and exemplified the neoclassicism of the period. Latrobe's large and simple forms contrasted with the small-scale treatment common in Adamesque works. Latrobe owed much to his materials—granite and marble, rather than the brick that prevailed at the height of the Federal style. He exploited the sheer size of the cathedral and the Exchange to achieve the monumental, and their interiors provided new experiences. Masonry vaults and domes created vast spaces enlivened by the intricate play of light and shadow from side and top illumination. For Baltimoreans of Latrobe's day, these sensations introduced new possibilities for public drama: In 1824, when the city greeted the touring Marquis de Lafayette on his historic return trip to America, authorities chose the city's most prominent building associated with its mercantile wealth—the Baltimore Exchange—for the reception in his honor.

Elevations, sections, plan, and detail of dome for a library in Baltimore. Watercolor drawings by Benjamin Henry Latrobe, 1817. Maryland Historical Society

In 1817 Latrobe drew floor plans and sections for a building to house the Library Company of Baltimore. Its geometric design features, smooth exterior planes, arched recesses, and soaring, vaulted interior spaces typified his genius and the neoclassical approach.

Monuments

To commemorate the men who had given their lives in defense of Baltimore in September 1814, city leaders the following year asked Godefroy to design a suitable monument. The architect worked with dramatic material. In preparing for a British attack (the enemy had burned Washington and clearly looked next to this home port of marauding privateers), citizens had worked as one, strengthening Fort McHenry and building new fortifications. On September 13, 1814, militia regiments from Maryland and nearby states fought and delayed British troops at North Point, southeast of town. Later than night and into the following morning, while red-coated soldiers waited to assault home defenses at what became Patterson Park, ships of the Royal Navy tried to pound Fort McHenry into submission. The result was a near thing, and Baltimoreans viewed the British departure as a triumph of the whole people.

Hence the theme of the Battle Monument, the first war memorial since antiquity to celebrate the common soldier rather than a commander. The commission gave Godefroy an opportunity to explore a variety of classical forms, experiment with scale and size, and recall and combine in unusual ways symbolic forms from ancient arts—Egyptian, Hellenistic, and Roman—that suggested a memorial purpose. He produced three designs: an obelisk, a sarcophagus, and a monument composed of combined symbols. The committee chose the last of these and built the monument as Godefroy envisioned it, on the square formed along Calvert Street between Fayette and Lexington, then called Washington Square, the city's most fashionable address and the site of the county courthouse. Several good views survive from the early nineteenth century, and one can see how well Godefroy tailored his work to its setting.

As a work of public art the monument registered a notable success. Its message: "Baltimore pledges eternal remembrance to the republican virtue of her sons." To convey it, Godefroy drew upon visual expressions of battle, civic virtue, death, and unity, all of which he executed in miniature, offering another study in scale, this time not of gigantic proportions but of a size reduced to the proportions of a decoration. The original elements, extracted

from the art and architecture of antiquity, went together in a new way. The three steps of the base referred to the years of the war, the thirteen courses of masonry in the marble base to the original states of the union. The sides and four false doors of the next element slanted inward, suggesting the form of a mortuary vault and the themes of dignity and eternity associated with ancient Egypt. Also Egyptian, a winged solar disk appeared in relief on the lintel of each door. For the shaft of the monument Godefroy chose an enlarged Roman fasces—a hand-carried bundle of rods, originally surrounding an axe, which denoted authority and military virtue in the ancient republic. The cords binding the rods together bore the names of the thirty-six soldiers killed in the city's defense (those of the three lost officers appeared above). In his overall design, Godefroy reduced the massiveness of Egyptian and Roman architectural forms to ornamental scale. A griffin guarded each corner of the base. At the top of the column stood a marble female figure representing the spirit of Baltimore. The statue, griffins, friezes, and other sculptural elements were carried out by Antonio Capellano. The city dedicated this monument, the first war memorial in the country of any distinction, in 1827.

Robert Mills, the third of the nationally distinguished architects to work in Baltimore during the first two decades of the nineteenth century, was born in Charleston, South Carolina, in 1781. He trained in engineering and studied architecture first with James Hoban, designer of the executive mansion in Washington, and then in 1803 won the friendship and encouragement of Thomas Jefferson, who soon after recommended Mills to Latrobe. Four years later Mills left Latrobe to follow his own career in Philadelphia, where he erected the Sansom Street Baptist Church, a bridge over the Schuylkill River, and a fine row of houses at Ninth and Locust Streets. He also designed the

Even as traffic and tall buildings overtook the place that became Monument Square, the Spirit of Baltimore, armed with a rudder and a cannon ball, continues to look down Calvert Street to the harbor, whence all her fortunes sprang.

LEFT:
Four studies of the Washington Monument, by Robert Mills, ca. 1815. Maryland Historical Society
RIGHT:
Elevation of the Principal Front, *watercolored competition drawing for the Washington Monument submitted by Robert Mills, 1814. Maryland Historical Society*

The Washington Monument, photographed for the Historic American Buildings Survey by E. H. Pickering, 1936. Maryland Historical Society

RIGHT:
Ornamental iron railing at the base of the Washington Monument. Photograph by E. H. Pickering, 1936. Maryland Historical Society

Monumental Church in Richmond, Virginia. His arrival in Baltimore in 1814 led to four notable commissions—an imposing monument to George Washington, a major church and residence, and a stylish row of houses. The monument not only influenced the planning of a whole section of the city but also became popularly identified as the symbol of Baltimore itself. The open competition for a suitable monument to Washington called forth a careful drawing of a triumphal arch by the French architect Joseph J. Ramée, who lived in Philadelphia and later planned Union College in Schenectady, New York; a design by Nicholas Rogers; and one by Godefroy. Mills's hasty sketch for an imperial column captivated the judges, and the commission was his.

If early plans had worked out, the Washington Monument would have risen next to the Battle Monument, but popular objection to placing Mills's dangerously tall, columnar design on Washington Square led Colonel Howard to donate a piece of land not far from his home, Belvidere, on land long known as Howard's Park. This verdant tract beyond the northern edge of town, celebrated by Saint-Méry and other visitors, had the advantage of high elevation. City dignitaries, supported by enthusiastic townspeople, laid the cornerstone there on July 4, 1815.

The Mills design—experimenting with the Roman celebratory column on a size and scale that typified neoclassicism—included six iron balconies set like rings on the shaft (curious accessories, which would certainly have destroyed its antique character as well as the simplicity of the silhouette). Extensive bronze reliefs and inscriptions relating the history and virtues of Washington would decorate the shaft. As built, Mills's Washington Monument was simpler, more correctly antique, and much more powerful than the prize-winning design. The base, at first envisioned as allowing passage of the street through a vaulted way (much like the old "courthouse on stilts") became a simplified block with four entrances. Instead of a four-horse chariot carrying Washington as an allegorical military figure, Mills asked the Italian sculptor Enrico Causici to portray the general as a man of peace, a standing figure facing Annapolis, the site of his resignation as revolutionary commander and thus his farewell to arms. The last piece of the statue went up in late November 1829. Rising 178 feet on a hill 100 feet above sea level, the Washington Monument became another landmark for ships sailing upriver from the Chesapeake Bay; it, too, helped to create one of America's first distinctive urban skylines. Foreign visitors flocked to climb the spiral stairway of 228 steps leading to an observation platform on the abacus of the column.

The unfluted Roman Doric column was the first such giant, freestanding structure to be raised in the New World. Architects in Napoleonic France had published several designs for huge columns of this type. Whether or not Mills knew of the Nelson Monument in Dublin or similar columns being installed in St. Petersburg and Paris (Lafayette is said to have admired the finished shaft as comparable to that in the Place Vendôme) or saw illustrations of hypothetical projects of this kind, his employment of it established Baltimore in the avant-garde of architectural taste.

The impressiveness of the Washington Monument owed a great deal to its location. On two sides the ground fell away, creating variety and attracting the eye. This topography encouraged the imagination, and, not surprisingly, Mills himself had a hand in a larger design for the context of the monument. As early as 1814, before work began, Mills recommended clearing 106-foot-wide, block-long approaches to the monument, from the north and the south, between what became Centre and Madison Streets, as well as opening 66-foot-wide avenues to the east and west. Writing the board of managers overseeing the project six years later, he again urged it to adopt "a plan of improvement of the square upon which the Washington Monument stands." Colonel Howard, he suggested, had approved of the plan and would willingly provide land enough for such avenues. After Howard's death in 1827, his heirs implemented these plans and laid out building lots on Monument Street and Charles Street.[8]

The size, simplicity, and lovely setting of Mills's Washington Monument made it forever impressive. Godefroy's Battle Monument—smaller, more complex, its message nonetheless legible in its collection of symbols—formed the principal element in the city seal. Together the two works inspired John Quincy Adams to compliment Baltimore as "the Monumental City."[9]

Monumental Churches

Begun in 1817, the First Independent (Unitarian) Church, on the northwest corner of Charles and Franklin Streets, stands as Godefroy's major Baltimore work and one of the city's finest monuments. It is the equal of any design produced abroad in the course of romantic neoclassicism, for it well embodies all the traits of the revolutionary new style. The elements of which it is composed may be counted on the fingers of one hand. The first element is a cube, bound round by two moldings, one at the height of the vaulted porch beneath the pediment and the other at the crest of the pediment. The second is the porch, a rectangle that appears to penetrate the cube and in part emerges from it. A wide flight of low steps and a screen of four Tuscan columns separate porch and building from the street. The third element is a large rounded apse. The fourth is the shallow coffered dome, fifty-five feet in diameter, which originally covered the interior and is visible from the exterior (the room has been modified internally to improve its acoustics). All exterior details are sub-

Between 1985 and 1993 the monument underwent extensive restoration. Its base houses a collection of documents and artifacts that shed light on its early history.

A Perspective View of the 1st
Independent Church of
Baltimore, *engraved in 1819 after a
drawing by Maximilien Godefroy.
Maryland Historical Society*

servient to these four major geometric elements, a principle of the design underscored by the stucco exterior, which unifies each unit and relates it to the others. The building can thus be understood as composed of visible interlocking volumes, a characteristic of neoclassicism. The only decorative element on the façade is a terra cotta sculpture in the pediment representing the angel of truth, fashioned by Antonio Capellano.

An inner vestibule and a colonnade led into a large space facing the broad apse, and geometric elements continued inside. Four great piers supported arches, pendentives (the triangular masonry that rises from a building's corners to support the base of a dome), and the dome. They also created four vast openings onto broad vaulted secondary spaces, including the apse, the whole forming a Greek cross at floor level. Squared by the piers, the space rose upward into the circle of the pendentives carrying the dome. This complex of inner spaces was brightly lit from a circular window at the center of the dome and from tall arched windows at two sides. Some of the interior effect arose from a Capellano illusionistic painting—swags of flowers and foliage on the side walls, coffers on the under side of the dome, and emblems in the pendentives evoking the arts and learning and the flight of time.

Interior of the Unitarian Church,
Baltimore, *drawn by William
Goodacre Jr., New York, engraved
and printed in London, 1831.
Maryland Historical Society*

FAR RIGHT:
*Detail view of portico, First
Unitarian Church. Photograph by
Jack E. Boucher, 1960. Historical
American Buildings Survey,
Library of Congress*

BOTTOM:
*Floor plan, First Unitarian Church.
Drawing by Michael F. Trostel*

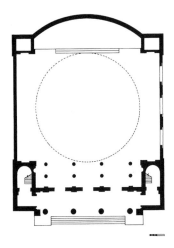

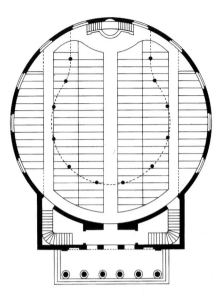

Meanwhile, Mills was not idle. While work on his monument slowly progressed, he raised another great Roman dome in 1817, this one for the First Baptist Church at South Sharp and Lombard Streets, on a budget of $50,000. The Baptists had their first meetinghouse as early as 1773 on a site later occupied by the Shot Tower, at President and Fayette Streets. Mills designed the new building, known as Old Red Top Church, as a cylinder with a low Roman-saucer dome and a portico with a simple Ionic colonnade. He combined these elements in more orthodox fashion than Latrobe had done ten years earlier in designing the cathedral (then half built) or than Godefroy was doing then in his Unitarian Church. The curved brick walls of the great circular space under the dome freely expressed the exterior. The rectangular porch joined this main member by means of a transitional vestibule block. Mills gave the dome an oculus in its center, and, though shielded by a monitor, it brought a great deal of daylight into the interior of the central space. The frieze of the porch Mills carried around the entire building as a unifying and strengthening member for its cornice, but aside from this element the main fabric of the church went undecorated. There were two levels of very plain windows and five equally simple doorways with arched transoms. Completed in 1818, the church demonstrated Mills's remarkable restraint.

Masterly Houses

Earlier, in 1815, Mills had designed a group of twelve three-story row houses on Calvert Street north of Centre Street. In a double pun, the public eventually named the houses Waterloo Row. The owner, the Baltimore Water Company, met financial defeat in the enterprise in the same year that Napoleon lost at Waterloo because the expensive houses went up too far north of the city to attract buyers. Tepid sales may also have been due to their innovatively plain style.

At Waterloo Row, Mills achieved a monumentality new to domestic architecture and expressed a new authority through form and design. He created a controlled design for the block-long front while introducing sufficient variety to avoid monotony. White freestone

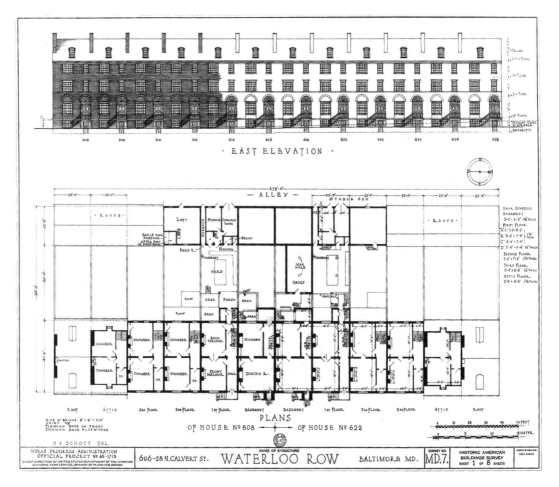

Waterloo Row, east elevation and floor plans. Historic American Buildings Survey, Library of Congress

stringcourses, which marked first- and second-story levels, and white wood cornices contrasted boldly with the flat, red-brick wall plane and unified the length of the block, serving as horizontals that held the arches and windows in place. Further emphasizing the flat, planar quality of the façade, the window openings were sharply cut, with narrow lintels and sills. The arched first-floor openings were wide, one for the door with its accompanying side-lights and arched transom; the other, of the same size, framing a wide tripartite window capped by a shallow, arched reveal. Tripartite windows also marked the main rooms of the second and third floors.

Waterloo Row's fanlights offered a signal reaction against the dainty elegance of the Federal style. Rather than the exquisitely detailed oval forms and looping arches and swags of the Adamesque, Mills chose regular geometrical shapes. Not only did his vocabulary of forms differ from that of the Federal; so, too, did the broader scale and precise definition of mass and void. This taste, described as "masculine" in its time, also sought a largeness of effect inside the house to equal that gained outside. Mills laid out the interiors of Waterloo Row simply and with careful attention to the placing of doors and windows. Austerity and precision show in broad wall surfaces defined by simple baseboards and shallow cornices, which stretch out with apparent muscularity, as though supporting the ceiling. Finely molded door and window frames run almost to the full height of the room. As Latrobe once remarked of Mills, "in the design of private houses, he is uncommonly excellent."[10]

Mills designed another residence of consequence, this one for John Hoffman (it later be-

Waterloo Row disappeared in the enthusiasm for urban renewal of the 1960s, and the cleared site remained vacant for many years. Fortunately, enough parts were salvaged to permit reconstruction of a typical first-floor double parlor at the Baltimore Museum of Art. There visitors can see how the clouded black marble mantle pieces and the prominent window casings act as visual focal points to emphasize the three-dimensionality and spaciousness of the two drawing rooms joined by a wide opening. Chandeliers hang from the plasterwork ceiling medallions, whose decorative details were larger-scaled and bolder than earlier Adamesque designs.

longed to George B. Hoffman), on the northeast corner of Franklin and Cathedral Streets, just north of Latrobe's cathedral and a block west of Godefroy's Unitarian Church. Beginning work on it in the late 1810s (it was completed in 1821), Mills used triple-sash windows on the first-floor front, one on either side of an entrance that featured a portico with classical semicircular roof, two Ionic columns, and matching wrought-iron fixtures for gas lamps. Mills added a porch along the rear, or Hamilton Street side, of the house. To avoid the delimiting impression of brick, he ordered the exterior stuccoed and brushed to give it neoclassical grandeur. Back buildings included stables and a summer kitchen. A recessed alcove and double entrance on Cathedral Street suggested that the two first-floor rooms on the west side may have drawn on a Latrobe plan for a house in Lexington, Kentucky, and one that Mills employed at Ainsley Hall, a house he completed in Columbia, South Carolina, in 1823. In both instances two large rooms met each other with semicircular walls, their exterior arcs leaving space for an alcove. Steps graced with a wrought-iron railing made a quarter-circle turn from the Hoffman House alcove, connecting to the sidewalk on its uphill side.

One cannot help but notice how many landmarks went up in so short a span of time. By 1820, all the celebrated architects were gone. Latrobe died that year. Godefroy had returned to France in 1819. Mills, after the Waterloo Row debacle (for which he was heavily blamed), returned to his native South Carolina and later worked in Washington, where his commissions included the capital city's Washington Monument, the great obelisk on the Mall. Latrobe's grand design for a library in Baltimore was never built. Yet under the direction of his son John H. B. Latrobe, an engineer and lawyer who lived in Baltimore and had his father's drawings, the south tower of the cathedral was completed in 1830–31, the north tower in 1840–41, and the portico in 1860–63.

John Hoffman house, as it appeared in a photograph, ca. 1880s. Maryland Historical Society

The Builder as Architect: Robert Cary Long Sr.

Enlarged in 1858, the Hoffman house was home to the Maryland Club until late 1891, afterward quartering the Maryland Academy of Sciences. It was torn down in about 1906.

The influence of Latrobe, Godefroy, and Mills lingered well after their departure, at first in the work of Baltimore builder-architect Robert Cary Long Sr., whose rise to prominence resembled that of his contemporary, Jacob Small Jr. Born in 1770, Long rose in Baltimore business as the owner of a lumberyard and workshop, serving on city committees and supervising construction of Nicholas Rogers's Assembly Room. He and Small thus typified the upward progress, still common in the early nineteenth century, of a carpenter or bricklayer turning to design, completing creditable buildings, and calling himself an architect. Eventually competing with the masters, Long left his own legacy of landmark buildings. He produced work influenced by both Federal and Latrobean neoclassical styles, blending conservative and daring elements in unexpected ways.

Long may have built many dwellings, as his obituary stated, but documentary evidence

*Robert Goodloe Harper springhouse, designed in 1827
by Benjamin Henry Latrobe.*

*Latrobe's own additional work in Baltimore included a springhouse (or dairy,
ca. 1812), all that survives from Oakland, the Robert Goodloe Harper country
estate that later formed part of Roland Park and the Baltimore Country Club.
Latrobe applied a delicate Ionic porch to a simple and functional rectangular
structure, creating a miniature Greek temple. This photograph was taken
after the building had been relocated to the grounds of the Baltimore Museum
of Art. Peale Collection, Maryland Historical Society.*

THE ROBERT OLIVER HOUSE
SOUTH GAY STREET, BALTIMORE, MARYLAND

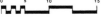

*Robert Oliver house on South Gay
Street, built 1805–7. Drawing by
Peter Pearre*

clearly marks two designs as his. One, a large house
for the Irish-born merchant Robert Oliver on South
Gay Street, went up in 1805–7. Long gave the
dwelling, which featured a ballroom, greenhouse,
and aviary,[11] a smooth, five-bay-wide front with a recessed central bay featuring a tripartite entry (suggestive of Latrobe and Mills). The doorway and sidelights were framed by narrow Ionic columns
supporting a partial architrave and an elaborate fanlight. Giving second and third floors equal elegance,
Long placed a similarly scaled Venetian window atop
the entryway and, even higher, a large arched triple
window to light the third story. His neoclassical de-
tails included decorative stone panels separating the upper stories in the recessed, central
portion of the façade.

In 1807, Long designed his first public structure, the impressive Union Bank, at Fayette
and Charles Streets. Like Godefroy in his work soon thereafter on the Commercial and
Farmers Bank, Long enjoyed the architectural freedom involved in designing a new kind of
structure. He conceived of a large (sixty-eight-foot-square) brick box that featured Ionic columns, marble pilasters, and the first figural sculpture to decorate a Baltimore building. The

Robert Cary Long Sr.'s Union Bank of 1807, as it appeared in Latrobe's Picture of Baltimore.

Long's Union Bank as captured in a photograph of 1885. Maryland Historical Society

---

The bank was demolished in the late nineteenth century.

---

two-story bank had a recessed vestibule set behind a screen of four full-height columns; similar columns set oddly in half-niches marked the corners, and matching pilasters articulated the side elevations. Plain, unadorned rectangular windows cut sharply into the smooth wall surfaces. Long also employed the fashionable Soanean devices of recessed wall panels and shallow, arched reveals to articulate the façade. While building the bank, Long twice borrowed Soane's 1798 *Sketches in Architecture* from the Library Company.[12]

No drawings of the interior survive and one can only surmise that it held at least one great hall—likely with a high ceiling, judging by the space between the first- and second-story windows—with smaller rooms for offices. In the Charles Street pediment a large freestone relief in the form of a lunette paid classical tribute to Ceres and Neptune, the ancient Roman deities of agriculture and the sea—and the sources of Baltimore's wealth. Even though his design was modeled on Soanean principles, the essentially untrained Long employed the tall, thin proportions of the Federal style for the elongated columns and pilasters that decorated the façade, leading Nicholas Rogers to dismiss the building as "wonderfully full of deformity, a sort of oyster in Architecture!"[13]

Long next entered a competition for a building to house the newly chartered University of Maryland College of Medicine. A lottery raised funds, and John Eager Howard supplied

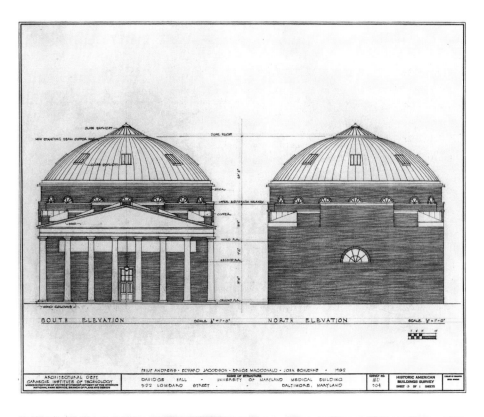

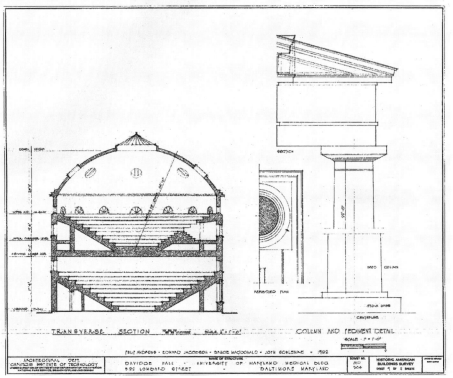

Davidge Hall, south and north elevations, as drawn for the Historic American Buildings Survey in 1962. Library of Congress

Medical College of Baltimore, or University of Maryland, *better known as Davidge Hall, portrayed in Charles Varlé,* A Complete Guide to Baltimore *(Baltimore, 1833). Enoch Pratt Free Library*

Interior of Davidge Hall. Medical Alumni Association, University of Maryland at Baltimore

Holliday Street Theatre, as it appeared in View of Baltimore, *lithograph by E. Weber & Co., 1848. Maryland Historical Society*

the ground at the corner of Greene and West Lombard Streets. Godefroy himself worked on a design, but Long's won acceptance. Work began in May of 1812, the college taking full occupancy the following year. Later named Davidge Hall, it commemorated the moving spirit behind the creation of the medical school, Dr. John B. Davidge.

In designing this building, the first one dedicated to higher learning in the city, Long took inspiration from the Pantheon, Agrippa's seat of the gods in Rome (as Mills soon did in designing the First Baptist Church, although in quite different proportions, and as Jefferson would do in conceiving of the Rotunda at the University of Virginia). A portico with eight Doric columns of stuccoed brick fronted Long's domed structure, a rectilinear box encasing a cylindrical rotunda. Long subdivided the exterior walls with advancing and receding planes that marked the rotunda's position, seemingly borrowing this treatment from Latrobe's nearby cathedral and the Bank of Pennsylvania in Philadelphia. A double-ended pantheon, the bank also provided a model for Long's front; behind the colonnade, the wall exhibited a long rectangular panel above a single doorway. Although the columns retained a Federal slimness, Long, in the manner of Latrobe, clearly strove for neoclassical expression.

The most impressive element of Davidge Hall, the sixty-foot circular anatomical theater, filled the width of the structure and rose into the dome. A large oculus and eight smaller windows, fitting into the circles of the rich stucco decoration, lit the interior. Circular seating platforms rose from the floor in auditorium style; they could hold, by inflated accounts, fifteen hundred persons. A similar room below served as a chemistry lecture hall. The extension on the front held the entrance hall and two rooms on either side for library, office, and teaching space.

Between 1811 and 1813, two doors away from the Assembly Room on East Lexington Street, Long rebuilt the Holliday Street Theater, a wooden structure erected in 1794. Rogers's treatment of the Assembly Room may have prompted Long's design, for the theater front adopted an equally neoclassical combination of high basement and tall, thin pi-

Baltimore Museum and Gallery of
the Fine Arts, as depicted in the
border of Thomas H. Poppleton's
Plan of the City of Baltimore,
1823. Maryland State Archives

The Peale Museum, as
photographed in the 1930s.
Enoch Pratt Free Library

lasters above. Long established the same clear hierarchy of openings: five arched recesses punctuated the scored basement, those at the center and ends containing doors. Tall, narrow windows lit the principal floor; a row of ocular windows lit the gallery. Above the cornice, a block-and-panel parapet marked the three central bays. The Doric order of the six pilasters came from Sir William Chambers's *Treatise on the Decorative Part of Civil Architecture* (1791), which Long borrowed from the Library Company, conveniently located in the Assembly Room, for six weeks in the late winter of 1812.

For Rembrandt Peale, son of the artist and naturalist Charles Willson Peale, Long in 1813–14 designed and built the first structure in the United States expressly intended as a museum. The Baltimore Museum and Gallery of the Fine Arts (later simply Peale Museum) went up only a short distance from the theater, north, along the east side of Holliday Street. Having no model for the design of a public museum, Long adapted the standard five-bay house plan, enlarging the center into a tripartite pavilion. Rusticated masonry laid in horizontal courses created the effect of an English basement similar to that of the theater's design. The central entrance employed a Latrobean motif, a screen of two Doric columns set before a recessed vestibule. Pairs of Ionic colonettes framed three large second-floor windows and carried a high entablature. Above, a rectangular stone panel, like those on Latrobe's cathedral, awaited relief sculpture or inscription.

The interior provided rooms simply finished, suitable for museum purposes, and Peale advertised the place as "an elegant Rendezvous for taste, curiosity and leisure."[14] The entrance led to a central hall with staircase and two rooms on either side. One large exhibition gallery filled the second-story front; rooms on the third floor served as Peale's painting studio, or perhaps as lecture halls. Museum exhibits offered a combination of "natural curiosities" and art, displaying stuffed birds, the skeleton of the giant mastodon the elder Peale had excavated in New York (along with his panoramic painting of himself lifting the curtain to share the discovery), Peale family portraits, live American Indians, Egyptian mummies, and later the notorious "Fiji Mermaid." At the back of the museum Long attached a small two-story building, which housed the family on the ground floor, with extra museum space above. Peale claimed that the museum and house cost $14,000, far more than he had anticipated. In 1816 he hired Mills to install a furnace to provide central heating, in accordance with the standards of modern comfort.

Long's major buildings included a church that replaced the old barnlike St. Paul's of 1784. Baltimore's Episcopalians, as if to compete with the Presbyterians and Catholics, spent the early years of the nineteenth century discussing a more monumental place of worship. In 1810 Nicholas Rogers submitted an old-fashioned design in the late English Baroque style for a "Temple of Divine Worship" with a projecting entrance, balustrade with statues of saints, and an enormous four-stage steeple, each stage with its own heavy decoration. Four years later, however, Long won the commission with a design for an up-to-date, neoclassical white-stuccoed brick church, the exterior of which carried complementary decorative elements of white freestone and marble. Following the pattern of the auditory church, which Sir Christopher Wren developed expressly for preaching, the body of the new St. Paul's was almost as wide as it was long.

Long combined older style Roman elements with more fashionable Greek forms. Over the portico rose a tall tower marked by the sequence of orders familiar from the Roman Coloseum; at street level, however, four pairs of Greek Doric columns gave the entrance a contemporary, monumental character. In the tower circular and octagonal stories successively marked by Ionic and Corinthian columns and composite pilasters built up to the small dome at the top. The Doric columns were among the first in Baltimore to be modeled on an ancient Greek example.

The largely white interior, furthered brightened by numerous windows, included touches of gold, yellow, and imitation marble. Such high coloration provided the brilliance and clarity emblematic of the Age of Reason, and, appropriately, some of the detailing drew directly from the Adam brothers, whose two-volume *Works in Architecture* Long also borrowed from the Library Company. Although the wide auditorium followed the Wren tradition in its breadth, two rows of tall columns running down the center of the nave created a longitudinal emphasis. The altar was set at the back of a broad apse; the pulpit stood at the axis in front of the apse, indicating the rector's place as leader of the congregation. Thus, within an auditory-church design, Long also created a setting suitable for high-church ritual, centering on the celebrant. While the blending of styles identified Long as a self-taught architect who made use of various reference and pattern books, it also showed originality; Greek taste soon predominated, and Long had sensed the trend before the neoclassical masters. In 1816 Rt. Rev. James Kemp, bishop of the Episcopal Diocese of Maryland, pressed for

Apostel St. Pauls, St. Paul's Protestant Episcopal Church, as designed by Robert Cary Long Sr. and built 1814–17. The engraving also depicts, below and right, the two predecessor buildings. Peale Collection, Maryland Historical Society

TOP, RIGHT:

St. Paul's Episcopal Church, from View of Baltimore, lithograph by E. Weber & Co., 1848. Maryland Historical Society

BOTTOM:

The Hamilton Street houses by Robert Cary Long Sr., as they appeared in the late twentieth century. The missing house on the right, or eastern end, lent symmetry to the ensemble. Photograph by J. Brough Schamp

Long's own house on Hamilton Street suffered demolition. Of the other six, which are still standing, two have undergone drastic remodeling and four have had only minor alterations.

completion of this building, making it the first in the country built as the seat of an Episcopalian bishop. The new St. Paul's recognized—and hastened—development out Charles Street from the center of the city; lots sold from church property quickly filled with housing.

In 1818 Long and George B. Hoffman merged properties they owned on the north side of Hamilton Street between Charles and Cathedral Streets and over the next two years built a row of seven brick dwellings, each three stories high, three bays wide, and two rooms deep. Because they lacked back buildings, Long placed kitchens and other service rooms in the basements. Although much smaller and less ambitious than Mills's nearby Waterloo Row houses, Long's houses clearly tried to emulate the work of the master. His façade design featured smooth brick walls with a stone stringcourse separating the ground level, with its regular fenestration pattern, from the upper two stories, each lit by a wide, tripartite window, a popular element at the time. Although Long sought the precision and clarity of Mills, he here reached beyond his competence. The ground floor seemed disassociated from the upper two-thirds of the front. The top windows hung from the cornice; the middle ones

floated uncertainly. Unlike Waterloo Row, and perhaps because of the street grade, Long's houses lacked continuous roof lines and the horizontal elements of the design (cornice and stringcourse) broke at the edge of each unit. The row seems to have been financed like Pascault Row, under a method used frequently in early-nineteenth-century Baltimore. Craftsmen and suppliers needed for construction and finishing contributed their skills and materials and were paid by receiving title to a house. Hoffman and Long retained one house each and Long took up residence in 1823.

Long executed one of his odder designs in about 1820, a residence on Bank Lane for William Gwynn, an Irish immigrant who edited the Baltimore *Federal Gazette* and dabbled in the city's literary life. Two stories tall and unusually deep, the house had a low-pitched roof and recessed first- and second-story front porches. Two Ionic columns supported the porch roofs, with matching pilasters framing the recessed entrance. On the first-floor façade, Long placed tall arched windows on either side of the central porch; smaller, squared attic windows lit the second floor. Gwynn named his house the Tusculum, and it served for a time as the meeting place for the Delphian Club of writers and poets.

Understudy: William F. Small

Several other projects of this period illustrated the lasting power of Latrobe's influence in Baltimore, all of them the work of William F. Small (son of Jacob Small Jr. and grandson of Small Sr.), who apprenticed with Latrobe for three years in Washington and in Baltimore between 1818 and 1820. In 1828 the federal government commissioned Small to draw up plans for completion of the master's (and his father's) Baltimore Exchange by adding a United States Customs Warehouse on the Water Street side of the building. Small complied, as one would have expected, with a wash drawing that lent detail to Latrobe's original vi-

Elevation and first-floor plan for Folly Quarter. Watercolored drawing by William F. Small, 1831. Maryland Historical Society

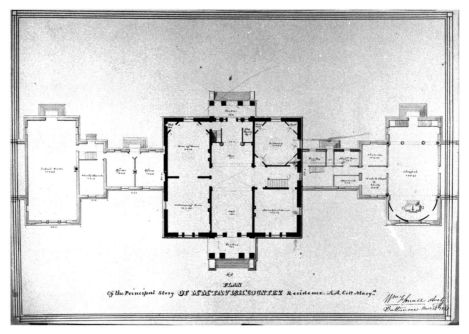

By an addition of 1865, the archbishop's house gained three semihexagonal bay windows in a faintly Tudor design, along with wings and a third story; in the late twentieth century, a new concrete veneer aimed to replicate the original stucco.

sion—smooth exterior surfaces, perfectly ordered window and door openings, and a presentation that Latrobe would fully have approved.

These plans never materialized, but Small continued his work by altering Peale's museum in 1830, when the city acquired the building for office space (his father then served as mayor) and by conducting experiments in adapting the neoclassical style to residential architecture. Both of his known house designs stood on Charles Street. While rows of red brick, Federal-style two-and-a-half-story row houses were still going up in working-class waterfront districts, Small's design for a house for the secretary of the city school-building committee, Jacob I. Cohen Jr., in 1830 featured flat, stuccoed wall planes and first-floor arched windows, set within shallow reveals. Exterior simplicity contrasted with the elegance of the interior. Small called for the typical Baltimore side-hall plan, parlor and dining room, with a demioctagonal back wall, to the right, the passage leading past the main staircase to pantry, breakfast room, and necessary at the far end of the structure. The kitchen apparently occupied a back building. Like the warehouse drawing, Small's design for the Roman Catholic archbishop's residence, which in 1829–30 went up on the east grounds of the basilica, facing Charles Street, complemented Latrobe's earlier work and stood fast by the neoclassical style. Small's original design called for a condensed five-part building, exterior stuccoed and scored to resemble stone.

Small's design in November 1831, for a country house in what was then Anne Arundel County, further illustrated the neoclassical sensibility that Latrobe had passed on to the younger architect. John McTavish, a native Scot who had married Emily Caton, a granddaughter of Charles Carroll of Carrollton, ordered a rural retreat that befitted his station and included quarters for private worship services. Small's design for the McTavish house, Folly Quarter, followed a five-part plan, a chapel with a rounded nave occupying one of the dependencies, a schoolroom, the other. With angled walls, Small created an octagonal library on the first floor, with an unusual triangular entrance and closets. The dining room on the opposite side of the house had similar angled walls overlooking the garden front. Small's design for the garden front followed the example of Latrobe and Mills. Recessed tripartite arched windows marking the dependencies and first-floor rooms of the central block recalled Small's work on the customs warehouse. For the main entrance façade Small designed a flat-roofed Greek Doric portico, which supported a windowed, second-story pavilion that extended slightly above the cornice line. Small's window arrangement, squat portico, horizontal pavilion cap, and low-pitched roof with a small cupola gave Folly Quarter a look of strength and understated elegance. It epitomized neoclassical ambition.

Elevation of the J. I. Cohen house on North Charles Street, watercolored drawing by William F. Small, 1830. Maryland Historical Society

4

THE REIGN OF THE
ROMANTICS, 1829–1878

"Baltimore is, I think, one of the handsomest cities to approach in the Union," declared Frances Trollope, an English visitor whose travel account made few kind references to Jacksonian America. "The noble column erected to the memory of Washington, and the Catholic Cathedral, with its beautiful dome, being built on a commanding eminence, are seen at a great distance." Another visitor, a Scottish woman who eventually settled in the United States, had written similar praise a few years before. "Spread over three gentle hills," said Fanny Wright, streets in Baltimore, "without sharing the fatiguing regularity and unvarying similarity of those of Philadelphia, are equally clean, cheerful, and pleasingly ornamented with trees." She had even climbed the Washington Monument. "Ascending to it," she reported, "we saw this beautiful little city spread at our feet; its roofs and intermingling trees shining in the morning sun, the shipping riding in the basin, and crowded round the point while, in the distance, the vast waters of the Chesapeake, and more near those of its tributary rivers, gleamed in broad lines of silver through the dark extent of forested plains, that stretched beyond the more cultivated precincts of the young city."[1]

These bucolic memories aside, the city continued to grow by being relentlessly commercial, increasingly industrial, and necessarily innovative. Private companies built toll roads radiating out from the city, including turnpikes connecting Baltimore to the federally funded National Road from Cumberland to the Ohio country. In 1828 a group of leading citizens incorporated the first railroad line in the United States with ambitions of linking Baltimore to the Ohio River. Two years later John O'Donnell's heirs established the country's earliest planned, large-scale industrial park at Canton. In 1832 Baltimore

Washington Place ca. 1830.
Watercolor by Robert Cary Long Jr.
Charles Howard's noteworthy
house stood just to the north and
east of the monument. Maryland
Historical Society

interests launched one of the country's fastest-sailing merchant ships, the clipper *Ann McKim*. Two years later they helped form the Philadelphia, Wilmington, & Baltimore Railroad and in 1846 launched a trans-Atlantic packet line, sailing between Baltimore and Liverpool. The A. S. Abell Company, the owner of the *Baltimore Sun*, dedicated the first cast-iron building in the country in 1851, the year of London's Crystal Palace Exhibition. Baltimore's population continued its steady rise: from 80,620 in 1830, to 102,313 in 1840, to 169,054 in 1850, and to 212,418 in 1860.

The "more cultivated precincts," as Fanny Wright phrased it, pushed away from the harbor as newcomers filled older housing. Old Town took on a role it played for a century or so, serving as the town's gateway and earliest home for newcomers. A great wave of Irish and German immigrants swept in during the 1840s. Ethnic violence sparked gang warfare, making the 1850s a decade of extreme political and racial violence. Some citizens sought stabler surroundings, moving out of the old city to new communities served by horsecar lines, which first appeared in 1859. Riding on tracks in the streets, the horse-drawn streetcars could travel twice as fast as a carriage and rapidly changed the way people traveled to jobs and visited friends.

As if in response to such swift urbanization, Baltimoreans began to care about parks. Besides the Howard family bequest that led to Mount Vernon Place, examples included new houses grouped around central parks. In the late 1840s developers of Franklin Square, on the city's western edge, offered building lots facing a landscaped common. Londoners knew the practice well. In Baltimore similar park squares, typically for the private use of surrounding homeowners, later appeared as the centerpieces of Union Square, Harlem Park, and Lafayette Square, on the west side of town, and in Johnson, Madison, and Collington Squares on the east side. Small public squares surrounded the city's many

View of Baltimore, *watercolor by
T. Tanssen, 1831. Tanssen's view
captured the breadth of the
northern limits of the city at the
time, from the jail on the east to the
Washington Monument on the
west. The rear of Robert Mills's
Waterloo Row figures prominently
in the center foreground. Enoch
Pratt Free Library, on extended loan
to the Baltimore Museum of Art*
RIGHT:
Baltimore City Spring, *as drawn
by August Köllner and lithographed
by Deroy, 1848. Maryland
Historical Society*

water sources or city springs. City Spring on Calvert Street near Saratoga was praised in
an 1858 guidebook as "a beautiful little park . . . enclosed by an iron railing and surrounded with umbrageous elm trees."[2]

In 1858, Baltimore mayor Thomas Swann formed a city park commission, which
urged the city to purchase Druid Hill, Nicholas Rogers's five-hundred-acre country estate about two miles north of the harbor. Baltimoreans thus joined the contemporary nationwide movement for urban parks. The choice was perfect. Open land at Druid Hill
protected Baltimore's latest major source of drinking water, a reservoir at the southern
end of the park formed by America's first large earthen dam. The beauty of the landscaped hills and woods arguably rivaled New York's newly planted Central Park. Druid
Hill Park and the city's new horsecars developed symbiotically: The rail lines encouraged
park patronage, and a one-cent tax on the nickel fare helped to defray the acreage's half-
million-dollar purchase price.

By October 19, 1860, the day the park was dedicated, a state-run police force had
brought comparative peace to the streets, and the people were ready to celebrate. The
event nearly brought out the whole town; according to an observer, "the entrance was
literally packed with people and vehicles, a continuous string of carriages, buggies,
hacks, wagons, and, in fact, every class of vehicle."[3] It seemed the dawn of a new age of
peace and pleasure.

DURING THE MIDDLE FOUR DECADES of the nineteenth century, architectural taste in Baltimore reflected the European affection for, and urge to revive, historic styles, which in its most exuberant forms became known as romanticism. An emphasis on feeling as opposed to reason, romanticism, at least in Britain, registered a reaction against the rapid and dehumanizing changes of the Industrial Revolution and the violent excesses of the French Revolution. But the cultural context for this new sensibility also included fresh achievements in history and archaeology. Romantics looked longingly to the past; and in the early nineteenth century, scholarship broadened their panorama. Knowledge of the arts in the ancient Near East, Egypt, Greece, Asia, and Europe throughout its history burgeoned. In the process of compiling this information, romantics came to regard buildings as revelatory of the nature of the society they were built to serve. An English historian put the concept into words in 1821: "The architecture of any people always forms one of the features by which we characterize them in our imagination," he said; from architecture "the earth derives its moral physiognomy."[4]

In this manner, the Greek style came to represent the order, learning, and stability of the ancient Greek democracies (in contrast to the decadence and political instability of the Roman Empire). The recent (1824) Greek war for independence—in which Lord Byron lost his life—solidified British romantic attachment to the democratic ideals of the ancient Greeks. The Gothic style of medieval churches seemed equally romantic, shrouded in mystery and the mysticism of early Christianity. Gothic ruins and churches became favorite motifs on transfer-printed china, which was popular in the American market, and the romantic novels of Sir Walter Scott fueled British and American fascination with the heroic days of yore. The religiosity of the Middle Ages seemed to make medieval styles perfect for the many new churches being built across the country. The truly ancient forms of Egyptian architecture seemed especially exotic and romantic, as did the lesser known forms of Moorish, Near Eastern, and Chinese building and ornament.

Not all styles were appealing. Since Greek architecture represented the ideals of democracy, the Roman-derived styles of the princely and monarchic Renaissance, baroque, and rococo periods seemed corrupt and therefore unworthy of revival or development. Like the neoclassical architects, the romantics also dismissed the Georgian, which seemed unrepresentative of deep feelings. In an era when more than one associational style was available for use, the concept of "style" itself increased in importance. Learned professionals and gifted amateurs offered public lectures on the meaning of architectural style and the differing attributes and associations of the styles now recommended for use.

In general, throughout America, the pure Greek style, as embodied in temple-form buildings, seemed ideal for the many public schools being built in the era of Jacksonian democracy. Newly successful businessmen and professionals sought the cachet that attended the use of Greek forms in their city and country residences. Medieval forms, which always seemed appropriate for churches, also came to be favored for cemetery ornaments and institutional structures that needed to suggest power, such as jails. Egyptian forms suggested quintessential power—massiveness and solidity, as well as association with mortuary practices—and found favor for tombs, cemetery ornaments, and public structures designed to safeguard valuable resources. By the 1840s another romantic form of architecture

Green Mount, *watercolor by*
unknown artist, ca. 1840.
Maryland Historical Society

An architectural curiosity of the
period vividly demonstrated the
sudden appeal of the Greek Revival
manner and the stylistic distance it
traveled from the Federal. In about
1825 Robert Oliver commissioned
someone, perhaps Robert Cary Long
Sr., who drew plans for and built
the Oliver town house, to place a
new entrance along the side
elevation of his country house out
the York Road, Green Mount. The
builder obliged with a Doric portico
that must have provided
conversation for many a visitor.

had surfaced as appropriate for both town and country residences. Italian villas in the countryside around Rome and Florence, with their asymmetrical massing and tall towers,
seemed the perfect model for the residences of America's newly rich manufacturing class,
which based its wealth on the newest technology but longed to create a home environment
belonging to another place and time. For their in-town homes and places of business, Americans copied the styles of Renaissance-period urban palazzos.

The romantic architectural styles of mid-century America were spread much like the earlier Georgian and Federal styles, namely, through builders' handbooks as well as expensive
folio volumes showing buildings of the past in fine detail. One of the most influential of
these publications, *Cottage Residences*, was first published in 1842 by Andrew Jackson Downing, a landscape gardener, architectural critic, and tastemaker; it was followed in 1850 by the
widely circulated *The Architecture of Country Houses*. Downing's volumes provided models
for rural houses in the Gothic, Greek, Egyptian, and Italian styles, complete with floor plans
and suggested ornamental details.

Although most "architects" were still self-trained, by mid-century America was producing more architectural professionals who designed important buildings, gained local and national recognition, and were sought out by wealthy clients in cities other than their own.
These men almost invariably practiced fluently in either the Greek or Gothic styles in the

1830s and 1840s and successfully took up Italianate forms in the 1850s. The center of the profession had moved to New York, where more people had more money to spend than anywhere else in America. Pre-eminent practitioners of the Greek Revival style for public buildings, Ithiel Town and Alexander Jackson Davis also provided romantic Gothic designs for churches and rural cottages. In New York, Richard Upjohn and James Renwick produced the most striking Gothic churches of the era: Upjohn's Trinity Church, 1839–46, and Renwick's St. Patrick's, 1853–58.

Commentators expected romantic designers—in due course and as history shows those of other ages to have done—to develop an architectural style of their own. Ironically, their acquaintance with history hampered the process; it encouraged the replication of past styles, eventually tending to stifle rather than encourage stylistic invention. It also invited loyalty to an idealized image of the past and a belief that excellence, enshrined in the buildings of an admired age and its style, could be restored through revival of that style.

Revivals: Greek and Gothic

Architects adopting the Greek Revival style copied ancient temple forms as well as the Greek versions of the Doric, Ionic, and Corinthian orders, all illustrated in the first volume of James Stuart and Nicholas Revett's *Antiquities of Athens* (London, 1762). They became more and more concerned about archaeological correctness, in terms of both design and ornament, and faithfully copied the forms of their ancient models. Earlier architects had experimented with Greek forms as well. Benjamin Henry Latrobe's springhouse at Oakland (ca. 1812) faithfully copied the temple on the Ilissus as depicted in the Stuart and Revett volume; Robert Cary Long Sr.'s temple-front Davidge Hall and St. Paul's portico illustrated the early Greek influence in Baltimore, as did Mills's First Baptist Church. Greek Revival–style buildings vividly illustrated the romantic penchant for idealizing the past and its architectural styles, as well as imbuing buildings with serious associational meanings. In America the style fully captured the popular imagination beginning in 1821, when Greek patriots revolted against Turkish rule, and the more so after 1824, when Lord Byron, the romantic poet, died in the service of Greek independence. Greek Revival influenced American public and domestic design for another forty years or so. Temple forms, with varied archaeological accuracy, inspired banks, courthouses, churches, plantation houses, and academic buildings across the country.

For other romantics, the Middle Ages, not pagan Greece, offered the highest examples of virtue and a much closer past to draw upon. The romantic impulse to revive medieval art and Gothic architecture became the style known as Gothic Revival. Architects favored asymmetrical compositions, massive stone construction, and the use of the Gothic pointed arch. Unlike frothy eighteenth-century Gothic Revival garden follies (when Gothic had been one of the various exotic styles that attracted rococo designers), the new Gothic Revival style demanded a direct relationship between ornament and structure, between the emotive and formal expression of the whole. Meaningless, applied ornament had no part in this revival. Most of all, Gothic style should reflect the visible bonding of design, religious faith, and northwestern-European history and culture (each nation had its own medieval version

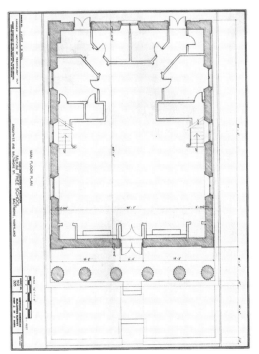

Isaac McKim's Free School, built
1822, as drawn by John Penniman
and engraved by A. W. Graham,
1838. Maryland Historical Society
RIGHT:
Main floor plan of the McKim Free
School. Historic American
Buildings Survey, Library
of Congress

The McKim Free School, the
most archaeologically correct
Doric structure in Baltimore, remains in use as a community center; First English Lutheran burned
in 1872.

of the style). Aggressive members of the movement used Gothic in an attempt to end the classical revival. Comparing their image of the Gothic past to the nineteenth century, whose modern buildings seemed to them to represent structural and artistic dishonesty, as well as being expressive of a secular, unjust, and inhumane society, these enthusiasts insisted that a revival of the Gothic style could impart order to the disorderly life and art of their time. Moderate adherents found Gothic suitable only for some purposes, churches in particular. Churches made a forceful, primitive statement of the relationship that should prevail between a building's function and its form. Baltimore builders and architects seized the moment to build soaring church spires and towers that still give the Baltimore skyline a strongly ecclesiastical cast.

The equal stature of both the Greek and Gothic Revivals in Baltimore architecture, as throughout the United States in this period, is perfectly exemplified by the erection, in 1832, as both styles were just beginning to make their influences felt, of both pure Greek temple-form buildings and a Gothic castle by local tastemakers.

As scholars published drawings of Athenian antiquities, the style associated with early, Democratic Greece—the Doric—seemed appropriate for the Jacksonian democratic government's first experiments with free public education. Local architect William F. Small, working with amateur architect William Key Howard, the son of John Eager Howard, designed Baltimore's first Greek temple building, the McKim Free School (endowed by Quaker merchant John McKim), in Oldtown in 1832. Working with McKim's son Isaac, Howard and Small copied the granite hexastyle Doric portico from the Temple of Athena and Hephaestus (popularly called the Theseum) in Athens, while the flanks of the school derived from the north wing of the Propylaea on the Acropolis. Such details were undoubtedly copied from plates in Howard's extensive architectural library. The columns—fluted, freestone

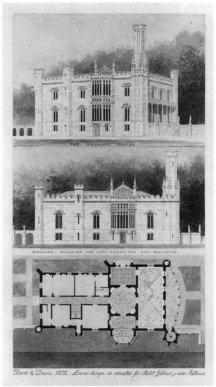

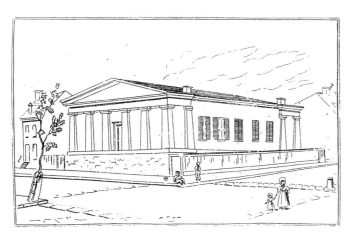

Male Public School Number 1, from John H. B. Latrobe's Picture of Baltimore, Containing a Description of All Objects of Interest in the City; and Embellished with Views of the Principal Public Buildings *(Baltimore, 1832). Maryland Historical Society*

RIGHT:

Designs for Glen Ellen, the Robert Gilmor house, north of Baltimore, by Ithiel Town and Alexander Jackson Davis, 1832. Gilmor's original, vaulting ambitions called for a two-story structure (top); *the house as built was revised to just one story* (center). *Metropolitan Museum of Art, Harris Brisbane Dick Fund, 1924 (24.66.17)*

monoliths—stood seventeen feet tall. The large, one-room interior space was not unlike that of a Greek temple. The imposing design of the McKim Free School, still standing today at Baltimore and Aisquith Streets, won Small the commissions for the first public schools to be built in the city. Public Schools Numbers 1–4, erected between 1832 and 1835, were all one-story Greek temple-form buildings designed in the Doric order, the plainest and simplest of the Greek orders, as befitted the serious purpose of the new schools.

William Howard's enthusiasm for Greek architecture had already manifested itself in the monumental town house he had built for himself in 1830 on the northeast corner of Charles and Franklin Streets, directly across from Godefroy's Unitarian Church. The tetrastyle Ionic portico, with its imposing full-height marble columns, was modeled on the Erectheum in Athens. Howard may also have collaborated with William Small on the Greek-temple design of the First English Lutheran Church (1832), on the north side of Lexington Street, west of Park Avenue, whose front was copied from Stuart's plates of the Ionic temple near the Illissus.

Also in 1832 a young Baltimorean, Robert Gilmor, commissioned two well-known New York architects, Ithiel Town and Alexander Jackson Davis, to design a picturesque Gothic "castle" and service structures for his extensive property in Towson, north of the city. An avid art collector like his uncle, Robert Jr., Gilmor often traveled abroad. On one English tour he had fallen under the spell of Sir Walter Scott's Abbotsford, a medieval-style mansion, and Horace Walpole's "Gothic" home at Strawberry Hill, on the Thames. For his rugged setting along the Gunpowder River, Town and Davis borrowed heavily from the houses Gilmor had visited, installing battlements, historically correct details on towers, and a two-story oriel window. Named Glen Ellen, after his wife, Ellen Ward Gilmor, the castle remained a Baltimore landmark for over a century, even though Gilmor, due to high construction costs, could only complete the center portion and the first and second stories of the rambling three-story design. The first Gothic Revival structure in Baltimore, Glen Ellen nevertheless partook more of the ornamental aspect of Gothic—as seen at Godefroy's St. Mary's Chapel, or indeed at Horace Walpole's Strawberry Hill—than the integrated structural principles that would characterize the Gothic Revival buildings of the 1840s.

The Architect as Historian: Robert Cary Long Jr.

The local architect who would best characterize the ease in shifting from one romantic style to another, for the design of churches, residences, and institutional buildings, was

The Patapsco Female Institute, *oil painting by an unknown artist, ca. 1835. The romantic yearnings of the age were perfectly captured in this view of the temple-form Patapsco Female Seminary on the top of the hill, with the Gothic Angelo Cottage nestled in trees at the bottom. Maryland Historical Society*

Robert Cary Long Jr. The son of the talented builder-architect Robert Cary Long Sr. enjoyed advantages unknown to his self-trained father. The younger Long attended St. Mary's College (doubtless passing many hours in Godefroy's chapel), then at age sixteen, in 1826, left for Europe to study architecture. But cholera raged there, so he returned to the United States, apprenticing in the New York architectural office of Martin Euclid Thompson and Ithiel Town, one of America's first important architectural firms. By then Town was well known as a pioneer in Gothic Revival architecture (Grace Church on New Haven Green, 1814) and an innovator in the Greek Revival style (the Doric-temple-front Connecticut State House, also on the Green, 1827). In 1828 Town left the partnership to join Alexander Jackson Davis, and young Long may have departed with him. Town opened his remarkable library on architecture to all who wished to study, and Long appears to have availed himself of the opportunity it offered.

In 1833 Town and Davis briefly opened a branch office in Baltimore. Although it soon closed, Long finally returned home three years later to assume his deceased father's practice. The young man brought with him a heady mixture of knowledge, talent, enthusiasm, and business sense. He had already acquired a grasp of the sweep of architectural history—the classical architecture of Greece and Rome, Gothic styles, the architecture of ancient Egypt, and perhaps even that of the Mayans in Central America. Having worked in a professional firm in New York, Long wrote from Baltimore in 1836 to support the founding of an American Institute of Architects. Later his lectures and publications interpreted European ideas about the relevance of historical styles to Baltimore audiences.

Long's earliest known work in the Baltimore area dramatically shows his dedication to the design principles of the romantic era. In the mid-1830s he received a commission to build a female seminary high atop a hill in Ellicott City. For this scholastic endeavor he chose the Greek Revival style and erected a stone temple-front building with Doric columns for the Patapsco Female Institute. At the bottom of the hill he created a whimsical Gothic folly known as Angelo Cottage and across the valley a Greek-style residence, with full-height, columned portico, for William Ellicott.

In Baltimore Long's reputation grew dramatically. Family anecdote credits him with

With its ruins stabilized, the Patapsco Female Institute, as well as archaeological findings nearby, is today interpreted as a historical and cultural resource by the local Howard County Historical Society.

Robert Cary Long Jr.'s design for the Baltimore City and County Record Office, 1836. Maryland Historical Society

entering the design competition for the British Houses of Parliament in the mid-1830s. Whether he did or not, in a mere twelve years Long had received some fifty commissions. Thirty-five of these were in Baltimore, but he also designed a large Greek-Revival structure for the Institution for the Deaf, Dumb, and Blind in Staunton, Virginia (1840); the Gothic-Revival St. Mary's Roman Catholic Cathedral in Natchez, Mississippi (1841); two Gothic Protestant Episcopal churches—St. Timothy's, Catonsville (1844), and the Church of the Ascension, Westminster (1845–46); and a monumental neo-classical mansion in Altoona, Pennsylvania (1844–46).

Long's hallmark—his mastery of many styles—made him a perfect architect for his times, but beneath his borrowing lay considerable originality. He seldom copied exactly the details found in the published illustrations he used as sources. In 1835, after fire had badly damaged the old City and County Courthouse in Baltimore, authorities decided to rebuild the courthouse and also to erect a separate fireproof record office behind it. (Until then, Baltimore had been curiously reluctant to put up governmental buildings; the jail of 1800 was largely a county project, as was the first courthouse, and proposals for a city hall went down to defeat as an unnecessary extravagance.) The city invited Robert Mills to submit proposals for the record office but in the end selected Long Junior for both the courthouse reconstruction and the new building. A year later he offered a daring scheme for the record office, using an Egyptian temple design that resembled an illustration in a romantic's travelogue. Overseers persuaded Long to submit a series of progressively simpler designs, and he finally produced a design that was unusual in its stark simplicity. The vaulted brick interior, which was acclaimed as absolutely fireproof, was sheathed on the outside in Baltimore County marble. Originally there were two short flights of steps leading up to the great iron doors. Its solid mass recalled an Egyptian structure or a Mayan temple.

Long's name has often been associated with Upton, a Greek Revival–style country residence designed by an unknown architect in 1838 for Edwin Ireland but soon sold to attorney David Stewart. It stood southwest of Bolton, on a hilltop that offered a splendid view. Not as vehemently Greek Revival as the temple front added to Green Mount, Upton's design included a two-story Greek Doric-style portico, with a second-story porch, at the rear

Upton, from a painting of the period. Peale Collection, Maryland Historical Society

of the house, looking southwest toward the city. Demioctagonal projections at both ends of the building—more common in earlier than later Greek Revival designs—illustrated the continuing influence of the Adamesque. Superb iron railings, bearing the Stewart crest of roses and thistle, completed the design.

In 1839 the lawyer David M. Perine asked Long to enlarge his country house north of the city, apparently specifying that he wished the renovation to stand with classical dignity. Long obliged with a two-story temple block of unusual width, with six full-height Doric piers (built of solid masonry) supporting a deep, south-side portico that extended across the entire central block of the house. Single bays at either end were marked by recessed panels containing full-length first-floor windows and attic windows above.

By 1843 Long, as well as romantic styles, were firmly established in Baltimore. In that year

As the city overtook the site, Upton became 811 West Lanvale Street and, eventually, a private school for pupils with special needs.

Entrance elevation of Mondawmin. Drawing by Michael F. Trostel

Mondawmin and its setting as recreated from late-nineteenth-century sources. Drawing by Michael F. Trostel

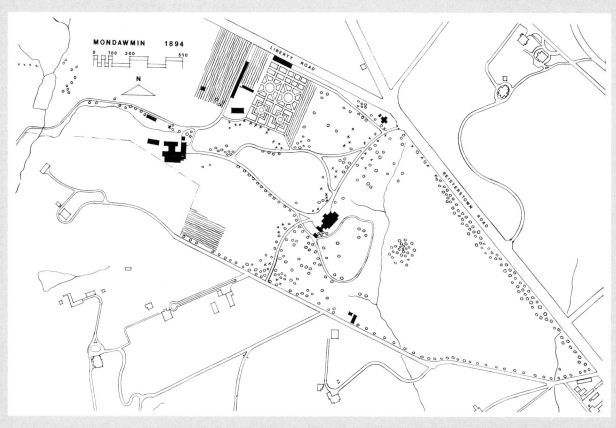

Long Junior may also have designed Mondawmin, the magnificent retreat northwest of the city commissioned by Dr. Patrick Macauley and completed in 1841. Combining neoclassical elements, such as advancing and receding planes, and sitting on a raised basement, the house featured a large botanical conservatory in one wing (Macauley served for a time as president of the Maryland Academy of Sciences) and an early Baltimore example of a porte-cochère at the front entrance—a portico large enough to provide passage for carriages and protect disembarking visitors from the weather.

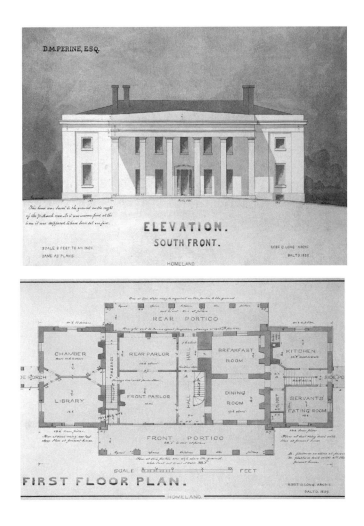

Elevation, south front, Homeland, and first-floor plan, watercolored drawing by Robert Cary Long Jr., 1839. Maryland Historical Society

alone, Long designed two major Greek Revival–style churches and his most important Gothic Revival church, and he presented lectures to different groups on the various styles of historic architecture. The same year local architect and builder Jacob Wall designed the Charles Street Methodist Episcopal church in the "Grecian style of architecture," with an Ionic tetrastyle portico copied from the temple on the Ilissus at Athens. (Although the *Sun* noted that the church was "unusually stylish for Methodists," the same denomination hired Wall a year later to build a Grecian-style church on Pennsylvania Avenue, near Lanvale.)[5] Also in 1843 local architect William Caldwell designed a Gothic-style hall for the Odd Fellows, which featured a grand Egyptian-style ceremonial room, with painted "views taken from tombs of the old Egyptian kings at Thebes."[6] The following year Long designed a battlemented Norman Gothic Church, to be followed in 1845 by both Gothic and Egyptian designs for the gates at Greenmount Cemetery (opened in 1839). Just a year later, in 1846, he introduced the new Italian villa–style to the city, in his designs for rebuilding the country house Homeland. He also suggested the new Italian mode for one of the city's most prominent cultural buildings, the Athenaeum, erected between 1846 and 1848.

In 1843 Long was preparing both Greek and Gothic designs for various congregations at the same time. That differing faiths considered both Greek and Gothic designs acceptable

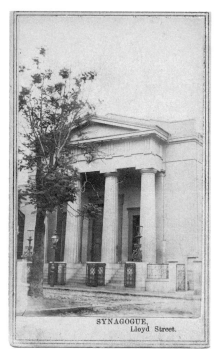

SYNAGOGUE,
Lloyd Street.

*Broadside announcing a series of
lectures on architectural taste and
history delivered by Robert Cary
Long Jr. in Baltimore in 1844. Left to
right, from the top, Long supplied
drawings of buildings typifying the
Egyptian, South Asian, Mexican,
Grecian, Roman, Romanesque
(Italianate), Saracenic (Middle
Eastern), and Gothic styles.
Maryland Historical Society*

TOP, RIGHT:
*St. Peter the Apostle Church,
designed by Robert Cary Long Jr. in
1843, as it appeared ca.1970.
Maryland Historical Society*

BOTTOM:
*Lloyd Street Synagogue, the first
Jewish place of worship built
expressly for that purpose in
Maryland and the third oldest in
the United States, as captured in a
ca. 1864 photograph. Ross J.
Kelbaugh Collection at the Jewish
Museum of Maryland*

testifies to the basic interchangeability of these designs in this era. For a Catholic parish in West Baltimore, begun as a kind of missionary church for the large number of Irish immigrants settling there to work at the Baltimore & Ohio Railroad yards, Long designed St. Peter the Apostle (1843–44) at Hollins and Poppleton Streets. A massive hexastyle temple-front building with huge stone fluted Doric columns supporting a deep entablature boldly articulated with metopes, St. Peter's became the cornerstone of a neighborhood that was just beginning its rapid growth. For the city's first Jewish synagogue to have a building designed expressly for worship—the Lloyd Street Synagogue (1845) at the corner of East Lombard Street in Old Town—Long created a smaller version of St. Peter's, now with a tetrastyle wooden temple-front portico. The bold metopes and pedimental moldings seem otherwise identical. The fluted columns were painted white to look like stone.

Despite these prominent examples of Greek Revival churches (including the earlier First English Lutheran Church), by 1840 most Baltimoreans, in company with the rest of the United States and Europe, had decided that Gothic best suited Christian worship. Local preference owed a great deal to the opinions and authority of Rt. Rev. William Rollinson Whittingham, who that year became bishop of the Protestant Episcopal Church in Maryland.

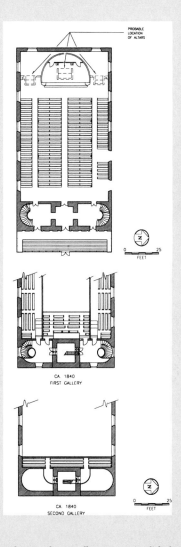

St. Vincent de Paul's Church, *as
it appeared in* View of Baltimore,
*lithograph by Ed. Weber & Co.,
1848. Maryland Historical Society*
RIGHT:
*St. Vincent's original floor and
gallery plans, based on research
conducted during restoration.
R. Christopher Goodwin &
Associates, Inc.*

Temple forms were also used by other architects at this time, but not all were as accomplished as those by Long. In 1840, on Front Street in Old Town, Roman Catholics who had formed the St. Vincent de Paul's Benevolent Association laid the cornerstone for a church to which they hoped to add an orphanage and a school. The temple-form design, with its Greek Doric pilasters supporting an entablature and pediment, was a flattened version of the kind of Greek Revival–style freestanding porticos Robert Cary Long Jr. was designing for both houses and churches at this time. The multistaged steeple, however, is a throwback to an earlier era, resembling the tall steeples of the First German Reformed Church and Long Senior's St. Paul's, built in 1803 and 1814, respectively. The church closely resembled plates that appeared in Asher Benjamin's The American Builder's Companion, first published in 1806 and updated through six editions by 1840. A design for a courthouse in the same volume illustrated a single-stage, polygonal domed spire, which builders could easily have seen and employed in designing the base; St. Vincent's prominent three-stage spire in any case had local precedent in a simpler, two-stage steeple that Fr. John Baptist Gildea, first pastor at St. Vincent's and likely overseer of construction, had ordered built at St. James Church in 1837. (See Thomas W. Spalding and Kathryn M. Kuranda, St. Vincent de Paul of Baltimore: The Story of a People and Their Home [Baltimore: Maryland Historical Society, 1995], 177–80.)

In 1974 the federal government added St. Vincent de Paul Church to the National Register of Historic Places. The church was fully renovated and restored in 1990.

Whittingham brought with him determined taste in church architecture. He was a scholarly gentleman, sympathetic to the ideas of the English Ecclesiological Society, which in the 1840s advocated a particular style of Gothic Revival in church building and church ceremony. Its conservative recommendations and the ferocity with which the members of the society pursued those who failed to accept their doctrines testified to their romantic enthusiasm. Insisting upon Gothic and the English parish church model (a nave with aisles and a chancel less tall and less broad than the nave), the bishop embarked on a campaign of church building, and from 1840 to 1850 every new Episcopal church in the diocese followed his lead. Whittingham and Long were acquainted; the young architect always treated the erudite bishop with the deference due to a religious leader, scholar, and potential client.

Long did much to bring the Gothic Revival to Baltimore church design. He pioneered in the use of the new material—cast iron—in interior framing, tall towers and spires, and decorative details. Romantic enthusiasm for sheer height—mountain peaks, towers, and balloon ascensions—helped to explain these structures. Until Eiffel built his tower in Paris, only church spires and a few monumental columns and obelisks offered the architect a chance to soar.

Long's work epitomized ecclesiastical Gothic design, and his most impressive churches, all of them brick, represented different medieval styles. Long's first Gothic commission was the Redemptorist Catholic Church of St. Alphonsus on Saratoga Street and Park Avenue, which he began in 1842 and completed two years later for the German Catholic community of the city, many of whom were new arrivals. Long called its style English Perpendicular, described by the *Sun* as the "third period of Gothic . . . the finest style of Gothic." The reporter continued, "the vertical character is seen in every part of it . . . all of its details seem to be 'struggling' upwards toward heaven."[7] The sharp profile of the spire carried considerable authority and assurance. Tower and spire—two hundred feet tall—contrasted brilliantly with Latrobe's neoclassical cathedral two blocks away. The original color scheme—walls painted a pale warm grey with decorative ornament brought out in coral pink—further enhanced the effect of the whole building.

German Catholic Church, Balto., *the design for St. Alphonsus drawn and etched by Robert Cary Long Jr., 1843. Maryland Historical Society*

The interior of St. Alphonsus, a virtuoso performance, suggests in its dense, glittering exuberance the fabulous interiors that the British architects Sir Charles Barry and Augustus W. N. Pugin developed for the Houses of Parliament a few years later. Even so, its old stained glass and fifty-foot-tall complexly clustered columns, soaring in dimness to the fan vaultings of which Long was so proud—he did not know, he wrote during construction, "of any church yet executed in this country that has a ceiling so elaborately ribbed as this one will be"[8]—the church gave an air of quiet mystery. Long pleased his German Redemptorist patrons with an interior plan typical in German churches (a large hall with a shallow, rounded apse containing the high altar and two flat apsidal areas on either side of it at the ends of the aisles, each equipped with an altar). Of Long's churches, St. Alphonsus was the grandest in size and detailing. It was his masterpiece.

With the construction of St. Alphonsus, Long launched a campaign in print to inform the

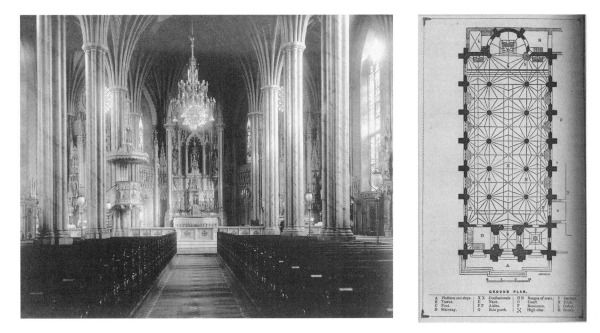

Interior of St. Alphonsus as seen in a late-nineteenth-century photograph. Courtesy of Phoebe B. Stanton

RIGHT:

Ground plan and vaulting design of Long's St. Alphonsus Church. United States Catholic Magazine 2 (May 1843): following 296.

public of what he was doing and to educate it in the use of historic styles. Long shared with Pugin, whom he characterized as the leader of the Gothic revival in England, the belief that no new architectural style developed after the Gothic. Greek and Gothic had reached perfection; after them, degeneration prevailed. In architecture, Long declared, "the law of imitation" had replaced "that of originality."[9] His churches, and his writings, revealed that he had read the contemporary English books and periodicals that appeared as interest in Gothic and its revival developed. Long clearly felt Pugin's influence. Mannerisms that characterize Pugin's style in the illustration of his buildings appear in Long's view of his proposed St. Alphonsus, and Pugin's "principles" can be detected in Long's architectural doctrine; like Pugin, Long announced that he would decry buildings that did not measure up to the standards he espoused. Comparison between Pugin and Long must note that Pugin's Church of St. Chad, Birmingham, and St. Alphonsus are coeval and that both are major early works by their architects. In his use of painted brick, however, and cast iron for tracery and other ornament, Long departed from Pugin's stern standards. In fact, Long's employment of cast iron structurally and ornamentally pioneered such uses in America. But in style alone, St Alphonsus stands as a major monument of the American early Gothic Revival.

Long's Franklin Street Presbyterian Church, commissioned in 1844 and completed three years later, at the northeast corner of Cathedral and Franklin Streets, drew directly from illustrations of Gothic-style churches published by Pugin and his son. Unlike St. Alphonsus, this church went without tower or spire; it stood as low and horizontal as St. Alphonsus was tall and slender. St. Alphonsus Church represented the influence of applied Gothic; but Presbyterians seemed to prefer the dubious warmth of English Tudor. Long made use of a rectangular plan, so well suited to Protestant congregations, but he conceived the façade as an entrance gate, quite in the manner of Anne Boleyn's Gate at Hampton Court, near London. The church was built in brick with stone doorways, cornices, and dressings, the brick painted to match. Gothic window frames and sashes were cast iron, filled with elegant cast-

iron perpendicular tracery, which, along with the well-buttressed and crenellated side walls, recalled parts of King's College Chapel, Cambridge. Long's version of English Gothic implied an antiquarianism rare at the time; for whatever reason, Franklin Street Church did not seem as American as its contemporaries.

By 1845 Gothic had grown so dominant that Long, in his independent fashion, proposed an Egyptian gateway for the recently established Greenmount Cemetery. It found no favor with the cemetery governors, who preferred Gothic, and Long complied, finishing the structure about two years later.

Between 1845 and 1848 Long introduced the new Italianate style (already popular in New York and London) to Baltimore, first in remodeling Homeland and then, majestically, in designing the city's Athenaeum. The first Perine house did not have a happy history. Long's drawing of the Greek design carries the later notation that the house burned in March 1843. "As it was unsuccessful at the time," he added, "it was supposed to have been set on fire."[10] Whatever the case, Perine again commissioned Long to rework the design, and in 1845 patron and architect collaborated on a quite different design, a modified rural villa of the Italian Renaissance. Long built on the end walls that had survived the fire, so the house retained its width. But in a new three-story design, he called for vertical reach, the second story narrower than the first and the third consisting of a central tower, each story stepped back from the one below. At Homeland Long's independent exercise in Italianate villa design clung to traditional symmetry, but it introduced Baltimoreans to the elements and forms that would dominate residential and commercial architecture for the next generation: tall chimneys, pitched roofs, and deep eaves supported by carved brackets. The Italianate style also came to include arched window and door openings, heavy door and window moldings, and ornamental iron balconies. Villas most often had vigorous asymmetrical designs, marked by towers, porches, and balconies.

In 1845 Baltimore's cultural leaders proposed the building of an Athenaeum—a single building designed to house the recently founded Maryland Historical Society, with its art gallery and library, along with two earlier-established subscription libraries, the Baltimore Library Company and the Mercantile Library. Neighboring Philadelphia was already building its Athenaeum, designed by John Notman, and Baltimore could not be left behind. The word *athenaeum* derives from the Temple of Athena in Athens and refers to an institution devoted to the arts and literature. The founders hired Robert Cary Long Jr. to design the building, and in October 1846 the foundation was laid at the northwest corner of St. Paul and Saratoga Streets. The *Sun* reported that above the rusticated basement "the second and third stories will be finished in the Italian style," with projecting balconies on all windows.[11] The three-bay-wide entrance façade on St. Paul Street had a dramatic, arched frontispiece carried on squat Doric piers. Beneath the wide fanlight, paneled bronze doors led inside. A low, hipped roof, with deep eaves and a modillioned and dentilled cornice, capped the eight-bay-long design. Because of the upward slope of Saratoga Street, the rear entry to the building opened onto the second

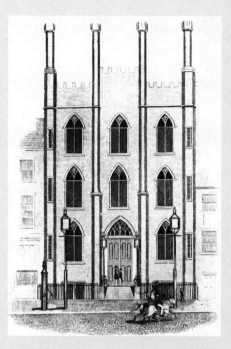

Variations of Baltimore Gothic. This view of the Baltimore cemetery on East North Avenue, taken from plans made by the architects Thomas Chiffelle and William Reasin in the late 1840s, shows the mix of crenellated Gothic, pointed Gothic, and Egyptian styles popular for funerary architecture at this time. Lithograph by A. Hoen & Co., ca. 1860. Maryland Historical Society

RIGHT:

The Odd Fellows Hall, designed by William Reasin, 1843, also showed the popularity of the castellated Gothic style in 1840s Baltimore. Engraving by S. A. Sands, 1846. Maryland Historical Society

Robert Cary Long Jr. designed a conservative, symmetrical Italianate façade for the 1845–46 rebuilding of Homeland. Maryland Historical Society

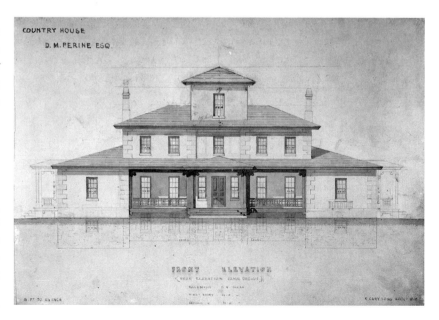

The third version of Homeland came down in 1924, when the property became another suburb developed by the Roland Park Company.

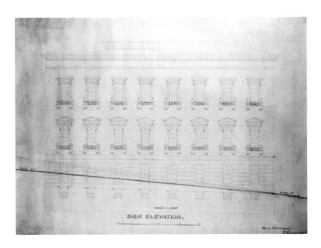

The Athenaeum, side elevation, on
Saratoga Street, drawn by Robert
Cary Long Jr., 1845. Maryland
Historical Society
RIGHT:
The Athenaeum, as it appeared
in a period print. Maryland
Historical Society

The Athenaeum served as the
headquarters of the Maryland
Motor Vehicle Administration
from 1918 until 1930, when,
ironically, it came down to make
way for parking.

---

floor. For his decorative details, Long drew upon the forms and details of the town palazzos of Florence and other northern Italian cities. The windows were elaborately framed—arched windows on the second floor had triangular pediments supported by pilasters; those on the third floor had flat lintels supported by wooden brackets. Each window sported a carved stone balcony supported by blocklike forms modeled on classical triglyphs.

Although many of the Greek Revival–inspired town houses near the cathedral and Mount Vernon Place have variously been attributed to Long, only one, the Samuel W. Smith house, at 505 Park Avenue, can definitively be assigned to him. It is also known that Long designed at least four Gothic Revival "cottage ornées" in the style popularized by Downing's pattern books. Fairy Knowe, built in 1843 west of the city for John H. B. Latrobe, son of the famous architect, who was the principal attorney for the B&O Railroad, combined Greek and Gothic motifs in its rambling design. When it burned in 1850 Latrobe quickly rebuilt it after a design, "A Plain Timber Cottage-Villa" (plate 25), from Downing's newly published *Architecture of Country Houses*. Evesham, designed for B&O president Joseph William Patterson, rose in 1846, north of Homeland and east of the York Road. Its steeply pitched gable roofs, picturesque chimneys, deep porches, and decorative cornice boards (bargeboards) set a model for later translations of the style. Two more Gothic Revival cottages, completed in 1848 by local builder Henry Curley after designs by Long, rose on Lanvale Street, west of Park Avenue, north of the old Grundy mansion, Bolton.

Long's last design in Baltimore may have been his work for the offices of the Baltimore *American* on West Baltimore Street, under construction in 1848. The Gothic storefront featured twin front gables decorated with quatrefoils and pinnacles, a cast-iron-columned street level, and an imposing pair of two-story-high front windows decorated with cast-iron panels and topped by elegant Gothic tracery.

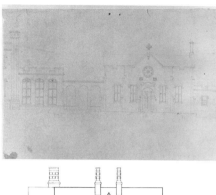

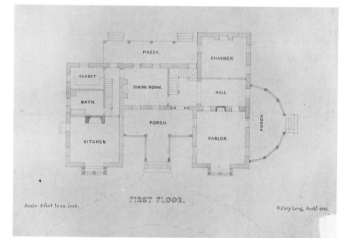

Throughout these busy years, Long also worked on the maintenance and completion of historic buildings. His father had assisted Godefroy in building St. Mary's Chapel; in 1840 the son made minor repairs to it and added the spire that Godefroy had intended to build. At Latrobe's basilica on Cathedral Street, Long Junior designed handsome iron railings to enclose the property.

In October 1848, he left the city to seek his professional fortune in New York. The *Literary World* of that city announced that Long, "late of Baltimore," had established an office at 61 Wall Street and offered "designs detailed in every way that could be ordered by mail and for all kinds of buildings and monuments."[12] He worked on a design for the Astor Library in New York, a commission that would have launched his New York career. Soon he became architecture critic for the *Literary World*, generously delivering his opinions on the work of others and what he believed to be the salient issues of style and performance. By 1849 he had embraced a new enthusiasm, delivering a paper at the New-York Historical Society on the ancient architecture of Central America and its "historical value and parallelism of devel-

The Baltimore American Building, West Baltimore Street, designed by Robert Cary Long Jr., ca. 1847. From George W. Howard, The Monumental City: Its Past History and Present Resources *(Baltimore, 1873).*

opment with the architecture of the old world." In it Long revealed himself to be the consummate architectural romantic. "In the Monuments of the Past we have the human deposites of the Ages, the truth of the Historical Past," he said. "Architecture in this view, is the geology of humanity."[13] In 1849, while superintending construction of a church of his design in Morristown, New Jersey, Long died suddenly of cholera.

Residential Architecture: Greek Interpretations

By the 1830s the center of Baltimore's fashionable life had moved north to the blocks surrounding the Washington Monument (completed in 1829), where it firmly remained until the late-nineteenth-century exodus to the new garden suburbs some miles north of the city. Apart from the land encircling the monument, donated by Howard to the city in 1814, the remainder of the acreage belonged to Howard's country estate Belvidere. Upon Howard's death in 1827, commissioners appointed by Maryland's General Assembly widened the streets flanking the monument and drew up a plat assigning the various thirty-foot-wide lots thereby created to his many heirs. Presumably, at this same time, the Howard heirs contacted Robert Mills, then in Charleston, South Carolina, for suggestions about how to lay out building lots on the newly widened Monument and Charles Streets. A few schemes survive in the collection of the Maryland Historical Society, each showing a different number of building lots carved out of the cruciform shape of the square. The family chose the design that allowed for parks to be laid out to the north and south and the east and west of the Washington Monument, even though this plan offered fewer building lots than another of the designs. Soon the north-south axis (Charles Street) bore the name Washington Place, the east-west axis (Monument Street) Mount Vernon Place, which natives eventually applied to the cross-shaped space as a whole.[14]

In 1829–30 two of Howard's sons, Charles and William, erected monumental Greek Revival–style town houses on their father's land. The temple-front residence built by William Howard on the northeast corner of Charles and Franklin Streets, across Charles from Godefroy's First Unitarian Church and just down the hill from Latrobe's cathedral, was by far the costlier and more pretentious. William Key Howard was a physician, but also a natural historian, engineer, surveyor, and well-traveled amateur architect whose architectural library may have been the most expansive in the state at the time.[15] He hired architect William Small to design his house, but he undoubtedly worked closely with him, poring over plates of Greek temples found in his extensive library. The massive five-bay-wide, two-story-and-attic house, facing onto Franklin Street, boasted a full-height portico with four striking Greek Ionic marble columns. The brick façade was stuccoed and painted a neoclassical light grey; wide marble steps led from either side to the deep portico. Two oriels, or bay windows, overlooked Charles Street as well as the garden on the east side of the house.

The same year William began work on his house, Charles Howard put up his own im-

*Watercolor of St. Mary's Chapel,
Robert Cary Long Jr., ca. 1840,
showing Long's addition of a spire
of his own design. The spire
eventually fell victim to wind and
weather. The Walters Art Museum*

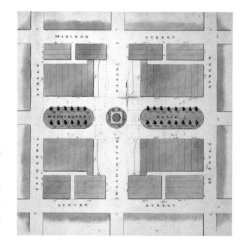

*Plans for the squares around the
Washington Monument, drawn ca.
1830. Washington Monument
Papers, MS 876, Maryland
Historical Society Library*

posing Greek Revival dwelling on the northeast corner of Charles and Monument Streets. Five bays wide, the grand house set the architectural style and tone for much of the future residential development in the area. It was described as being "three stories and attic" in height, and instead of the steeply pitched gable roof associated with the Federal style, it boasted a much-lower-pitched roof, with the top story lighted by stylish, narrow, "attic" windows, a feature that came to be closely identified with the Greek Revival style. Unlike his brother's two-story temple-front portico, Charles Howard's house was marked by a much less ostentatious, single-story Ionic portico.

A few years later a similar house rose on the south side of Monument Street, west of Cathedral Street. Built for merchant (and later French consul) George C. Morton, the two-

William Howard house,
as photographed by architect
Laurence Hall Fowler in the late
nineteenth century. The John Work
Garrett Library of the Johns
Hopkins University
RIGHT:
Baltimore, Washington's
Monument, *as drawn by August*
Köllner and lithographed by Deroy,
1848. The Charles Howard house
stands to the right of the
monument. Maryland
Historical Society

In 1910, when the William
Howard house came down,
Alexis Shriver contrived to sal-
vage the four thirty-ton Cockeysville marble portico columns
and haul them twenty-five miles
to his estate, Olney, in Harford
County, where they still stand.

story-and-attic house featured a central, four-columned Greek Ionic freestanding portico; a tall basement; full-height front windows with cast-iron balconies; and a low-pitched hipped roof with rooftop balcony. Like the Charles Howard house, the Morton house was origi-nally painted grey, in imitation of stone. The still undeveloped nature of the area around the Washington Monument is strikingly seen in a painting (ca. 1839) of an encampment on West Monument Street. All that can be seen among the grassy fields are the Washington Monu-ment to the left, the Morton house opposite, and beyond, the spires and dome of Latrobe's cathedral.

By the late 1830s a few three-story-and-attic houses with Greek-ordered porticos had gone up on the south side of the square, and by the early 1840s, building was in full swing. One of the earliest documented houses, built in 1842 by William Tiffany, a commission mer-chant, still stands on the north side of Mount Vernon Place, a few lots west of Charles. Its design showed an evolution away from the plainer Greek Revival façades of the Charles Howard and Morton houses. The unknown architect gave it a tall, scored English basement, with the upper levels articulated by a central, shallowly recessed bay marked by a pedi-mented second-floor window. Traditional features, however, included the freestanding four-columned Doric portico, closely resembling the form of the earlier Ionic portico on the Morton house, and the low-pitched roof with broad frieze and attic windows (later owners added the balustrade). That the house was almost complete by September 1842 is docu-mented by an account of a *"Dreadful Accident"* which appeared in a local newspaper on the sixth, detailing the collapse of the scaffolding used by the four men painting the façade, some of whom were "very seriously" injured.[16]

The new style of the Tiffany house was soon reflected in a number of massive, five-bay-wide Greek Revival–style town houses that went up in the 1840s near both the Washington Monument and Latrobe's cathedral. Although only a few of these can definitely be attrib-uted to known architects, newspaper accounts describe many others as the work of obvi-ously accomplished master builders. For example, a long article in the *Sun* in February 1846 described the five-bay-wide, two-story-and-attic house at the southeast corner of Park Av-

George C. Morton house, as it appeared in a painting by an unidentified artist, ca. 1839. Maryland Historical Society

Morton house, as photographed ca. 1900. Robert Hicks Collection, Enoch Pratt Free Library

RIGHT:

Tiffany-Fisher house, photographed by Laurence Hall Fowler, ca. 1900. The John Work Garrett Library of the Johns Hopkins University

In the early years of the twentieth century, the Tiffany-Fisher house became the Mount Vernon Club, whose governors then added more elaborate interior fittings on the main floor and replaced original windows with larger-paned versions.

enue and Centre Street as being under roof, with interior work progressing. The house was being built for John R. Ricards, Esq., a wholesale dry goods merchant, by Ira Brown, master builder. A year later the New England–born hardware merchant Enoch Pratt completed his very similar five-bay-wide, two-story-and-attic house on the southwest corner of Monument Street and Park Avenue. Although the architect is not known, the exterior design adhered to basic Greek Revival principles. The Greek Ionic-style portico was older than the house, having been fashioned in a Baltimore marble yard in the 1830s for a house in Washington, D.C. When the owner decided he could no longer afford the elegant design, Pratt bought it at a reduced cost. On the interior of his home, however, Pratt spared no expense. The two wide parlors, with their full-height windows opening onto cast-iron balconies, were separated by two pairs of highly decorative fluted Corinthian columns. Fine Italian

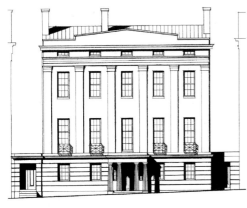

TOP:

A Greek Revival–style house that stood on the southeast corner of Park Avenue and Centre Street, built in 1846 for John R. Ricards, as photographed by Laurence Hall Fowler in the early twentieth century. The John Work Garrett Library of the Johns Hopkins University

RIGHT:

Pratt House double parlor. Maryland Historical Society

BOTTOM:

The home of Gustav W. Lurman, an import merchant, on West Franklin Street, as originally built. Architect unknown. Drawing by Peter Pearre

marble mantels and elaborate plaster ceiling medallions completed the formal rooms. Across the hall, in true romantic fashion, Pratt commissioned a Gothic library, with built-in Gothic-style bookcases and probably the most finely crafted plaster ceiling in the city, with its ribbed arches and cusplike pendants.

A more stylish five-bay-wide, three-story-and-attic house, the residence of commission merchant Gustav W. Lurman, rose two blocks south, on West Franklin Street, opposite the cathedral. Here, the scored basement and articulated wall planes resembled those of the Tiffany-Fisher house. Six full-height Doric pilasters set off the five bays, which supported a deep entablature, above which five narrow attic windows peeked out from a tall parapet, which hid the low-pitched gable roof. Paired, fluted Doric columns formed a deep stone portico, and the tall first-floor windows opened onto cast-iron balconies. A light grey painted stucco exterior added to the house's neoclassical grandeur. Immediately to the west, a much smaller three-bay-wide house, built for attorney William F. Frick, also boasted a massive stone Greek Doric portico, combining fluted columns with wide stone piers. In the same block local architect John Hall designed an even grander four-story, three-bay-wide house for Thomas Swann, president of the Baltimore & Ohio Railroad. Above the dramatic stone portico, with its paired Ionic columns, a tall, tripartite window with trian-

Doric portico of the W. F. Frick house, West Franklin Street. The John Work Garrett Library of the Johns Hopkins University

Thomas Swann house, West Franklin Street. Designed by John Hall, as collection bills attest. Drawing by Peter Pearre

RIGHT:
Portico of the Thomas Swann house, as photographed by Laurence Hall Fowler at the turn of the twentieth century; interior, showing the domed circular stairwell and part of the natural history collection. Garrett Library of the Johns Hopkins University

gular pediment (supported by carved brackets, as at the Athenaeum) marked the central bay; flat-linteled pediments set off the other two windows of the principal floor. Like other houses nearby, the building had a scored English basement, a smooth façade with sharply cut window openings, and a parapet hiding the low-pitched roof. Inside, the dramatic, circular stair hall in the center of the house was lit by an elegant dome supported by Corinthian columns.

Prosperous times and the rising fortunes of the new manufacturing elite brought about a flurry of fine town-house construction in the late 1840s, much of which captured the attention of local newspaper writers, proud of the accomplishments of their bustling city. In the spring of 1846 a grand three-story-and-attic residence, with an English basement, was in progress on the south side of Mount Vernon Place, west of Charles. The *Sun* pointed out that the house, built by a New York architect and builder for a recent resident of that city, Capt. James J. Ryan, was in the "New York style of erecting buildings." The three-bay-wide house had a ten-foot-deep, balconied piazza running across the entire rear of the building for the full three stories, providing an airy view of the undeveloped land to the south and the cathedral beyond. The house had an Ionic portico, tall granite steps, and full-height first-floor windows opening onto richly ornamented iron balconies, much like the Morton house. The interior, no doubt reflecting New York taste, featured a grand double parlor separated by sliding doors and an elaborate circular stairway leading up two and a half flights and capped by "an elliptical stained glass dome." Elegant tall niches for statuary marked each corner of the stairway. As was common in houses of this type, the kitchen and dining room were located in the high basement, and a "bath house" occupied the second floor rear.[17]

Just around the corner, on the west side of Charles Street, south of Monument, local architect John R. Niernsee was putting the finishing touches on a similar three-bay-wide house, designed for B. H. Latrobe, the engineer son of the famous neoclassical architect.

Marble steps led to a marble-pillared Greek portico, beyond which lay a double parlor and grand staircase. Niernsee emigrated from Vienna, and he had studied architecture and civil engineering in Prague before coming to the United States about 1838. He worked as an office draftsman for the Baltimore & Ohio Railroad and in 1846 began designing expensive town houses around Mount Vernon Place. Another identified master builder, Samuel Hess, was credited with a three-story house on the west side of Park, north of Franklin, "adjoining a fine row to the north." Hess was also responsible for a three-story-and-attic house built for attorney J. J. Lloyd, Esq., on the east side of Park, between Centre and Franklin, which was to be finished that spring. Two doors north, on the east side of Park, north of Centre, Hess

505 PARK AVENUE ELEVATION

Façade and first- and second-floor plans of the Samuel W. Smith house, 505 Park Avenue, designed by Robert Cary Long Jr., 1848. Drawings by Michael F. Trostel and Peter Pearre

Much altered, the Smith house still stands.

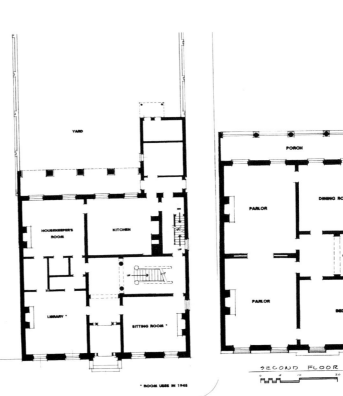

SECOND FLOOR PLAN

had almost finished two adjoining three-story houses, with twenty-eight-foot fronts, which had marble steps leading to each "surmounted with a handsome portico with circular fluted pillars in front." These two were for business partners A. B. Reilly and R. W. Pendleton, who owned a wholesale dry goods firm.[18]

By 1848 the *Sun* was bragging that dwellings "little short of regal palaces in point of splendor are springing into existence like magic," calling attention to the "immediate neighborhood of the Washington Monument" for the large number of these "beautiful abodes of wealth and luxury." Like the B. H. Latrobe house, the three described were designed by "John R. Niernsee, Esqr., architect," and the *Sun* estimated their joint cost to exceed $60,000, a princely sum in an era when very substantial three-story town houses could be erected for less than $10,000. Just completed for Edmund Didier, the president of an insurance company, a house on the north side of Mount Vernon Place, just east of Cathedral (now 16 West), had a "chaste Greek front and portico" and an interior decorated with a "profusion of carved ornaments and stucco work." To the east a luxuriously finished house for commission merchant George Tiffany boasted an exterior ornamented with an elaborate cast-iron balcony. Inside, the house featured marble floors throughout the first floor and halls and salons decorated with rich wood carvings and stucco, along with numerous sculptures and statues of "celebrated masters." The grand stairway was lighted by a dome of stained glass. The third house, built for dry good merchant John H. Duvall, stood "nearly opposite" (at 5 West Monument, later purchased by William Walters). Here the reporter concentrated on the interior conveniences, available in these years only to the very wealthy. The house had hot air furnaces, an ample supply of hot and cold water, and bathrooms, all supplied by "Messrs. Hayward & Co., the major plumbing contractor of the day."[19]

Only a few weeks later, another just completed "magnificent dwelling" received attention in the newspapers. The one town house that can definitely be attributed to Robert Cary Long Jr., the four-story, five-bay-wide house still stands at the northeast corner of Park Avenue and Hamilton Street, just a block and a half west of the cathedral. Built for Samuel W. Smith, nephew of the revolutionary officer and United States senator Sam Smith, it is similar in overall form to the model established by the Tiffany house, with a scored English basement and the main floors articulated with pedimented windows and shallow reveals. The house was notable in 1848 because its scored basement and window lintels were "painted in imitation of the brown stone so extensively used in the northern cities." When completed in December 1848, the *Sun* heralded it as "one of the finest specimens of architectural skill." Long combined "elegance and convenience, as well as all the recent improvements introduced in such buildings." Its front on Park Avenue occupied fifty-three feet; its carriage house and stable ran "to a considerable depth" on Hamilton Street; Long gave the interior a "magnificent finish," the newspaper noted, employing stained glass windows, "rich and elaborate marble work," and various evidences of the highest style and finest workmanship. Willing to invade Smith's privacy in order to give readers a sense of the building's grandeur, the *Sun* added that the house had cost more than $30,000, a staggering sum.[20]

In the same Mount Vernon and Cathedral Street area patrons with less money to spend would opt for a simpler portico with wooden columns, or even a simple pediment set above wooden pilasters with Greek-ordered capitals. In search of guidance, speculative builders or

Detail, Baltimore, Md. U.S. Genl. Hospital, Newton University; *lithograph by E. Sachse & Co., 1864. The Greek Revival row houses adjoining the hospital on the north side of Lexington Street at Calvert have pilastered doorway enframements and squat Doric columns supporting the front stoops. Maryland Historical Society*

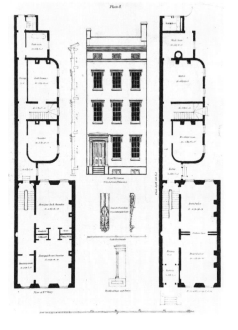

Greek Revival–style three-story town-house plans. From John Hall, A Series of Select and Original Modern Designs for Dwelling Houses *(Baltimore, 1840). Maryland Historical Society*

those working for private clients could turn to an 1840 publication by John Hall, an English-born Baltimore cabinetmaker who had taught himself architecture. Hall stated in the preface to his volume—apparently the only one of its kind to appear south of the Mason-Dixon Line until many years later—that his illustrations derived from houses built or being built in Baltimore and Philadelphia. Plate 8, with its narrow attic windows, closely resembles several houses on the south side of Mount Vernon Place, west of St. Paul Street.

Hall also provided detailed drawings of the decorative elements found in ancient Greek buildings, such as anthemions (floral or leaf patterns), acanthus (thistle) leaf brackets, and the proper forms of columns and capitals for each of the ancient orders: Doric, Ionic, and Corinthian. Copying also from published English designs, he supplied plates that explained to builders how to correctly use Greek orders with their proper ornamental details. Hall's sample interiors reflected the development of a feature new to Baltimore's residential architecture—the "double parlor," or front-and-rear-parlor plan. With a wide opening between them, freestanding full-height columns marking the break, this floor plan provided spaces conducive to entertaining. High ceilings, columns, elegant marble mantels decorated with Greek motifs, walls painted a neoclassical buff, and glittering gaslight chandeliers all combined to make an impressive setting for an evening's pleasure.

By the mid-1840s, when more housing was needed for the many German and Irish immigrants flooding into the city, speculative builders put up long rows of only two-bay-wide, two-story-and-attic houses, modeled on their Greek Revival Mount Vernon Place predecessors in exterior form, but lacking any ornamentation or interior detailing except for plain Doric mantel surrounds. Houses such as these filled many blocks in Fells Point, Federal Hill, and west Baltimore near the Baltimore & Ohio Railroad yards. Along with double-parlor

912–920 Lemmon Street, part of a row of two-story-and-attic houses built for immigrant railroad workers a half block from the Baltimore & Ohio Railroad yards in west Baltimore. Drawing by David Gleason & Associates

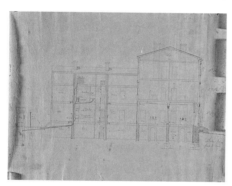

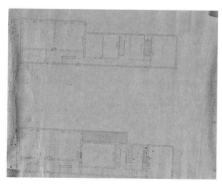

Designs for a three-story Greek Revival–style Baltimore town house and back building, architect unknown. Façade, section, and floor plan. Baltimore Museum of Art

floor plans, these working-class rows had the lower-pitched roofs and narrow attic windows of their prototypes, a design change that allowed for extra room on the upper story, a considerable boon to these large families, many of whom also took in boarders. A typical row went up in the 900 block of Lemmon Street, a half block north of the B&O yards, in 1848. The speculative row was built by Charles Shipley, who also put up grand three- and four-story houses a few years later facing Franklin Square. Both Irish and German railroad workers lived in the Lemmon Street houses.

Residential Architecture: Italianate Interpretations

By 1848, when Robert Cary Long Jr. left Baltimore, John R. Niernsee had already received important residential commissions, and that year, in partnership with J. Crawford Neilson, he oversaw construction of what would prove to be probably the most magnificent house on Mount Vernon Square. A Marylander who had been trained as an engineer in Belgium, Neilson began his career working as a railroad engineer; the two young architects met in the engineering department of the B&O Railroad. At the request of wealthy banker Dr. John Hanson Thomas, the firm designed a house for the prominent southwest corner of Charles and Monument Streets, a building that would introduce elements of the Italianate style to urban residential architecture. The five-bay-wide, two-story-and-attic house at 1 West Mount Vernon Place was essentially Greek Revival in form—almost a perfect cube, it featured a grey-stuccoed exterior, a classic portico with four fluted Corinthian columns of Baltimore County marble, a slightly recessed central bay, and small, square attic windows. But the Thomas house sported some new stylistic details not generally associated with Greek style, harbingers of new tastes soon to make their appearance in local architecture. These Italianate details, already introduced to the city by Long's Athenaeum, included a cornice with deep eaves supported by carved brackets, decorative roof-line ornaments, and windows with pediments made of cast iron and supported by brackets, causing local writers to praise the building's modern effect.

View of Baltimore City, colored lithograph by E. Sachse & Co., 1850, one of the earliest bird's-eye images of the city. The John Hanson Thomas house, to the right of the monument in this view, had just been completed. Maryland Historical Society

A gift to the city from Mr. and Mrs. Willard Hackerman, the Thomas (now Hackerman) house was restored in the late twentieth century as part of the Walters Art Museum and serves as an exhibit area for Oriental treasures of the Walters collection.

Thomas (later Hackerman) house as it appeared in an 1885 photograph with its original grey-stuccoed exterior. Maryland Historical Society

Apparently not concerned with cost and aiming to make a bold artistic statement, Hanson and his architects chose the richly elaborate Corinthian order for both the portico of 1 West Mount Vernon Place and its interior fittings. They apparently achieved their desired effect, because the *Sun* characterized the house as "elegant and princely," with a Corinthian portico of the "purest white Italian marble"; a grand hall with dome supported by Corinthian columns; pure white walls and elegant stucco work finished in the "chastest Corinthian style"; and the long parlor with its high ceilings and pairs of Corinthian columns "finished with white China polish."[21] The house boasted a large basement furnace, bathrooms, and a third (or attic) floor reserved for domestics. Unusual for this early date and indicative of a spare-no-expense attitude, the house also had the new gas lighting. Soon Niernsee & Neilson's expertise in interpreting the newly popular Italianate style would make a dramatic impact on the appearance of both Mount Vernon Place and the surrounding countryside.

As the Thomas house was nearing completion, architect Thomas Dixon was in process of erecting the first Italianate-style row of houses in the city, Waverly Terrace in Franklin Square. As the grand, four-story row on the east side of the square neared completion in 1851, the *Sun* described the row as "much handsomer than any yet finished in this city, and displaying the pure Italian style of architecture." Named in honor of Sir Walter Scott's novels, the row ran the entire length of the block with a unified composition consisting of a scored ground level, a principal floor with full-height "French casement style" windows opening onto a "highly ornamented cast iron" balcony that ran across the entire façade. Principal floor windows were "dressed with architraves and cornices . . . painted and sanded to represent brownstone." There was a "bold block cornice" with scroll-

*Waverly Terrace, the east side
of Franklin Square, built in 1851.
Peale Collection, Maryland
Historical Society*
RIGHT:
*A house in Waverly Terrace,
showing the elaborate cast-iron
fencing and balconies. Peale
Collection, Maryland
Historical Society*

sawn modillions set against a frieze, and the fronts were coated with "genuine mastic, the first ever done in this city," to resemble brownstone.[22]

Meanwhile, Niernsee & Neilson were busily at work bringing the elegancies of brownstone to monumental town mansions, filling the few remaining lots near Mount Vernon Place. A recently marketed building material, brownstone had been highly endorsed in 1846 by Robert Dale Owen, who adopted it for James Renwick Jr.'s new Smithsonian Institution in Washington; it was also popular for residences in New York. By the late 1840s Baltimore builders were using brownstone for façade trim and also imitating its effect by covering brick with an imitation stone or mastic and painting it to look like brownstone, as at Waverly Terrace. In the Thomas house, Niernsee and Neilson had merely experimented with Italianate flourishes, but within a few years they embraced the full-blown Italian town palazzo style so popular in London and New York City. In 1852 the firm built a brownstone-front house on the northwest corner of Cathedral and Monument Streets for Decatur Miller, a tobacco and commission merchant. The *Sun* especially praised its "magnificent" stair, crafted of rich, massive rails and balusters and set in a large elliptical hall, lit from above by a stained-glass dome. Not surprisingly, the fine painting, graining, and white work in the house was done by Messrs. Walsh and Kerns, who had painted the ceiling of Grace Church, also by Niernsee & Neilson.[23]

At about this same time architect Louis Long built an even grander five-bay-wide brownstone palazzo just around the corner, at 105 West Monument Street. Here, too, principal-floor French windows opened onto stone balconies. A tetrastyle stone Doric portico, with

105 West Monument Street, designed by Louis Long, ca. 1852. Photograph by J. Brough Schamp

deep entablature, led to the arched entryway. Second-floor windows had arched stone hoods, apparently a Long trademark, and stone, balustered balconies. Long was also responsible for the monumental three-story, five-bay-wide John Irving Griffiss mansion just north of the Miller house on Cathedral Street. Resembling the Renaissance palaces of Florence, this brownstone faced the street with high, rusticated basement and a formidable façade, featuring tall windows with heavy moldings and projecting hoods. First-floor windows opened onto shallow balconies with carved-stone balusters. Instead of the low-pitched gable roofs of Greek Revival–style houses, the new Italianate palazzos had flat roofs with deep eaves supported by elaborately carved brackets, as at Waverly Terrace.

By the beginning of 1855 Niernsee & Neilson had completed two more impressive brownstone dwellings, this time on the eastern side of the square, at 10 and 12 East Monument Street. The *Sun* noted them as "grand and costly." The house built for Albert Schumacher (10), "of the Roman style," had a "handsome central front [bay window] with piazza of brownstone." Its vestibule was finished in "mosaic marble panel work"; the two parlors were octagonal in form; and the stairs, unusually, continued in a curved flight up to the third floor, at the top of which a "magnificent and spacious dome" rested upon three Corinthian columns. The front room on the second floor was fitted up for a library, which opened out onto the piazza and had bookcases and drawers of elaborately carved oak; the rear room was a boudoir, its walls finished in "panel work of silk and gold." The house next door, for William Mayhew, was also in the "Roman style," but with a "plain" front. Both houses had the usual back buildings—with the kitchen on the basement floor, the dining room and pantry on the first floor, and chambers, baths, and water closets on each of the two floors above.[24]

Not long after Niernsee & Neilson had finished its elegant brownstones, Richard France hired Louis Long to build him a brick house next door, as well as a row of six Italianate four-story, three-bay-wide brownstones extending eastward down the hill to St. Paul Street.

Many of the new industrialists and railroad men of the 1850s built country seats just as the landed gentry, shipowners, and merchants had done a generation earlier. Often turning to the same architects who designed their town homes, these wealthy Baltimoreans established a taste for Italianate villas, as first publicized in the works of Andrew Jackson Downing. One of the most popular designs in Downing's *Architecture of Country Houses* was an Italian villa designed in 1845 by Richard Upjohn for Edward King, of Newport, Rhode Island. It featured asymmetrical massing, a larger and a smaller tower with arcaded windows, balconies, arcaded loggias, and deep eaves supported by brackets.

William Wyman, a merchant who had purchased the old Homewood mansion and land surrounding it, apparently spied this illustration; in 1851 he approached Upjohn in New York about building a similar villa for him on one of his hilltops. The two never reached an agreement and Wyman returned home determined simply to hire a local builder and to copy the design from Downing's book. Along the way, he asked a cousin from Boston to obtain construction details from the Newport carpenter who had built the original house for King. Completed two years later, Homewood Villa—closely resembling its prototype—lent Upjohn's weight to Italianate developments in Baltimore, which Niernsee & Neilson and other local architects and firms promoted as well.

In 1852 the wealthy merchant Johns Hopkins asked architects, probably Niernsee & Neilson, to overhaul his Federal-era country house, Clifton (about two miles east and south of the Wyman house), in the manner of an Italian villa. The designers obliged him by adding a third story, a deep, arcaded veranda that ran around three sides of the house, and, on the west side, a tall arcaded and balconied tower that rose over a vaulted porte-cochère. From atop the new tower, one could see the distant harbor. Grand Italianate villas like these often sat in the middle of vast parklands, rolling hills that exemplified romantic aspirations, and formal gardens. Hopkins concerned himself with horticulture; the five hundred acres surrounding Clifton included an artificial lake, orangery, ornamental garden structures, and a large collection of statuary.

Niernsee & Neilson also designed the villa that Thomas De Kay Winans built in 1853 near the Baltimore & Ohio Railroad yards, west of the city. Son of the B&O engineer and locomotive builder Ross Winans, Thomas not long before had returned from Russia a wealthy man, having overseen construction of the czar's rail line between Moscow and St. Petersburg. Named Alexandroffsky, for the site of Winans's offices in Russia, the house and grounds demonstrated the effects of joining extravagant wealth with romantic taste. The four-story

William Wyman house, Homewood Villa, after a design by Richard Upjohn, featured in A. J. Downing's Architecture of Country Houses, *1850. Peale Collection, Maryland Historical Society*

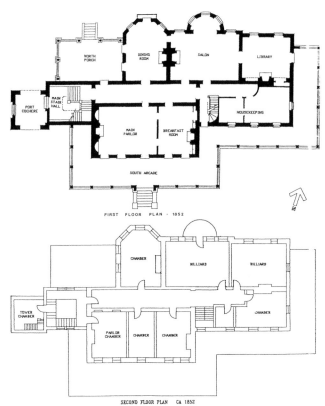

Clifton, as remodeled by Johns Hopkins in the Italianate-villa style. Ferdinand Hamburger Archives, Milton S. Eisenhower Library, The Johns Hopkins University
RIGHT:
Conjectural floor plans, Clifton, ca. 1852, based on a Baltimore Sun *article of February 5, 1852. The main parlor and breakfast room made up the original house (1798). A new exterior wall created the hallway behind those rooms ca. 1801. A rear projection with bay window can be dated ca.1812. Friends of Clifton Mansion*

villa featured towers on both the entrance and garden fronts, projecting bows, and semicircular, arcaded porches marking each level. Although the villa was located within the city, near his locomotive car works on West Pratt Street, Winans installed trees that would reach towering heights around it and lined his garden with replicas of classical statues. His extensive gardens, apparently open to the public, warranted special mention in a contemporary guidebook under the heading "Walks and Promenades." The writer noted that "multitudes of visitors from far and near come to visit it, and gaze upon its beauty and magnificence." The mansion was "adorned with the most exquisite specimens of American, European, and classic art . . . while the spacious grounds surrounding it are tastefully laid out and adorned in a style that would do credit to the home of a European prince." The writer went on to praise the "extensive range of green houses, conservatories, etc . . . filled with the rarest productions of nature from this and other climes," while the gardens were filled with "statuary, bowers, fountains, foliage, and birds."[25] The same architects were also responsible for a second Italian villa, Crimea, built for Winans west of the city on Windsor Mill Road sometime before 1860.

Norris Gershon Starkwether, a Philadelphia architect in Baltimore to oversee construction of his design for the Gothic First Presbyterian Church, prepared a number of Italian villa designs for country houses in Baltimore and Howard County which featured wraparound

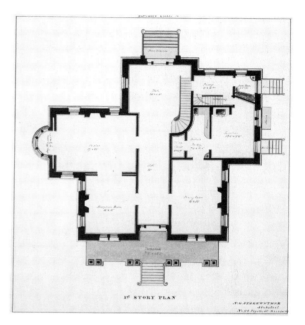

TOP:
Detail from Alexandroffsky
Schottisch, *a sheet music cover
published in 1856 by George Willig
Jr., with the song dedicated to Mrs.
Thomas Winans, celebrated and
handsomely depicted the Winans
house in west Baltimore. Maryland
Historical Society*
BOTTOM AND RIGHT:
*Front elevation and first-floor plan
of a villa for Mrs. John Campbell
White, watercolor by N. G.
Starkwether, 1857. Maryland
Historical Society*

porches, banks of arcaded windows, fussily-detailed towers and spires, and deep roof brackets that, in combination, began to resemble the "steamboat Gothic" decorations so popular for Mississippi River vessels. For Mrs. John Campbell White, the wealthy, widowed daughter of one of the Hampton Ridgelys, he created in 1857 a bound presentation album of beautifully executed watercolors showing the different elevations and floor plans for a stone Italian villa that was never built. A similar Starkwether design was used for Grey Rock, near Pikesville, built in 1857–61 for Richard Maynard, and, based on style, Starkwether may also have been the architect for the lavish north Baltimore villa belonging to Felix Agnus, publisher of the *Baltimore American*. Reversing the name of his newspaper, he called his estate Nacirema.

Starkwether also gave his distinctive Italianate touch to William Small's old City Hotel on Monument Square. Renamed Barnum's City Hotel, the popular establishment after 1857 sported extra floors, extravagant Italianate window lintels, cast-iron balconies, a flat roof with deeply projecting, bracketed eaves, and a central tower.

Not to be outdone, in 1857 Edmund G. Lind and his new partner, William T. Murdoch,

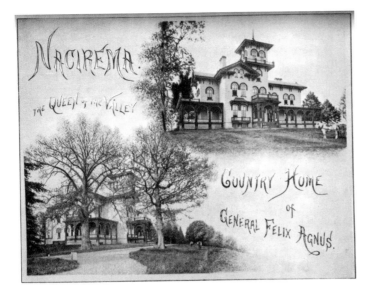

designed a sprawling Italian villa for the wealthy sportsman William McDonald. Guilford, as it was called, boasted just about every delight of the Italianate country villa, including an asymmetrically placed six-story arcaded and balconied tower, bay windows, deep porches, loggias, portes cochere, balconies, window hoods, and deeply bracketed eaves. A lover of good horseflesh, McDonald also had the architects design the stables and requested special accommodations for himself there.

North of McDonald's Guilford another kind of Italianate country house was built for Stephen Broadbent in 1857–58. Later called Evergreen and best known as one of the homes of the Garrett family, the imposing two-story house was classically symmetrical, without protruding towers, porches, bay windows, or balconies. Nevertheless, it showed the rich detailing of the Italianate style in its deep, bracketed cornice, cast-iron window hoods, cupola, and elaborate Roman-arched entryway. But the most striking feature of the house, boldly advertising its grandeur, was the striking full-height, tetrastyle Corinthian portico, built on a scale not seen since William Howard put up his Greek Revival town mansion at Charles and Franklin Streets.

Other Romantic Forms of the 1850s

Baltimore entered the second half of the nineteenth century still enamored of the Greek and Gothic and fast embracing the new Italianate style. Romanticism had matured; bor-

Guilford was demolished in
1914 to make way for the restricted residential community of
the same name, developed by
the Roland Park Company.

LEFT:
Evergreen, as it appeared
in 1930. The John Work
Garrett Library of the
Johns Hopkins University
RIGHT:
Cornice detail, Evergreen House.
Photograph by Marion E. Warren

Open to the public by appoint-
ment, Evergreen House, much
modified, forms part of the
Historic Houses of the Johns
Hopkins University.

rowings from, and improvisations upon, the arts of the past had increased. The tumult of
new ideas and stylistic possibilities—during the Great Exhibition of 1851 American attention
focused on London and its new architecture—meant that the resources architects might
draw upon had grown in quantity, complexity, and sophistication. One building that especially mirrored the attitudes of the age was the Italianate-style Maryland Institute for the

Baltimore, *drawn by A. Weidenbach, colored lithograph by Hunckel & Sons, 1861. Peale Collection, Maryland Historical Society*

This 1861 lithograph superbly summarizes the romantic eclecticism of the pre–Civil War era. Enclosed within the most elaborate of Gothic arches are views of the bustling port city and some of its major monuments and latest architectural achievements–the gothic gates to Greenmount Cemetery, the Gothic First Presbyterian Church, and the Odd Fellows Hall; the new Italianate villas of Johns Hopkins and Thomas Winans; the Italianate Camden and Calvert Street railroad stations; as well as those earlier monuments of the classical revival, Latrobe's cathedral, Mills' Washington Monument, and Godefroy's Battle Monument and Unitarian Church. The print radiates a sense of pride in achievement as well as an uplifting moral tone and suggests a future full of optimism, Victorian energy, and moral industriousness —a future that would see Baltimore become one of the major industrial centers of the post–Civil War United States while retaining a commitment to cultural, educational, and scientific advancements that would give the later city its particular distinctions.

Promotion of the Mechanic Arts, whose new building opened in 1851 on Market Space, replacing the old Centre Market. Designed by William Reasin, a teacher at the institute, the arcaded first story still provided space for an open-air market, but upstairs, the halls were designed to present "annual exhibitions of American industry," which, like the London exhibition, would glorify progress. The facility boasted the largest hall in the city (260 feet long by 60 feet wide, it could hold six thousand persons)[26] and soon became the place to hold important large events; both Presidents Franklin Pierce and Millard Fillmore were nominated there.

The Maryland Institute also sponsored a School of Design, which apparently met a great local need. In its first year about one hundred pupils enrolled in the "sketching or ornamental department," thirty in the "architectural class," and twenty-two in the engineering class, though only half of the engineering students "attended regularly." No matter whether students planned on an architectural or engineering career, they had to begin with sketching and ornamental design, which gave a "freedom to the hand and an exactness to the eye which mere instrumental drawing never can." It was also thought that this initial class laid the background for future work by improving "both the taste and the judgment in the use of ornamental embellishment."[27]

In the relatively prosperous 1850s, Baltimoreans built no fewer than eight major churches, which, in originality and modernity, echoed the spirit of the age. For Grace (later Grace and St. Peter's) Church, one block west of Mount Vernon Place on Monument Street, in 1850 Niernsee & Neilson became the first Baltimore architects to opt for brownstone for a church

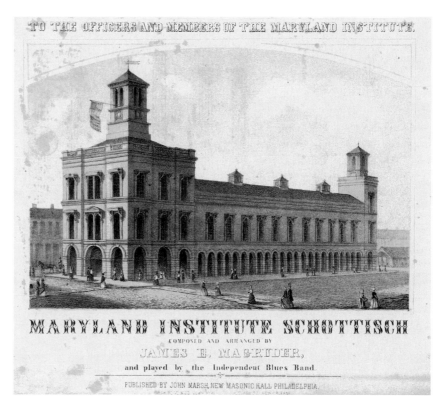

Maryland Institute Schottisch, lithograph by A. Hoen & Co., 1854. A sheet music cover shows the building as erected in 1851. Maryland Historical Society

Church of St. John the Evangelist, *designed by John C. Neilson, 1855. Lithograph by E. Sachse & Co., 1856. Maryland Historical Society*

Further examples of the robust Italianate style in antebellum Baltimore: Neilson's Church of St. John the Evangelist, built in 1855, stands at Eager and Valley Streets, directly south of Greenmount Cemetery. In 1862, the now city-owned Druid Hill mansion also received an Italianate facelift. John H. B. Latrobe provided design direction, giving the remodeled house wide verandas and a distinctive cupola. In 1869 R. Snowden Andrews gave Eastern Female High School, at Orleans and Aisquith Streets, Italianate end towers and a deeply bracketed cornice.

Druid Hill Mansion House, *in an early photograph. Maryland Historical Society*

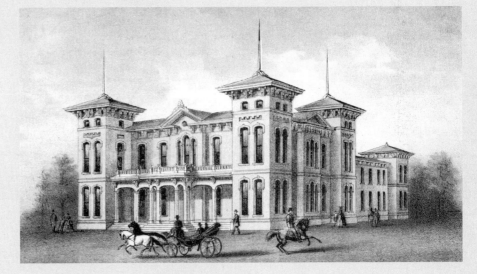

Eastern Female High School, *designed by R. Snowden Andrews. Lithograph by A. Hoen & Co. Maryland Historical Society*

design. By then available by rail from quarries in New Jersey, New York state, and the Connecticut Valley, brownstone was light in weight, easily cut by hand or by machine, and much easier to handle than the heavy local granite and marble. It had been popular as a building

material for so short a time that no one could yet foretell its durability or the effect of soot upon it. (By the later 1850s, however, most architects knew that the brownstone on New York's City Hall had already begun to deteriorate and it actually remained popular in Baltimore for only about a decade.) At Grace and St. Peter's the architects abandoned the traditional simple rectangular church plan in favor of a fully three-dimensional form, employing the boldly projecting vestibule, transepts, and semidetached sacristy of the picturesque rural parish churches of England (Grace Church followed plans for John Notmans' St. Mark's, Philadelphia, which itself derived from a much-discussed London church by Benjamin Ferrey). Regrettably, the parish failed to build Niernsee's planned spire. The nave roof, lending so much character to the exterior silhouette, rests on an excellent hammer-

Niernsee & Neilson's Grace and St. Peter's Church, 1852. Enoch Pratt Free Library

beam construction within, which is in turn supported by a good version of an English Perpendicular nave arcade.

Niernsee and Neilson immediately surpassed the brownstone Grace Church with the monumental Mortuary Chapel for Green Mount Cemetery, which went up between 1851 and 1856. They designed a remarkably open, strongly buttressed octagonal structure, which mourners entered from a porte-cochère. A dramatic spire (102 feet to the tip of its fleuroned pinnacle) rose above the chapel. Although the brownstone wall gave it mass and weight at the base, the freestanding pinnacles, flying buttresses, and tracery of the spire forecast a

growing concern among the Gothicists to achieve height as well as establish mass. More emotional than intellectual in its appeal, the structure looks much like some of the imaginative Gothic edifices in the paintings of American Hudson River school landscape artist Thomas Cole. It is not a coincidence that, as a student, Niernsee had spent time sketching the Cologne Cathedral.

Although many parishes preferred the understated rural parish church style advocated by the Protestant Episcopal community, a magnificent marriage of the minds between one of the city's wealthiest congregations and innovative Philadelphia architect Norris Gershon Starkwether led to the most significant Gothic Revival church built in Baltimore since Long's St. Alphonsus. Trained as a master builder in his native Vermont, Starkwether worked first in Massachusetts during the 1840s and by 1850 was established as an architect in Philadelphia. He was called to Baltimore in 1853 by the Presbyterian congregation that had built the old "two-steeple" church downtown but now desired to move uptown to be near its fashionable pa-

Mortuary Chapel for Greenmount Cemetery. Peale Collection, Maryland Historical Society

trons. The new First Presbyterian Church would be located on the northwestern corner of Park Avenue and Madison Street, near Mount Vernon Place. For the exterior of the new edifice Starkwether chose New Brunswick freestone and created an elaborate, decidedly perpendicular interpretation composed of tall spires and pinnacles and an immense needle-

First Presbyterian Church,
designed by N. G. Starkwether, 1853.
Color lithograph by John F. Watson,
Philadelphia, 1853. Maryland
Historical Society
RIGHT:
Interior of the First Presbyterian
Church, the nave and altar viewed
from the choir balcony. Photograph
by Lanny Miyamota, September
1958. Historic American Buildings
Survey, Library of Congress

sharp steeple not completed until 1874. It possessed the dry and rigid geometry of American Gothic as executed in wood or brick—or as interpreted in stone by Richard Upjohn, a New York architect and then dean of American architects, in Trinity Church (1839–46), lower Manhattan. According to a Baltimore guidebook that recorded the construction in detail, Starkwether succeeded in building "the most massive and scientifically arranged cast iron frame work ever done in this country or any other." The writer went on to describe the church as being in the "Lancet Gothic" style and deemed it one of the "most elaborate in its detail in this country."[28] Inside, tall, narrow, pointed arches frame the altar and doorways, which are decorated with complex tracery, and a series of groined ceiling arches end in cusped pendants, further articulating the interior space.

An especially interesting contribution to local church architecture of the period followed the loss, in 1854, of the elder Long's neoclassical St. Paul's, which burned, its exterior walls alone surviving. Before the ashes were cold, the parish called in Richard Upjohn, who departed from the mode of the English parish church in which he had worked and would continue to work successfully. Upjohn gave Baltimore its first approximation of an Italianate basilica. He gutted the building, leaving the walls intact, while creating a new Charles Street entrance.

The architect had just returned from Italy, and his design reflected lessons he had drawn from twelfth-century Lombardic basilica designs. Upjohn's perspective rendering of the façade and tower—illustrating not only Italianate asymmetry but also its proportion and balance—juxtaposed a low, timber-roofed basilica, extending back from Charles Street, and a six-story campanile, or bell tower, on the northern side, articulated with pairs of blind arches. The façade of the church, with its triple-arched portico, adopted features of the old classical building; otherwise, St. Paul's reveled in its differences. The design for the campanile closely followed that of San Giorgio in Velabro, Rome. Upjohn divided and embellished the Charles Street exterior by means of recessed panels, pilasters, and ornamentation that accentuated his Lombardic inspiration. Sadly, St. Paul's never achieved its promise. It was beautiful in its original design, but only the first two stories of Upjohn's projected tower were ever completed.

Fondness for various historical styles tended to, but did not invariably, follow a building's use. Just as Greek Revival in the 1830s and 1840s seemed suited to impressive town residences, school buildings, and courthouses, Gothic in the 1840s and 1850s seemed most appropriate for churches but also, as if answering morally kindred purposes, for orphan asylums, homes for the aged, female seminaries, jails, and firehouses.

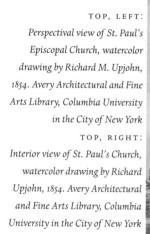

TOP, LEFT:
Perspectival view of St. Paul's Episcopal Church, watercolor drawing by Richard M. Upjohn, 1854. Avery Architectural and Fine Arts Library, Columbia University in the City of New York

TOP, RIGHT:
Interior view of St. Paul's Church, watercolor drawing by Richard Upjohn, 1854. Avery Architectural and Fine Arts Library, Columbia University in the City of New York

BOTTOM, LEFT:
St. Paul's Church as built, as seen in a 1903 photograph. Library of Congress

BOTTOM, RIGHT:
The interior of St. Paul's in the mid-twentieth century. Courtesy of Phoebe B. Stanton

Until 1858, when the city finally established a paid fire department, volunteer fire companies dotted the city, all of them boisterous, but some of them attentive to the designs of their station houses. Five years before the city takeover, "Old Number Six," the Independent Fire Company at the corner of Gay and Ensor Streets, commissioned the firm of William H. Reasin, a Harford County native with experience working with iron (and the architect of the Maryland Institute), and Samuel B. Wetherald to design and build a tower to stand beside the two-story firehouse. Their structure rose four stories above the station roof line to a height of 103 feet; it also added a fashionable touch. With its tall, slender arched openings and delicate roof balustrades, it resembled a Venetian Gothic campanile. In 1874 the tower received rusticated-concrete reinforcement at its base.

Another group of architects, Dixon, Balbirnie & Dixon, seemed to specialize in embattled Tudor styles for institutional buildings but also produced the Greek Revival Baltimore County Courthouse and elegant Italianate row houses. Thomas Dixon, a native of Wilmington, Delaware, had arrived in Baltimore in the 1840s and practiced alone until he was hired by James and Samuel Canby, also of Wilmington, to help them design the buildings for Franklin Square—the city's first planned residential public square. The Canbys had acquired the thirty-two-acre tract from the heirs of Dr. James McHenry in 1835, and four years later they shrewdly donated two and a half acres in the center of the tract to the city, with the proviso that the area be kept a public square forever. The first building to go up, designed by Dixon, was an Aged Women's Home for widows at the northwest corner. The *Sun* described it as "Tudor Gothic" in style and praised the "embattled parapets" that capped the finely carved stone roof line.[29] Next Dixon designed a group of paired houses for the west side of the square and Waverly Terrace, on the east. By 1853, Dixon, now joined by his brother James and the Scottish-born Thomas Balbirnie, completed the Baltimore Orphan Asylum just west of the Aged Women's Home in the "Roman style."

In 1852 the firm designed the Tudor-style Lutherville Female Seminary ten miles north of the city, the centerpiece of a new railroad summer colony founded by two Lutheran ministers, Dr. John G. Morris, pastor of the First English Lutheran Church, and Dr. Benjamin Kurtze, former pastor of Zion Lutheran. All proceeds from the sale of lots in the commu-

Independent Fire Company, *tower designed by William Reasin and Samuel Wetherald, lithograph by A. Hoen & Co., 1853. Maryland Historical Society*

The station and tower escaped demolition in 1960; today it houses a fire-fighting museum.

Lutherville Female Seminary, near Baltimore, Md., *colored lithograph by E. Sachse & Co., ca. 1864. The cottage that housed the school's founder stands to the left of the main building. Maryland Historical Society*

The original building burned in 1911, but it was rebuilt and served as the Maryland College for Women. It is now a retirement home.

nity went to support the seminary. Tall octagonal turrets framed the pointed arch entryway, extending the vertical reach of the building, as did the ninety-six-foot-high Gothic-style cupola placed over the central block.

A few years later the Dixon firm was tapped to design a new jail for the city and again returned to the crenellated Tudor style to suggest the castlelike fortress that would both safely hold prisoners and at the same time deter potential criminals, loathe to be incarcerated within such massive walls.

By mid-century Baltimore city fathers realized that the old jail had grown too small, even as humanitarians condemned it for poorly serving the health and well-being of the prisoners. In 1855 the Dixon brothers and Balbirnie won a competition for plans for a new jail, receiving $500 as their award. In preparation for this project, they declared that they had examined the designs of the new Pennsylvania State Penitentiary, the Albany County Penitentiary, the new Boston City Jail, as well as a number of modern prisons in Great Britain. The following year, however, before the Dixons (Balbirnie having departed the firm) could present detailed building specifications, the city commissioner in charge of building the new jail obtained completely new plans from the Boston inventor, engineer, and sometime-architect Gridley J. F. Bryant. Bryant's elaborate Romanesque design called for marble decoration, superfluous towers, and other expensive features, and would have proven quite costly. The city council and newly elected mayor, Thomas Swann, overthrew Bryant's plans and admonished the commissioner, saying that "while honest labor can often hardly find shelter in a hovel, it is scarcely befitting that a palace should be raised at the public charge for the accommodation of felons and offenders."[30]

The Dixons completed their specifications, and John Maxwell & Company finished the building in December 1859. Containing three hundred cells in each of two wings off of a central block for offices, it emphasized such practical features as security, ventilation, heating, and sanitation. The Dixons made much use of granite for the walls, slate for the roof, and cast and wrought iron for all structural members except the rafters. Great masonry vaults supported the main floor. Functional for its time, the jail also possessed considerable distinction in design. The cellblocks, lighted by tremendous lancet windows, flanked a square

Of Dixon's original jail structure, only the warden's residence, on Madison Street, remains.

LEFT:
Baltimore City Jail, *as completed in 1859. Lithograph by A. Hoen & Co., ca. 1877. Maryland Historical Society*

RIGHT:
The city jail as it appeared in a late-nineteenth-century photograph. Peale Collection, Maryland Historical Society

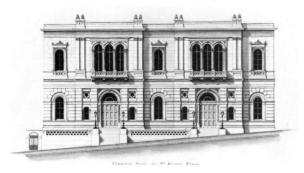

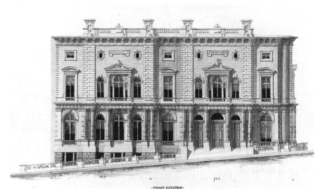

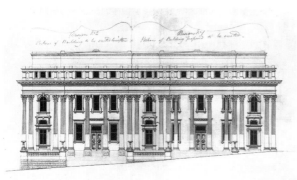

Peabody Institute competition drawings, 1857. J. Crawford Neilson's entry (top) and one submitted by the architect William Baldwin Stewart; below, an early Lind & Murdoch design, left, and the winning design by the same firm, façade and perspective views. Initially only the first three bays facing Monument Street were built. Archives of the Peabody Institute of the Johns Hopkins University

central mass boldly defined by octagonal and square crenellated watchtowers of English Tudor flavor. A Baltimore newspaper described its grey stone exterior and crenellated towers as "decidedly appropriate."[31]

In the mid-1850s Mount Vernon Place supplied the logical site for the proposed Peabody Institute. Massachusetts-born George Peabody had risen as a merchant in Baltimore; his gift of $1.4 million to found a school of music, a library for scholars, an art gallery, and rooms for lectures and exhibitions deserved the best site available, and found it at the southeast corner of the square.

Forced to address the relationship among cost, style, and function, the trustees of the institute, like most Baltimore patrons of architecture between 1850 and 1875, ruled out the extravagant stylistic flourishes and exotic possibilities that distinguished English and Continental design during the same years. Robert Cary Long Jr. may have sensed this situation in moving his practice to New York. Baltimore patrons were unwilling to accept the terribly unusual or spend money to indulge in it. Announcing the search for an architect to design a building to house the institute, the Peabody trustees specified that they would not consider Gothic. They probably had in mind something that resembled the Renaissance Revival–

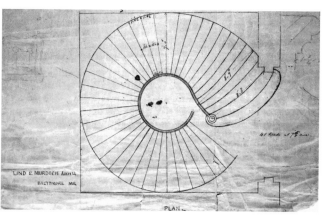

*The original building of the
Peabody Institute as it appeared
ca. 1869. Archives of the Peabody
Institute of the Johns
Hopkins University*

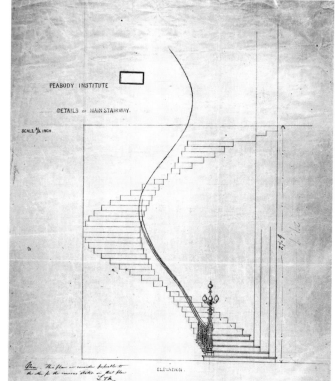

*Lind's spiral staircase, Peabody
Institute, overhead view and
section. Archives of the Peabody
Institute of the Johns Hopkins
University*

style new clubhouses on Pall Mall in London, many of them the work of Charles Barry. The trustees traveled abroad, often to England, and surely knew these clubs; they may equally have thought of India House, Hanover Square, New York (1850). In March 1857, they sponsored a major competition, announced in Boston, New York, Philadelphia, Washington, and Baltimore newspapers, offering cash prizes for the best designs. The job was challenging because the site selected sloped dramatically downhill in two directions, south on Charles and east on Monument Streets. The trustees specified that they wanted a two-story building with a brownstone façade (later changed to marble) to house a library of one hundred thousand volumes, a fifteen-hundred-seat lecture hall, an art gallery, a concert hall, and rooms for the historical society.

By the fall they had received at least thirty-four designs from more than seventeen architects—in New York, Albany, Lexington (Virginia), and Baltimore—and in the spring of 1858 Lind & Murdoch's final plans, for a dignified, Italianate-style clubhouse design, were approved.

Edmund Lind was a native of London who had attended the Government School of Design and been apprenticed to John Blore, who designed a new façade for Buckingham Palace in the 1840s. He arrived in New York in 1855 at age twenty-six and, seeking work, was hired by N. G. Starkwether as an assistant and reported to Baltimore. Starkwether put him to the task of completing the First Presbyterian Church (the walls were only five feet high at the time). Lind resigned after six months, forming a partnership with William T. Murdoch, a draftsmen working in the same office.

The firm struggled to prepare a design that could be fitted into the available space and still be appropriate to the scale and ambition of the developing neighborhood. They kept the Peabody Institute to two stories, about the height of the Thomas house across Charles Street. Even so, the formal marble building dominates the residences nearby. The original building extended seven bays down Charles Street and three bays along East Monument Street. As with Barry's London clubhouse designs, the decorative elements of the façade combine both Palladian and more freely rendered Italianate design motifs. A stone balustrade supported by brackets encircles the roof. Centrally located wide, arched doors, framed by pilasters supporting a full entablature, with a boldly designed Palladian window above, set the tone for the elegant façade elevations. The corners of the slightly projecting end bays on the Charles Street façade, as well as the central bay on Monument Street, were set off by wide-angle quoins, while a series of deep moldings marking the second-floor level provided a strong horizontal accent, echoing the line of the roof balustrade. Windows in the end pavilions have heavy projecting pediments (either triangular or segmentally arched) supported by long scrolled brackets. An iron railing with a Greek-key motif graces the Charles Street façade.

Inside, Lind & Murdoch faced a principal problem in the need for a two-story lecture hall (later concert hall) whose interior space would not be obstructed by load-bearing walls or piers. The architects and trustees turned to iron, still an innovative building material, but one that could also be shaped into decorative details to harmonize with the style of the building. Horizontal iron supports bear the weight of the upper floors, but iron was also used to create a splendid cantilevered cast-iron spiral staircase, which rises the full height of the building at the east end of the entrance lobby, which also features a marble floor and a series of plaster caryatids cast in 1861 from a wooden original prepared by a local carver, James I. Randolph. Randolph worked from an illustration, not of a Greek, but of a Roman example. The cast-iron decoration, generally rococo in character, carried patterns of plants, flowers, and vines.

Completed in 1861, the building was not dedicated until the Civil War had ended. At that ceremony, in 1866, a throng of civic-minded adults and all city school children assembled to honor George Peabody.

The Grammar of Ornament

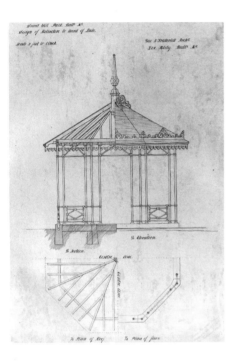

Other traces of romantic preferences can be found in the association between the rough and leafy texture of landscape and exotic architectural styles. In the eighteenth century kings, czars, and others of wealth had built ruins and Oriental pavilions amid the landscapes of their estates. When Druid Hill Park became the property of the city, George Aloysius Frederick, a native of Baltimore who apprenticed with Lind & Murdoch, relied upon this tradition when he designed the park's bandstand and the small Chinese and Moorish-style pavilions, which served as way stations on the park's railroad line.

But of all the possibilities romanticism provided, none better suited Baltimore taste than neo-Grec, a style made possible by the academic side of romanticism. In 1856 Owen Jones, English architect, theorist, and aesthetician, published *The Grammar of Ornament*. In it, with the aid of gloriously colored lithographs, he discussed the history of ornament through the ages (the volume later interested Louis Sullivan and Frank Lloyd Wright). This was historicism at its best, for Jones opened with a set of rules, deduced from study of the past, governing how ornament should be used. The rules foreshadowed the principles of modern design. Jones's illustrations did not show whole buildings but rather extracted bits of ornament from many sources—pottery, manuscripts, metalwork, and architectural decoration. His plates on Greek ornament helped to establish neo-Grec style, which, because much of its decoration was incised, made it ideal for use on cast iron. Its designs could also be gently modified to recall Gothic. All neo-Grec decorations derived from Greek art, but they were not used as the Greeks had used them; the alphabet was Greek but the vocabulary was not.

Ornate cast iron had already established itself in Baltimore as a romantic flourish. Dixon & Dixon employed fancy iron balconies and fencing in their design for Waverly Terrace and manufacturing firms like Bartlett-Hayward specialized in delicate castings for balconies and exterior porches of the kind that Baltimoreans of high taste began adding onto both older and new structures in the 1850s. And designers of churches such as Robert Cary Long Jr. and N. G. Starkwether had been using structural cast iron to open up nave interiors for three decades.

In 1875, when the Peabody Institute trustees undertook to build a fireproof four-bay-wide eastern addition as a library wing (giving the building its enduring cubic form), they once again assigned the task of designing it to Edmund Lind, who turned to neo-Grec style for the interiors. From the beginning, the trustees had wished to unite the new building with the earlier one as seamlessly as possible, and now they had the chance also to make repairs to the interior and exterior of the old structure, the insufficient slope of whose roof and poorly designed skylights had produced leaks. The departure of both the library and a temporary guest, the Maryland Historical Society, opened up the second floor

Peabody Institute exterior, with eastern addition following Lind's original design, as completed in 1878. Archives of the Peabody Institute of the Johns Hopkins University

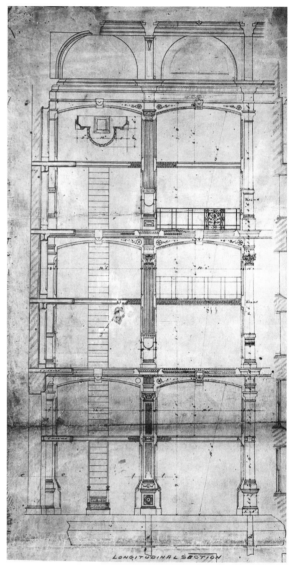

Edmund G. Lind's 1878 sectional drawing of two bays of the interior of the Peabody Library shows neo-Grec ornament that would be cast in iron by Bartlett, Robbins & Co. Archives of the Peabody Institute of the Johns Hopkins University

of the original building to adaptive new uses. Some of the space so acquired would house the conservatory of music, which had been located elsewhere.

In 1878, as the new library building was being finished, Lind had the front of the institute cleaned and its woodwork repainted, and he continued the balustrade that ran along the north front and west side of the original building across the roof line of the new library. The north front of the old and new buildings joined so expertly that they appeared as one. Provost Nathaniel H. Morison believed that the new combined building would "rival the Pantheon itself in durability and permanence."[32] Indeed, the library wing represented remarkable and distinguished interior design, allowing the visitor to look up to five tiers of or-

Interior of the Peabody Library, as it appeared in the mid-twentieth century. News-American Collection, Marylandia and Rare Books Department, University of Maryland Libraries, University of Maryland, College Park

namental cast-iron balconies on all sides of the reading room. The book-laden stacks give glory to the space; with such rich and lavish detailing, Lind created a bibliophile's dream. He also made a wonderful statement of neo-Grec style. With his brilliant interior and the decorated bronze main doors of the building, neo-Grec attained quiet and refined splendor in the city.

The interior of the Peabody Library combined building for efficiency and decorating in iron. Here the old and the new united—an altogether romantic aspiration.

5

INDUSTRIAL DESIGNS, 1840–1917

As a center of industry, Baltimore competed energetically during much of the nineteenth century with New York and Philadelphia, cities that eventually far surpassed the Queen City of the Patapsco. Waterborne commerce continued to account heavily for industrial growth, directly and indirectly. "A forest of shipping covered the spacious harbour," wrote a British visitor in 1855, "comprising every species of craft, from the noble Baltimore clipper to the spruce and gaily painted fishing boats, which were spreading their sails and skimming rapidly over the waters, flashing under the morning sun."[1] Shipping produced some of the profits that capitalized the factories and trade ties that supplied markets for manufactured goods. Clothiers made inexpensive garments for sailors. Textile mills specialized in cotton duck, the material of sails, and by mid-century, mills in the Jones Falls Valley rivaled the more famous factories of Lowell, Massachusetts. Copper processed in Baltimore sheathed the hulls of wooden ships as a guard against barnacles, marine grasses, and ship worms. After about 1850, when Baltimoreans and others perfected canning technology, Baltimore canned goods provisioned nearly every departing ship.

During the Civil War, the needs of the federal government had a selective but powerful impact on the industrial growth of the city. The War Department issued orders in unprecedented quantities for cotton duck (to make army shelter tents, among other things); ready-made, standard-sized uniforms; leather shoes for troops and iron shoes for horses; iron for cannon, artillery shells, and the plates Horace Abbott used in manufacturing the USS *Monitor* in Canton. Military demand made supplying foodstuffs highly profitable. Inflicting damage on the Lincoln administration's rail ties east from Washington, Confederate forces kept Baltimore & Ohio Railroad workers busy repairing damage to track and rolling stock.

After the war, the B&O Railroad gave Baltimore an advantage in direct rail connections to Appalachian coal. Water-powered milling soon gave way to steam. The clothing factories of the city made themselves the ready-to-wear giants of the postwar period, their strongest markets to the west and in the rebuilding South. Baltimore deserved its reputation as premier producer of cast iron and canned food.

"Modern industry turns toward manufactures," observed Daniel Coit Gilman, president of the Johns Hopkins University, in 1893, "and Baltimore has the fair variety of establishments which employ a large number of persons. Its silverware has been famous for three generations. Its porcelain has acquired a wide reputation; its bells chime in hundreds of towers. The printer's craft is held in honor; lithography thrives; furniture and clothing and manifold minor articles are produced in great quantities; iron foundries, copper works, oil-refineries, Bessemer furnaces, sugar-houses, and machine-shops employ large amounts of capital. The type-setting machine, one of the most ingenious pieces of mechanism mankind has invented, is a Baltimore invention."[2] Between 1870 and 1890 the number of industries established in Baltimore had tripled, and capital investment had increased by a multiple of six in everything from men's clothing and shoes to fertilizers, copper, and steel. "It is doubtful if any other large city of the United States shows an equal diversification in its industrial standing," boasted a newspaper report of 1894. "With such a magnificent exhibit (aggregate wages of $45 million a year paid to 100,000 workers) it is not remarkable that competing cities regard Baltimore's growth and development with sentiments of alarm or that capitalists should be attracted here with sanguine prospects and a settled conviction that they will materialize into a golden reality."[3]

Baltimore in 1889.
Lithographed and published by
Isaac Friedenwald, Baltimore,
Maryland. Maryland
Historical Society

Local leadership stood firmly behind progress. "The whistle and bell of a locomotive mean far more than the undisturbed trill of a singing bird," Mayor James H. Preston exclaimed in 1913. "The rumble of a freight car is prosperity's favorite music. The rush and din of whirling machinery are the melody that thrills a business man's soul." That thing "which produces," he concluded, "is of more importance than that which adorns."[4]

Baltimore firms employed men, women, and children of diverse origins. The Chesapeake Marine Railway & Dry Dock Company, which Isaac Myers and other African-American entrepreneurs founded in 1868, shortly after the war, carried white as well as black workers on its payroll. (Myers also founded the first black labor organization, the Colored Caulkers Trade Union Society.) In 1870, when black males gained the right to vote, African Americans made up 15 percent of Baltimore's population. After 1867, when the Baltimore & Ohio Railroad established connections with the North German Lloyd Line and built a pier and extensive railroad yards at Locust Point, many laboring families from Europe swelled the city's population. Ships carried flour and tobacco east and returned with eager immigrants; many boarded B&O trains to midwestern cities, but many others remained. In certain years, more newcomers landed at Locust Point than at any place in America with the exception of Ellis Island. Many found jobs in the new manufacturing industries springing up around the waterfront, making their homes in Fells Point, Canton, and East Baltimore, as well as Locust Point. By the turn of the century this part of Baltimore offered a potpourri of ethnically rooted enclaves—Welsh, Bohemian, Polish, Lithuanian, Italian, and Greek.

Those immigrant families who stayed in Baltimore clustered by ethnic group and preserved old ways, building churches (the first Polish Catholic Church, St. Stanislaus in Fells Point, went up in 1880) and developing safety nets for survival in a strange new environment. They clung to ethnic clubs, read native-language newspapers, sent children to parochial schools, and banked and borrowed at their own savings and loan societies. By 1910, Eastern Avenue became known as the Polish Wall Street. In those years ethnic Catholics in Baltimore had a good friend in James Cardinal Gibbons, son of Irish-immigrant parents, whom the church had invested as cardinal in 1886.

Many of the newcomers moved into both old and newly built row houses in neighborhoods surrounding the harbor and its growing industries; northeast of the city near the breweries; and southwest, near the Mount Clare railroad yards and businesses related to the butchering and processing of pigs and cattle. Typical row houses often occupied a lot only twelve to fifteen feet wide. Affordable, they typically stood within walking distance of one's place of work. Some companies, like the William Wilkens Steamed Curled Hair and Bristle Manufactory, out the Frederick Road, built row houses and then rented them to their workers. When families decided to buy a home, they borrowed at favorable rates from the savings and loan associations that their ethnic group had established. The ground rent system continued to place home ownership within reach of all but the lowest-paid workers. Home ownership thus became commonplace among Baltimore's working families—more so, perhaps, than in comparable American cities of the time.

NEVER TERRIBLY FAR from nineteenth-century Baltimore's houses, churches, stores, and schools, a gritty collection of seemingly austere buildings emitted coal smoke, steam vapors, dust, and lint. They were building blocks in the economy that produced the wealth that accounted for the city's "finer" architecture. Some carried the smell of spices, coffee, fish, or produce as it passed through or was processed. Around, between, and inside them ran railroad tracks, with locomotives giving off their own smoke, steam, and screeching sounds.

Baltimore was built on numerous and diverse industries, industries housed in buildings even more varied than the work performed inside. Yet whatever their differences in use, shape, and age, Baltimore's industrial structures—generally, and especially early on—shared one common feature: They were designed strictly to enclose a production process in the most effective and efficient way possible. The surviving Shot Tower in Old Town, completed in 1828, offers a fine example. This single tower enclosed the entire production process from beginning to end. Fires melted lead at the tower's top, workmen poured the molten metal through a sieve, and the lead drops, cooling and solidifying as they fell the length of the 234-foot-high brick shaft, formed spherical lead shot. Once operated by the Phoenix Shot Company, it was one of four such towers in Baltimore and among only about thirty-two in the country at the time. Here form followed function long before the phrase became an architectural axiom.

Functional buildings did pose problems, however. Industrial design reflected a complex combination of considerations: how materials were to flow through a production process; where the power came from and how it was transmitted; what kind of machinery the plant used, where it was placed and how supported; how raw materials were to be received and stored; how finished goods were shipped out; how many workers were needed; how much was to be produced—and the list went on. There were also more straightforward problems, such as site characteristics and land value. Sometimes the owners of remotely located plants needed to provide housing and social and spiritual sustenance for workers. Furthermore, many of these factors changed over the years, requiring additions, alterations, recycling, and replacing. Often the result was a disparate collection of buildings reflecting two or three eras of industrial design fashions and construction techniques.

Conventional aesthetics and architectural fashion were usually considered last, if at all. For the most part, the beauty of these buildings rested on how gracefully they juggled the various demands their function placed on them. Some, of course, could combine utility with some degree of superficial architectural refinement—particularly those "clean" industries located in spots visible to the public, for example, certain warehouses, breweries, and the garment trade's loft buildings. But for several of Baltimore's most important industries—milling, canning, shipbuilding, steel making, petroleum refining, and chemical manufacturing—the production process was everything and the architecture essentially nothing.

In the beginning, the city's industry grew out of the happy geographic conjunction of the fall line and a fine natural harbor. In the days before steam power or railroads, such a location was vital. The rushing streams of the Patapsco River, Jones Falls, and Gwynns Falls provided power, while the nearby harbor gave access to distant markets and minimized the grueling wagon haulage over mud-bogged roads. Baltimore's earliest industries (as distinguished from craft shops) thus grew up either around the harbor or along the streams flowing into it. At the waterfront were warehousing, shipbuilding, and businesses that used materials brought in by water.

Mills in the Valleys

Water-powered mills, most of which originally ground flour, were built along the streams. Baltimore's first true industry, flour or grist milling, began in 1711 on the Jones Falls east of what is now Franklin Street and Guilford Avenue, and until 1830 Baltimore and its environs produced more flour than any other region in the country. Millers later moved farther from the city to points where water flow (or "fall" conditions) was even more favorable. Beginning in the 1850s, steam engines slowly supplemented or replaced the more limited and less reliable water power. For the most part, however, the mills remained along the waterways, where they had already established facilities and built up worker communities—and where the water could be fed into boilers. Railroads served both the Jones Falls and Patapsco Valleys and delivered the coal for their new steam power. Partly for safety and partly for efficiency, steam power plants were generally housed in separate buildings; various systems of belts and drive shafts connected them with the production machinery.

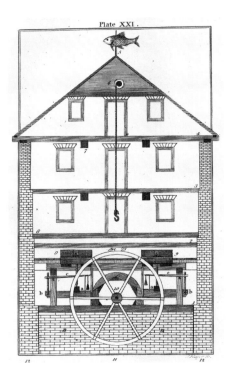

Plate XXI.

Thomas Ellicott's drawing of an "automated" flour mill that he built in Prince William County, Virginia. The image appeared in part five of Oliver Evans, The Young Mill-Wright and Miller's Guide *(Philadelphia, 1795). Enoch Pratt Free Library*

Flour manufacturing, especially when water provided the motive force, relied on gravity: Rushing water powered millstones by means of a waterwheel and a system of shafts and gearing that translated horizontal motion from the waterwheel to vertical motion for the stones. Grain fell through chutes and hoppers into the turning millstones, and the resulting flour dropped into bins. All of this movement required considerable vertical space, plus space and sufficient support for heavy stones and machinery. In 1787 Oliver Evans, a Delaware-born mechanic of unusual genius who had established himself in Baltimore, developed a system of internal elevators and conveyors that allowed one person to handle the entire grist-milling or flour-making process. Nearby millers soon adopted the design (leading, eventually, to patent-infringement claims).

Thus flour mills, which were usually three- or four-story buildings, with loading and unloading doors on the upper floors reached by hoists, supplied Baltimore and its immediate environs with their first custom-designed industrial structures. They could be built of stone, brick, or wood, but their external form was unadorned and functional, and virtually all of them adhered to the same interior layout, which necessarily included heavy wood framing.[5] On the Baltimore County bank of the Patapsco River Valley, about twelve miles west of Baltimore, the brothers Joseph, Andrew, and John Ellicott built a huge mill in 1772. With new roads reaching westward, the Pennsylvania natives prospered, and Ellicotts' Mills grew into one of the major American flour-milling centers of its day. The original building burned in 1809, whereupon the Ellicotts replaced it with a smaller structure. Samuel Owings's brick

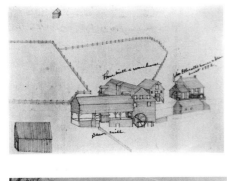

Upper Mill, built in about 1793 on the upper Gwynns Falls and one of three such mills Owings operated in this area, probably used Oliver Evans's automated system from the start. In 1888 its millstones were replaced with steel roller units. Rockland Mill, built of local "Falls Road stone" in 1813, made use of Slaughterhouse Branch where it flowed into the upper Jones Falls, at Falls Turnpike Road and Old Court Road. Owner and workers lived in a cluster of nearby houses of the same stone construction. Dating from 1856, the stone Orange Grove Mill drew its power from the Patapsco about three and a half miles below Ellicotts' Mills while snuggling against the B&O's main railroad line. The structure stood four stories high, plus two levels of attic, and measured 150 by 175 feet. In 1860 it advertised itself as the largest grist mill in Maryland. A Corliss steam engine replaced water power in 1873, and ten years later steel roller equipment took over from the old millstones.

The same proximity of harbor and fall line which stimulated flour milling powered Baltimore's early textile industry. The raw material, southern cotton, arrived in Baltimore principally by way of coastwise shipping and, eventually, via the B&O and its terminals on the Ohio-Mississippi River system. For power, textile plants originally relied on the Jones Falls and Patapsco River. The basic multifloor flour mill design, with its heavily supported flooring, sometimes sufficed for textile manufacturing, and a few early flour mill operators adapted their buildings after calculating that textiles produced higher profits.

Typically, however, textile mills followed their own patterns. The various types of specialized carding, spinning, weaving, and other processing machines were layered vertically on the floors, powered by belts driven by horizontal rotating shafts above them; these shafts in turn were geared to a vertical shaft turned by the waterwheel. As the beating heart of the mill, the line shafts dictated a long, narrow structure so that machines could be grouped nearby. Even more important, the long-and-narrow design was necessary so that workers would be near windows, to get maximum natural light. Other industries that depended on belt-powered machinery adopted this same basic layout.[6]

LEFT:

Rockland Mill, rear view showing the waterwheel, ca. 1900. News-American *Collection, Marylandia and Rare Books Department, University of Maryland Libraries, University of Maryland, College Park*

RIGHT:

Orange Grove Mill ("Mill C") as portrayed in George W. Howard, The Monumental City: Its Past History and Present Resources *(Baltimore, 1873).*

At Ellicotts' Mills, a six-story steel and concrete mill built in 1917 became Maryland's last operating flour mill, closing in 2000. Rockland Mill and its nearby village underwent renovation and restoration in 1930 and 1983, all milling equipment having long since disappeared. The Orange Grove mill burned in 1905, and its owner, Charles A. Gambrill & Company, abandoned it, leaving only overgrown ruins for later archeologists to explore.

Textile milling in Baltimore traced its origins to 1808, with the construction of two mills on nearby waterways. First to open was the Union Manufacturing Company mill on the Patapsco at Oella. Washington Cotton Factory on the Jones Falls in the area that later developed into Mount Washington, then a rather remote six or seven miles from the city center along the Falls Turnpike Road, soon followed. The Washington design and stone construction closely followed that of New England mills, such as Slater's in Rhode Island, as well as the "long-and-narrow" dictum. Fifteen bays long and three and a half stories high, it had a gabled roof punctuated by dormer windows. One large dormer featured a door and exterior beam for hoisting material to the top floor. Like its flour-mill predecessors, its exterior appearance was strictly functional, not much different from a huge stone barn with windows; the sole adornment was a small belfry at its east end, which summoned workers living in the small adjacent company town. The five-story Union Mill building, with its large waterwheel, was flanked by a range of worker housing, from imposing houses for owners or foremen to row houses for the ordinary workmen.

Baltimore-area textile mills came to specialize in cotton duck, canvas, and sailcloth, among other things, since the port and its own shipbuilding industry provided ready markets. These markets expanded dramatically after the Civil War, and by the late nineteenth century, mills in the Jones Falls and Patapsco Valleys collectively accounted for about 80 percent of the world's cotton-duck production. Older plants were expanded or replaced, the Washington mill receiving extensive brick additions.

The cotton-duck mills were concentrated along the Jones Falls immediately north of Baltimore. Together with other industries, such as the large Poole & Hunt foundry and machine works at Woodberry (dating from 1853, the firm manufactured textile-milling and mining equipment, steam engines and boilers, and had cast the columns and brackets that went into the building of the U.S. Capitol dome), the mills made this Jones Falls corridor the greatest single industrial concentration in Maryland during the late nineteenth century. In this case "industrial" did not necessarily mean austere and ugly. The new mills built after the Civil War marked not only a shift from water to steam power but also a visual transition from the crude, utilitarian design of mills like the Washington to con-

Interior view of the "Old Slater Mill." From George S. White, Memoir of Samuel Slater *(Boston, 1836).*

Washington Cotton Factory, built in 1809–10, as it appeared in the late twentieth century; the ruggedly attractive south façade. Courtesy of John W. McGrain

RIGHT:

The Union Manufactories of Maryland on Patapsco Falls Baltimore County. *Maximilien Godefroy sketched this model mill complex, which included housing for managers and workers as well as laundry and brick kiln, ca. 1810. Maryland Historical Society*

By the late twentieth century, Washington Mill had drawn notice as the country's third-oldest surviving mill structure and one of the best examples of early textile-mill architecture. Restored in the early 1990s, it houses specialty shops.

scious aesthetic forms—even if the basic "long-and-narrow" designs did remain, often in larger sizes.

Mill owner Horatio Gambrill pioneered in combining some surface beauty with large-scale production. In 1866 at Woodberry, on the Jones Falls above the city limits, he completed the first section of his Druid Mills, building a long two-story stone structure that nestled into the hillside (the sloping site exposed the basement level on the west end). Its principal aesthetic touch was a three-and-a-half-story Italianate stone bell tower, with arched windows and entranceway, quoined corners, and inset round louvered vents. First- and second-floor doorways on the east end also were arched.

Gambrill doubled Druid's size in 1872 by adding a similar single-story stone mill building on the north side, its basement floor also partially exposed. Processes were divided between the two long blocks, with the 1866 building housing rope-twisting, carding, drawing, and

BOTTOM, RIGHT:
Druid Mills, Baltimore County,
Md. *The Woodberry plant as it
appeared in Howard,*
Monumental City, *179.*

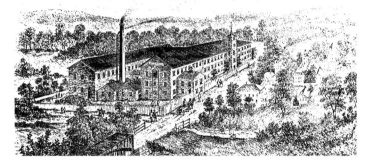

*The decorative detailing of the
Druid Mills tower, as photographed
in the late twentieth century.
Photograph by John W. McGrain*

slubbing machines and the newer building being devoted to weaving. Steam powered from the start, the complex included a boiler house built between the two blocks. When fully completed in 1872, Druid Mills claimed to be the state's largest stone mill and the country's largest single cotton-duck producer.

Downstream from Druid Mills and different in design, Clipper Mill formed part of William E. Hooper's local empire. Originally a flour mill, the first building on the site was converted to cotton-cloth production in 1837; it burned in 1854. Hooper rebuilt Clipper Mill on the site in 1855; it, too, burned, in 1865, but was quickly rebuilt. Over the next twenty years an unusual string of brick buildings replaced the originals; their similar architectural features, however, lent homogeneity to the complex. Various new units were added end to end, creating an impressively long, low single line. First came a three-story mill with boiler house and unusual multifaceted stellar-form brick chimney; then, in 1870, a long two-story west-end addition. A longer, narrower two-story picker house lengthened the east end in 1875, and finally, in 1885, Hooper added housing for twisting machinery to the west end. Hooper's building superintendent, Reuben Gladfelter, apparently served as the designer; in any case, the consistent use of tall, paired arched windows, high roof monitors, and all-brick construction united this conglomeration, and a single wooden Italianate ventilating cupola punctuated the gabled roof line.

In 1877, off Union Avenue at Clipper Road in Woodberry, Hooper created the most strik-

Mount Vernon Mills, from a late-nineteenth-century letterhead.
Enoch Pratt Free Library

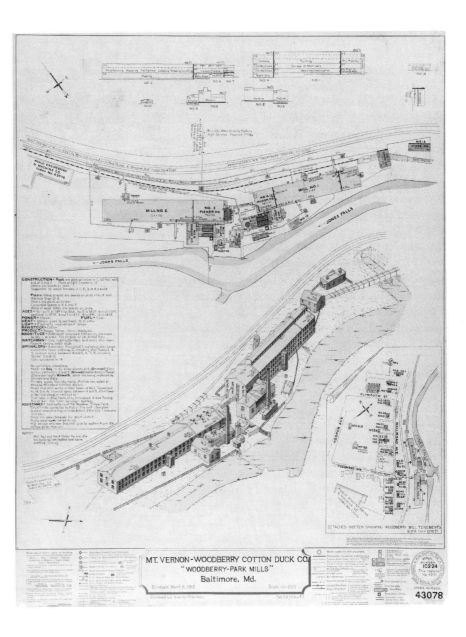

Mt. Vernon–Woodberry Cotton Duck Co., "Woodberry-Park Mills," Baltimore, Md., as documented for an insurance survey of 1912. Sections of buildings, top, indicate work flow by floor.
Baltimore Museum of Industry

ing of the Jones Falls textile mills, Meadow Mill. Unlike either the Clipper or Druid Mill complexes, Meadow Mill architecturally resembled the typical late-nineteenth-century New England mill. Its main brick building—four stories high, to house all of the necessary textile machinery without further expansion—unquestionably marked the epitome of mill aesthetics in Baltimore. Again, Gladfelter most likely called for the elaborate Italianate lintels over the windows and ordered a striking steepled belfry to rise from a large, square central-stair tower. At the front of the mill Hooper planted and carefully manicured a flower garden. Subsidiary buildings included a steam-engine house, pump house, and three-story picker house, all similarly designed and built at the same time; in 1907 the company added a two-story packing building.

Not many structures deviated from Baltimore's industrial textile-building design, but the W. J. Knox Net & Twine Company plant at 1800 Johnson Street in South Baltimore, built in 1905, offered one example. Steam powered and without any earlier ties to a waterway, the Knox plant stood inland, near the harbor and adjacent to a main rail line. Electric lighting reduced the need for natural light, so the four-story brick building was considerably wider than its predecessors and laid out in an L-shaped pattern. Most significant, it incorporated the "slow burn" factory design principles that insurance company engineers in the 1870s devised to minimize the effects of fire—iron interior columns, an almost-flat roof, stairways placed in corners rather than in a central tower, large windows, and a complete lack of ornamentation or other aesthetic treatment.

Dickey Mill, Oella, ca. 1915, after the installation of the new railroad material-moving system. Courtesy of Charles L. Wagandt

W. J. Dickey purchased the buildings of the old Union Manufacturing Company at Oella in 1887, five years after the company had linked the two early-nineteenth-century stone buildings with a new brick one. In the fall of 1914 the Sun *reported the installation of a new electrical railroad that connected service buildings and promised improved efficiency. The entire complex burned in 1918; the new brick factory was built in 1919 and expanded in 1941.*

Railroads Discover Art

Baltimore pioneered in railroad construction, which dramatically eased freight haulage and reduced its cost. The Baltimore & Ohio Railroad incorporated in 1827 with the aim of linking the city with the Ohio River; a year later the Baltimore & Susquehanna formed with the object of reaching the Susquehanna and central Pennsylvania. More than two decades elapsed before either road reached its goal, but by 1832 both lines were operating through nearby valleys and serving the newly developing mills. The B&O reached Cumberland in 1842 and by the late 1840s carried an ever-growing flow of bituminous coal into the city to fuel industry and fill the holds of ships.

In the earliest days passenger stations were not a priority for the undercapitalized and financially overstretched railroads. Originally both the B&O and B&S pragmatically used existing buildings for their Baltimore terminals; beyond the city, stations were mostly non-existent. Freight needed protection from the weather and from theft, and the B&O built a

Ellicott City Station, Baltimore & Ohio Railroad, ca. 1900. The B&O Railroad Museum, Inc.

RIGHT:
Calvert Station, Baltimore & Susquehanna Railroad, 1850. Peale Collection, Maryland Historical Society

few freight depots. Passengers often waited for trains at hotels or taverns near the track—much as they did for stagecoaches.

Such was the case at Ellicotts' Mills, thirteen rail miles west of Baltimore, to and from which point in May 1830 the B&O offered the country's first scheduled public railroad service. Within a year the line had built a depot building there to serve as a freight house and operating office (several years later it also housed a locomotive). Passengers used the adjacent Patapsco Hotel (built in about 1830) until 1856.

The freight house was a purely utilitarian two-story stone warehouse with five large freight loading doors facing the street on its ground level. The railroad line, built on filled land, ran behind the building at the second-floor level, with a freight siding entering the building at its east end. Freight was then hoisted up or down between the rail cars on the second floor and the ground-level wagons. Jacob Small Jr., by this time a former Baltimore mayor and the railroad's superintendent of depots, probably designed the building. Over the years the station was modified both externally and internally; its interior loading track was removed and the end door sealed over with stone (probably in the 1850s), and in the 1880s it received some decorative wood trim and multicolored glass windows. The stone hotel that served as the first passenger station also survived, albeit in reconstructed form. Another example of these primitive hotel-stations, a stone tavern later known as the Valley Inn on Falls Road near Brooklandville, served as a Baltimore & Susquehanna "station" from 1832 to 1906, when a new station was built across the street.

In the 1850s the railroad industry, earlier having struggled to develop its technology and finance costly construction, began to acquire greater economic power, and to make this success fully visible Baltimore railroads decided to build fashionable new architect-designed terminals and stations. In 1850 the Baltimore & Susquehanna completed its twin-towered Italianate Calvert Station, designed by Niernsee & Neilson as the company's passenger and freight terminal and headquarters office. Its style recalled Upjohn's new St. Paul's Church, though without as much refinement. That same year the Philadelphia, Wilmington & Baltimore opened its Italianate-style President Street Terminal, designed by then-railroad-engineer Isaac Ridgway Trimble and especially notable for its curved wooden Howe truss roof supports.

Local architect Joseph F. Kemp, designer of elegant brownstones on Cathedral Street as well as chief draftsman and architect of the B&O Railroad in the 1850s, designed and oversaw construction of the B&O's grandiose Camden Station. Like the B&S's Calvert Station, Camden, which the company intended to rival contemporary London stations, originally served as a passenger and freight terminal and as the B&O's executive headquarters. Workers had completed most of the flamboyant three-story Italianate main building fronting on Camden Street by 1857. Kemp's original plan called for a tall, central tower and one-story flanking wings, extending on either side to both Eutaw and Howard Streets. These were to be "fitted up with ticket offices, baggage rooms, refreshment rooms, and private rooms for lady passengers." Through these wings passengers could directly enter the inner portion of the depot. The newly built depot extended over the entire block-long space between Howard and Eutaw and Camden and Barre Streets, with a suspension roof supported on columns running back from the main building. The interior was to be divided into three sections: "In the center, running the entire length of the lot, will be the platforms for passengers and tracks for passenger cars. Upon the line of Eutaw street will be a platform for the receiving of freight, and a similar one upon the line of Howard street, for the delivery of freight."[7] Between 1865 and 1867 Niernsee & Neilson added the pair of now two-story flanking wings, capped by towers, and probably oversaw construction of the soaring 180-foot central tower, which provided an emphatic exclamation point until the 1880s, when it was taken down as being unsafe. The station subsequently underwent many alterations.

*Calvert Station, border detail from
E. Sachse & Co.'s* Bird's Eye View
of the City of Baltimore, *1869,
Maryland Historical Society*

*President Street Terminal,
Philadelphia, Wilmington &
Baltimore Railroad, border detail
from E. Sachse & Co.'s* Bird's
Eye View of the City of
Baltimore, *1869.*

Calvert Station came down in
1949, making way for a new
Sunpapers building. In 1992, as
part of the adjacent new baseball
stadium project, Camden Station
underwent cosmetic exterior
restoration to its 1865 form.
More slowly, President Street Terminal (better known as Station)
was also repaired, reopening in
1997 as a Civil War museum.

Baltimore can also claim the country's earliest railroad shop site at Mount Clare, on the city's near-west side. It began as a stable and carriage repair shed in about 1829; a forge and machine shop followed in 1833, as the railroad began to adopt steam power, and by 1834 Mount Clare workers were building the line's own locomotives. Here New York native Peter Cooper assembled his tiny engine, later called Tom Thumb, the first American-built loco-motive. The complex often changed and expanded; first, when coal traffic began flowing in the late 1840s, again after the Civil War, and almost continuously from the 1880s into the early twentieth century, as the railroad adjusted to both growth and downturns.

During the second half of the nineteenth century, Mount Clare, then one of the country's largest and most comprehensive railroad shops, offered a prime example of a fully inte-grated complex designed to make the company largely self-sufficient. In it B&O employees built more than six hundred locomotives from scratch, as well as thousands of freight and passenger cars; repaired, rebuilt, and modified the system's locomotives and cars; fabricated bridge components, including the pioneering iron truss design of Wendel Bollman; and made numerous small parts, repaired furniture, and did all of the company's printing. At its height in the 1920s, some three thousand workers went to Mount Clare each day; the com-plex stretched the equivalent of ten blocks along the south side of Pratt Street.

In 1882, one of Baltimore's most distinguished post–Civil War architects, Ephraim Fran-cis (E. Francis) Baldwin, designed Mount Clare's most memorable structure, the Passenger Car Shop, one of the most distinctive industrial buildings anywhere. Baldwin was an aston-ishingly versatile architect who designed many residential, commercial, ecclesiastical, in-dustrial, and institutional buildings in Baltimore. He is best remembered, however, for his railroad work. Born in upstate New York, Baldwin had grown up in Baltimore, the son of a civil engineer who sent the boy to Mount St. Mary's College in Emmitsburg. After gradu-ating, Baldwin served as an apprentice in Niernsee & Neilson's busy office and then, be-

Mount Clare "roundhouse," the passenger car shop as it appeared in the 1920s. The B&O Railroad Museum, Inc.

RIGHT:

Mount Clare Passenger Car Shop, interior with workers, 1910. The B&O Railroad Museum, Inc.

Since 1953 the Mount Clare shops have served as the centerpiece of the B&O Railroad Museum, its breathtaking interior restored to an approximation of its original colors. Three other historic buildings form the museum complex: The small brick Mount Clare station, built in 1851; a large brick rectangular shop building, dating from 1870; and a long, narrow two-story brick building built in 1884 as a shop office and employee library.

tween 1867 and 1873, formed a partnership with a onetime Princeton student and fellow former intern, Bruce Price, whose family had moved to Baltimore from Cumberland in the early 1850s. By 1874, when Niernsee and Neilson went their separate ways, Baldwin had taken over as the B&O's principal architect. He had also accepted as a draftsman and apprentice a native Baltimorean and graduate of St. John's College, Josias Pennington. Baldwin's work for the B&O included many attractive stations, some railroad-owned resort hotels, and various routine commissions.

When the B&O asked Baldwin to design a shop for building and repairing railroad passenger equipment, Baldwin clearly did not consider the assignment at all routine. A devout Roman Catholic who also produced many ecclesiastical buildings, he created an airy, soaring circular structure, truly a secular cathedral, which may well be his masterpiece. Almost universally called a roundhouse (more accurately, a twenty-two-sided polygon), the building has an unusual layout: a central turntable servicing twenty-two radial tracks. Although roundhouses were commonly built to store and service locomotives between runs, few heavy car–repair shops followed this pattern; most were conventionally rectangular and served by parallel tracks, which entered from one or both ends. The round layout offered a major advantage by minimizing the internal switching of cars; a car could be left at a single location until work was completed, undisturbed by the movement of other cars in the shop.

Completed in 1884 at a cost of $100,000, the shop was an experiment in brick and iron fireproof construction. The neatly proportioned brick lower story supports a slate-roofed dome 245 feet in diameter through an intricate and novel system of radial trusses and twenty-two iron columns, the whole combining to produce a design of strength, utility, and lightness. Baldwin designed a building of the grandest scale—perhaps "the largest passenger car shop in the world" and, for many years, "the world's largest circular industrial building"[8]—235 feet in diameter and 123 feet from the floor to the top of its unusual, lanternlike circular clerestory and cupola. Built at a time when artificial lighting was still relatively primitive, the building lets in a maximum of natural light, both from above and from its large

Mount Royal Station, ca. 1950.
Peale Collection, Maryland
Historical Society

LEFT:
Ornamental grillwork and
structural-support details from the
train shed at Mount Royal Station.
The B&O Railroad Museum, Inc.
RIGHT:
Detail of grillwork, Mount Royal
Station. Peale Collection, Maryland
Historical Society

ground-floor windows. Baldwin specified a light color of paint for the interior, whose height far exceeded any practical needs but created a stunning visual effect.

In the late nineteenth century, as the city expanded northward, it became clear to the B&O that it needed another passenger station. As part of the line's extension of service to Philadelphia, the railroad burrowed a tunnel under Howard Street from Camden Station to a new residential area along Mount Royal Avenue, and there in 1896 opened a magnificent new station.

The work of Baldwin and Pennington, whom the older man had admitted to partnership in 1883, the station featured heavy granite walls and a tremendous clock tower, thereby demonstrating the influence of Henry Hobson Richardson, a Louisiana-born architect then practicing in Boston. Richardson's massive churches, libraries, courthouses, and jails had revived, while also modifying, the Romanesque style; Richardsonian Romanesque featured strong arches, heavy horizontal lines, corner turrets, and careful attention to exterior and interior details. At Mount Royal, Baldwin & Pennington followed Richardson while achieving fine contrasts—a rugged stone exterior offset by the light girders of the train shed and delicately ornamental grilles screening the platform. The interior became famous for its atmosphere of a comfortable sitting room, a feature that pleased both departing and returning travelers. Well lighted, the great hall also featured polished marble columns, well-scaled oak paneling, a huge functional fireplace, massive oak benches and rocking chairs, all of which created an air of southern hospitality.

Standing in a deep hollow, the building has the rare architectural distinction of being visible chiefly from above, as one would view a model. As a result, the massing of the low hor-

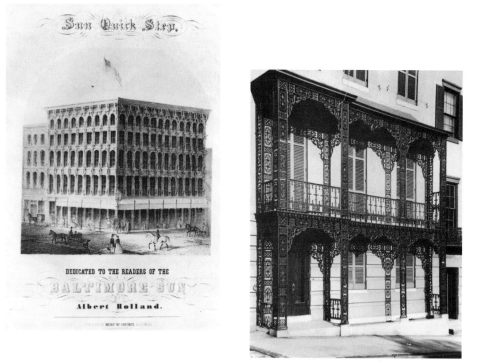

LEFT:

Sun Iron Building as it appeared on the sheet music for the "Sun Quick Step," colored lithograph by A. Hoen & Co., 1854. Maryland Historical Society

RIGHT:

Decorative cast-iron work, typical of Baltimore's local and export product, on a house facing South Washington Place. Peale Collection, Maryland Historical Society

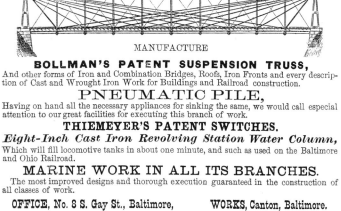

Advertisement for Patapsco Bridge and Iron Works. From Howard, Monumental City, 218.

izontal features against the soaring tower gives it a daring and dramatic aspect and enhanced monumentality.

Architectural cast iron—in many ways emblematic of the nineteenth century's marriage of industry and aesthetics—had strong Baltimore connections, first because of the prominence of Peter Cooper's Canton ironworks, where skilled workmen designed and built the earliest American locomotives. By the middle of the century Baltimore had become a center for the production of architectural iron, both structural and decorative, as in the internal supports and interior detailing of the Peabody Library. James Bogardus of New York had gone further, experimenting with iron in putting up building façades. A few years later, Arunah S. Abell, owner of the *Baltimore Sun* and pioneer in the use of the telegraph in journalism, decided to follow suit, and in 1850 he engaged New York architect R. C. Hatfield to design a newspaper building on this bolted-iron principle, five stories high with a maximum amount of glass in its iron front. Bogardus & Hoppin of New York received the contract to build the "Sun Iron Building," which became the proud predecessor of many iron-framed and iron-fronted business buildings in the city. Meanwhile, structural ironworks were also being exported—in 1849, the firm of Price & Company made and shipped to San Francisco the iron frame of a hundred-room hotel, three stories high and some two hundred feet long. Less than a decade later Poole & Hunt of Baltimore made the cast-iron columns and much of the structural ironwork for the new dome of the United States Capitol.

Indeed, for a time after the Civil War, Maryland was one of the great iron-producing states. At least two firms specialized in building iron bridges, the chief of which, before 1880, were the St. Charles Bridge across the Missouri River, the Rock Island Bridge over the Mississippi, and the Varrugas Viaduct, built in the Andes for a Peruvian railroad. Baltimore companies produced iron shop-fronts, demountable houses, galvanized iron roofs, patent ventilating skylights, and miles of iron cornices, window lintels, porch railings, and balconies to ornament commercial and domestic buildings throughout the United States. Baltimore structures of the period offer particularly fine examples of this local production.

TOP:
Detail, Baltimore & Ohio Railroad tidewater terminus, elevators, etc., Locust Point. From Howard, Monumental City, *facing 320.*

BOTTOM:
Brown's Wharf warehouse complex in Fells Point dates to the 1820s and was used mainly for storing coffee, an import that became one of Baltimore's most important staples after the Civil War. Courtesy of Mary Ellen Hayward

Warehouses, Waterside and Railside

Storing goods was as important as making them, since raw materials and finished products often needed temporary storage as they moved between rail and ship or between manufacturer and market. Baltimore was not only a major port but also a significant regional domestic distribution center, making warehousing one of its earliest, liveliest, and hardiest industries.

A warehouse was intended to provide dead storage space secure from weather, theft, fire, contamination, and other hazards, so the buildings were sturdily built, usually of heavy masonry, simple in layout, with as much open floor area as possible and ceilings high enough so that goods could be stacked. Windows provided rudimentary lighting and ventilation but were often smaller and less numerous than needed for factory work. Larger warehouses were often sectionalized, with fire walls between. The earliest

Miraculously, Brown's Wharf survived into the 1990s, when, like
other such waterfront relics, it
was overhauled for
adaptive reuse.

warehouses were located largely on or near piers, but once railroads became important in-land carriers, rail access was usually also a necessity. Until the late nineteenth century the lack of elevators limited a building's height to three or four stories; with the advent of high-capacity freight elevators, warehouse capacity could be increased by building upward, reaching eight stories in some cases. Warehouse architecture emphasized stolid strength and an air of impregnability, with massive rectangular forms sometimes offset by aqueduct-like arched effects; cast-iron doors and shutters often drove the point home.

In many cases, nineteenth-century Baltimore-area warehouses specialized in specific large-volume commodities passing through the port—tobacco from Southern Maryland for export, and imported coffee and sugar. The export grain elevator was a particularly spe-cialized form of warehouse; as its name implies, it was, in effect, a bulk warehouse elevated above the ground so that grain could easily flow by gravity into a ship's hold. Baltimore's vitality as a port came to be based heavily on export bulk products, predominantly coal and grain, brought in by rail to ship-side storage and transfer facilities. After the Civil War the B&O built large waterfront export elevators at Locust Point. Across the harbor at Fells Point, the competitive Northern Central Railway built a small elevator in 1868, replacing it with progressively larger ones at Canton after 1873. Both railroads also established inland elevators for the domestic trade.

The Brown's Wharf complex off Thames Street in Fells Point offered a typical example of early ship-oriented warehousing, in this case for the coffee trade. Twin warehouses were built in 1820 and 1822—simple, unpretentious three-story brick structures distinguished mostly by their steeply sloped shed roofs. An addition of 1868, fronting on Thames Street, had more architectural flair—arched windows, arched doorways on each level, and some elaborate brickwork.

Baltimore nonetheless lost some noteworthy industrial relics. Among the finest, the U.S. Appraisers' Stores—a massive rectangular structure of brick, four stories high, with brick

LEFT:

*U.S. Appraisers Stores: elevation
on Gay Street. Historic
American Buildings Survey,
Library of Congress*

RIGHT:

*U.S. Appraisers Stores: section A–B.
Historic American Buildings
Survey, Library of Congress*

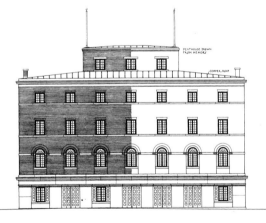

ELEVATION on GAY ST.

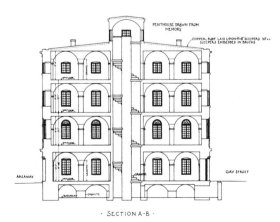

· SECTION A-B ·

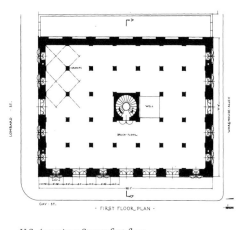

U.S. Appraisers Stores: first-floor
plan. Historic American Buildings
Survey, Library of Congress
RIGHT:
Scene outside the Appraisers' Stores
building in the 1930s, showing
window and door details.
Historic American Buildings
Survey, Library of Congress

vaults supporting each floor—stood for many years on the southeast corner of Gay and Lombard Streets, diagonally across from the Baltimore Exchange. Robert Mills himself completed work on it in 1839. The building's simple cornice and the stringcourses between the stories reminded one of the nearby Baltimore Exchange. The familiar aqueduct motif could be seen at the second-story level, where the arched window lintels connected to the horizontal band. The building expressed strength and protection; in addition to heavy masonry, the lowest story carried heavy cast-iron shutters to make it as secure as possible.

Another great warehouse, the building known as the old Sugar House, once stood at the corner of Aliceanna and Chester Streets. Built in 1849, this brick structure had tightly grouped windows and more vertical emphasis than the Appraisers' Stores. The end wall rose in a series of rectangular steps, like the fire walls seen on contemporary Greek Revival houses. Iron shutters and doors, iron frames and window lintels with delicately molded patterns, were all used in a competent architectural manner without denying the fundamental qualities of strength and endurance that iron connotes.

Sugar House, as drawn in the 1930s:
the elevation on Aliceanna Street.
Historic American Buildings
Survey, Library of Congress

The late nineteenth century produced progressively larger warehouses, most tied to rail lines and several of them the work of notable local architects. In 1853 Niernsee & Neilson designed a new tobacco warehouse on the south side of Barre Street between Charles and Light Streets for William Gail. Later, the Gail & Ax Tobacco Company became the American Tobacco Company. In 1887 Charles L. Carson, son of the well-regarded Baltimore builder Daniel Carson, designed a tobacco warehouse at 429 South Charles Street for the Marburg Brothers tobacco-processing company. The eight-story brick and stone structure, styled in a restrained

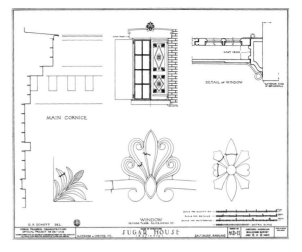

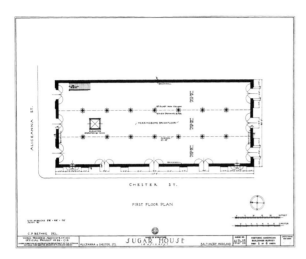

Sugar House: first-floor plan. Historic American Buildings Survey, Library of Congress

RIGHT:
Sugar House details. Historic American Buildings Survey, Library of Congress

The Appraisers' Stores building survived the 1904 Baltimore fire, no more damaged than adjoining steel-framed structures. It was demolished in 1939. The Sugar House came down in July 1974.

version of the Romanesque manner that Carson often employed, became part of the expanded facilities of the original Gail & Ax warehouse.

For the B&O, E. Francis Baldwin designed railroad warehouses, including one for tobacco on Fort Avenue, a three-and-a-half-story, 80-by-317-foot brick structure built in 1879–80. It belonged to the B&O's extensive Locust Point import-export terminal complex. As the B&O's export tobacco business grew, Baldwin designed a larger, six-story, 283-by-204-foot tobacco warehouse for the railroad at Henderson's Wharf, on the Fells Point waterfront. Completed in 1898, the structure oddly had no direct track connection with other B&O lines. Railroad cars were ferried across the harbor from Locust Point on car floats and were unloaded directly into the warehouse on its water side or transferred to a peculiar little switching spur on the building's street side. The warehouse itself had arched, street-side loading doors, arched windows covered with iron shutters, and an elaborate brick cornice.

All nineteenth-century Baltimore warehouses paled before the B&O's enormous Camden Warehouse, the grandest of its kind in the city, if not the country. Located adjacent to the Camden passenger terminal, this high-capacity structure had to be squeezed into a narrow site between railroad yards on the east and South Eutaw Street on the west. The result was a striking long, tall, and slim configuration. Only 51 feet wide, the eight-story brick structure stretched four blocks (1,116 feet) along South Eutaw Street. Inside, this warehouse provided 430,000 square feet of storage space—the equivalent, boasted the railroad, of a thousand boxcars. The hulking building was built in phases, beginning in 1898 and ending in 1904. Baldwin likely served as architect, although this has not been documented. In 1905 the railroad added a five-story office building at the north end, sacrificing the original west wing of Camden Station in the process. As completed, Camden Warehouse consisted of six vertical sections, each separated by a fire wall and served by one or two large hydraulic elevators. Breaking up the long exterior expanse, recessed arches capped the sixth-floor windows, and granite stringcourses marked the second- and sixth-floors levels, with panels of

Round corner detail, Levering & Company coffee warehouse (Chase's Wharf), Thames Street at Caroline. The Levering & Company coffee warehouses dated from 1869–79. The four-story brick main structure, completed last, originally had arched windows and loading doors and modestly elaborate brickwork on its street façade; its upper-floor cast-iron loading doors testified to the lack of internal elevators. Baltimore Museum of Industry

G. W. Gail's Tobacco Works, Barre Street, from Robert Taylor's 1857 Map of Baltimore City and Baltimore County. Baltimore County Public Library

G. W. Gail & Ax Tobacco Factory incorporated Gail's earlier tobacco works (at far left). Baltimore Museum of Industry

The southern end of the Marburg (formerly Gail & Ax) tobacco works, viewed from the southwest corner of South Charles and West Lee Streets. When federal researchers took this photograph in the 1930s, ownership had passed to the Pierre Lorillard Company. Industrial buildings like this one had for many years encroached on the distinguished early-nineteenth-century row housing in the foreground. Historic American Buildings Survey, Library of Congress

Henderson's Wharf in 1932. The B&O Railroad Museum, Inc.

The Gail & Ax warehouse came down in the 1970s and is now the site of the Harbor Court Hotel; the Marburg warehouse was demolished in 1989. The B&O's Fort Avenue warehouse expired in a spectacular fire in early 1996. Abandoned by the railroad in the early 1970s, Henderson's Wharf was adapted for reuse as a hotel-apartment complex.

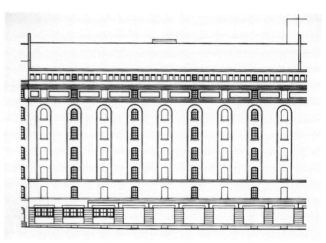

Camden Warehouse and yard, east side, as it appeared in the 1920s. The B&O Railroad Museum, Inc.
RIGHT:
Camden Station, warehouse, partial west elevation. Historic American Buildings Survey, Library of Congress

Camden Warehouse continued in use until 1974, after which it endured almost two decades of abandonment and failed reuse proposals. It was finally rescued by the Maryland Stadium Authority and made an integral part of the Oriole Park at Camden Yards complex in 1992.

decorative brickwork above. Just as the B&O's Mount Royal Station visibly expressed the grandeur of the age of rail travel, the vast Camden Warehouse, certainly impressive as architecture, also symbolized the high tide of railroads at the turn of the century, when they hauled virtually all the nation's intercity freight.

Canning Chesapeake Harvests

In the nineteenth century Baltimore became a major center of the American canning industry, eventually claiming to be the canning capital of the world. Chesapeake Bay oysters explained its genesis; from the 1850s onward, the city developed a virtual monopoly on oyster packing. In order to keep busy during the warm months after the September-to-April shellfish season, packers diversified into fruit and vegetable canning, drawing on the fertile fields of nearby Anne Arundel County and the Eastern Shore and on exotic imports, like pineapples from Central America. Every winter yielded millions of oysters, a delicacy shipped to restaurants across the country. In summer, boats brought peaches, tomatoes, shoe-peg corn, and various fruits and vegetables from Maryland's bountiful farms. By 1870 more than one hundred packing houses employed men, women, and children to do the work not only of processing the food that filled the cans but also of making the cans themselves, the colorful paper labels that covered them, and the boxes they went into. At century's end mechanized equipment had split canning and can-making into specialties. Two national can-making companies evolved; as late as 1940 Baltimore made more cans than any other city.

The industry naturally clustered around the harbor, east from Fells Point, along Boston Street to Canton, and across the basin, at the foot of Federal Hill—close by the piers where oysters and produce arrived and near rail transportation. Neither canning companies nor can-makers developed truly distinctive building designs; their plants were primarily boxes to contain production-line machinery and materials—low-rise buildings (one to three stories), often with central clerestories running the length of the building above the main roof,

The Baltimore Museum of Industry later incorporated most of the Platt complex (including a postcannery 1967 addition) into its museum facilities, which include a "living history" exhibit of nineteenth-century canning.

their windowed walls providing light and ventilation to workers below. Canneries usually had separate steam plants and adjoining storage buildings. Typical of many industries, the canning and can-producing plants over time became complexes of buildings, each new addition resulting from increased production or the advent of new machinery or processing techniques.

One of the earliest surviving canneries, the onetime S. B. Platt oyster-packing plant at 1415 Key Highway, typified such operations—and how they expanded by patching new structures onto old. A two-story brick head house was built in 1864, housing offices above and working space below. Architecturally unremarkable, it was distinguished mostly by a projecting second-floor-front turret with Italianate cornice. Behind it, a single-story brick shed provided a large open work area, with wooden roof-trussing above. In 1900 Platt built a two-story brick addition at the rear of this building, with ground-level loading doors for shipping by wagon and rail. The back of the complex opened directly onto the west side of the harbor, where boats bringing in oysters and produce were unloaded and their cargo cleaned in wooden sheds.

The Platt firm and other canneries tended to be medium-sized specialty businesses, but the can-makers expanded into large-scale, national producers. The American Can Company plant at Boston and Hudson Streets was one of them. It supplies a fascinating case study of how an industrial complex progressively evolved under the simultaneous spurs of a constantly growing business and new developments in structural design, such as the use of poured concrete for the 1924 signature building. American Can's buildings cover the entire history of the can-making operations on that site, illustrating three eras of industrial-plant architecture. Even before American Can took over the site, the Abbott Ironworks had produced plates for the Union Navy's ironclad *Monitor* there.

The Norton Tin Plate and Can Company, a pioneer in fully mechanized can production, established the first can-producing plant on the site in 1895. Norton's original factory, a fairly ordinary two-story brick structure with a wide central clerestory and gabled roof, had tall, narrow second-story windows and ground-level loading doors opening onto the all-

Aerial view of the American Can Company buildings, 1938. Baltimore Museum of Industry

The American Can plant closed in the 1980s, but at the end of the century adaptive reuse saved the principal structures and smaller outbuildings for offices, restaurants, and specialty shops.

important railroad siding (the plant, like most in this area, was reached from railroad tracks laid directly in Boston Street, a harking back to the 1830s, when all of Baltimore's railroads entered the city over streets). Norton became part of the newly formed American Can Company in 1901, and a year later the firm expanded its plant by adding an unexceptional-looking two-story brick building with ground-level loading doors onto its south end. It, too, featured tall, narrow second-story windows typical of the era and had a flat roof with monitors. In 1913 American Can built a large, three-story addition on the north side of the original 1895 plant, this one clearly a twentieth-century industrial design. Its exposed, reinforced-concrete supports made it one of Baltimore's first such structures. Large multipane "industrial" windows maximized natural lighting and ventilation. Inside, fully automated specialized machinery produced "sanitary cans." Another functionally attractive combination of concrete and brick with large rectangular windows, a separate four-story building for closing-machine operations and offices completed the American Can establishment in 1924. Part of its top three floors were built out over a railroad siding and loading dock.

Architectural Fashions for the Garment Industry

After the Civil War the sewing machine enabled Baltimore's well-established clothing business to mechanize, making the city a leading producer of ready-made clothing. In 1900 only New York exceeded the city's output of men's clothing. Roughly twenty thousand Baltimoreans then worked in the needle trades, most of them laboring in residences or modified residences under contractors and subcontractors who "sweated" profits from immigrant labor by promising more work than the competition in less time. But in the early twentieth century, true factories began to be built which housed hundreds of skilled and semiskilled men and women. Designers of such structures realized that, even where mechanized, the garment industry remained heavily labor intensive, with many workers operating individual small cutting and sewing machines. Loft buildings—high, open-floored structures that covered the equivalent of several city lots—met the need for vast square footage and ample storage space for bolts of cloth and finished products.

All built within thirty years of one another, the buildings that made up Baltimore's loft district clustered along Howard, Eutaw, and Paca Streets north of Pratt, an area easily reached by workers from all parts of the city via the new streetcar system and only a few blocks from both the docks at the basin and the B&O's Camden Station freight yards. The Johnston Brothers & Company Building (1880) stood at 26–28 South Howard Street and the Rombro Building (1881) next door, at 22–24 South Howard Street. The Strauss Building went up at 40–42 South Paca Street in 1887. Four Erlanger Buildings (1890s) occupied the 500 block of West Pratt Street. In 1896 the Hamburger Brothers Clothing Company built a loft structure at 16–20 South Eutaw Street, just west of the Sonneborn (later Classic Uniform Company) Building, at 10–14 South Eutaw (1896). After 1905 the Rosenfeld Building stood at 36 South Paca Street. Interspersed in this area, sometimes in the same buildings, were manufacturers of straw hats, umbrellas, and other accessories, as well as shoes, cigars, and pharmaceuticals.

Practical minded but ambitious, the owners of these companies—Leonard Greif, Henry Sonneborn, J. Schoeneman, and the Strouse brothers among them—aimed to present a fashionable image. They asked for buildings with more than routine architectural attention. An imposing brick and red sandstone structure with terra cotta decoration, the Brigham and Hopkins Building (1884) illustrated classic Romanesque design: round-arched, rusticated openings extending through the second story and narrower, round-arched motifs for the windows above. Regularly spaced square windows provided light to the attic story. Six years later Charles L. Carson drew plans for another Romanesque monument, the Strouse Brothers (later Marlboro Shirt) Building at 414–418 West Lombard Street. Carson took as his model H. H. Richardson's Romanesque Marshall Field Wholesale Store (1885–87) in Chicago. He enclosed the six open-loft floors of the Strouse Building in brick, red and brown sandstone, and terra cotta, with Romanesque arches over the fifth-floor windows. Four monumental round-arch openings graced the ground floor at the corner of Lombard and Paca Streets, extending to the second-floor level. Inside, wooden columns and beams supported the floors. In 1906 the factory received a large addition on its east side, framed with structural steel. By then engineering pragmatism ruled, and the addition hardly matched the majesty of its Richardsonian predecessor.

The Brigham and Hopkins hat factory, 413–421 West Redwood Street, as it appeared in the pages of The Trade, Commerce, and Manufacture of Baltimore *(Baltimore, 1887). Baltimore Museum of Industry*

Like the newer additions at the American Can plant, the Henry Sonneborn & Company Building on the northwest corner of Pratt and Paca Streets represented modern early-twentieth-century industrial construction. Sonneborn, an immigrant German merchant who entered the industry before the Civil War, had already proven himself an innovator, leading the way toward consolidating the work of garment manufacturing and also recognizing the right of labor to organize. He commissioned Baltimore architects Otto Simonson and Theodore W. Pietsch to design the new building, which integrated suit manufacturing in one plant, eliminating the need to contract out piecework, and accommodated some seven thousand workers on its nine floors. When it opened in 1906, it advertised itself as the largest clothing factory in the world. Besides reinforced concrete, the large buff brick building—ten bays on Pratt Street, eleven on Paca—employed electricity, indoor sanitation, and steam heat during the cold months. Simonson and Pietsch did their best to beautify the

Henry Sonneborn & Company garment factory as seen in a 1936 photograph. Baltimore Museum of Industry

The Sonneborn (later Paca-Pratt) building was renovated and adapted for office use in 1986–87. Collectively impressive, the massive survivors of Baltimore's loft district still huddle closely together within a six-block area directly north of Camden Yards. They rank among the city's distinguished buildings; the 400 block of Redwood Street would make a delightful vista in any city.

hulking structure. They designed the two corner bays of the Paca Street façade as wide, horizontally rusticated pilasters. The Paca Street entrance featured six stone pilasters and a split pediment. A deep roof cornice enriched with dentils topped the building; narrower cornices marked the second and eighth floors. Although Sonneborn's factory looked much like a typical early-1900s office building, its large industrial-style windows and railroad siding in the rear identified it as a factory.

Old-Country Brewing Palaces

From the mid-eighteenth century onward Baltimore had a substantial German population, which surged after the Civil War, thanks in large part to an 1867 agreement between the B&O and the North German Lloyd steamship line, which carried Maryland tobacco to Bremen and returned with immigrants. The Germans debarked at the B&O's piers at Locust Point. With them came both the production skills and the market for lager beer.

Brewing in Baltimore began with John L. and Elias D. Barnitz, father and son, at Hanover and Baltimore Streets in 1748, and by 1800 at least nine breweries had appeared (and others had already disappeared). In the late 1860s brewing became a truly heavy industry, one dominated by families and brand names like Wiessner, Beck, Bauernschmidt, Wunder, Eigenbrot, and Gunther. About sixty distinct breweries operated in the city at one time or another, but the golden age of Baltimore brewing arrived with technological innovations during the 1870s and 1880s. Lager brewers faced the need for cooling through various parts of the production process; the industry thus pioneered the development of steam-powered mechanical refrigeration (traditionally, the product and materials were kept cool in underground vaults or by ice). Steam power also aided with various brewing functions. Plants soon moved from the city's center to outlying locations near major highways, where more space was available and where grain and other materials could be brought in more readily. Unlike many industries of the time, brewing had little need of railroad access; brewers sold largely to the local market and obtained their raw materials from nearby sources or from the port.

That golden age had no better visual expression than the John F. Wiessner brewery on the corner of Gay and Lanvale Streets. An immigrant from Bavaria, Wiessner built his first brewery in Baltimore in 1863. By the mid-1880s business had blossomed to the point that he needed a larger and improved plant. The dazzling replacement, perhaps the work of Charles Stoll of Brooklyn, New York, opened in 1887. "The design is entirely unique in brewery architecture," said the major trade magazine at the time, "while at the same time its interior arrangements and practical utility of each of its departments have not been sacrificed in the least to mere architectural effect."[9] Unique it surely was. Eclecticism run rampant, this ebullient Victorian confection defied architectural analysis but clearly symbolized the zenith of local brewing and brewery architecture. Fronting Gay Street on what was originally a two-acre site, the five-story brick and stone structure sprouted three ornate wooden towers of

Advertisement for the George Bauernschmidt Brewing Company. The elaborate brewery of 1887 in the background featured all the modern equipment known to the industry, including an ice machine. Colored lithograph, A. Hoen & Co., ca. 1890. Maryland Historical Society

TOP, RIGHT:
John F. Wiessner & Sons Brewing Company as it appeared in about 1880. Maryland Historical Society
BOTTOM:
Wiessner & Sons central pavilion and ornate tower, photographed in the late twentieth century. Courtesy of John W. McGrain

different sizes and exotic shapes. There were arched windows, round stained-glass windows, a profusion of pilasters, and various forms of decorative brickwork and woodwork.

The inside, however, was the very model of a modern 1880s-era brewery. The building had an iron framework and was laid out to take full advantage of gravity flow for the various processes, with raw materials stored on the upper floors. There were three major vertical sections—a central portion flanked by two wings. The central portion incorporated Stoll's patented malt-storage towers and a large area for malt storage, with malt-milling and cleaning machinery. Upper floors of the north wing, used for hops storage, were served by a large platform elevator; below were two Linde mechanical refrigeration units (of 50 and 100 tons capacity), advertised as the first ice machines in Baltimore. The south wing included a ground malt hopper and large, iron tubs for mash. Bottling equipment came later;

originally, outside contractors bottled the product. Wiessner's own mansion stood opposite the brewery on the west side of Gay Street, a large three-story building designed not only to house the Wiessner family but also to serve as a temporary home for newly arrived workers from Germany.

Wiessner's business prospered and the brewery eventually expanded to cover a total of five and a half acres east of Gay Street. Additions included a bottling plant and two-story stable in 1900, a four-story brick and stone warehouse in 1901, another addition in 1906, and a garage in 1910 (motor vehicles had begun to replace the traditional dray horses used for deliveries). Prohibition closed the plant and ended Wiessner's ownership; after repeal of the Eighteenth Amendment, the American Brewery bought the operation and replaced much of the earlier equipment.

Equally elegant but more conventional, the Henry Eigenbrot brewery of 1873 also stood six stories high and was three bays wide, with arched windows, curved brickwork, and fancy cornice and pilasters. A similar but more elaborately detailed hops-storage building stood adjacent to the brew house; three stories high in front, it rose to four stories in the rear. Several other brick buildings in the same style completed the impressive complex, which loomed over a block at 101–117 Willard Street. Otto C. Wolfe of Philadelphia, a brewery architect, designed the Brew House in 1896 and the refrigerated storehouse in 1897.

The Wiessner brewery closed for good in 1973. In the summer of 2001 city officials announced plans to redevelop the brewery, mansion, wagon house, and stables as a senior living center.

Today the Eigenbrot Brewery still stands in this off-the-beaten-path part of West Baltimore.

Structures for Street Railways

A thick web of street railways made Baltimore work in the nineteenth and early twentieth centuries. Following the horsecars, cable and then electrically powered trolleys did much to build the city and bind it together. Streetcars carried workers to their jobs, shoppers to stores, and everyone to theaters and amusement parks. The cars were as essential to industry as were raw materials and machinery; they were also an industry in themselves, with plants to produce power for their operations and shops to build and repair equipment. Mechanical power came in the 1890s, first in the form of cable traction and then electricity.

Baltimore's brief and economically disastrous fling with cable power produced several unique and surprisingly long-lived structures. The cable streetcars took their power from endless moving cables that lay beneath the pavement between the rails. The cables in turn were powered by stationary steam engines in six strategically placed power houses (one of them the former Epworth Methodist Church, undoubtedly the country's only ecclesiastical power house). The most impressive of them, completed by the Baltimore Traction Company in 1891, stood on Druid Hill Avenue at Retreat Street. A ponderous Romanesque-style stone and brick building with turrets and stone arches, it housed two 500-horsepower Corliss steam engines, cable-winding equipment in its northerly section, and a storage and repair barn large enough for almost forty streetcars. In only five years, however, the Baltimore Traction Company gave up on cables and electrified its lines.

Electrification brought dramatic expansion in streetcar lines, which soon reached far be-

Cutaway view, Baltimore Traction Company railway cable power house, this one placed in a former Methodist church in 1892. From Street Railway Journal, *March 1894, 160.*

Baltimore Traction Company railway cable power house on Druid Hill Avenue, photographed in the late twentieth century. On the left, the low-lying car house. In the main building, at the right, a pair of steam engines powered the cables. Photograph by Herbert H. Harwood, Jr.

For many years employed for other uses, the fortresslike buildings on Druid Hill Avenue, along with three other former cable power houses elsewhere in the city, still stand, giving Baltimore the country's best collection of relics from this street-transportation era.

MIDDLE AND BOTTOM:
United Railways & Electric Company Power Plant on Pier 4, as it appeared in the early twentieth century, and detail of brickwork. Baltimore Streetcar Museum; Baltimore Museum of Industry

yond the built city. Development followed, as did the consolidation, in 1899, of a myriad of independent street railway companies into a single company—appropriately named the United Railways & Electric Company. The new UR&E instantly found itself faced with a massive modernization and rebuilding program. To centralize electric power generation for the entire city streetcar system, the UR&E built a huge new coal-fired steam power plant on Pratt Street, roughly at the center of the company's system, near the harbor and unlimited water for its boilers, and at a point where it could take on coal either directly from barges or by rail via the B&O's Pratt Street freight line.

The company developed the plant in several stages, beginning with an existing section facing Pratt Street built in 1895 by a predecessor company. Inside, steam engines drove generators. In 1901 a higher boiler house was added directly to the south, providing space for thirty-two boilers, its four smokestacks rising 192 feet above water level. On its west side a complex steel framework structure aided in transferring waterborne coal to the upper part of the plant, where gravity then fed it into the boilers. This 151-foot-high unloader and conveyor was the plant's most interesting and innovative feature; the company claimed it to be the most efficient of its kind at the time. A final rear portion of the power plant, built in 1903, housed the turbo-generators, which replaced the original engine-generator equipment. The entire complex rested on pilings driven deep into the harbor.

In deference to its commanding size and location downtown at the harbor, the complex received some aesthetic attention, although not much more than a typical turn-of-the-century power plant. Each section had its own architectural style, the most elaborate being the northerly unit. It appears that E. Francis Baldwin designed at least part of the plant, as perhaps did another architect active in Baltimore, Henry F. Brauns. Since there were four sections in total (counting the replacement of the original building), two or more architects easily could have been involved.

In addition to power, the United Railways & Electric Company required a centralized heavy maintenance shop to replace the scattered and obsolete plants of earlier companies. It needed large acreage in order to lay out a facility that could both cope with all of the system's repair and rebuilding work on a single level and provide extensive outdoor room to store materials and cars, which by the late 1920s numbered about thirteen hundred, all of them passing through the shop at one time or another.

The margin note on the left:

In 1921 the streetcar company decided to switch to commercial power and sold its Pier 4 plant to Consolidated Gas, Electric Light & Power, the city's utility company. Smoke from its coal-fueled generators continued to float over the harbor until 1973, when Consolidated's successor, the Baltimore Gas & Electric Company, shut it down. All interior equipment was subsequently removed, along with the external coal-transfer steelwork, leaving three cavernous empty shells topped by the four landmark stacks. Developers since then have attempted various commercial adaptations.

Interior view of the Carroll Park shops of the United Railways & Electric Company, the clerestory visible above the repairmen. Baltimore Streetcar Museum

The UR&E selected a site that fronted on Washington Boulevard (then called Columbia Avenue) west of Bush Street, directly south of Carroll Park. Baldwin designed the shop complex, which consisted of a matching pair of huge four-bay-wide buildings, each 475 feet long and 360 feet wide. Together they provided 342,000

Today the Carroll Park shops
continue to serve their original
purposes for the state-operated
bus system, the lineal
descendant of the UR&E.

square feet of covered area. Tall windows on the sides of the building provided abundant natural light and ventilation, as did a clerestory above. The building housed a car-erecting shop, an electric-motor erecting shop, a paint shop, a cabinet shop, a machine shop, two blacksmith shops, an electric-motor armature room, a storeroom, and a power station. The Carroll Park shops, completed in 1901, proved exceptionally well-suited for their job.

A final part of the UR&E's turn-of-the-century consolidation and modernization program was the construction of seven large fireproof car houses, or carbarns. These went up over a seven-year period, from 1907 to 1913. They served primarily as regional operating centers: Active cars were stored and inspected between runs, and most crews were based there. Typically they were designed to store between seventy and a hundred streetcars safely on a single level and to provide inspection facilities, operating offices, and crew rooms. The largest and most elaborate among them, Park Terminal, opened in 1909 at Druid Hill and Fulton Avenues. Once again Baldwin was the designer of the large brick, steel, and concrete mass, which sported squared towers with bold, dentilled cornices and castellated tops, horizontal bands of light stone contrasting with the dark brick, and decorative stonework and terra cotta around many of the windows. Unlike most carbarns, Park Terminal had two floors. Its ground floor tracks included turning loops for the several car lines that terminated there, a passenger waiting room, a crew locker room, and a crew restaurant. Upstairs were offices, a crew reading room, and a bowling alley.

*Park Terminal in the late twentieth
century. Photograph by
Herbert H. Harwood, Jr.*
RIGHT:
*Track layout, Park Terminal.
Baltimore Streetcar Museum*

Park Terminal closed to streetcars
in 1952. Serving other uses, it
and five of its sister structures still
survive.

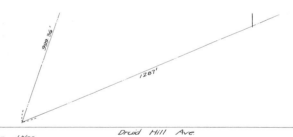

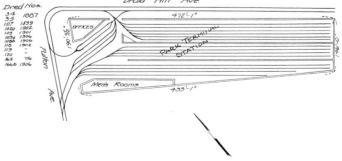

6

ECLECTIC CITY, 1865–1904

In the years after the Civil War great waves of immigrants—eastern and southern Europeans but also ex-Confederates and former slaves—swelled Baltimore's population, which rose from 267,354 in 1870 to 332,313 in 1880. In 1888 the city annexed twenty-three square miles and 38,000 people; two years later the federal Census Bureau reported that 434,439 people lived within the new city limits. At the turn of the twentieth century, the number of Baltimore citizens exceeded half a million. While working hard, the typical Baltimorean could take pleasure in the many popular amusements that developed late in the century. Trolley lines led to parks and picnic grounds on the city's fringes. German residents developed shooting and picnicking parks, which also relied on public transportation. Horse racing at "Old Hilltop," the Pimlico Race Course, resumed in 1870; after 1873 the racing season included a new stakes race, the Preakness. The city purchased the old Carroll mansion and property in the southwest and opened it as a park in 1890, just as it had done with the Rogers estate, Druid Hill. Meanwhile, national railroad connections made it possible for new professional baseball teams to travel and play in the first organized league. In 1882 a local brewery owner, Harry Vonderhorst, sponsored a team that he soon named the Orioles. Stands at his Union Park, near Twenty-fifth Street and Greenmount Avenue, seated about six thousand spectators. For three seasons in the mid-1890s, the Orioles reigned as champions of the new professional game.

The 1870s and 1880s were also noted for particularly high levels of cultural and educational achievement, often aided by impressive local philanthropy. In 1873, the College of Notre Dame of Maryland opened, becoming the first Catholic women's college in the country. In 1876 the Johns Hopkins University began as the first true research university in the Americas. Four years later the African American Centenary Biblical Institute (1867) became Morgan College, and four years after that, in 1884, the Woman's College of Baltimore opened, later to be known as Goucher College. In 1886 Enoch Pratt presided over the opening of his library system—the country's first free public circulating libraries— including a central Baltimore location and four branches. The Johns Hopkins Hospital, soon to become one of the nation's leading teaching and research hospitals, opened in 1889. That same year Henrietta Szold organized a Russian night school in Old Town in an effort to teach the English language and American history to newly arrived Eastern European Jews; it was a forerunner of night schools everywhere.

In 1896 *Harper's Magazine* published a long essay in which Stephen Bonsal praised the citizens of "the new Baltimore" for having "that air and bearing of civic pride which Plutarch says somewhere is characteristic of the sons of famous cities, and which . . . is so enviable and makes so much for happiness."[1]

Baltimore and the Proposed Extension of the City Limits, map by F. Klemm, 1872. Peale Collection, Maryland Historical Society

WHILE ADDING a heavier industrial dimension to Baltimore's economy, maintaining the city's commercial position, and contributing heavily to the advancement of learning, medicine, and public libraries, Baltimore's two postwar generations also did a great deal of building. Like their contemporaries in rival cities, Baltimore's builders and architects generally followed the latest fashion, as set abroad or in New York, borrowing stylistic motifs from a wide range of popular styles. The postwar building boom coincided with the development of new materials and construction methods, the development of new building types to house different kinds of civic and economic functions, and a widespread dissemination of architectural ideas through the print media—all of which worked to transform the architectural landscape of the city.

Rapid economic expansion created a demand for new types of buildings, including large-scale commercial buildings, warehouses, and offices. A burgeoning population in a mature city called forth institutions, both public and private, that required buildings appropriate to their new function and high-profile image. New construction materials, like iron (and later steel), and new technological advances (like the elevator) made this innovative architecture possible. The near-simultaneous flowering of several eclectic architectural styles, widely published in trade journals and popular magazines, offered architects and their clients an unprecedented range of choices.

In the second half of the nineteenth century, architectural fashions were reinvented in a new age of stylistic borrowings. No longer attracted to discrete historical styles that came with specific romantic associations (Greek, Gothic, Egyptian, or Italian Renaissance), a new generation of professionally trained architects looked for inspiration to contemporary work abroad. In Paris, the architects of Napoleon III were rebuilding the city, creating wide boulevards and national monuments like the New Louvre, completed in 1857. With its high mansard roofs, elaborate stone dormers, majestic rows of arches and double columns articulating the granite façade, and rich sculptural decoration, the Louvre became a principal architectural glory of Second Empire Paris and a worldwide symbol of cosmopolitan fashion.

City Hall, designed by George A. Frederick, in an image ca. 1862. Maryland Historical Society

As a result, when Americans decided to build impressive new civic and commercial buildings after the Civil War, they frequently turned to Second Empire models. Especially popular were Second Empire city halls and government buildings.

During the same years in England, tastemaker John Ruskin praised the metaphysical virtues of Gothic forms—particularly the Venetian, with its richly polychromatic façades—in two seminal publications, *The Seven Lamps of Architecture* (1849) and *The Stones of Venice* (1851). Following these principles, architect William Butterfield introduced what would come to be known as the High Victorian Gothic style to London in his 1850 design (completed 1859) for All Saint's Church, Margaret Street. The red brick exterior was patterned with black brick and broad bands of stone, and there was a similarly colorful interior. In America, this colorful, eclectic Gothic style seemed perfect for banks, churches, and large-scale institutional buildings like schools, hospitals, and orphanages. At the same time the English architect Richard Norman Shaw created a highly original style, taking as inspiration the late medieval domestic architecture of the late seventeenth and early eighteenth centuries, a style called Queen Anne after the monarch who assumed the throne in 1702. In America, the precepts of the Queen Anne style were most commonly translated into residential architecture.

Later, in the 1880s, "creative eclecticism" expanded to include forms derived from Romanesque architecture (as translated by the seminal American architect Henry Hobson Richardson) and the French Renaissance of François I (turned into "chateauesque" designs by New York architect Richard Morris Hunt). Still other architects turned to the French Beaux-Arts for guidance; when American millionaires wanted showy palazzos, they tended to desire a return to monumental classicism, and their tastes soon influenced what would be deemed appropriate for civic buildings at the turn of the century.

Second Empire Tastes

As the Peabody Library symbolized Baltimore's coming of age intellectually and culturally, so too did the new City Hall, on which work began soon after the Civil War had ended. Both buildings relied for their effect upon the creative and daring use of structural iron in combination with traditional architectural design and building techniques. Both buildings were the work of young architects, just beginning in their professions, who had won a major design competition.

Baltimore had been without a city hall since its incorporation. At the outset of the Civil War the mayor and city council governed two hundred thousand people from a group of converted houses and the building that originally served as the Peale Museum, on Holliday Street. This arrangement seemed too apt a reflection of Baltimore's disorderly antebellum reputation, and just before the war, city officials announced a city hall design competition. The winner, George A. Frederick, was at the time a complete unknown and not yet twenty years old.

Frederick's ambitious City Hall provided more than 100,000 square feet of interior space, making it larger than Latrobe's Exchange. The architect called for lofty ceremonial chambers for elected magistrates and practical offices for a small army of clerks. Every room had natural light. In the center, the rotunda rose 119 feet through three levels marked by the

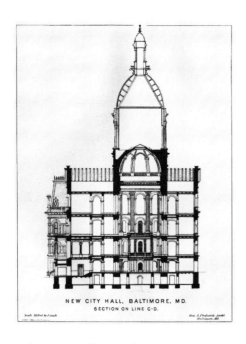

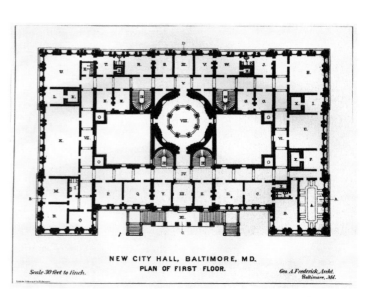

Baltimore City Hall, sectional view and first-floor plan, drawn by George A. Frederick. Historic American Buildings Survey, Library of Congress

Doric, Ionic, and Corinthian orders to an interior dome; beyond that point, a monumental exterior dome and cupola reached a height of 227 feet. Construction got under way in 1867—on an entire city block along Holliday Street, between Fayette and Lexington—and the project became a major community effort. Hugh Sisson, proprietor of the steam marble works that had supplied material for the South Carolina state capitol, laid a special rail line to bring 600 tons of white Cockeysville marble to the site. Philip Hiss made the furniture. Wendell Bollman, the Baltimore & Ohio Railroad's bridge-building genius, engineered the 130-ton cast-iron dome, with iron supplied by the local firm of Bartlett-Robbins. In 1873 George W. Howard, celebrating Baltimore past and present in *The Monumental City,* declared that the new building would "be one of the handsomest and most imposing edifices in the country" and would also "reflect credit on our City, the materials for its construction, to the minutest item, having been obtained within the limits of the State, and the work upon it, having been done altogether by the artisans of Baltimore."[2] On completion of the building in 1875, auditors determined that it had cost far less than the amount budgeted.

Frederick called his design Renaissance, but in fact he combined a Renaissance-detailed main building with a French roof, newly made fashionable by Napoleon III's Second Empire, especially the New Louvre. Howard accurately pointed out that the new design accorded "with the Roman style, very materially modified by modern innovations, of which the French roof is a prominent feature."[3] The window openings of the main building, inspired by the work of the Italian Renaissance painter and architect Sebastiano Serlio, recalled Palladio's basilica in Vicenza. The division of the façade into five parts by means of projecting central and end bays also bespoke the influence of the Second Empire. Frederick's building lacked the clustered chimneys and superimposed orders that later blossomed in Philadelphia's City Hall, possibly the grandest American exemplar of the style, and was also more conservative than the Second Empire Boston City Hall of 1862–65, and the State, War,

and Navy Department building (later Executive Office Building) built next to the White House between 1871 and 1875. For his tall, slender dome, Frederick may have been inspired by Italian or French sources or by the dome of the Charlottenburg Palace in Berlin, or he may have looked closer to home—to Thomas Ustick Walter's recently completed dome for the United States Capitol.

"In beauty of design," proclaimed Mayor Joshua Vansant, "in its architectural proportions, in the execution of the work of the building—exterior and interior—in its great strength, in the materials used in its construction, and in its perfect ventilating adaption, it is questionable if its equal can be found in the United States, save in the Capitol building at Washington."[4] With its dedication Baltimore's citizenry took a giant step closer to the goal of building an orderly, honorable city.

Most of the important buildings erected in the late 1860s and early 1870s took their tone from Frederick's design for City Hall and all were the work of established architects in the city. Frederick moved from his work at City Hall to design the office building for the city's German-language newspaper, the *German Correspondent,* at the southwest corner of Baltimore Street and Post Office Avenue (now Custom House Avenue), completed in 1869. Three stories high, with its Baltimore Street arcaded marble façade resembling the arched openings of City Hall, the prominent structure also boasted a fashionable French roof. From this site one of the leading dailies of the city gave testament to Baltimore's continuing Germanness. Because of his own ethnic roots, Frederick seemed to be the favored architect of the city's German community. In 1873 he designed the German Orphan Asylum, at Aisquith and Orleans Street, a three-story building with French roof whose massing closely resembled that of City Hall, with its projecting end and center pavilions. (In this later building, however, the window detailing showed the influence of the new Ruskinian Gothic style.)

On the southwest corner of Baltimore and Light Streets, on the site of the historic Fountain Inn, Niernsee & Neilson designed a totally French-inspired new hotel, the Carrollton, completed in 1873. Six stories high, with a tall French roof marked by Second Empire–style dormer windows, the

TOP:

Interior view of the dome, Baltimore City Hall. Historic American Buildings Survey, Library of Congress

BOTTOM:

German Correspondent Building, designed by George A. Frederick, completed in 1869. From George W. Howard, The Monumental City: Its Past History and Present Resources *(Baltimore, 1873), 60.*

Carrollton was the first "modern" hotel to be erected after the Civil War, and it remained a prominent feature of the city for many years. Its full-page advertisement in Howard's *Monumental City* described it as the "only Hotel in Baltimore of the new Style, embracing Elevators, Suites of Rooms, with Baths, and all conveniences; perfect ventilation and light throughout," suitable for the businessman and tourist alike. It boasted an elegant "Office and Exchange Room, with Telegraph, &c.," available for use by the "merchants and citizens of the City," as well as a "Ladies' Entrance on Baltimore Street," connected with "beautiful Drawing Rooms" to give families "more than the usual degree of quietude and seclusion."[5] Ladies and gentlemen freely used the gigantic lobby.

Thomas Dixon and his new partner Charles Carson were responsible for the boldly

TOP:

The German Orphan Asylum, at
Orleans and Aisquith Streets,
designed by George A. Frederick,
1873. Colored lithograph by A. Hoen
& Co., 1874. Maryland
Historical Society

RIGHT:

The Carrollton Hotel, Baltimore
and Light Streets, designed by
Niernsee & Neilson and opened in
1873. Peale Collection, Maryland
Historical Society

BOTTOM:

Baltimore American Building,
designed by Dixon & Carson, built
1873–75. From A History of the
City of Baltimore, Its Men and
Institutions *(Baltimore: Baltimore*
American, 1902), frontispiece. Enoch
Pratt Free Library

French Baltimore American building of 1873–75, in terms of design a more ornate version of City Hall, but with a front of cast iron. Built for the city's second-ranked newspaper, directly across the street from the epoch-making Sun Iron Building, this ornate, iron-fronted structure seemed determined to steal attention from its rival. Four stories, with iron columns framing all the windows and crowned by a dramatic French roof, the American building also drew attention to itself with a bold two-story tower set at the corner and two secondary towers at either end. The line of the roof, with its pinnacled dormers, towers, and elaborate cresting rails, suggested less the France of the Second Empire than the chateau-building France of the sixteenth century. Graciously, the *Sun* approved of the building, noting that it was "a conspicuous improvement in this central locality, in which improvement was begun with the erection of the Sun iron building twenty-five years ago." The account reported that the printing operation took place in the basement, while the composing rooms occupied the tall, mansard stories. The counting room, on the first floor, was "lofty and richly ornamented . . . decorated in elegant taste, with paneled ceilings, frescoed walls, ornate cornices, and mahogany counter." All floors were served by a "duplex water elevator."[6]

Following quickly in the footsteps of the Sun Iron Building and the Baltimore American's even bolder statement, scores of commercial iron-front buildings went up along Baltimore Street during these years. From Paca Street east to South Street, groups of stately, cast-iron Renaissance town palazzos, some with French roofs, marched down Baltimore Street, offering the kind of merchandise that Baltimore was becoming famous for—men's and ladies' clothing, dry goods and notions, straw hats, and umbrellas. Many of these businesses belonged to wholesalers (whose largest market was in the rebuilding South), but they often had retail counters with fixed prices to cater to the local marketplace.

The ability of cast iron to be molded into intricate ornament produced lavish Italianate façades that rose four or five stories. Strong and slender cast-iron framing and new improvements in plate-glass technology allowed for spacious storefronts with huge windows showing off the tempting wares inside. Cast-iron construction supplied vast interior spaces for the storage and display of merchandise. The large front windows admitted much natural light, but inside, hanging gas fixtures illuminated the shelves of goods.

In 1853 William Reasin, working directly with James Bogardus, designed a five-story iron front for Ephraim Larrabee & Sons, a wholesale leather merchant, on South Calvert Street. He also worked with Bogardus on the latter's other Baltimore project, a building on West Baltimore Street for Samuel Shoemaker, local superintendent of the Adams Express Company.

The five-bay-wide, four-story Italianate Fava Fruit Company was built in 1869 at the northwest corner of Charles and Camden Streets, originally for the W. R. Thomas Oyster and Fruit Packing Company, and possibly designed by Niernsee & Neilson. Much simpler than the Sun Iron Building, without engaged columns and a bracketed cornice, the Fava building nevertheless made good use of repetitive, arched window designs and strong vertical and horizontal accents to create a striking, rhythmic composition. Its wide, street-level metal awnings, which sheltered goods that had been set outside for inspection and loading, were typical on buildings used in the wholesale fruit and vegetable trade.

Bartlett, Robbins & Company, which provided the ironwork for the Baltimore American building, also supplied material for many of the iron-front commercial buildings downtown and, from its foundry at Pratt and Scott Streets, shipped iron fronts to many other cities. The G. R. Vickers office building, on Redwood Street near South Street, perfectly represented the aesthetics of the age—three stories of Italianate arcades capped by an elegant French

G. R. Vickers' office building, cast-iron front by Bartlett, Robbins & Company, stood on German (Redwood) Street near South Street, on South Gay Street. From Howard, Monumental City, *255.*

RIGHT:

Hurst, Purnell & Company's iron-front building on Baltimore Street, designed by Dixon & Carson in 1877. From Howard, Monumental City, *739.*

The Fava Fruit Building came down in 1976, but it was saved and re-erected as part of the expansion of the Baltimore City Life Museums in 1995–96. Two beautiful postwar iron fronts survive at 305 and 312 West Baltimore Street; another stands at 300 West Pratt Street.

roof. Bartlett, Robbins was also responsible for the four-story, nine-bay-wide warehouse on South Gay Street, built in 1873–74 for the L. W. Gunther Company, tobacco and cotton commission merchants. Architects also had their hand in designing iron fronts: Dixon & Carson designed storefronts for Hurst, Purnell & Company on Baltimore Street in 1877 and for Daniel Miller & Company at Sharp and Liberty Streets in 1880.

Owing to the swift rise in the city's population, the postwar building boom also produced blocks of new housing, most of it row houses, and the builder-entrepreneurs who shaped much of Baltimore's urban landscape continued to put up structures that echoed the styles of more expensive buildings. Italianate rows began to appear with fashionable mansard roofs, as on the southern portion of the west side of the 1200 block of St. Paul Street. Other homeowners, like Enoch Pratt, decided to "modernize" their houses by adding a "French roof," which he did in 1867, probably under the direction of Edmund Lind. But the experiment was short-lived, and builders settled in to producing block after block of the familiar three-story, flat-roofed Italianate row house that had become popular before the Civil War. Now, pressed-brick façades (a particularly fine and hard brick, which didn't need painting) were standard, with white marble or brownstone trim, and marble steps. Expensive houses still boasted cast-iron ornament for window hoods, balconies, and stair railings, but most three-story Italianate row houses relied only on their elaborate Renaissance-style wooden cornices for decoration, with deep eaves supported by bold, scroll-sawn brackets.

Speculative developers continued to create parklike residential squares to make their nearby improvements more valuable. However alike they appeared to the untrained eye, blocks of Italianate housing typically were the work of several builders, each producing small differences in the finished sets of buildings, particularly at the cornice line. In hundreds of such blocks, Baltimore achieved unusually harmonious urban architecture. So many blocks of three-story, red-brick Italianate row houses went up in the late 1860s and 1870s that, in the hard times that followed the Panic of 1873, newspapers complained that the city lacked

Enoch Pratt house, exterior as remodeled in 1867. Maryland Historical Society

enough two-story houses to serve working families. A miniature, two-story version of the popular Italianate row house soon emerged, complete with marble trim, steps, and a boldly carved wooden cornice (all such decorative features made affordable by steam-powered saws). Inside, however, the two-story version lacked the amenities of its larger cousin—notably, central heating and inside plumbing. Far smaller than the three-story houses with their two- and three-story back buildings, these twelve- to fifteen-foot-wide houses contained only six small rooms.

When builders put up two-story Italianate houses for workers (many of them newly arrived immigrants), they built them near their workplaces. Such houses thus ringed the waterfront, from Locust Point and Federal Hill to Fells Point and Canton. As factory neighborhoods sprang up to the northeast (breweries), the southwest (railroad-car building and slaughterhouses), and to the north, beyond the city's boundaries, in the mill towns of Hampden and Woodberry, two-story Italianate houses followed.

In the 1860s, seventies, and eighties, on the narrow streets running down the center of most residential city blocks (by 1851 all of these former "alleys," with evocative names, bore respectable street names), even smaller versions of Italianate row houses went up. This pat-

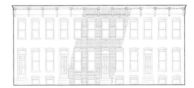

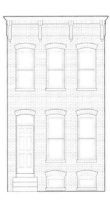

LEFT: *Mansard-roofed row houses of the type built in Baltimore in the 1870s. Computer-assisted drawing by Rosalie Fenwick*

MIDDLE: *27 South Stricker Street, a fancy Italianate three-story row facing Union Square, built between 1857 and 1858. Computer-assisted drawing by Rosalie Fenwick*

RIGHT: *A typical two-story Italianate row house of the 1880s. Computer-assisted drawing by Rosalie Fenwick*

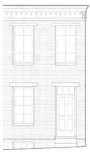

The 1600 block of West Lemmon Street, small houses in the Italianate mode, built by Jacob Saum, 1871, on a narrow street just south of Union Square. Computer-assisted drawing by Rosalie Fenwick

tern of land use continued throughout the century. Always only two bays wide (eleven or twelve feet) and sometimes only two rooms deep, these houses built for the most recently arrived immigrant groups still boasted the bracketed cornices that allowed them to claim relationship with the fashionable houses lining residential squares.

Fresh Ideas, New Professionals

The 1870s brought both a new professionalism to Baltimore architecture and a range of new styles from which to choose. Although professionally trained architects had worked in Baltimore in the 1840s and 1850s, their level of training generally depended on fruitful apprenticeships with established architects or a tour of study abroad. The self-confidence and self-consciousness of the profession coalesced in 1857 in New York with the formation of the American Institute of Architects, which aimed to "unite architects in fellowship . . . to combine their efforts so as to promote the aesthetic, scientific, and practical efficiency of the profession and to make the profession of ever increasing service to society."[7] Among the founding members were the already successful Baltimore architects Edmund G. Lind, designer of the Peabody Institute, and John R. Niernsee, designer of Baltimore & Ohio Railroad stations and elaborate Italianate-style brownstones around Mount Vernon Place. By 1870, with prosperity booming in Baltimore and more young architects arriving to take up work, five more Baltimore architects had joined the Institute, including J. Crawford Neilson (Niernsee's longtime partner), Thomas Dixon (of the city jail project), John Murdoch (Lind's former partner), Nathaniel H. Hutton, and Charles E. Cassell.

On December 10, 1870, these seven men, along with eight other architects and three engineers, joined together to form the Baltimore Chapter of the American Institute of Architects, one of the first six local chapters to be established in the country. Both Lind and Niernsee had obtained professional training in Europe and were eager to share with their apprentices and colleagues the formal recognition that such experience made possible. Charter members included Richard Snowden Andrews, who had worked in the office of Niernsee & Neilson before the war, during which he served as a Confederate artilleryman; George A. Frederick and Francis E. Davis, both apprentices with Lind & Murdoch; the B&O architect E. Francis Baldwin and Baldwin's partner Bruce Price, who had studied briefly in Europe after leaving Princeton; Charles L. Carson, Thomas Dixon's apprentice and later partner; Jackson C. Gott, who had apprenticed with a master builder in his youth; and Henry Brauns, designer of the large factory for the Knabe Piano Works in 1869. At first they held their monthly meetings in the offices of Hutton & Murdoch on Lexington Street, a few doors east of Charles, but they soon moved to permanent headquarters on the third floor of the William Lorman house (later converted by George A. Frederick to use by the Central Savings Bank), at the southeast corner of Charles and Lexington, in the heart of the enclave of architectural offices at this corner.

Establishing the AIA formally set architects apart from others in the building trades—the carpenters, masons, bricklayers, and self-tutored master builders who had contributed so much to Baltimore's built environment—and presumably also from engineers, who typi-cally concerned themselves more with function than form. However, three of the Baltimore founders, John E. Ellicott, John Wilkinson, and J. C. Wrenshall, nonetheless called them-selves engineers, and in all, the original members were a diverse lot with a wide range of ex-perience.

In the 1870s, other architects, many young, won election to the Baltimore chapter, mak-ing its professional influence increasingly important. Baldwin's associate Josias Pennington became a member not long after the chapter's founding. After service in the Union army and informal training, some of it self-directed reading in architecture, the Baltimore native Benjamin Buck Owens joined the chapter in 1873. His work later consisted of residences, churches, and industrial structures, notably, in the 1890s, plant and worker housing for the Pennsylvania Steel Company at Sparrows Point. George Archer, a Harford County native and Princeton graduate, took an apprenticeship with Frederick in about 1873, opening his own practice and joining the chapter in the spring of 1875. South Carolina–born Joseph Evans Sperry arrived in Baltimore in 1868, at the age of fourteen, and began an apprentice-ship with Dixon & Carson. He became an AIA member in 1875. John Appleton Wilson be-came a member of the chapter in 1876, after graduating from Columbian College in Washing-ton, studying architecture for two years at MIT, and working for a short time in Baldwin's offices. He, too, opened his own practice in 1877. These individuals formed a core group of architects and engineers who are credited with most of the major buildings erected in the city through the end of the century.

The national chapter of the American Institute of Architects began holding annual meet-ings in host cities with local chapters in 1868. They also began publication of the *Quarterly Record,* which contained reports on the activities of local chapters. In 1876 Baltimore hosted the ninth annual meeting in the Maryland Historical Society's headquarters in the Athenaeum building, where papers were given, drawings exhibited, and convention business discussed. Richard Morris Hunt chaired the meeting, in the absence of President Richard Upjohn, and the annual report was given by Henry Van Brunt (of Ware & Van Brunt), of the Boston chapter. Each local chapter gave its report, as did the Publications Committee and the Professional Practice Committee. The latter was given approval to publish a "tract on competitions" for distribution among the chapters. The main subject of discussion involved ensuring that there be an exhibition of architectural drawings at that year's Centennial Ex-hibition in Philadelphia, and it was resolved that the individual chapters should take such means as would be necessary in order to be properly represented at the Exhibition.[8]

When most of these gentlemen received their training, little formal architectural educa-tion was available in America. Edmund G. Lind, a native of Great Britain, trained in archi-tectural offices there; John R. Niernsee reportedly studied engineering and architecture at the University of Prague. Charles E. Cassell was trained as a naval architect and received a degree in engineering from the University of Virginia. In the absence of formal architectural training, most Baltimore architects of this period served apprenticeships in established Bal-timore offices—a process that may have contributed to a conservative tendency that has been noted in the city's design. Indeed, the list of "begats" is practically biblical. Charles Car-son received a practical education in the construction trades at the feet of his father, builder

David Carson, and spent nine years as the junior partner of Thomas Dixon before he became known as one of Baltimore's most prominent late-nineteenth-century designers in his own right. R. Snowden Andrews and E. Francis Baldwin both studied with Niernsee & Neilson; George A. Frederick entered the office of Lind & Murdoch when he was sixteen years old and worked briefly for Niernsee & Neilson before opening his own office at age twenty. Frank E. Davis worked for Lind & Murdoch before establishing his own practice in 1870; Joseph Evans Sperry was just sixteen when he first advertised his practice; his youthful enthusiasm may have been ill-advised, as he soon took down his shingle and went to work for E. Francis Baldwin to gain a few more years' experience.

As the century progressed, formal academic programs, foreign travel and study, and architectural publications offered opportunities for local architects to gain a broader perspective. Locally, the Maryland Institute offered courses in drafting from an early date; the Baltimore architect William Minifee, active in the 1840s, later taught at the institute and published a widely used textbook on architectural drawing. William H. Reasin, the designer of the institute, also taught there until his early death, just after the Civil War. Later Baltimore architects also held places on the institute's faculty and helped train aspiring practitioners; Charles Carson, for example, headed the drawing program before his death in 1891.

In 1865 the Massachusetts Institute of Technology established the first academic architectural program in the United States, and two Baltimoreans, J. B. Noel Wyatt and J. Appleton Wilson, joined the first set of students in the early 1870s. William R. Ware, the founder of MIT and, later, of Columbia's architecture school, based the course of study on the precepts of the well-known Ecole des Beaux-Arts in Paris. Two of America's foremost architects, Richard Morris Hunt and Henry Hobson Richardson, studied at the Ecole, Hunt in the 1850s and Richardson a decade later. The Ecole supplied professional training unattainable elsewhere, set high standards of draftsmanship, and introduced new ideas of monumental planning and composition. Its regimen of instruction by textbooks and "exercises in Historical Research, Historical Drawing, and Historical Designing" conveyed principles with firm bases in the classical past. In 1871 Wyatt entered the atelier of Emile Vaudremer, where Louis Sullivan had studied some years before, and remained for a term of three years.

Together with academic programs at home, architectural trade publications in these years offered a supplement to, even a substitute for, the foreign travel and study that long had been the chosen path to architectural sophistication. Following the example of the British *Building News*, first published in 1854, *American Architect and Building News* began monthly publication in New York in 1876. It supplied detailed drawings and beautifully rendered illustrations of the most stylish work being produced in New York, Paris, London, Rome, and throughout America. Like the architectural pattern books relied upon by previous generations, these widely circulated magazines provided examples of the latest trends for architects to emulate or adapt. By the late 1870s the usual phenomenon of stylistic time lags no longer obtained; a Baltimore architect could see something inspirational in *American Architect and Building News* and have his new building up within a year or two of its models' erection.

Trade magazines played an invaluable role in this creatively eclectic period, when popular styles drew on a variety of historic inspirations, often mixing forms and details, materials and massing derived from a wide range of "pure" historical styles. They regularly published carefully drawn examples of all variety of architectural parts and forms as interpreted in a wide array of historical styles, as well as detailed pictorial essays on all of the important architectural styles of the past.

It is rarely possible to attribute a building of this postwar era to a particular designer based on style alone; all competent architects could work in many styles, and this versatility was at the root of their professional stature. It was a period when "style" carried less interpretive meaning (e.g., Greek temples being appropriate for democratic public education) but was rather more to be enjoyed, in its excess, fine craftsmanship, rich materials, and vivid combinations. In an era of business growth and general economic prosperity, buildings grew larger and more pretentious. They could be larger because of new technologies and continuing engineering inventions. They assumed their pretensions from the monumental styles from which they derived; they called even more attention to themselves by the expensive and elaborate stylistic flourishes that adorned their façades and enriched their interiors.

Members of the firm pause for a photograph, probably for promotional purposes, in the office of Joseph Evans Sperry, ca. 1900. Courtesy of Michael F. Trostel and Peter Pearre

A city whose prosperity was fueled by the success of the Baltimore & Ohio Railroad, expanded foreign shipping, and the growth of large industries supported by immigrant labor thought big and created large buildings to meet the expanded needs of this expanding society. Tall office buildings, large department stores, monumental churches, impressive hotels, new schools and colleges, and major institutional buildings like the Johns Hopkins Hospital and the Enoch Pratt Free Library assumed the new scale of the mature economy and the successful city. But almost all of these structures owed as much to the new technological innovations of engineers as to the rich imagination of architects.

The choices of two young men beginning their careers in the early 1870s are especially illustrative of the new professional opportunities open to those desiring to become architects. James Bosley Noel Wyatt, a native Baltimorean who graduated from Harvard in 1870 and briefly studied architecture at MIT before departing for Paris in 1871 to complete Ecole des Beaux-Arts training, returned home in 1874 to work in the office of E. Francis Baldwin, who then practiced alone. By March 1877 Wyatt and Joseph Evans Sperry had formed a partnership, which flourished for many years and whose work illustrated the various styles Baltimore architects employed in the last decades of the century. By contrast, just as academic aesthetics pulled architects in one direction, materials science and electricity called technical men in another. After forming a partnership with John Murdoch in 1867, Nathaniel Henry Hutton, a founder and the first AIA chapter secretary, left in 1873 to open a new office, this one with his older brother, William Rich Hutton, a renowned civil engineer. The younger Hutton seems eventually to have chosen engineering over architecture; he resigned from the AIA in 1876, when he occupied the chapter president's chair, and spent the last years of his career as chief engineer of the Baltimore Harbor Board.

High Victorian Gothic and the Picturesque

Beginning in the 1850s some English architects were turning away from traditional classicism and embracing much more vivid forms of building. Influenced by the writings of the social reformer and architectural critic John Ruskin, English ecclesiastical and public architecture came to be dominated by a style known as High Victorian Gothic, which sought a freer and more creative use of traditional Gothic forms. Buildings like the highly imaginative and colorful London church St. James the Less, by G. E. Street (1858–61), relied for impact on asymmetrical massing, vivid polychromy carried out in red and black brick, and picturesque roof lines. G. G. Scott's Albert Memorial, begun in 1863, epitomized for many the High Victorian period, combining strong color contrasts and monumental forms with rich Gothic details, such as pointed arches, pinnacles, and spires. The first Ruskinian Gothic building in the United States, the National Academy of Design in New York, followed closely upon the heels of the London examples, going up in 1863. The architect, Peter Wight, designed the building in the Venetian Gothic mode, with pointed arches marked by broad bands of contrasting colored stone and the walls diapered in colored stones. In the late 1860s the Boston firm of Ware & Van Brunt designed a quintessential High Victorian Gothic building (and one of the largest), Memorial Hall at Harvard College. Following Butterfield's example, the massive structure has walls of red brick with black brick banding and a huge tower with a pyramidal roof.

Christ Episcopal Church, northwest corner of St. Paul and Chase Streets, designed by E. Francis Baldwin and Bruce Price, 1869. Enoch Pratt Free Library

In the 1870s contemporary writers in Baltimore spoke more and more frequently of the "monotonous style of architecture so disagreeably prevalent," referring to Italianate row houses and their "classically styled brethren."[9] George Howard, in *The Monumental City,* went so far as to suggest that popular tastes had been "completely fettered" by "arbitrary rules." He applauded Ruskin's efforts as having created "a complete revolution in the science of architecture abroad," but equally credited the "ambitious efforts of our energetic architects" for having created an entirely new system of architecture, "not referable to any particular style, but a combination of many which may be described as distinctly American."[10] In Baltimore, the newspapers most often referred to such new buildings as "picturesque." The style embodied a wish to draw freely from Gothic and other forms, avoid the symmetrical (with its classical associations), and experiment with picturesque shapes, colors, and materials. Picturesque architects aspired to find artistic beauty and nobility of character in natural forms, through contrasts of color and texture, and through the handcrafted work of contemporary artisans.

The style first appeared in 1869–70 with the design of several new churches in the Mount Vernon area, to be followed in the next few years by some truly monumental institutional and business buildings. Architects opted either for a restrained French Gothic manner, which relied on rock-faced white marble façades, crisply cut carved-stone Gothic ornament, and steep, picturesque roof lines, or they chose the richly polychromatic and boldly massed Ruskinian model.

Christ Church, at the corner of St. Paul and Chase Streets, designed in 1869 by E. Francis Baldwin and his partner at the time, Cumberland native and former Niernsee & Neilson apprentice Bruce Price, introduced picturesque French Gothic design, often called Norman Gothic, to the city. Its details are elegantly restrained and carried out in rough-faced white marble—narrow lancet windows, carved stone trefoils, pointed-arch doorways and window lintels, stone columns with leafy medieval capitals, and carved stone rosettes. The massing is asymmetrical, with a tall, main tower and secondary, smaller towers and spires. Baldwin & Price also designed a stone Gothic church for St. Ann's Catholic parish in what was then Baltimore County, on the York Road (later Greenmount Avenue at Twenty-second Street). It, too, had asymmetrically massed towers of different heights, as did St. Martin's Roman Catholic Church, the work of local architect Eben Faxon, in West Baltimore. A similar, white marble French Gothic–style church designed by Thomas U. Walter, the architect of the dome and wings of the United States Capitol, went up in 1871 at the southeast corner of Eutaw Place and Dolphin Street, for a Baptist congregation. Walter designed the church free of charge.

In these same years the firm of Nathaniel Henry Hutton and John Murdoch drew plans

St. Peter's became the new home of the Bethel African Methodist Episcopal Church in 1911, as the city's black elite moved to homes in northwest Baltimore near Pennsylvania Avenue.

LEFT:
Eutaw Place Baptist Church,
southeast corner of Eutaw Place
and Dolphin Street, designed by
Thomas U. Walter, 1871. From
Howard, Monumental City, *41.*

RIGHT:
St. Peter's Episcopal Church,
northwest corner Druid Hill Avenue
and West Lanvale Street, designed
by Hutton & Murdoch, 1870. From
Howard, Monumental City, *456.*

for two other rock-faced white marble Gothic churches, St. Peter's Episcopal, at West Lanvale Street and Druid Hill Avenue (now Bethel A.M.E.), and Brown Memorial Presbyterian,
at 1316 Park Avenue. Both designs reflected Norman Gothic influences in their restrained ornamental details and carved stone ornament, as well as their asymmetrical massing and
towers and spires of varying heights. For both buildings Hutton & Murdoch broadened the
naves so as to increase the general seating area. At Brown Memorial they marked the space
with huge stained-glass windows set under wide relieving arches. The design for St. Peter's,
however, called for round-headed Romanesque windows, a tall tower marked by rows of
round-arched windows and capped by a graceful spire, and a secondary castellated tower.

The most striking High Victorian Gothic church built in Baltimore was the 1872 design
of Thomas Dixon and Charles Carson, his partner since 1871, for the Mount Vernon Place
Methodist Church, the last jewel to be fitted into Mount Vernon Square (on the former site
of Charles Howard's Greek Revival town house). The massive asymmetry of the broad central nave, flanked by towers of varying heights, and the Gothic vocabulary match the form
of the French Gothic churches previously discussed. But what is different here is the rich
polychromy of the exterior, created by combining green serpentine Baltimore County

*Mount Vernon Place Methodist
Church, designed by Dixon &
Carson, 1872. Peale Collection,
Maryland Historical Society*

marble with red and buff sandstone trim. The compelling polychromatic
effects also enhance the boldly interpreted, more elaborate carved stone
decorations on the various spires and towers, framing the windows, and
marking the vigorously sculpted triple entryway. None of the colorful
stones used took kindly to carving, so the details have an appropriately naturalistic look, unlike the fine, crisp carving of Christ Church. Native flora
and fauna adorn the triple entryway and add an intimate, earthy touch—
birds eat local berries and corn, squirrels feast on acorns, and a tiny mouse
relishes grain.

The façade is distinguished by the fine springing line of the tremendous
relieving arch of sandstone, within which is framed a magnificent rose window. Fortunately the architects recognized their responsibility to create a
pleasing design for the west side of the church—marking the view along
Washington Place—and there produced a varied if crowded design with an
interesting strip clerestory. Inside, slender cast-iron columns support
pointed arches separating nave from side aisles, creating a spacious effect,
which is completed by a plaster, fan-vaulted ceiling and clerestory windows.

Almost all of Baltimore's important architects produced Ruskinian High
Victorian Gothic buildings in the 1870s. Niernsee & Neilson's YMCA Building, which the
firm designed in late 1872–73 for the triangular lot on the northwest corner of Charles and
Saratoga Streets, made a bold statement with its red brick and striking sandstone trim framing groups of triple-arched windows and its dormered mansard roof topped with towers,
turrets, and an elaborate ironwork cresting rail. The main façade was marked by corner
towers with tall roofs, and the entrance was flanked by two Gothic-inspired turrets, which
also rose beyond the roof line. Both the entire first story and the corner tower were stone.
To help support the activities of the Y, the ground floor was outfitted as retail spaces and
storerooms, to bring in revenue. Upstairs, a grand hall and lecture room, triangular in shape,

rose three stories in height, ringed with galleries and capable of seating twelve hundred people. The building contained classrooms and a library on the third floor, while the fourth was devoted to the two gymnasiums. Described at its time of erection as having "something of a collegiate character," the building clearly brought to mind similar uses of the High Victorian Gothic style on campuses like Harvard and Yale.[11]

In 1874, on the west side of the 500 block of North Howard Street, the same office oversaw completion of the even more ornate Academy of Music. Not dissimilar to the YMCA in its design components, the façade featured the polychromy of red brick with sandstone trim, sets of triple-arched windows, and a steep French roof of polychromatic slate with dormer windows, finials, and a fancy iron-work cresting rail. The building was designed to provide a grand concert hall, opera house, and theater for the city, combining features offered in other, older buildings, such as Ford's Opera House and Concordia Hall, into one modern building with greater seating capacities. The marble-floored entrance hall was flanked by two "exquisitely frescoed" and brilliantly lighted cafes and led to two 14-foot-wide grand stairways "beautifully painted in decorated panels." The stairs led to the 100-foot-long concert and lecture room, with arcaded galleries, a dancing floor, and a seating capacity of twelve hundred persons. The main feature of the building was the Grand Opera House, with its lobby, galleried auditorium, and large stage. The ceiling boasted elaborate frescoes, a "Crystal Dome," and a great crystal chandelier with 240 candle-shaped burners lit by an electric battery. The walls were traced in gilt and colors, and the "tout ensemble" was "the expression of highest art and the most cultivated taste."[12]

Dixon & Carson followed a Venetian Gothic, Ruskinian example for the office of Alexander Brown & Sons, completed on West Baltimore Street in the early 1870s. The architects richly banded the façade, using contrasting colors of stone to accentuate the pointed arches,

arcaded windows, floor levels, and elaborate cornice piece. The same firm's 1874 St. James
Hotel, which stood on the southwest corner of Charles and Centre Streets, more closely resembles English High Victorian Gothic styles, with a polychrome façade and an abundance
of steep dormers and pointy turrets that made the firm's nearby Mount Vernon Place
Methodist Church look tame.

In the mid-1870s George A. Frederick designed the massive polychromatic Abell Building, facing Eutaw Street and extending the entire block south from Baltimore to Redwood
Streets. Its owner, Arunah S. Abell, founder of the *Baltimore Sun,* built it as a speculative venture, rightly expecting clothing manufacturers and their suppliers to move into the area. It
opened in 1879 with cast iron from Bartlett, Robbins & Company (in the same neo-Grec
style used at the Peabody Library) framing the storefronts on the ground level. Frederick
trimmed the exuberant five-story brick structure above with banded patterns of bluestone
and white-marble trim, intricate brickwork, and decorative terra cotta details. Its expanse—
six bays on Baltimore Street and nineteen bays on Eutaw Street—produced a breathtaking
effect.

Late-nineteenth-century Baltimoreans pointed with great pride to institutions that transformed American higher education and medical science—the Johns Hopkins University,
Hospital, and, eventually, Medical School. Clustered near the intersection of Howard and
West Monument Streets, the university buildings attracted little notice in their day. The architecture of the hospital, however, attracted great interest at the time and has become
closely identified with the city itself. The Johns Hopkins Hospital provides a classic example
of Ruskinian High Victorian Gothic.

The Hopkins trustees appointed John Rudolph Niernsee, then in his sixties, as architectural consultant, and in 1876 he drew up plans based on a revolutionary idea developed by
the army physician and student of hospital design John Shaw Billings. The scheme proposed

twenty or more buildings arranged on fourteen acres of land "crowning one of the hills upon which Baltimore is built." Billings laid out the hospital with the idea of combating "hospitalism," the spreading of infections that plagued conventionally designed structures. He called for a main building with double wings facing Broadway, its rear (beyond a detached apothecary) leading to a garden space along which flanking wards would stand, connected by covered walkways but separated so as to admit light and air. Boilers of 80,000-gallon capacity heated the buildings with hot water in winter; ventilation in the warmer months relied on large windows but included a system of electrical exhaust fans. Interior spaces employed curves, avoiding right-angle corners and moldings above panels, which collect dust. Billings derided cheapness and speed of construction as false economies.[13]

Work on the administration building began in June 1877, following a design the trustees had accepted from the Boston firm of Cabot & Chandler. It featured local red brick set off by bands of Cheat River stone, a fine-grained blue stone; a picturesque roof line offering a vivid massing of tall chimneys, towers, turrets, and dormers; a projecting central bay marked by tall pilasters framing sets of triple windows, with a clock set in the end gable above an entrance portico, and polygonal end bays. Molded brick and terra cotta panels decorating the cornice line and set beneath window groupings showed the latest design motifs—naturalistic carvings and the obligatory sunflowers of the contemporary Queen Anne style. The high central tower, its roof sheathed in copper and topped by a spire, gave notice of the building's presence from the harbor and for miles around. Beneath, skylights lit an impressive galleried rotunda. The two

Home to clothing and dry-goods wholesalers until 1891, the Abell Building for many years thereafter provided a home to Friedenwald Lithographers, printers of various bird's-eye views of the city. It remains standing today.

Abell Building, designed by George A. Frederick and completed in the late 1870s. From Howard, Monumental City, *832.*
RIGHT:
Original block plan of the Johns Hopkins Hospital, design by John Shaw Billings and John R. Niernsee, 1876. Alan Mason Chesney Medical Archives, The Johns Hopkins Medical Institutions

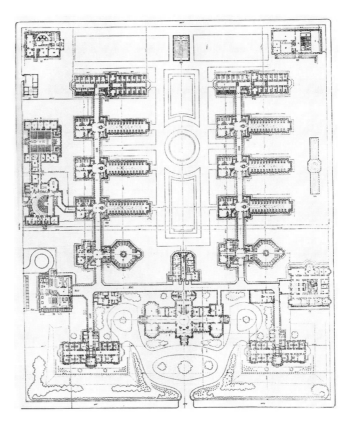

The domed rotunda of the
administration building.
Photograph by Edwin
Remsberg, 1997

RIGHT:

The Johns Hopkins Hospital
administration building and, in the
foreground, the Wilmer building,
designed by Cabot & Chandler of
Boston, as it appeared from the
southwest ca. 1890. Maryland
Historical Society

In 1977 the hospital adopted a
new building plan, which left
standing only the original main
building and the advanced Marburg and Wilmer wings.

end towers boasted lesser spires. During construction Niernsee served as overseer, parceling out work to building firms in Baltimore and Washington. The project went on for twelve
years and ran into a combination of rising costs and lagging endowment income. As built,
the hospital realized just one of the rows of wards Billings and Niernsee had envisioned, but
it still gained fame as the most modern hospital in the world. It helped bring about such
medical advances as the use of disinfectants, which made isolated wards unnecessary.

Another important civic building that owed its existence to Baltimore's philanthropists,
the Enoch Pratt Free Library, rose in Victorian Gothic splendor in 1882–83. Designed by
Charles Carson, by then working independently, the library, fronting on Mulberry Street,
near Cathedral, featured a tall central tower capped by a polygonal roof with details reminiscent of Richardson's Trinity Church. The two-story front, carried out in "roughened"
Beaver Dam white marble, with "polished granite pillars and pilasters" supporting the
arched windows, showed an amazingly free and creative use of decorative forms derived
from classical, Renaissance, Venetian, and Romanesque sources and made a vivid contrast
to its highly restrained Greek Revival residential neighbors.[14]

Noting that the style of architecture was "Romanesque," the *Sun* called attention to the
busts of Shakespeare, Scott, Webster, Irving, and Franklin above the windows, as well as the
bas-reliefs of History, Poetry, and Eloquence just below the roof of the central tower. The
writer was equally enthusiastic about the interior. The broad, round arch of the entrance,
supported by pinkish marble columns with black marble bases and white capitals, led
through heavy mahogany doors to a hallway with dove-colored marble wainscoting and
enameled tile walls, in hues of blue, buff, chocolate, white, and black. The first-floor main
rooms, where books were shelved, were finished in old oak, "including counters, window

frames, and antique chimney pieces," with floors of marble. The reading room on the second story was a huge space—thirty-seven by seventy-five feet with a twenty-four-foot-high ceiling, decorated with frescoed walls, marble wainscoting, and a heavily paneled ceiling with gilt molding at the cornice line. The large arched windows had circular transoms of stained glass bearing portraits of well-known European writers and poets.[15]

Enoch Pratt Free Library, Mulberry Street, west of Cathedral Street, designed by Charles Carson, 1882. Lithograph view from "In and About Baltimore," Harper's Weekly, *September 7, 1889.*

Carson also designed the four identical branch libraries that opened at the same time, in a brick version of Romanesque architecture with buff stone trim and tall slate roofs. All of the buildings were fireproof, as was the main library. The branches fulfilled Pratt's expressed intention of serving the needs of people, "rich and poor, without distinction of race or color."[16] Citizens could check out books from libraries conveniently located in northwest Baltimore, near the Lafayette Market; in West Baltimore, near the Hollins Market; in south Baltimore, near the Cross Street Market; and in Canton, near the Canton Market.

Not surprisingly, Baltimore's biggest corporation, the Baltimore & Ohio Railroad, built the first tall office building in Baltimore. Designed by Baldwin & Pennington and finished in 1882, the B&O headquarters building stood seven stories tall on the northwest corner of Baltimore and Calvert Streets and confronted the heart of the city with eclectic bluster. Built of red brick with dark bluestone trim over an iron frame, it combined the same High Victorian Gothic color contrasts as the Abell Building, with even fancier ornamental details. It boasted banks of alternating arcaded and rectangular-cut windows, all trimmed in stone; broad stone belt courses; and a gigantic two-story mansard roof capped with elaborate terra cotta cresting and marked by multiple dormers. Decorative terra cotta panels were set beneath the windows, in the brick dormers, and in the main piers. In the original design, the Baltimore Street façade boasted a tall clock tower with soaring spire, but this was replaced by a second pavilion mirroring that of the Calvert Street façade.[17] The two-story entryway was fortresslike, with heavy granite plinths, decorated by sculptured railroad-car wheels, supporting paired polished granite columns and a massive pediment of bluestone. *American Architect and Building News* noted that "the color of the entire mass is dark" but that this was relieved by "the fanciful coloring of the roofwork," with its second tier of dormers, roof angles, and elaborate cornice carried out in two shades of very light brown brick, the lighter "exactly the tint of the yellow terra-cotta cresting crowning the black slate roof."[18] Few Baltimore façades have ever been "busier" or more complicated; the showy boldness of the design clearly announced the national importance of the railroad.

Illustrating well the penchant of the time for architectural flourish, the federal government erected a new Post Office building, just east of the Battle Monument in the early 1880s; it may have been the most purposefully picturesque and eclectic building in the city. A massive, four-story stone structure capped by a busy roof line replete with tall tower and many smaller turrets, it established a formidable federal presence on Monument Square. Replacing three-story town houses—including what once had been Guy's Monument House Hotel—it also completely changed the scale of the square. Impressive though the structure may have been, much discussion arose in the newspapers in 1883 regarding the extensive

Baltimore & Ohio Railroad Building, northwest corner of Baltimore and Calvert Streets, designed by Baldwin & Pennington and completed in 1882. Enoch Pratt Free Library

RIGHT:

United States Post Office, east side of Monument Square, completed 1884. From The Monumental City, the Liverpool of America: A Souvenir of the 121st Anniversary of the Baltimore American, *2 vols. (Baltimore,1894–95), 1: [1]. Enoch Pratt Free Library*

This post office came down in 1930 to make way for a new post office and federal courthouse.

changes made to the original design by the supervising architect, James Green Hill. The *Sun* complained that the original design, which would be an "ornament to the city" and bear comparison with City Hall—"the great municipal structure of white marble alongside of which it is to stand"—had been stripped so bare of ornamentation as to no longer warrant the public funds contributed. The paper called upon Charles E. Cassell to ascertain the facts and then published his detailed analysis of the design changes. Cassell concluded that the changes marked a serious reduction in the amount of carving and other sculptural decoration promised in the original design and complained that the new version would be "commonplace" and "severely plain." Apparently the uproar had some effect, for the building as finished reintroduced some of the ornament originally called for.[19]

Picturesque and Queen Anne Housing

Devotees of the eclectic style applied their art to entire residential quarters of the late-nineteenth-century city, as the area known as Mount Vernon expanded farther and farther north to the city's old boundary, now known as North Avenue. Along and parallel to Charles and St. Paul Streets, from Chase Street north to the Jones Falls, two large properties became available for development in 1873. Here, along the 1000 to 1300 blocks of Maryland, Charles, St. Paul, and Calvert Streets, spacious lots were purchased by both individual homebuilders and by speculative developers. A fashionable neighborhood quickly came into being, one that offered ready employment for the city's growing number of architects and patrons who could afford the best that architects had to offer. The highly praised results offered picturesque and varied streetscapes that Baltimoreans could be proud of. Similar development occurred slightly later on Eutaw Place, the city's other prominent residential area.

Bruce Price and E. Francis Baldwin built the first picturesque houses in the Mount Vernon area, a group of three houses erected in 1872, just west of their Christ Church. They designed the houses according to compatible French Gothic standards, employing local white marble and enhancing their façades with all kinds of decorative Gothic details—boldly framed, pointed-arch doorways and windows; columns with carved lintels; carved stone trefoils; and, above it all, pointed roof dormers set into a steep French Gothic mansard. Soon Dixon & Carson had designed a similar group of three marble-fronted houses on the east side of the 1100 block of St. Paul Street (just around the corner), with steep mansard roofs, medieval-style dormers, and Gothic incised decoration on the stone door and window lintels. In 1877 A. S. Abell hired Charles Cassell to design a group of ten very expensive French Gothic picturesque-style marble-fronted and mansard-roofed dwellings on the southwest corner of Charles Street and present-day North Avenue. Replete with ornamental stone carvings of gargoyles, lions' heads, and stone capitals, the houses, priced at $15,000 to $20,000, were noted by the *Sun* as among the most expensive in the city. That same year the building developer George Blake hired Dixon & Carson to design a row of eight marble-fronted houses with elaborate Gothic detailing in the 1200 block of St. Paul Street.

Meanwhile, British architects were ransacking the late-medieval English past for fresh forms, admiring cottage-style red brick and stucco and half-timbered exteriors, turrets, terra cotta panels, molded and cut brick, colored glass in old sashes, and wrought-iron balconies. One of them, Richard Norman Shaw, created what came to be known as the Queen Anne style, combining asymmetrical massing, variegated roof lines, red brick decorated with glazed tiles, terra cotta, carved brick ornament, and stained glass. For decorative elements, designers like William Morris Hunt preferred to draw upon natural forms for inspiration, interpreted through handcraftsmanship. Sunflowers became favorite forms of this Aesthetic movement and were used in all manner of ways to decorate façades. Natural leaf forms, twining vines, and flowers were also popular. Shaw's design for the New Zealand Chambers in London (1871–72) became the model for many urban Queen Anne residences in America soon after it appeared in *Building News* in 1873. A few years later, an architectural critic in New York announced in *Harper's* that the Queen Anne style was "a delightful insurrection against the monotonous era of rectangular building."[20] In America, the precepts of the Queen Anne style most commonly found their way into residential architecture.

The Queen Anne style arrived in Baltimore in 1876, when John Appleton Wilson designed a house on the southeast corner of St. Paul and Biddle Streets for William T. Wilson, his cousin. A year later the architect designed a matching house on the northeast corner of the same intersection, this one for George C. Wilkens, an English-born civil engineer who later became general manager of the Pennsylvania Railroad. The Wilkens house, which the *Sun* called "very striking," had an exterior of pressed brick, some black brick and tile, black mortar, a black slate roof with red bands, and "a handsome wrought iron balcony." Its interior imitated decorative elements in the height of British Shavian fashion: tile-lined fireplaces,

12–16 East Chase Street, designed by Bruce Price and E. Francis Baldwin, 1872. Photograph by J. Brough Schamp

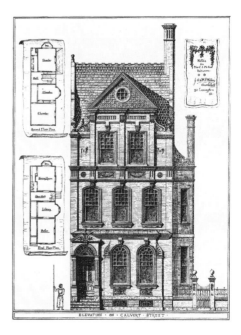

TOP:

George C. Wilkens house, northeast corner of St. Paul and Biddle Streets, designed by J. Appleton Wilson, 1876. J. Appleton Wilson Collection, Maryland Historical Society

RIGHT:

McKim house, 1035 North Calvert Street, designed by J. Appleton Wilson and completed in 1879, when this elevation and plan appeared in American Architect and Building News. *Courtesy of Mary Ellen Hayward*

BOTTOM:

East side of Belvidere Terrace, designed by J. Appleton Wilson, 1878, as it appeared in the late twentieth century. Photograph by J. Brough Schamp

glazed pictorial tile facings, elaborately carved hardwood mantels (those on the first floor having "mirrors, shelving, etc."), and plaster in all rooms sand finished "for decoration."[21]

Wilson's forays in the Queen Anne manner included two major commissions for Catherine L. McKim, one of the heirs of the last five and a half acres of the Howard estate, Belvidere. The McKim family had occupied Belvidere since 1843; in the mid-1870s, they decided to develop this prime property; they demolished the old house, and the city then extended Calvert Street through the grounds. Wishing to have a new house built for herself, Mrs. McKim hired Wilson to design it, as well as a row of fourteen adjacent houses. Her own home came first, and Wilson gave its façade a more sophisticated and complex design than that of the Wilkens house, articulating the façade with bands of brick and terra cotta ornaments and making use of specific details as seen in Richard Norman Shaw's New Zealand Chambers and other published English examples. Completed in 1879, the house faced Calvert Street with a gabled façade that bore richly carved stone and terra cotta details. *American Architect and Building News* praised its finely executed front, "of the finest quality red pressed brick, laid in red mortar, with all string courses, mouldings, etc. of 'Peerless' brick, which give nearly as true and sharp a line as cut stone." All of the other "decorations, carved work, sills, etc." were of "red terra cotta from Perth Amboy, New Jersey." The basement was of red granite, with roofs "of black slate with red terra cotta crestings."[22]

South of the McKim house on the same block, Wilson, by this time in partnership with his cousin William, designed a row that completed one side of a double file of Queen Anne houses, an ensemble that became known as Belvidere Terrace. Using three different façade designs, the Wilsons grouped the houses in sets of 3–2–4–2–3, the four dwellings in the cen-

House of Ross Winans, east side 1200 block of St. Paul Street, designed by McKim, Mead & White, 1882, as it appeared in American Architect and Building News, *April 30, 1887. Maryland Historical Society*

ter being of white marble, the rest of red brick. The three houses on each end replicated the Dutch-gable roofline of the McKim house and boasted highly elaborate wrought-iron balconies and large terra cotta panels decorated with sunflowers, one of the symbols of the Aesthetic movement, which had spawned such architecture.

On the west side of the street, the firm of J. B. Noel Wyatt and Joseph Evans Sperry designed a row of twenty-three houses for another member of the family, Rev. R. A. McKim. The architects composed their block face of no fewer than seven different façade designs, carried out in red brick with brownstone trim, consisting of varied combinations of arched and pedimented doors and windows, Dutch gables, and end gables. Both rows made use of stylish multipaned upper windows, molded and cut brick, and terra cotta sunflower decorations. The Baltimore correspondent for *American Architect and Building News* praised Belvidere Terrace on its completion in 1882 as architecturally the "handsomest" of any block in the city.[23]

A Visit from McKim, Mead & White

Just as Baltimore's young architects were influenced by what they read in *American Architect and Building News* or London's *Building News,* when a trend-setting, nationally famous architect came to town, they sat up and took notice. In the early 1880s, Stanford White, of the important New York firm McKim, Mead & White, journeyed to Baltimore to design a majestic chateau in the 1200 block of St. Paul Street for Ross R. Winans, grandson of the pioneer builder of steam locomotives for the B&O Railroad of the same name and son of Thomas DeKay Winans, the builder of Alexandroffsky, in west Baltimore.

White brought to Baltimore his own firsthand knowledge of the work of Henry Hobson Richardson, who was pioneering a new American style of architecture based on adapting the style and honesty of materials of pre-Gothic Romanesque architecture to the institutional needs of the growing country. The first American architect to design with polychromatic, rock-faced stone—his Trinity Church on Boston's Copley Square went up in the early 1870s—Richardson had also used High Victorian Gothic trim on the earliest parts of the building. By the 1880s, however, he had fully embraced the naturalism of round-arched Romanesque forms and massing.

For the Winans house White combined features of the Richardsonian Romanesque style with the more fanciful "chateauesque" designs favored by the New York architect and Ecole-trained Richard Morris Hunt. He gave his client an impressive, castlelike structure, which relied on both rock-faced stone and wide, round Romanesque arches for effect but which also included allusions to the medieval chateaus of the French Renaissance of François I. The façade of the house—brownstone on the first story, pressed brick with brownstone trim above—bespoke vigorous asymmetry. Anchored by a three-story turret articulated by multipaned, leaded windows and naturalistic terra cotta panels, the three-story structure boasted steeply pitched gable roofs, tall chimneys, and a mélange of medieval and highly original decorative details. The arched entryway and bold arched window suggested Romanesque influences, but the adjacent windows with their iron grates harked

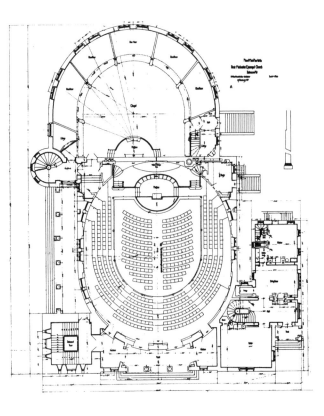

First Methodist Episcopal Church,
northwest corner St. Paul and
Twenty-second Streets, designed by
Stanford White ca. 1884 and
completed in 1887. Lovely Lane
Church Archives

RIGHT:

First Methodist Episcopal Church,
gallery and parsonage floor plans,
ca. 1883, McKim, Mead & White.
Lovely Lane Church Archives

back to the medieval. The steep French roof was punctuated with boldly designed dormer windows decorated with elaborate terra cotta pediments, one with the date stone "1882."

To the south of the house White provided a walled garden and separate carriage entrance. The rich interior details included elegant burnished oak, teak, and mahogany woodwork, often with rich carvings; a lavishly ornamented staircase with parquet walls; inlaid wood flooring; elaborate and ornate fireplaces; tapestry-covered walls in the first-floor hall; and delicate chandeliers. Clearly, Winans spared no expense, and the house, with its tower, corresponding rounded-bay at the rear, steeply pitched roof, excellent ironwork and stained glass, and tall, distinctive chimneys, attracted much notice. In the spring of 1887 it, too, appeared in the American architects' magazine of record.

While at work on the Winans house White designed one of the great Baltimore churches of the period, and, through it, clearly showed the power of Romanesque forms on the eclectic imagination. In 1884 the First Methodist Church, trying like so many other congregations to keep pace with the migration of its members, elected to move north from Lovely Lane to a site beyond Boundary (later North) Avenue at what became St. Paul and Twenty-second Streets. The Reverend Dr. John F. Goucher, well educated and traveled, chaired the new building committee, and the commission for the church went to White, who arrived in Baltimore carrying a sketchbook full of notes on medieval French and Italian buildings. He had assisted Richardson in Boston by overseeing completion of the master's Trinity Church, but Lovely Lane represented his first independent ecclesiastical design. White shared Richardson's enthusiasm for emphasizing the rugged masculine character of stone, laid up in large, simple Romanesque masses with round-arched openings, as opposed to the thinner, smoother walls, pointed arches, and sharper accents of mid-nineteenth-century Gothic church construction.[24]

Following his mentor's example, White designed for Lovely Lane a large, simple, massive form, executed in masonry, which gave an overall impression of weight, strength, power, and durability. As in Richardson's work, the development of the building's overall form proceeded from an understanding of its intended purpose, with the plan organized to suit the function. In this case the pastor desired a large preaching space, and White obliged by creating an oval-shaped auditorium with a balcony extending around three sides.

Goucher Hall of the Women's College of Baltimore, with Lovely Lane Church in the background, west side of St. Paul Street, north of Twenty-second Street, designed by Charles L. Carson and completed in 1887. Maryland Historical Society

Richardson freely used historical ornamental motifs from various European sources, but he combined them in creative new ways that he felt enhanced the sense of a building's purpose. (At Trinity Church, for example, he used sources from Auvergne in the east façade, Provence on the west front, and modeled the tall, pyramidal lantern on the Old Cathedral of Salamanca in Spain.) White's tall, rugged granite bell tower on the southeast corner of the church, tapering slightly as it rises with fortresslike pierced openings, traced directly to the little-known twelfth-century brick church of Santa Maria in Pomposa, near Ravenna. White eliminated the Lombardic detail but kept the stringcourses, the corner extrusions, and the curious flared, conical roof. Growing out of the body of the church rather than merely standing next to it, the tower dramatizes the finely three-dimensional structure. The coarsely textured wall surfaces of this building are perfectly complemented by the symmetrical pattern of the heavy red-tiled roof. By its sheer force of design, White's First Methodist Church, completed in 1887, may approach Latrobe's cathedral as Baltimore's most monumental structure. The early-twentieth-century architectural critic Lewis Mumford rated the tower as "surely one of the finest that has been erected in America."[25]

Adjacent to Lovely Lane Church, on the north, Methodist elders built the campus of the Women's College of Baltimore, founded in 1885 by Rev. Dr. John F. Goucher, and later renamed in his honor. Goucher asked Charles Carson to design a college building to harmonize with the church, and two years later builders completed the similarly rock-faced granite Romanesque Goucher Hall, roofed in red tile like the church. Broad Romanesque arches define the entrance portico and the second-story windows, and ornamental detail is kept to a minimum. Two other compatible Romanesque buildings, Bennett Hall and Catherine Hooper Hall, rose a few years later to the north. Both were designed by McKim, Mead & White, with White identified as the architect in charge.[26]

Publicly Romanesque

The firm of Wyatt & Sperry produced Baltimore's finest Richardsonian commercial building, the Mercantile-Safe Deposit & Trust Company of 1885–86. Carried out in red brick with light red freestone trim, this highly ornamented bank building is distinguished from other commercial structures in the city by its bold, expressive, Romanesque features: simple, heavy massing, broad roof planes, dramatic windows, and finely carved stonework detail. Two huge, round-arched windows dominate the fortresslike brick mass of the façade, which was illustrated in *American Architect and Building News* in May 1885.[27] Squat, medieval stone columns flank the wide entranceway, frame a set of first-floor windows, and mark the panels beneath the huge arches. Inside, the grand banking floor was lit by skylights. In a stroke of great fortune for the city's architectural heritage, the building survived the 1904 fire, although the interior had to be entirely rebuilt.

Another building sporting huge, rounded arches reached completion in 1888, the department store designed by Baldwin & Pennington for the Hutzler Brothers Company on North Howard Street. Many German-Jewish fortunes had been made in the dry-goods business, and as the city's population grew in the last decades of the century, the smaller dry-goods houses began to expand into elegant, palatial department stores. Hutzler Brothers began business in 1858 in an old house in the 200 block of North Howard Street, later bought two adjacent houses and linked them together, and in 1874 expanded again. By 1886, with business booming, they decided to build on a much larger and more dramatic scale. They tore down everything they owned on several corner lots and commissioned Baldwin & Pennington to design Baltimore's first planned department store, a marvel of picturesque design.

The *Sun* praised the store as "one of the largest and best-arranged buildings of its kind in the United States," noting that the design was "Romanesque," and carefully described both exterior and interior details. The buff stone exterior was set off by the copper that framed the windows of the polygonal bays to each side of the main entrance block and by a copper-

LEFT:

Mercantile-Safe Deposit & Trust Company, northeast corner of Calvert and Redwood Streets, designed by Wyatt & Sperry in 1885. Maryland Historical Society

RIGHT:

Hutzler Bros Store, *212–218 North Howard Street, designed by Baldwin & Pennington, 1886. From* Frank Leslie's Illustrated Weekly, Supplement, *October 27, 1888. Courtesy of Arthur J. Gutman*

·HUTZLER·BROS·STORE·

and-slate-covered turret capping the oriel, which marked the northern corner. At the center of the building rose a three-story-high Moorish arch leading to a vestibule laid in mosaic tiling and opalescent glass. Elaborate stone carving, consisting of foliage, arabesques, and occasional heads, marked the various floor levels, and atop it all a band of windows set between clusters of stone pillars supported a pediment bearing the "figure of the Goddess of Justice" and the firm's name, carved in relief on "flowing bands." Inside, novel chandeliers of polished steel and brass, designed by the Hutzlers, lighted a selling floor half an acre in size, its open spaces and upper galleries supported by slender iron columns. Hutzler called it the Palace Building.[28]

By the late 1880s Baldwin & Pennington had become particularly associated with the Richardsonian Romanesque style. In 1889 they designed a new home for the Maryland Club just north of Mount Vernon Place, at the southeast corner of Charles and Eager Streets. Much more restrained in interpretation than the Hutzler building, the structure—with its rock-faced Beaver Dam marble façades, asymmetrical massing, corner turret, and varied roof lines, all carried out in red tile—nonetheless established a commanding presence. Three wide arches marked the entrance front; arcaded loggias at the third-floor level carried out the Romanesque themes. Squat medieval columns supported the central arch and flanked the wide marble steps. Baldwin & Pennington's Romanesque Mount Royal Station followed only a few years later.

Similar Romanesque design features appeared in the Associate Reformed Church, at the northwest corner of Preston Street at Maryland Avenue. Designed by Charles Cassell and constructed in 1889, the church featured a circular plan, with massive, roughly-textured walls of Port Deposit granite enlivened with layered levels of arcaded windows, a deep semicircular porch with paired, round-arched entryways, the whole capped by pitched and conical red-tiled roofs. As at Lovely Lane, the complex was dominated by the central, auditorium-style space.[29]

Today, Hutzler's Palace Building stands empty, at 212–218 North Howard Street.

LEFT:
Maryland Club, southeast corner of Charles and Eager Streets, designed by Baldwin & Pennington, 1889. Enoch Pratt Free Library

RIGHT:
Associate Reformed Church, northwest corner of Maryland Avenue and Preston Street, designed by Charles Cassell, 1889. Enoch Pratt Free Library

In 1937 the Associate Reformed
Church became the Greek
Orthodox Cathedral of the
Annunciation, which it
remains to this day.

Two other striking, rock-faced white marble Romanesque-style religious structures were completed during these years. Beginning in the late 1870s Baltimore's wealthy German-Jewish elite had begun to build impressive homes along Eutaw Place, the Berlin-like boulevard that ended at the entrance to Druid Hill Park. Naturally, they needed their places of worship to follow them from East Baltimore to this new neighborhood, and the several different congregations hired architects who had already designed impressive homes in the neighborhood.

The first synagogue, the work of Charles Carson in 1890–91 for the Baltimore Hebrew Congregation, graced the northeast corner of Madison and Robert Streets, a half block west of Eutaw Place. Its design featured a cruciform shape with central dome and wide, round arches marking the entryway and nave window. The most striking features, however, were the two very tall towers at the front of the church which rose high above the dome, "in minaret form," and were topped by open arcades set beneath smaller domes. The *Sun* noted that from the outset the congregation had wanted a design in the "Byzantine" style, unlike anything yet built in the city, and had sent a building committee to New York, Albany, Philadelphia, and Washington, D.C., to examine the finest examples of Byzantine architecture in the country. The committee felt it appropriate to take the temple design from Oriental sources, "in accord with the origin of the religion in whose service it is built." The building was constructed of Port Deposit granite, with a dome-shaped roof of red and brown Spanish tiles and sandstone carvings. The interior, with its round arches, vaults, dome, and richly carved capitals, seemed the perfect embodiment of Byzantine architecture.[30]

Baltimore Hebrew Congregation Synagogue, northeast corner of Madison and Robert Streets, designed by Charles L. Carson, 1890. The Jewish Museum of Maryland, 1987.109.2

Similarly Romanesque in inspiration, with the same touch of Byzantine flair in deference to the client, Joseph Evans Sperry's Oheb Shalom Synagogue went up at the northeast corner of Eutaw Place and Lanvale Street in 1891–93. Sperry carried out the massive exterior in rock-faced Beaver Dam marble; it featured multiple banks of round-arched openings similar to those Cassell had used at the Associate Reformed Church. The towering red-tiled central dome marked the city skyline from all directions and covered an interior resembling that of a mosque. Two smaller domes topped the corner towers of the almost biblical fortresslike façade. Inside, Sperry provided a brightly lit open sanctuary, a central court with a second-story balcony surrounding it on three sides. This wonderful Moorish-inspired space could accommodate more than two thousand persons in prayer. Both synagogues were among the most impressive places of worship in Baltimore, their size and majesty helping to identify their neighborhood for generations.

Although by the early 1890s new architectural styles had made an appearance in Baltimore, certain types of projects still seemed best suited to Romanesque interpretation. In 1894 Jackson Gott designed a new Maryland penitentiary, adjoining Thomas Dixon's old City Jail east of the Jones Falls. Built on a massive scale a few years later, the forbidding building closely followed Richardsonian Romanesque models. A multistory administration building capped by a soaring pyramidal roof and marked by conical corner turrets anchored two wings of four-story cellblocks. Window units in both the main block and the prison

Oheb Shalom Synagogue, northeast
corner Eutaw Place and Lanvale
Street, designed by Joseph E. Sperry,
1891. The Jewish Museum of
Maryland Institutional Archives

TOP, RIGHT:
Maryland State Penitentiary,
designed by Jackson Gott, 1893, as it
appeared in American Architect
and Building News, no. 929 (1893).

BOTTOM:
Western High School, Lafayette
Avenue and McCulloh Street,
designed by Alfred Mason, 1895.
Enoch Pratt Free Library

The Maryland Prince Hall Masons
acquired Oheb Shalom temple in
1960 and have maintained it
ever since.

wings were framed by round-arched openings that matched the wide, round arches of the
entryway and its flanking windows. The sentrylike shape of the corner towers was echoed
in the piers that marched down the front of each cellblock.

Schools, too, seemed to convey the right message of stability and strength if designed in
the Romanesque style. In 1895 the city awarded Alfred Mason, an early member of the Baltimore chapter of the AIA, the design contract for Western High School at Lafayette Avenue
and McCulloh Street. The looming four-story turreted structure was built of red brick with
carved Seneca stone trim and sported a very picturesque roof line. Many details resembled
those of the penitentiary: the central tower with its pyramidal roof, the wide, round arches
articulating entrance ways, the corner turrets with conical roofs, and the fenestration pattern, with vertical groups of windows capped by round arches.

Late Picturesque Houses

As Richardsonian Romanesque designs began to make their influence felt in the architecture of Baltimore churches and other major buildings, the tenets of the style began to be
adapted for row-house design as well. By the mid-1880s, in both the fashionable Mount Vernon and Eutaw Place neighborhoods, architects were designing individual town houses and

impressive rows featuring rock-faced stone façades of varying colors, often with projecting, rounded bays capped with stone porches and sometimes corner turrets. There seemed to be no end to the elaborate stonework, stained glass, and carved terra cotta ornament embellishing these houses, for which no expense was spared. Unlike the white marble or light-grey Port Deposit granite preferred for institutional buildings, row-house builders experimented with the green serpentine stone used for the Mount Vernon Place Methodist Church, sandstone, brownstone, and red granite, thus giving their houses a more solid and substantial appearance.

Dixon & Carson's row, built over the course of the 1880s on the west side of the 1200 block of North Charles Street, perfectly summarizes the shifts in taste of these years. The developer George Blake first hired the partners in 1881 to design a group of four four-story houses at the northernmost end of the block. These Gothic-style houses resembled those the pair had done earlier in the 1200 block of St. Paul Street. The first two, of white marble, seemed usual enough, but the next two had façades of "a serpentine stone of greenish color" from Chester, Pennsylvania, the *Sun* reported, thereby giving the houses a "novel and striking" appearance. Quickly recovering his investment, Blake next asked Carson alone to complete the row. His next group of four houses, built in 1883, with brownstone and dark green stone façades, dazzled the viewer and illustrated the stylistic shift away from marble to picturesque stone.[31] Carson and Blake completed the row by the late 1880s in rock-faced brownstone and red Seneca stone, and this last group of houses featured the wide, round-arched openings associated with the Romanesque style.

TOP:

West side, 1200 block of North Charles Street, designed by Dixon & Carson, 1881–85, in the late twentieth century. Photograph by J. Brough Schamp

BOTTOM:

Eutaw Place, from the northwest, 1903. Library of Congress

Similar dark, rock-faced-stone late picturesque-style houses went up on Mount Royal Terrace and on Eutaw Place, designed by the same core group of architects for the city's wealthiest clients. By the 1880s the newly developing upper portions of Eutaw Place were the residential place of choice for Baltimore's wealthy German-Jewish community. Owners of the city's primary department stores, dry-goods businesses, and garment manufactories—the Hutzlers, Hochschilds, Bragers, Gutmans, Strouses, Sonneborns, and Hechts, to name a few—built town palaces on Eutaw Place that rivaled the scale and luxury of Stanford White's Winans house. The 1800 block of Eutaw Place, developed in the late 1880s, has some of the largest and most elaborate picturesque-style houses in the city, anchored by the monumental David Hutzler mansion, at the northeast corner of Laurens Street, designed by Thomas C. Kennedy in 1887 for Martin Hawley and purchased a decade later by Hutzler. The forty-five by eighty-two-foot mansion was constructed of red granite with an irregular roof line of red tile, a "round corner outlook tower," copper roof finials, and broad arched Romanesque doorways. The *Sun* noted that all of the rooms were finished in different woods.[32] At a cost of $70,000, the house vied in grandeur with most any built in the city.

On the west side of the block, at 1802, the fifty-foot-wide Ohio sandstone mansion Charles Carson designed in 1889 for the banker German H. Hunt boasted a corner tower, two-story bay, wide-arched entryway, and multigabled roof line. In the same year Charles Cassell de-

David Hutzler house, northeast corner of Eutaw Place and Laurens Street, designed by Thomas C. Kennedy, 1887. Enoch Pratt Free Library

TOP, RIGHT:
Interior, David Hutzler house. Courtesy of Frank R. Shivers

BOTTOM:
German H. Hunt house, 1802 Eutaw Place, designed by Charles Carson, 1889. From The Monumental City, the Liverpool of America, *2: facing 4. Enoch Pratt Free Library*

signed a pair of houses nearby for the prolific builder Joseph Cone, at 1804 and 1806 Eutaw Place, each being thirty-five feet wide, with rock-faced white marble façades distinguished by rounded bays, wide-arched entrances, carved stone panels, flat roofs, and an asymmetrical façade composition. The newspapers noted that the pair was finished in the greatest luxury, with mahogany woodwork on the first floor as well as marble baths. A few years later Cassell designed three more thirty-six- foot-wide houses in the block for Cone which showed the later picturesque period's fondness for darker stones. The house at 1810 Eutaw Place is built of granite with brownstone trim; 1812 is of red granite and 1814 of rock-faced marble. Each façade is different, but the composition of the whole group is harmonious and very picturesque, with wide, round-arched openings, recessed entryways, bands of stone-work in contrasting colors with carved decorations, and a mixture of squared and rounded bays capped by appropriate roofs marked by dormer windows. More modestly scaled, rock-faced stone row houses with similar features, carried out in brownstone, granite, or marble, lined the upper blocks of Eutaw Place toward North Avenue and beyond, leading to the entrance to Druid Hill Park on Lake Drive.

The architects most closely associated with picturesque-style residences on Eutaw Place often designed their clients' downtown places of business as well. Carson built residences in the 1880s for Levi Strauss, Levi Witz, and Solomon Frank; business buildings for Joel Gutman, Frank, and Strouse & Brothers, and in 1890 he designed the Baltimore Hebrew Congregation Synagogue at 1901 Madison Avenue and the Mishkan Israel Synagogue in the 2200 block of Madison. Cassell designed Posner's department store (later Stewart's) in 1899. By the 1890s Sperry had emerged as the architect of choice for the German-Jewish community, designing Oheb Shalom, the Har Sinai Temple at Bolton and Wilson Streets, and the McCulloh Street Temple, along with the Joel Gutman and Hochschild, Kohn department stores and, later, Jacob Epstein's Baltimore Bargain House, at Liberty and Baltimore Streets.

Returning to Renaissance Roots

Even as local architects and their patrons were embracing Romanesque forms and building eclectic picturesque houses, New York architect Stanford White was in the process of bringing yet a new architectural style to town. In 1884 Robert Garrett and his wife, the former Mary Sloan Frick, hired White to remodel their Greek Revival–style townhouse at 11 West Mount Vernon Place. The house had been given to them as a wedding present in 1872 by Garrett's father, John Work Garrett, longtime president of the B&O Railroad. In 1883, when the elder Garrett died, Robert succeeded him as company president and also faced a social decision: whether to remain at Mount Vernon Place or move to one of the fashionable new neighborhoods in or just outside the city. The Garretts decided to stay, bought the house next door to the east, and commissioned White to combine the two old houses into one.

Over the next nine years, White completely rebuilt the houses, inside and out, and gave the pair a completely new façade, one that introduced the new Renaissance Revival style to the city. Just as the eclectic, picturesque style had been a reaction against the monotony of the classically derived Italianate style, now a return to symmetrical, refined classicism seemed

View of West Mount Vernon Place showing the Robert Garrett house as designed by Stanford White in 1884. Lithograph from "In and About Baltimore," Harper's Weekly, September 7, 1889, 716.

an appropriate antidote to the wilder excesses of the High Victorian Gothic, the Queen Anne, and their highly picturesque interpretations. McKim, Mead & White had first returned to Renaissance forms in their 1883 Villard houses, built for railway magnate Henry Villard in New York City. Actually, the design encompassed a group of houses arranged in a U shape facing Madison Avenue. A true High Renaissance Italian palazzo (modeled after the Cancelleria Palace, ca. 1500), the blocklike structure had simplified lines; a smooth, flat façade; symmetrically placed door and window openings; and a low, hipped roof. In Renaissance palazzo style, the building had a rusticated basement, with arched openings, and pedimented windows on the two floors above. The firm had recommended the use of a light-colored stone for the façade, to heighten the classical appearance, but Villard had insisted on the popular brownstone.

The Garretts, too, preferred brownstone, but otherwise, the façade design is strictly academic. The flat roof, with its classical cornice and deep frieze, complemented the horizontality of the composition, which the wide window groupings and belt courses between floors further accentuated. Classical details abounded: pedimented windows, a block modillion cornice set above a frieze decorated with swags, Corinthian columns articulating the porch, and balustrades running across both the main and porch roofs. The "monstrous" entrance, which protruded onto the sidewalk, departed so severely from Mount Vernon Place norms as to rouse neighbors, particularly the owner of the building to the west, who complained that it eliminated his first-floor view of the Washington Monument and sued to halt construction (Niernsee testified that this extension perfectly suited the design).[33]

Carved staircase with skylight, Robert Garrett house. Maryland Historical Society

White gave the Garretts, or Mary Garrett demanded, an interior that eclipsed any in Baltimore. Beyond the controversial entrance portico the mosaic-floored vestibule welcomed visitors with a fountain and an oversized Tiffany stained-glass window. One then proceeded into an oak-paneled two-story hall, with an impressive fireplace and a balustraded gallery along three of its sides. The formal dining room lay to the rear of the hall, in the original house. To the east, White created a spacious, well-lit (by the new bow window) drawing room by combining the front and rear parlors of the old house the Garretts' had just purchased. White filled it with furniture he ordered from Paris. A carved wooden spiral staircase, brightened by a Tiffany skylight, rose to the floors above. The family dining room, its walls covered in tapestry, and a room for the after-dinner entertainment of female guests, its walls red and ceiling domed, occupied the first floor of the Garretts' original house. Newly designed bedrooms were in the new house.

While working on the Garrett house White designed another Renaissance Revival–style house in Baltimore which was to have a much greater effect on local architecture. The Reverend Dr. John F. Goucher hired White to build a new dwelling for himself in the 2300 block of St. Paul Street, just opposite the college buildings. Instead of the grey stone, Romanesque-influenced style of the college, White gave Goucher something entirely different—a massive Renaissance town palazzo of yellow Pompeian brick topped by a flat roof, classical modillion cornice, and stone balustrade. The square, five-bay-wide block was crisply symmetrical, with three ranges of arched and pedimented window openings, belt courses, and a central, third-floor stone balcony. Florentine in exterior design, the house on the inside duplicated the opulence of the Winans residence. White chose woods and marbles for their unusual colors, and, to show their intrinsic beauty, he presented them with a maximum of polished surface.

Even before the Goucher house was completed in 1892, other local architects were fol-

TOP:

Dr. John F. Goucher house, 2313 St. Paul Street, designed by McKim, Mead & White, 1892. Photograph by Mary Ellen Hayward

BOTTOM:

Phoenix Club, 1505 Eutaw Place, designed by Charles L. Carson, 1890. The Jewish Museum of Maryland Institutional Archives

The Phoenix Club, closed in the 1950s, was demolished in 1963 to make way for a union hall.

lowing its lead in their institutional, row-house, and town-house designs. J. Appleton Wilson designed two Renaissance Revival–style rows in 1890, one just south of the Associate Reformed Church at Maryland Avenue and Preston Street, the other in the 1100 block of Calvert Street. The latter was chastely academic, carried out in brown brick with white marble trim, with a flat roof, elegant balustrade and modillioned cornice, sharply cut window openings, round-arched marble entryways, and two Palladian windows.

In 1890 Charles Carson provided a classically influenced design for the clubhouse of the Phoenix Club, an elite social organization for the city's German-Jewish business leaders, at 1505 Eutaw Place. With a first floor of brownstone and upper floors of red brick set in black mortar with brownstone trimmings, the symmetrical façade featured a classical entrance portico; a principal floor lit by wide, arched windows articulated with pilasters; and a central, third-story loggia. Delicate balustrades framing window balconies, connected by belt courses, provided the horizontal notes to the composition, which was topped by a low, red-tile roof with Italian-style dormers. Slightly projecting bay windows, with stained-glass transoms reminiscent of those at the Garrett house, marked the ground-floor level.

The opening of the club seemed such an important occurrence that the Baltimore *Sun* gave it a complete page of coverage, including a drawing of the façade. The newspaper reported that "the architecture is the Italian renaissance, and this has been faithfully carried out even to the smallest details." Inside, the *Sun* noted that the rooms "will be superbly arranged for social purposes and richly furnished." The main hall was "floored with mosaic work and paneled in quartered oak." To the north lay the reading room, "finished in ivory white," with Mexican onyx mantel surround and to be furnished with "massive mahogany" pieces; on the south side the ladies' reception room was finished in "oiled mahogany" and would have "gilded and crimson furniture." Behind the reading room there was a social hall, a "general place for lounging and smoking," with a private dining room adjoining. A café extended across the entire rear of the building. The second floor contained the major rooms—a grand banquet hall occupying the entire front, with a music gallery at mezzanine level, and, at the rear, a magnificent grand ballroom, also with mezzanine gallery, as well as a stage on the east side and a dome of opalescent leaded glass, from which hung a gilded chandelier. Private dining and card rooms were located on the mezzanine level between the second and third floors. The basement contained a gymnasium, billiard room, bowling alley, wine cellar, barber shop, and toilet rooms; space on the fourth floor was reserved for servants' sleeping quarters.[34] That same year Carson also designed the Levi Witz house, a Renaissance Revival–style town house at 1800 Eutaw Place.

Meanwhile, Mount Vernon Place experienced a spectacular resurgence. The Garretts, having stayed there, joined forces with William Walters in relandscaping the west square of Mount Vernon Place, installing a fountain, and setting out bronze sculptures. In the decade after 1885, well-to-do young people bought many of the comparatively plain, forty-some-year-old Greek-Revival houses in and around the four squares, enlarged the interiors, and

George Graham house, southwest corner of Washington Place and Madison Street, designed by George Archer, 1888, and behind it, the Stafford Hotel, designed by Charles E. Cassell, 1893. Peale Collection, Maryland Historical Society

upgraded plumbing and mechanical systems. Several owners of houses on the north side of West Mount Vernon Place also hired architects to remodel their homes with new Renaissance Revival façades.

A half block away, in 1888, George Archer designed a new white marble town house at the southwest corner of Washington Place and Madison Street for George Graham; it harked back to the chateauesque forms of the Winans house but also showed some classical detailing. It is most notable for its corner turret with conical roof and the deep end wall facing Madison Street, which features an end gable framing two of the upper stories and centered on a Richardsonian Romanesque round-arched window. The Ionic-columned granite portico with its roof balustrade, the classical friezes that provide horizontal accents to the façade, and the swag frieze beneath the roof turret are all classical in inspiration and reflect the influence of the nearby Garrett house.

As White finished work on the Garrett house, in 1893, Mount Vernon Place braced itself, with some vocal objection, for the construction of a new hotel. The Stafford Hotel went up, despite resistance, on the western side of North Washington Place, on land that had belonged to Dr. William A. Moale, a descendant of the Moale who first pictured Baltimore as a fledgling port. Charles Cassell designed the ten-story hotel, whose exterior combined terra cotta, brownstone, and yellow brick and followed the example of the Beaux-Arts-trained American architect Louis Sullivan. For his design, Cassell used an essentially classical vocabulary, articulating the façade with pilasters, sets of arched windows, and balustraded balconies. The use of brown Roman brick for most of the façade was in keeping with other city exercises in Renaissance taste; the brownstone base recalled an earlier era, but the wide terra cotta frieze near the top of the building bespoke a knowledge of the latest fashions. "The main entrance leads to a tiled hallway decorated in Romanesque designs," the *Sun* reported, after commenting on its "commanding position" on Washington Place. "Soft mono-tints of the walls and ceilings are relieved with friezes and borders in conventional patterns flecked with gold."[35] Cassell followed the Stafford with the nine-story Renaissance Revival–style Severn Apartments, at the northeast corner of Cathedral Street and West Mount Vernon Place. Built of Roman brick with brownstone trim, the building drew all its details from the classical vocabulary: deeply projecting bracketed cornice, stone panels decorated with swags, and balustraded balconies.

Business, Technology, Taste

By the 1880s business—whether wholesaling, retailing, financing, or overseeing industry and transportation, all of growing importance in the Baltimore economy—brought noteworthy developments, forcing ever more people together in ever larger buildings. In the national marketplace then emerging, businesses tended to combine and grow larger, calling for more floor space. Tall buildings thus responded to the needs of corporations; with hundreds of clerks in a home office doing paperwork for perhaps thousands in remote locations, big companies needed big office buildings and could afford to build them. The simple fact of public transportation also encouraged larger buildings. Horsecars, then trolleys, dispersed residents but also brought them together, promoting downtown districts for work and shopping. By the 1880s even the remarkable iron-front buildings of the 1850s and immediate postwar period seemed too small.

Building larger of course required and hastened the development of new technologies. Not accidentally, the mechanical systems of buildings—of vital interest to architects and engineers alike—grew increasingly complicated as each group pursued its separate lines of professional interest. Elevators, central-heating systems, plumbing, and artificial illumination had all been worked out by the 1850s; without them, the revolutionary big-floored, five-story buildings of the period would have been impossible. Buildings have "an internal architecture," as a late-twentieth-century construction engineer put it simply. "The mechanical systems are—and have been—the heart of the building."[36]

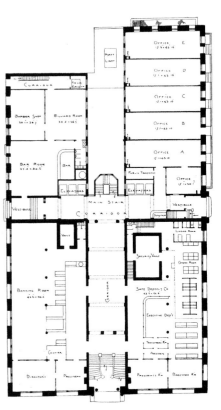

Equitable Building, 10 North Calvert Street, designed by Joseph E. Sperry, 1891. Illustration of exterior, first-floor plan, and main corridor, from Equitable Building, Baltimore: A Description of Baltimore's Greatest Business Structure *(New York: Art Publishing Co., 1893). Enoch Pratt Free Library*

Before the 1870s, however, those systems were inadequate for larger buildings: While every five-story iron front had an elevator, for example, safety considerations in Baltimore and elsewhere kept passengers out of elevators until the early 1870s, when, at Hutzler's and elsewhere, improved elevators lifted people effortlessly to one well-lighted, well-heated floor after another. Every iron front had piped-in water and water closets, but water pressure in the municipal system was too low for water closets or lavatories on upper floors. Central-heating systems relied either on the ability of hot air to rise (and it could rise only so far before cooling) or on high-pressure steam boilers (which had a disturbing tendency to blow up). Even gaslight, the safest and most reliable of these mid-century technologies, left workers competing for window space; without incandescent mantles, which an Austrian chemist-engineer patented in 1885, gas lamps gave only a dim, flickering flame. These and other factors added up to a de facto height limit of five stories in Baltimore until the seven-story Carrollton Hotel showed that the mechanical contractors of Baltimore could heat, light, plumb, ventilate, or elevate any building that ironworkers could frame.

Unfashionable in appearance and perhaps undernoticed, the Blackistone Building (later the Manufacturers' Record Building) appeared in 1889 on the northwest corner of Lexington Street and Guilford Avenue and paved the way for the many tall commercial buildings that were to follow. George Archer served as local supervising architect, working under Henry Van Brunt, a Richard Morris Hunt–trained designer and architectural essayist who had established a partnership with Frank M. Howe, with offices in Boston and Kansas City. The Blackistone, apparently Van Brunt's only Baltimore building, illustrated the point that tall structures would emerge not from iron-front buildings, in which the iron carried no weight, or even from buildings with cast-iron beams or columns, in which the walls still bore most of the building's load, but from principles first established in reinforced-masonry pier construction. The Blackistone seems to have been the first structure in Baltimore to make use of structurally independent skeletal supports, one of America's greatest contributions to the art of building and a concept that led to metal-skeleton buildings (the original object was not taller buildings but comparative fire safety). The Blackistone followed the example of William Le Baron Jenney and William B. Mundie's Home Insurance Company office building in Chicago, completed in 1885—even though in 1891 a leading authority wrote that the skeleton system "may be said to have been incubated, rather than invented, and the simple, triumphant method of constructing the most marvelous of modern buildings is found upon examination to be but an enlarged use of preceding methods."[37] Bessemer-process steel eventually replaced cast and wrought iron and masonry as the materials for skeleton construction. Stronger than iron—higher in carbon content and having greater tensile strength—steel enabled builders to construct higher than ever before.

Baltimoreans adopted the skeleton frame readily, delighting in the ability to express the might of their business community in monumental architecture. Now that technology allowed them to go higher, architects had to devise ways to adapt current popular styles to these new forms. With the Renaissance Revival now established as the highest fashion, architects of early skyscrapers devised a system of treating the vertical expanse of a building like a classical column—with a base, shaft, and capital. For the Equitable Building at 10 North Calvert Street, Joseph Evans Sperry in 1891 designed a granite "base" of three-story-high

FIDELITY AND DEPOSIT COMPANY.

LEFT:
*Fidelity & Deposit Company,
northwest corner of Charles and
Lexington Streets, designed by
Baldwin & Pennington and
completed in 1894. From* History of
the City of Baltimore *(1902), 106.
Enoch Pratt Free Library*
RIGHT:
*Continental Trust Building,
southeast corner of Baltimore and
Calvert Streets, designed by Daniel
H. Burnham, 1899. Maryland
Historical Society*

arches capped by classically cut windows and an egg-and-dart cornice. Above, the "shaft" consisted of six floors articulated with paired windows and tall, five-story arches, all carried out in buff brick. The "capital," also in buff brick, with its flat roof and modillion cornice, had a frieze of classically carved leafy ornament. Inside, with its barrel-vaulted corridors, coffered ceilings, and elaborate classical decoration, the building offered an elegant setting for the business done there. Designed as an office building with the amenities businessmen expected, it featured, on the first floor—in addition to the banking rooms and offices—a barber shop, a billiard room, and a bar, a Turkish bath below, and a restaurant on the top floor. The design elaborated on the architect's iron-framed Marlboro Shirt Building from the previous year, mingling various elements of the Italian Renaissance style with the kind of Romanesque that Richardson had made popular.

Baldwin & Pennington's Fidelity & Deposit Company Building, completed in 1894, showed a more traditional approach to architecture. Eight stories tall, the steel-framed building was encased in a Romanesque-style façade of rock-faced granite with a roof line decorated by French-style dormers and a small Romanesque tower. Located on the northwest corner of Charles and Lexington Streets, the eight-story building resembled Richardson's iron-framed Cincinnati Chamber of Commerce, completed two years earlier.

An economic downturn in 1893 dampened new construction for years, but in 1899, with prosperity restored, the important Chicago architect Daniel H. Burnham began work on the Continental Trust Building on the southeast corner of Baltimore and Calvert Streets. Employing steel-skeleton framing, Burnham followed the "skyscraper" model he had helped invent. Rising sixteen stories, the building had a base of rough granite, articulated with large, arched windows; a highly fenestrated eleven-story brick shaft, with openings arranged in groups of three between tall pilasters, and a terra cotta capital composed of a classical cornice with deep, carved frieze. Although highly characteristic of the stripped down, "Chicago style" skyscraper developed and perfected by Richardson, William LeBaron Jenney, Louis Sullivan, and John W. Root, the design yet retained elements of classical styling: the Renaissance Revival pediments over some of the windows and the row of columns at the top, under the frieze. Nevertheless, the lower-level arches and the triple windows in each bay are characteristic of the Chicago style. The finest marble, mahogany, and bronze graced the public-business spaces within. Completed in 1901, the Continental Trust briefly stood as the tallest building south of New York.

Beaux-Arts Classicism

By the mid-1890s the popularity of the Renaissance Revival style as popularized by McKim, Mead & White and the return to neoclassicism championed at the 1893 Chicago World's Fair ensured that the classical vocabulary once more commanded American architectural imaginations. The fair's design impresario, Daniel Burnham, decided on a neoclassical theme and invited architects throughout the country to submit designs—with impressive results. Quickly erected in wood and coated with white plaster (giving the fair its colloquial name, the "White City"), fair buildings occupied a park fronting on Lake Michigan and framing a formal basin, beyond which planners created a massive lagoon by moving tons of earth. Frederick Law Olmsted, near the end of his career, designed a picturesque island for the center of the lagoon. The World's Fair illustrated new forms of city planning, which became known as the City Beautiful movement; mostly, its structures offered Americans a splendid display of monumental classical architecture. In late spring of 1893, when one of the Baltimore newspapers interviewed Benjamin Buck Owens on the topic of Baltimore's architectural taste and his professional practice, Owens commented on the local "tendency" toward the classic styles. "I regard the World's Fair buildings as wonderful examples of the architectural profession," he said further. "That they will form models for the builders' art for many years to come is a foregone conclusion."[38]

For residentially scaled structures like Stanford White's Goucher house or Charles Carson's Phoenix Club, the restrained forms of the Renaissance Revival seemed a perfect fit. But at the turn of the new century, as Americans, including Baltimoreans, were planning imposing new public structures, "restrained" was not appealing. Taking inspiration from the "beautiful white city," with its templelike visions reflected in a blue lagoon, architects thought of words like *bold, monumental,* and *grand.* Such attitudes corresponded exactly with the long-respected teachings of the Ecole des Beaux-Arts in Paris, which had trained Richardson and Hunt and supplied models of instruction for the new American architectural schools. The Ecole taught that all architecture should be modeled on the classical past, but it also believed that architecture evolves, that change is guided by immutable principles. Classical forms, images, and symbols learned from the past could yet be combined in new interpretive forms to create a magnificent and valid national architecture. The broad latitude of this thinking allowed virtually any classical style to be adopted as "American," from Roman and Greek temples to Venetian palazzos to Louis XIV chateaus.

Baltimore Courthouse, west side of Monument Square, designed by Wyatt & Nolting, 1894. Maryland Historical Society

Looking upward, one could readily appreciate the classical details of the Wyatt & Nolting courthouse. Baltimore City Planning Department

Renovated in the 1950s and then partially restored, the Clarence M. Mitchell Jr. Courthouse, as officials named it in March 1985, continues to serve the citizens of Baltimore City today.

When Baltimore announced plans to build a new courthouse in 1894, most of the country's major architectural firms submitted plans. J. B. Noel Wyatt and William Nolting, partners since 1887, won the blind competition with a design that made the courthouse, begun in 1898 and completed in 1901, the first American public building to turn the vision of the Chicago Fair into local reality. Facing the west side of Monument Square and filling the entire block to the west, the courthouse sat on a base of rusticated local granite with the upper stories carried out in white Beaver Dam marble. In true Beaux-Arts style, with neoclassical details interpreted in a bold, original manner, the massive grace of the building suddenly made its eclectic neighbors, like the Post Office building, look fussy. Issuing a clear call to republican virtues, the courthouse combined forms from the Greek, Roman, and Italian Renaissance vocabularies that, blended together, copied no exact historical models. The creative combination of classical elements thus formed a new architectural style that seemed emi-

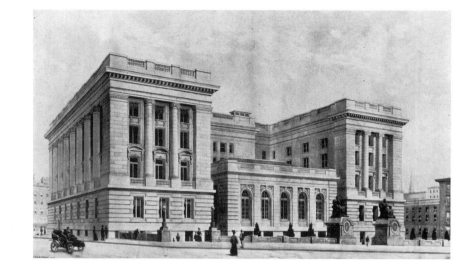

Hornblower & Marshall's perspective drawing of the United States Custom House, Gay and Lombard Streets, 1901. From the Catalogue Exhibition, Architectural Club of Baltimore, 1907, *held at the Peabody Institute Galleries (Baltimore: Williams & Wilkins Co., 1907). Enoch Pratt Free Library*

nently suitable for impressive public buildings. Greek Ionic columns mark the central portion of each façade, set above a rusticated basement with arched windows. Above, Renaissance-style pedimented windows combine with Beaux-Arts-style ocular windows as well as the square-cut windows associated with the Greek style. A richly balustraded cornice tops the whole composition. Inside, elegant and richly finished marble stairways, columns, open courts, and balconies, as well as symbolic, painted murals, bespoke the importance of the building. So entrenched did classical stylings become in Baltimore that, late in the twentieth century, federal judges declared, and an observer noted, "that they did not feel comfortable in a courthouse that had no columns and other classical appurtenances."[39]

For a United States Custom House at Gay and Lombard Streets (after demolition of Latrobe's Baltimore Exchange in 1902), the Washington, D.C., firm Hornblower & Marshall used much the same vocabulary Wyatt & Nolting had first employed in the courthouse—a rusticated base, three-story engaged columns articulating the main floors, and a flat, balustraded roof line. The classical forms, however, derived entirely from Rome and the Re-

Alexander Brown & Sons building, southwest corner of Baltimore and Calvert Streets, designed by Parker & Thomas, 1901. Maryland Historical Society

naissance. A graduate of the Ecole, Joseph C. Hornblower and his firm had already designed several buildings in the capital, including the Natural History Museum of the Smithsonian Institution. Begun in 1901, their well-proportioned and thoroughly columned grey-granite exterior (over a steel frame) compared favorably to any Beaux-Arts structure in the country and appeared in *American Architect and Building News* a year later.

Both the courthouse and the customshouse offered fine examples of another important element of Beaux-Arts-style buildings and the City Beautiful movement: the collaboration between architects, sculptors, and painters to create beautiful, thoroughly decorated, and symbolic public buildings, in the manner of the great Renaissance masterpieces. Beaux-Arts architects believed that their duty lay in celebrating and imparting inspirational values and that monumental painted murals were the perfect medium. For their Renaissance Revival–style Boston Public Library (1888–92), opposite Copley Square from Richardson's Trinity Church, McKim, Mead &

Belvedere Hotel, 1 East Chase Street, designed by Parker & Thomas and completed in 1903. Maryland Historical Society

RIGHT:

The luxuriant Palm Room of the Belvedere, photographed ca. 1910. Maryland Historical Society

White commissioned Puvis de Chavannes, John Singer Sargent, and Edwin A. Abbey to paint allegorical and illustrative murals, with associated sculpture by Augustus Saint-Gaudens. John La Farge worked at Trinity Church. Wyatt & Nolting asked La Farge to decorate their courthouse and he obliged, creating a mural entitled *The Lawgivers*, which depicted a gathering of the leaders of the world's four great religions—Moses, Emperor Justinian, Mohammad, and Confucius. For the Custom House, New York artist Francis David Millet created a sixty-eight-by-thirty-foot allegorical mural, *The Evolution of Navigation*, admiringly portraying all forms of seaborne commerce. Decorative trim throughout the room gave symbolic significance to local flora—corn, dogwood, oak—and fauna, with seahorses and scallop shells framing painted vignettes. (Ironically, Millet went down on the *Titanic*.)

A much more modest interpretation of Beaux-Arts design appeared in 1901 on the southwest corner of Baltimore and Calvert Streets, opposite Burnham's rising Continental Trust Building. A new office for Alexander Brown & Sons, the building was the work of a new firm, both of whose partners had trained at the Ecole. Douglas H. Thomas returned to Baltimore in 1899, at the age of twenty-eight, after studies in Paris and work in Boston. Grandson of the B&O president who in 1850 had built the distinguished town house at 1 West Mount Vernon Place, Thomas in 1901 joined with an Ecole classmate from Boston, J. Harelston Parker, to form Parker & Thomas, with offices in both Boston and Baltimore. The two-story "fireproof" Alex. Brown structure, built of concrete with brick and marble facings, used elements of English Georgian design—red brick and white marble—to create an aura of trust, responsibility, and good taste. Inside, a grand interior featured a large banking room lined with balconies with bronze railings, all beneath an impressive domed ceiling.

One of Parker & Thomas's most important commissions led to a Beaux-Arts triumph in Baltimore, the Belvedere Hotel, which went up not far from the site of Howard's old home—with the same, if differently spelled, name. French classical in inspiration, with its tall mansard roof and sculptural dormers, the Belvedere, finished in 1903, also showed a hint of the neo-Georgian style to come in its mainly pink-brick exterior with white stone angle quoins and window enframements. The main body of the hotel rises above a two-story rusticated base; above, one of the truly eye-catching "capitals" in town—a thirty-five-foot-high mansard roof with elaborate dormer windows—marks the skyline for miles around. The sculptural quality of the dormer windows, cornice, and other roof decorations are typical hallmarks of the Beaux-Arts style, but in this case they are mainly created using terra cotta and iron to simulate stone. Parker & Thomas carried out the interior in the best Beaux-Arts manner, with inlaid marble floors, rich Louis XVI–style plasterwork, and gilded chandeliers lavishly treated with cut crystal. Henry James, who headquartered at the Belvedere when he came to Baltimore in 1904, deemed it all "imposingly modern yet quietly affable."[40]

Planning the Bucolic: City Beautiful and Suburbia

Baltimore's development in the early years of the twentieth century benefitted from the national City Beautiful movement, which came into being formally in 1899, claiming inspiration from the design principles of the 1893 Chicago World's Fair. Reflecting the theories and philosophies of the Ecole des Beaux-Arts, the movement aimed to improve cities by better planning—coordinating the development of impressive groupings of public buildings, efficient transportation, sewerage, and lighting systems—the whole enhanced by the continued creation of public parks and tree-lined parkways and by adorning public spaces with statuary. Frederick Law Olmsted, creator of New York's Central Park and a pivotal figure in the history of American landscape architecture, had promoted the building of broad parkways to connect important civic or cultural structures and lead to large parks. In addition to being beautiful and adding an important relaxing element to urban life, parks and parkways also helped the city "breathe" by cleansing the foul air emanating from tenement districts and crowded downtown areas.

Late-nineteenth-century Baltimore boulevards or parkways included Eutaw Place, whose broad, grassy median strip, ornamented with sculpture, invited one in the direction of Druid Hill Park, as did the 1600 and 1700 blocks of Park Avenue, laid out in about 1870.

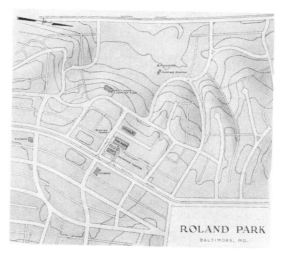

Plan for Plat Number Two, Roland Park, created by Frederick Law Olmsted Jr. and opened in 1901, boasted curving roads that took advantage of the hilly site's natural topography. The plan included the location of the shopping center, the Baltimore Country Club, several churches, the electric railway along Roland Avenue, and its carbarn. Peale Collection, Maryland Historical Society

City plans as early as 1851 called for wide, tree-lined boulevards with median strips to be created along the city's boundary lines, forming a "belt" that would provide fresh air, recreational spaces, and pleasant drives and walkways around the entire city. Complicated negotiations with Baltimore County proved the plan's undoing. Tree-lined Broadway led from Fells Point to North Avenue and, via

Harford Road, to Clifton Park, which the city established in 1895 after having purchased Johns Hopkins's country estate.

One of the most elegant Baltimore boulevards, Mount Royal Avenue, laid out in the 1870s and 1880s, was designed to link the new reservoir at Druid Lake and its developing neighborhood to the parks and distinguished residences of Mount Vernon Place. It was soon lined with noteworthy public structures—the Lyric Opera House, the B&O's Mount Royal Station, and Corpus Christi Church—along with impressive groupings of newly built picturesque row houses. With its grassy median, rows of trees, many fine sculptures, and eclectic collection of handsome buildings, Mount Royal Avenue represented City Beautiful design at its best, exemplifying the unifying power of gardens, sculpture, and architecture in an urban setting.

Wealthy Baltimoreans had always had summer houses outside the city; in the late nineteenth century, they could consider as never before living beyond the city year-round, in places designed with nature and escape in mind. Early summer communities developed for the upper-middle classes as early as the 1850s, along the rail lines that led out of the city, most notably to Mount Washington and Lutherville, to the north. By the 1870s horsecar service allowed Baltimoreans to move to the new row-house neighborhoods developing around parks and squares east and west of downtown; it also encouraged the growth of rural neighborhoods like Waverly, Catonsville, Pikesville, and Govans. The pace of suburban development picked up once electric streetcar lines began to extend beyond North Avenue and east and west of the city limits in the 1890s.

Newspapers described suburban life as idyllic, and developers rushed to expand the list of bucolic destinations. The late 1880s brought three new summer suburbs: Walbrook, Ruxton, and Sudbrook Park. To convert 204 acres of the former James Howard McHenry estate near Pikesville into the garden suburb of Sudbrook, Olmsted himself (the firm now included his son, Frederick Law Olmsted Jr.) prepared plans that featured winding roads, large, irregular lots, an abundance of communal open space, and generous plantings of trees. The community was serviced by the Western Maryland Railroad, which took workers downtown, and by the village of Pikesville, which provided food and services. Walbrook, in west Baltimore, only offered conventional narrow lots laid out in a gridiron pattern, but Ruxton Heights (also on a rail line) sited lots on gently curving streets on the hillsides just east of the tracks.

None of these communities aspired to offering year-round living. A few years later, however, an international syndicate acquired 550 hilly acres just north of the mill village of Hampden and extending along the Jones Falls Valley. Taking as its name the Roland Park Company, the principals sought to develop the hilly, picturesque landscape into an ideal garden suburb. Already served by the local "Ma & Pa" Railroad, the syndicate soon opened its own electric streetcar line, which ran regularly from City Hall to Roland Park. The company arranged for a local school (later the Roland Park Country School), built a small shopping center, and opened a country club.

Its first development, called Plat Number One, was located east of Roland Avenue and north of Cold Spring Lane, near the new railroad station. The first lot sold in June 1892, but sales proceeded so slowly that the company decided to build some sample houses to inspire purchasers' imaginations. These were all in the by-then well-established "shingle style," first introduced in New England by Henry Hobson Richardson and McKim, Mead & White in the 1880s. Regular in design, clad in simple shingles (harking back to early colonial forms), the restrained exteriors represented a reaction against the excesses of High Victorian Gothic and Queen Anne forms. Varied roof lines, corner towers, and rounded shapes were still popular, but now smooth-shingle surfaces with little ornament of any sort unified complex massings. Broad verandahs extending along whole façades further united the composition, as well as relating the houses (and owners) intimately to their natural setting. Agreeably informal, with rooms of various shapes and sizes loosely grouped about a central hall and opening freely into one another, the spacious houses seemed perfect for the city's newly planned suburb.

George Miller house, Roland Avenue, designed by Wyatt & Nolting, 1900. Peale Collection, Maryland Historical Society

Unfortunately—possibly because of aftereffects of the Panic of 1893, possibly because of Baltimoreans' natural conservatism—lots and houses in Plat One did not sell briskly. In 1897 Edward H. Bouton, the company manager, turned to the Olmsted firm in New York to plan for Plat Number Two, west of Roland Avenue. Frederick Law Olmsted Jr. became personally involved with the project and, making use of ideas first developed by his father, took advantage of the site's woods, hilly topography, and open, swift-flowing streams to create perhaps one of the greatest of the nineteenth-century garden suburbs. He laid out streets encircling the hills, retaining as much of the original grade and forestation as possible. According to company regulations, houses had to be set back at least thirty feet from the street, could have no stables or outbuildings, and had to cost at least $3,000—a measure to ensure the high tone of the neighborhood. This last rule soon became a requirement stipulating that homeowners obtain company approval for their architectural plans, thus ensuring high quality and compatibility.

By the time Plat Number Two opened in 1901 Roland Park had emerged as *the* new residential area in the city, with business and professional men vying for lots and hiring architects to build ever more impressive houses. Wyatt and Nolting received many of these commissions, having built houses for themselves in the community; they constructed a half-timbered English Tudor–style set of shops in 1895 and the Roland Park Country Club in 1897. With its smooth surfaces and rounded bays, the Miller house, on Roland Avenue at Elmhurst, completed in 1900, demonstrated the firm's proficiency in the late shingle style. As the new century opened, Roland Park became the site of the finest residential architecture created in the city, with AIA members offering creative versions of the various revival styles coming into vogue as well as continued original expressions of more academic versions of the shingle style.

7

MODERNISMS, MODERNISTS, AND MODERNITY, 1904–1955

Henry James, the Massachusetts-raised writer and critic who attended law school during the Civil War and after 1876 made his home in London, returned to the United States in 1903–4, traveling from Boston to Palm Beach, and later publishing his impressions. He, like so many visitors before him, found Baltimore charming and peculiar and its architecture worthy of comment—in his own self-conscious manner.

He arrived in June, when he supposed most important Baltimoreans to be out of town. "Houses were everywhere closed," he wrote,

> and the neat perspectives, all domiciliary and all, as I have hinted, tending mildly to a vague elegance, were the more neat and the more elegant, though doubtless also the more mild and the more vague, for their being so inanimate. A certain vividness of high decency seemed in spite of it to possess them, and this suggestion of the real southern glow, yet with no southern looseness, was clearly something by itself—all special and local and all, or almost all, expressed in repeated vistas of little brick-faced and protrusively door-stepped houses, which, overhung by tall, regular umbrage, suggested rows of quiet old ladies seated, with their toes tucked-up on uniform footstools, under the shade candlesticks of old-fashioned tea-parties.

He noticed the squares on which so many houses faced; "it was as if the virtuous dames had drawn together round a large green table, albeit to no more riotous end than that each should sit before her individual game of patience." He described Mount Vernon Place as being like the telltale treasure one finds in a drawing room while waiting for the host to appear: "The top of the central eminence," James called it, "with its air of an

Edward W. Spofford's bird's-eye view of 1911 depicts the city after it was rebuilt following the 1904 fire. Maryland Historical Society

ample plan and of sweeping the rest of the circle," a place he considered the city's "documentary parlour" and worthy of touching and examining. Robert Mills's monument to Washington he admired for its "high column . . . surmounting figure and spreading architectural base"; "this presence was for all the world, like that of some vast and stately old-fashioned clock, a decorative 'piece,' an heirloom from generations now respectably remote, occupying an inordinate space in proportion to the other conveniences."[1]

James toured the city at a time when it continued building and began serious rebuilding, often in a manner he approved. But the building resulted from various fundamental changes that made him and his style seem hopelessly out of date, including steady population growth and two world wars. During the half century between 1905 and 1955, half of Maryland's population lived in Baltimore City. Citizens there assimilated diverse new people while benefitting from a generally solid, because highly diverse, economy. By 1904 the Maryland Steel Company had built some eight hundred houses in a planned village, Sparrows Point, for workers in the largest steel plant on tidewater in the world. In 1910, when the population of Baltimore stood at 558,485, the number of Russian- and Eastern European–born persons peaked at 24,798. The city gained 124,000 people by means of another annexation of surrounding county territories in 1918.[2] Many thousands of workers and their families had settled in Baltimore then because of the war-related industrial buildup. That same year, the United States Shipping Board built more than five hundred houses in a planned village, Dundalk, for the workers at Bethlehem Steel's Sparrows Point shipyard. In 1920, there were 733,826 people who made Baltimore their home; in 1930, the Italian-born population struck an all-time high at 9,022. In 1940—as the city prepared for another world war and for the booming activity that meant for the city in terms of steel making, shipbuilding, and, after the arrival of the Glenn L. Martin plant at Middle River in 1929, aircraft manufacturing—the population stood at 859,100 (in the metropolitan region the figure exceeded 1.1 million).

Rising population and other factors accounted for a new, more systematic approach than in the past to large-scale urban issues. In 1903 city mayor Thomas G. Hayes announced a plan to build Baltimore's first sewer system. Baltimore was the last big city in the country to have sewers, and the mayor spared no expense to make the new system America's most modern and scientific—and, if possible, beautiful. By 1906 a pilot plant was operating in Walbrook; three years later the plant in Back River was up and running. The advent of sewers brought immediate improvements in overall living conditions. The privies that once filled alleys became unnecessary. The achievement of sewerage, in turn, sparked many women's clubs and other organizations to lobby to have the alleys paved and regularly patrolled for rats, treated for mosquitoes, and otherwise rid of disease-spreading vermin.

Meanwhile, the irresistible rise of the horseless carriage confronted Baltimoreans with another and highly serious planning issue. The number of motor vehicles in Maryland soared from 55,000 in 1910, to 100,000 in 1920, and to 300,000 in 1930, with at least half of them in Baltimore. Not entirely in keeping with the spirit of the City Beautiful movement, several important dealers established themselves along Mount Royal Avenue, several of them between Charles and Cathedral Streets, making their showrooms convenient to the elite of Mount Vernon and Bolton Hill. In 1906 the short-lived Baltimore firm of William Gordon Beecher, Clyde N. Friz, and Charles Gregg designed the most distinguished and expensive among them, an immense headquarters building for the Automobile Club of Maryland on the southwest corner of Mount Royal Avenue and Maryland Avenue. Besides offering dining and amusements for member motorists, the three-story brick and concrete structure, which cost $100,000 and became known as "The Garage," housed an automobile showroom. By 1917 fifty dealers in the immediate neighborhood were offering for sale sixty-five different brands of automobile.

"The Garage," auto showroom at Mount Royal and Maryland Avenues, designed by Beecher, Friz & Gregg, 1906. From Catalogue Exhibition, Architectural Club of Baltimore, 1907, held at the Peabody Institute Galleries *(Baltimore: Williams & Wilkins Co., 1907). Enoch Pratt Free Library*

The popularity of the automobile transformed the face of the city as it did the nation. After the annexation of 1918, the mayor appointed a City Plan Commission and a Public Improvements Commission, principally to deal with burgeoning automobile traffic: "To say that city planning is a traffic problem is as truthful a generalization as may be made," admitted members of the City Plan Commission in 1919.[3] They decided to rank roads according to capacity, from "arteries," which radiated from downtown to the suburbs, to "laterals," which connected the arteries, to "minor streets," which formed the city's many neighborhoods. This system both caused and clarified a problem that still vexes traffic engineers: what to do when the "arteries" converge in the old downtown business district? One planner proposed building a series of elevated highways to connect the eastern and western sections of the city. Controversy immediately ensued (and financial skulduggery was revealed), but at least one such road was built, the Orleans Street Viaduct. Completed in the 1930s,

Orleans Street Viaduct, 1939, showing the new Preston Gardens on the left. Photograph by Hughes & Co. Maryland Historical Society

this 2,200-foot-long, four-lane expressway carried traffic over railroad tracks, Preston Gardens, and Calvert Street and provided an appealing entry to downtown Baltimore.[4]

While these roads did help traffic flow between downtown and the suburbs, they also battered old neighborhoods. Baltimore progressives eventually organized efforts at city planning. In 1934 the architect W. W. Emmart completed a city-housing study that pointed with concern to a belt of "blight" around the city's commercial core. He observed that these areas fostered "crime, delinquency, and dependency"; he urged city leaders, public and private, to devise ways of dealing with the problems of unemployment and a decaying physical core.[5]

BETWEEN THE GREAT FIRE OF 1904 AND THE 1950S, when the city more or less accepted the International Style, *modern* meant different things to three generations of Baltimore citizens—often at the same time. At first the city's leaders, like their progressive counterparts throughout America, embraced the various revivals of the times; early in the century *modern* meant the neoclassicism of the French Ecole des Beaux-Arts and the picturesque irregularity of Loire Valley chateaus, Cotswold manor houses, and Gothic cathedrals. In 1908–9, for example, Roland Park Company architect Edward L. Palmer designed a row of five houses on University Parkway just south of Roland Avenue employing an innovative use of new materials, poured-in-place concrete—modern in method, one might say—but their façades resembled fifteenth-century English cottages. At the same time, many Baltimoreans rebelled against what they dismissed as Victorian fussiness and found inspiration for their "modern" buildings not in the 2,400-year-old temples on the Acropolis in Athens or in early-modern Europe but in the brick and frame structures built on the shores of the colo-

Edward L. Palmer's English-style concrete row houses on University Parkway, 1909. Maryland Historical Society

nial Chesapeake. This approach to the modern produced striking neo-Georgian structures, the "tasteful" toning-down of earlier flamboyant residences such as Evergreen House, and the continued construction of the Baltimore row house. Later, for yet others, *modern* meant the whimsy of Art Deco or the streamlining of *Art Moderne*. Beginning in the 1940s, Alexander Smith Cochran and a few other Baltimore architects and clients rejected these "modernisms" as hidebound, in favor of liberal politics, nonrepresentational art, and the flat roofs and glass walls of the Bauhaus.

All these approaches, of course, mirrored the architectural history of America at large. To the distress of some and the delight of many others, twentieth-century Baltimore followed national trends; it did not start them. The few exceptions, such as the peculiar "Russian Theater" at Evergreen, were so odd that they may truly be said to prove the rule.

"Dov'era e com'era": Building after the Fire

The Baltimore Fire of 1904 destroyed more than fifteen hundred buildings in a 140-acre area—roughly the expanse of the town in 1730. Rebuilding began immediately, and in only a few years some fourteen hundred brick buildings assessed at $13 million before the fire had been replaced by slightly more than half the number of structures assessed at almost twice the earlier figure. It would be convenient if one could say that the fire and subsequent reconstruction prompted a change in Baltimore's architecture; but they did not. The buildings built in 1905 and soon afterward looked like the buildings built in 1903 and before. The "burnt district" was essentially replaced, duplicated in a manner similar to what happened in Venice at about the same time; in 1902, when the five-hundred-year-old campanile at San Marco suddenly collapsed, the mayor, scion of a ducal family, said it would be rebuilt *"dov'era e com'era"* (where it was and as it was).[6] Following this precept, those who guided Baltimore's rebuilding, including members of the Brown, Warfield, Garrett, Jenkins, and Black families, set out to preserve a sense of "continuity" through the use of tried and true architectural styles.

Three early-twentieth-century structures—there were many others—well demonstrated such attention to continuity in Baltimore building. For a marble-clad temple completed in 1907, the Savings Bank of Baltimore (later First Union National), Parker & Thomas took inspiration from the Erechtheum on the Acropolis, including its pleasing Ionic col-

Baltimore's business district following the great fire of 1904. Maryland Historical Society

"The Heart of Baltimore," from Baltimore Today (Baltimore, 1916). When Baltimore businessmen rebuilt after the fire, they retained their allegiance to traditional styles, notably those of the revivalist Ecole des Beaux-Arts, as this photograph of the reconstructed "burnt district" attests. Maryland Historical Society

Schloss Building, 1904. Maryland Historical Society

A rare example of postfire whimsy, George Archer's design for a new shop for the merchant-tailors Joseph Schloss & Son, replacing one lost in the fire, adopted a northern-European medieval look, thus befitting the firm's advertised craftsmanship in the Old World tradition. Occupying a twenty-seven-by-seventy-eight-foot lot at 5 East Lexington Street, only a few doors away from the architect's office, the red-brick, step-gabled building stood on a granite foundation and featured Indiana limestone trim. Archer's elaborate entrance—framed by stone posts and lintel, embellished with a broken-scroll pediment— drew on the Georgian vocabulary; his steep mansard roof with its prominent deep gables derived from Belgian-Dutch-German examples. In any event, Archer met his clients' Rhineland wish beautifully. The first-floor interior featured weathered oak beams, oaken furniture, and a large fireplace at the back of a large salesroom, behind which a stairway led to a mezzanine. Cutters and sewers worked on the well-lighted floors above. Archer's design for the Schloss Building first received notice in an exhibit the Baltimore Architectural Club and Municipal Art Society cosponsored at the Peabody Institute in December 1904 and appeared thereafter in a catalogue published by the Maryland Institute. Irma Walker, "Baltimore Rises from the Ashes: George Archer and His Step-Gable Schloss Building," Maryland Historical Magazine 87 *(fall, 1992): 316–22. Maryland Historical Society*

Savings Bank of Baltimore, designed by Parker & Thomas and completed in 1907, as it appeared on a postcard of the day. Popularly known as "the temple of thrift," the bank building, according to the postcard, was "the finest example of Greek Ionic architecture in the U.S." Maryland Historical Society

RIGHT:

Emmanuel Church, as it appeared after its Flemish-Gothic facelift, ca. 1920. Enoch Pratt Free Library

umns and a frieze embellished with lions' heads. "There is nothing comparable to a huge colonnade," declared the *Architectural Record*, since the early 1890s the nation's leading professional journal, "for the impression it makes on the popular mind."[7] Likewise, for most Baltimoreans of this period, Gothic remained the only proper style for a church. When, in 1912, the Jenkins family decided to give Corpus Christi Church, on Mount Royal Avenue, a new, much higher, octagonal stone spire, it retained the rather free-wheeling Gothic style of the original church. In about 1920, the vestry of Emmanuel Episcopal Church at Cathedral and Read Streets commissioned Boston architect Waldemar H. Ritter to remodel the building's façade. Ritter changed it from English Gothic Revival to the more exotic Flemish Gothic, thus "clearly illustrating," in the words of one later observer, the Baltimoreans' "pictorial attitude toward architecture."[8]

Most noticeably, Baltimore's postfire commercial architecture evinced a continuing and thorough Beaux-Arts spirit. Charles Adams Platt, an architect drawn to cinquecento models, left his own elegant mark on the city. Born into a venerable New England family in 1861 and largely self-trained in architecture, Platt first gained renown as a designer of formal Italianate gardens for New England's wealthy. When he turned to architecture, his love of Italy found expression in his houses. He often stated that he wished to build American villas "in the Italian sense."[9] He almost always incorporated at least one loggia or pergola in the final design. (Later in the century the consummate American modernist Frank Lloyd Wright described Platt as "a very dangerous man" because "he did the wrong thing so well.")[10] Platt gained an introduction to Baltimore through his sister, who in the early 1890s hired him to "modernize" the splendid town house, built in 1851 by John Hanson Thomas, which she shared with her husband, Francis Jencks, at 1 West Mount Vernon Place. Platt added a bay window on the east side of the house, thereby admitting light to the dining room, created a conservatory at the rear of the house, and replaced the clear-glass skylight with a Tiffany design. He also added a Renaissance-style fireplace to the dining room, the most specifically stylistic of his changes. He moved easily among the city's establishment for decades.

Platt was but one of many nonresident architects to find work in Baltimore as the city

In the late 1980s the current owner of the Thomas-Jencks-Gladding residence, Willard Hackerman, donated it to the Walters Art Museum to house its Asian art collection; it opened to the public in 1991.

reveled in early-twentieth-century prosperity. John Russell Pope, who graduated from the Ecole des Beaux-Arts in 1900, obtained his first commission from the owner of the Garrett mansion on Mount Vernon Place. Robert Garrett died in 1896, and in 1902, with a prenuptial property agreement in place, his widow married Dr. Henry Barton Jacobs. Soon afterward the couple decided to remodel their "cottage" in Newport, Rhode Island—a house that Richard Morris Hunt had designed in 1872. For the task they selected the untested Pope, whose uncle had attended Harvard College with Dr. Jacobs (in letters Pope referred to his clients as Aunt Mary and Uncle Jake). The work at Newport went well, and in 1905 Mary Garrett Jacobs hired Pope to enlarge the McKim, Mead & White town house. Pope increased the breadth of the dwelling (already one of the largest houses in the city) half again by adding a vast supper room, a library, a private theater/ballroom, and a separate bedroom for Dr. Jacobs. Pope later added an enclosed rear conservatory, which housed doves, palm trees, and a little stream. Although he carried out the gilded interiors in the then-fashionable extravagant French style (complete with gold-plated bathroom fixtures), he retained the original reserved brownstone façade, a surface so perfectly in keeping with the dignity of Mount Vernon Place.

Since those persons who sat on the boards of Baltimore businesses often also served as trustees of the city's cultural institutions, these structures, too, embraced Beaux-Arts design. In 1905 Henry Walters, surviving son of William Walters and, like his father, an avid

Mrs. Jacobs died in 1936, Dr. Jacobs in 1939. The Garrett-Jacobs house became home to the Engineering Society of Baltimore in 1961.

LEFT:

Walters Art Gallery, begun in 1905, completed in 1909. Maryland Historical Society

RIGHT:

The main entrance to the Walters Art Gallery soon after its opening, Renaissance details much in evidence. News-American Collection, Marylandia and Rare Books Department, University of Maryland Libraries, University of Maryland, College Park

BOTTOM:

The interior court, Walters Art Gallery, ca. 1935. The Walters Art Museum

collector of art, commissioned a young New York architect, William Adams Delano, to design a gallery to house the growing Walters collection. Walters, wishing to place it on the southwest corner of South Washington Place, had bought the four mid-nineteenth-century houses that occupied the site. A distant relative of Walters and a 1902 graduate of the Ecole, Delano chose as his interior design model the Palazzo dell'Università, or Palazzo Balbi, a sixteenth-century structure, and for the exterior the seventeenth-century Collegio dei Gesuiti, both in Genoa. Walters surely approved; years later, Delano recalled that Walters told him he would give the young man the commission "providing you do what I tell you."[11]

Another cultural landmark of the day, the Maryland Institute, College of Art, completed in 1908, copied no existing palace but did attempt to distill a sensibility from a distant place and time: the Venetian *canale grande*, circa 1400. Pell & Corbett, a New York firm, gave the building gleaming white marble walls, a decorated attic story, and four stone memorial medallions, one with the city seal, one with the state's, and two others honoring institute benefactors Andrew Carnegie and Michael Jenkins. Carnegie gave generously toward the costs of building the institute, as he did with libraries across the country; Jenkins donated the land the institute stood upon, stipulating that the new structure be "of suitable character and one which would not clash architecturally" with nearby Corpus Christi Church. He seems to have been perfectly comfortable, and other Baltimoreans may have been equally willing to juxtapose Gothic and Renaissance. In any case, the arched windows of the institute, lighting the *piano nobile*, combined to make so perfect a Venetian palazzo that in front of it one half expects to see not parked cars but moored gondolas.

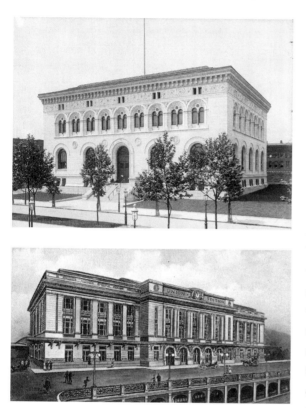

TOP:
Maryland Institute, College of Art, completed in 1908, in important ways a sister building to the Walters, as it appeared in an early-twentieth-century photograph. Maryland Historical Society
BOTTOM:
An early postcard view of the "New Union Station," later, Pennsylvania Station, completed 1911, emphasizes the formal setting of the imposing neoclassical building. Maryland Historical Society

After 1911, one could stand on the steps of the Maryland Institute and look east, across the Jones Falls Valley, and see the neoclassical façade of Pennsylvania Railroad's Union Station, the work of New York–based Kenneth M. Murchison. The station's Beaux-Arts exterior of granite and terra cotta and the cast-iron marquee running along the front and two sides belied its innovative plan. Murchison's design placed a waiting area for passengers above the level of the tracks, with stairs leading to separate platforms. This plan may have marked a first in America; because it greatly eased passenger flow, it quickly became the norm for stations throughout the country. The interior featured marble walls, bronze candelabra and sconces, the nation's most complete Rookwood-of-Cincinnati tile interior, and a cast-iron balcony at the mezzanine level of the two-story lobby, lighted by three domes of stained-glass skylights.

Baltimore gained a much-beloved bit of historicist eccentricity in 1911, when Isaac Emerson, millionaire manufacturer of the upset-stomach remedy Bromo-Seltzer, returned from a European holiday and commissioned Joseph Evans Sperry to design a new headquarters and factory for his pharmaceutical company on the northeast corner of Lombard and Eu-

The Emerson Tower, northeast corner of Lombard and Eutaw Streets, designed by Joseph Evans Sperry, 1911. Maryland Historical Society

The bottle came down from the tower in 1936, and the adjacent factory gave way to a parking garage in 1969.

taw Streets. Emerson's itinerary had included Florence, where the Medici family's Palazzo Vecchio, built between 1298 and 1314, deeply impressed him. He asked Sperry to recreate the Palazzo, and the architect complied. The heroic, 288-foot campanile, or bell tower, seemed to defy the old rule about the form of industrial architecture doggedly following function. But it did have a pragmatic purpose. Its clock face spelled B-R-O-M-O-S-E-L-T-Z-E-R in huge letters, and the tower supported a 51-foot-high, 27-ton revolving blue Bromo-Seltzer bottle. Lighted from within by 596 electric lights, the bottle could supposedly be seen as far away as the Eastern Shore.

More conventional towers—skyscrapers—did not emerge from files of ready-made designs, so architects continued to search for the most appropriate form for these novel structures. At first most Baltimore architects, like their counterparts across the nation, chose a columnar composition by using different sections to create a "base," "shaft," and "capital," a comfortable neoclassical approach wholly in keeping with Beaux-Arts principles.

The twenty-two-story Baltimore Gas & Electric Company Building of 1916 exemplified this compositional scheme. Parker, Thomas & Rice (Arthur Rice had joined the firm in 1907) designed a decorative tour de force, with a four-story base (eight-foot-tall allegorical figures representing Knowledge, Light, Heat, and Power mark the fourth story), thirteen-story shaft, and elaborate two-story "capital" of arched windows. When illuminated at night, it left no doubt about its classical-Greek inspiration.

While the *Sun* praised the city's new tall buildings as "signs of modern business spirit in Baltimore," not everyone agreed. H. L. Mencken, for one, viewed them with suspicion. The changes he witnessed in the Baltimore skyline between the 1910s and 1930s had been forced on the city, he believed, by "boosters, boomers, go-getters, and other such ballyhoo men." The changes and ballyhoo types alike horrified him. "In what way, precisely, has the average Baltimorean benefitted" by the new construction? he asked rhetorically in 1923. "So far as I can make out, in no way at all." Modern skyscrapers spelled disaster for the city: "There was never any need of them here," he fumed, "and the downtown area would have been much more sightly and comfortable without them. They were erected only because all the other big towns, following New York and Chicago, were erecting them. It seemed a disgrace to certain persons that we shouldn't have any, and so they went up." Such behavior was apostasy to Mencken, who, like all true Baltimoreans, believed that one of the city's greatest charms was that it was not New York. Nonetheless he deemed BG&E's skyscraper the best of a bad lot, mostly due to its sense of "spectacle."[12]

True to the Beaux-Arts tradition, and with little murmur from Mencken, the city in 1933 completed a new home for the Central Branch of the library he loved—a three-story Renaissance palazzo on Cathedral Street between Mulberry and Franklin Streets. The original central branch had faced Mulberry Street (the southwest corner of the new building occupied its lot). Heavy if not forbidding in appearance, with Romanesque windows and much eclectic ornamentation, it had grown too small for the needs of the library and had also outlived its stylistic appeal. The library directors in 1933 instructed the architects to "depart from

the traditional institutionalism of the past," to avoid the look of a "fortress or mausoleum," and instead to give the library "a dignity characterized by friendliness rather than aloofness."[13] Down came the daunting old building, along with several mid-nineteenth-century Greek Revival town houses; up went a spacious and elegant building whose large, nearly sidewalk-level windows obviously answered the directors' call for light and beckoning openness. Principally designed by Clyde N. Friz, a Michigan-born MIT graduate who had moved to Baltimore in 1900 to work with the firm Wyatt & Nolting (and who had worked on "The Garage"), the new structure featured a first-floor lobby whose ceiling rose the full height of the building. Further in keeping with Beaux-Arts sensibility, Friz decorated the lobby with imposing marble columns and murals illustrating episodes in Maryland history.

Even city officials of the day attuned themselves to prevailing taste. In 1915 the public works department selected an Italianate neoclassical design for the most prosaic of structures, the Montebello Filtration Plant. The work of various architects and engineers and thoroughly utilitarian in purpose, in 1928 the structure greeted the eye with arched windows, red brick walls, terra cotta trim, green-tiled roofs, and imposing towers.

Municipal Arts, Parks, and Verdant Suburbs

One of the overarching concerns of modernists of all stripes was the need for greater urban and regional planning, an impulse that gave rise to voluntary civic-improvement groups and fostered ongoing efforts to plan residential communities, whether functional places for workers or, for business and professional families, impressive retreats within reach of the downtown.

Among cultural groups, few proved as effective as the Municipal Art Society of Baltimore, which the career diplomat and scion of a Baltimore tobacco-exporting family, Theodore Marburg, and others had organized in 1899. Socially prominent and civically committed members undertook a series of city-wide City Beautiful embellishments early in the century. They took special interest in Mount Vernon Place. Furious at the height of the Stafford Hotel and concerned about preserving the character and visual unity of the squares around the Washington Monument, the society in 1904 persuaded the General Assembly to pass an "anti-skyscraper" measure, which prohibited the construction of buildings, other than churches, more than seventy feet higher than the bottom of the monument. Though opponents immediately challenged the act, the Court of Appeals upheld it, preserving what seems to have been one of the first zoning laws in the nation.

Earlier that year, on February 5, 1904—the same day firemen finally contained the disaster downtown—Marburg forwarded to the mayor a comprehensive Olmsted brothers report the society had commissioned on the subject of parks in the undeveloped parts of the city and its surrounding suburban zone. Accompanied by maps and illustrations, the 120-page report urged the city—for the enumerated purposes of exercise, neighborly recreation, and the enjoyment of outdoor beauty—to create numerous small parks and playgrounds, expand existing city parks, and develop parkways as approaches to or connectors among parks. Already-existing greenways impressed Henry James during his visit to the city that same year. Travel in "wonderful little Baltimore," he wrote, whether from "a noble eminence or . . . from one seat of the humanities, one seat of hospitality to another," consisted mainly "of prompt drives through romantic parks and woodlands that were all suburban yet Arcadian."[14]

The Olmsteds pointed out that parks sufficient to offer rest from the built environment and the tribulations of industrial life had to be secluded, spacious, and accessible, and he suggested that Baltimore rely on stream valleys as the mainstays of its park system. "From the landscape point of view it frequently happens that a great deal of charming scenery is to be found along the stream," the Olmsteds observed; "the water itself is interesting, the trees along the stream banks are apt to be numerous and well developed, and the valley landscape is generally self-contained and full of interest." In many cases, they said, such land would be less valuable for other purposes and thus less expensive to acquire. Water-channel parkways helped to abate the threat of floods. Parkways that followed streams provided the "most convenient and pleasant lines of travel." The Olmsteds hoped to overlay the city with a labyrinth of walks, drives, and open spaces in which Baltimoreans of every background could encounter "the colors of foliage, flowers, earth, rocks, walls, sky and everything we see out of doors."[15]

While Preston Gardens in St. Paul Place was not an Olmsted project, it did reflect Beaux-Arts and City Beautiful thinking. Begun in 1915, when the city marked centennials of the Battle of Baltimore and the dedication of the Washington Monument, this pet project of Mayor James H. Preston involved widening St. Paul Street between Lexington and Hamilton Streets and replacing five blocks of Federal-era houses with a landscaped park, complete

Although never fully adopted, the Olmsteds' ambitious city parks plans led eventually to Wyman and Herring Run Parks, additions to existing parks, and a partially completed Stoney Run Parkway (later San Martin Drive). It also laid the groundwork for state purchase of the lower Patapsco River Valley. In 1926 the Olmsteds submitted another proposal, this one calling for the extension of Druid Hill Park up the Jones Falls Valley to Lake Roland. For various reasons, only Cylburn Park and Robert E. Lee Park—the latter incorporating land willed to the city by the Garrett family ever materialized.

Preston Gardens, an effort both to move traffic and provide green space to downtown, pictured not long after its completion in 1919. Enoch Pratt Free Library

RIGHT:

Three early-nineteenth-century houses on East Pleasant Street, not far from Preston Gardens and across the street from the house that once belonged to the Riddell-Carroll families, shortly before their demolition in the 1930s—part of the price of downtown progress. Enoch Pratt Free Library

with curving stone steps, winding pathways, and, eventually, a statue of John Mifflin Hood, president of the Western Maryland Railroad.

The Municipal Arts Society also pressed for a new home for the Baltimore Museum of Art, which had incorporated in 1914 and afterward occupied rooms in the town mansion of Mary Garrett, at the southwest corner of Cathedral and Monument Streets (it was her brother who, in 1887, had employed Stanford White to refurbish two houses into one and add a brownstone façade at 9–11 West Monument, a half block away). In 1919 the trustees announced a search for an architect to design the museum. Among them and the museum founders were many of John Russell Pope's Baltimore friends—the Fricks and the Garretts, Michael Jenkins, Henry Walters, and Theodore Marburg—and, not surprisingly, Pope won the commission. It brought him to a genre for which he later won renown as the architect of the National Gallery in Washington and the Tate Gallery in London. On what became Museum Drive, Pope devised a building that served as a model for all such future commissions—a biaxially symmetrical structure with a slightly projecting central portico that boldly announced the main entrance. Behind, just as the carefully graded limestone façade suggested, lay a large central hall—possibly based on the ancient Theater of Marcellus—flanked by regularly arranged gallery spaces. This arrangement marked a distinct improvement over previous American museum designs; for the first time galleries, instead of being clustered together, were separated by hushed open spaces, which heighten the museum-goer's ability to see and to contemplate.[16]

Pope's final important Baltimore commission also came about through the Garrett-Frick family. In 1933, anticipating the bequest of Mary Frick Jacobs's collection of Old Master paintings, museum officials asked the architect to enlarge his own building. He repeated the original structure's general architectural design, creating an enclosed court behind the main hall, with galleries of various shapes arranged around it.

Meantime, in the still-rural northern precinct of the city, the Roland Park Company undertook the development of Guilford in 1913 and Homeland in 1924, forming a set of contiguous communities covering fourteen hundred acres. The brick and stone houses in Guilford tended to be larger and grander than the older, generally frame dwellings of Roland

*Charlcote house, the residence of
James Swan Frick, Esq., in
Guilford, designed by John Russell
Pope and completed in 1914. From
Views of Residences, the Roland
Park and Guilford District
(Baltimore, n.d.). Enoch Pratt
Free Library*

Park; those in Homeland, generally brick, did not quite aspire to the grandeur of Guilford. In Guilford, Mary Frick Garrett Jacobs's brother, James Swan Frick, deserves credit for what may be Pope's finest building in Baltimore, Charlcote House, completed in 1914. Frick bought six large lots—totaling four and one-half acres—due north of the intersection of Charles and St. Paul Streets, and he evidently gave Pope free rein in design. To ensure privacy, Pope built a brick wall around the entire site. He then placed the house toward the rear of the property and perpendicular to the entrance gates, thereby creating a small, private forecourt. The other principal façade faces south, with a bowed and pilastered section that overlooks the substantial garden and echoes the overall shape of the site. The house's simple cruciform plan features a large entrance hall leading to an ample, sun-filled drawing room with smaller reception rooms placed around. Pope kept the interior trim simple, somewhat suggestive of the Adamesque, and at Frick's request managed to incorporate several mantels the client had saved from an early-nineteenth-century downtown house. In all, Pope gave Frick a unified, well-integrated creation, which the contemporary critic Charles S. Keefe accurately called "one of the finest" houses in America.[17]

The success of Guilford and Homeland brought imitation. In 1922 the brothers Robert and John Garrett created the Blythewood Company to develop a community adjacent to and east of Roland Park. Leading architects again came to the fore. The partners Wyatt and Nolting had built houses for themselves in Roland Park; in 1924, on Blythewood Road, Charles Platt designed an immense brick French chateau for the diplomat and bon vivant Gilman D'Arcy Paul.

In addition to individual planned communities, Baltimore now and then gained what might be called a planned community within a planned community. Edgevale Park, an inward-facing courtyard development designed by the Roland Park Company's architect Edward L. Palmer Jr., went up just east of Falls Road in 1910–11. Palmer lifted his design virtually intact from the buildings of the English architect Charles Francis Annesley Voysey, whose best work, beginning in the 1890s, featured horizontal lines, hipped roofs, mullioned windows, roughcast white walls, sloping buttresses, and strap-hinged wide doors. Around the turn of the century, Voyseyesque buildings such as the Edgevale Park group appeared in most

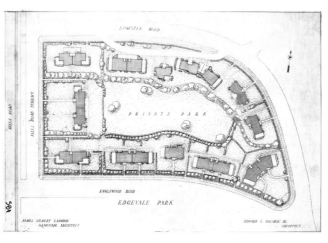

TOP, LEFT:
Edgevale Park as completed. Peale Collection, Maryland Historical Society
TOP, RIGHT:
"A Group of New Houses for Roland Park," designed by Charles A. Platt. From House & Garden, *April 1903, 194.*
BOTTOM:
Site layout, Edgevale Park, designed by Edward L. Palmer Jr., 1911–12. Peale Collection, Maryland Historical Society

major American cities and suburbs. The identity of the architect of the Beaux-Arts houses and Italianate gardens that line Goodwood Gardens, another of Roland Park's communities-within-a community, remains a mystery. Platt signed a sketch and site plan that appeared in a magazine in 1903, but Wyatt may finally have designed the block's classically derived houses and gardens.[18]

The Georgian Revival and Laurence Hall Fowler

"The young men nowadays," Edith Wharton declared in 1903, unless embroiled in state politics or municipal reform, seemed likely to be "going in for Central American archaeology, for architecture or landscape-engineering; taking a keen and learned interest in the pre-revolutionary buildings of their own country, studying and adapting Georgian types, and protesting at the meaningless use of the word 'Colonial.'"[19] Wharton rightly associated architecture in her day with adventure. At the time, many American architects were looking backward to their own past, pruning the list of places, objects, and events that a civilized person needed to know about and working out a new architecture of simplicity, light, coolness, and decorum. The Georgian Revival was an architectural revolution, and Baltimoreans were in the forefront.

Like the medieval revivals of the 1840s and fifties and the learned eclecticism of the 1870s and eighties, the Georgian Revival was more than a movement in architectural taste. By 1890 the traditional upper classes of older cities like Baltimore were feeling pressure from new European immigrants, whom they could not outvote, and from new American plutocrats, whom they could not outspend. Closing ranks, they launched the Social Register (and in Baltimore the Blue Book) and founded organizations such as the Daughters of the American Revolution and the Colonial Dames. Inspired by the great deeds of their forebears, reforming patricians evangelized with buildings that marked a return to a fancied eighteenth-century Golden Age. As the movement matured, houses once more resembled those of Georgian America or Georgian England.

Following this trend and its yearning for the colonial past, Baltimore architects increasingly found inspiration in distinctly American building traditions: clean lines and designs with traceable, local origins. Maryland displayed its eagerness to return to tradition in 1907, when the state building at that year's Jamestown Tercentenary recreated Homewood House. By the same token, if on a much smaller scale, Billy Baldwin—a native Baltimorean who eventually became known as the dean of American interior decorators—recalled his parents' decision in about 1913 to remodel the original "rather gloomy interior" of their Goodwood Gardens house. They painted the black oak walls white; "the Jacobean furniture was thrown out and chaste Hepplewhite mahogany brought in."[20]

During the first four decades of the twentieth century, the career of one architect, Laurence Hall Fowler, embodied the Georgian Revival movement in Baltimore architecture. Born in 1877, the year the Johns Hopkins University received its charter, Fowler completed undergraduate studies at Hopkins and then proceeded to Columbia University's School of Architecture, where he received his M.A. degree in 1902. He worked briefly in New York before embarking on a European Grand Tour. The young man got as far as Paris, where, applying for admission to the Ecole des Beaux-Arts, he demonstrated his awareness of the symbolic nature of the classical orders by discussing the Temple of Apollo at Delphi. Though admitted, he departed for home in 1904, before obtaining a degree, perhaps believing that the great

Laurence Hall Fowler's drawing desk. The John Work Garrett Library of the Johns Hopkins University

fire would give ambitious architects plenty of work. Back in Baltimore, he found employment with the firm of Wyatt & Nolting, but in 1906 he opened his own office at 347 North Charles Street. He kept his one-man operation going there for the next forty years.

At Columbia and in Paris, Fowler drank deeply from the cup of historicism, and throughout his career he steadfastly looked to the past for inspiration. Fluent in the neo-Georgian (or neocolonial), English Renaissance, shingle, chateauesque, Italianate, and Spanish Mission styles, Fowler soon drew praise for his work. He became, for most Baltimoreans, the ideal modern architect. Mencken in his column predictably praised Fowler's design for a restaurant called the Dutch Tea Room (sadly, no images of it seem to have survived): "It has color, it has character, it has distinction—and buildings of distinction are almost as rare in Baltimore as Prominent Baltimoreans of sense."[21]

While Fowler's commissions ran the gamut of building types, he truly excelled at house design, and between 1906 and his death he produced roughly sixty dwellings in and around Baltimore. He recognized that when he designed houses for his well-to-do, if unassuming,

TOP:

Greenwood, Charles Street Avenue,
designed by Laurence Hall Fowler
for John E. Deford, completed 1914.
Architectural Forum, *October*
1924, pl. 52. Enoch Pratt
Free Library

RIGHT AND BOTTOM:

Greenwood, entrance hall, which
was distinguished by "refinement of
detail, and Adamesque dining-room
details. Architectural Forum,
October 1924, pl. 53. Enoch Pratt
Free Library

clients, exterior simplicity could mask studied and sometimes spectacular interior details. He often contributed to this effect by purchasing furniture for his clients—William and Mary chairs or amply legged Elizabethan dining tables. He always began design work with study of worthy historical models; the Thomas Goodwillie house of 1913 relied, as Fowler wrote in his project file, on "early nineteenth-century neoclassical American architectural precedents."[22] In 1914, on a prominent hill north of the city line on Charles Street Avenue, he completed a white-columned brick mansion, Greenwood, for the Baltimore attorney John E. Deford. The building later won national praise. "Not only are the decorative details of this house successfully carried out in the Georgian style, but the brickwork has been given unusual thought and study," declared the *Architectural Forum*. "The walls, which are broken by niches, panels, string courses, and corner piers in a manner reminiscent of Wren's Queen Anne Orangery at Kensington, show the variety of treatment possible in brick architecture when handled by a skilled designer who understands and appreciates the merits of his medium."[23] Also completed in 1914, the William A. Dixon house on Wendover Road in Guilford "derived from American Georgian forms," Fowler wrote, specifically "from the Virginia plantation house Westover." It drew praise from Keefe for being "very pleasant and comfortable."[24]

Fowler was among twenty-four local architects who, along with out-of-towners Pope, Henry Bacon, and Cass Gilbert, entered a 1921 competition to design a memorial commemorating Maryland citizens who had lost their lives in the Great War. The selection committee chose Fowler's proposal, a modified Greek Revival temple somewhat reminiscent of Bacon's contemporaneous memorial to Lincoln in Washington, D.C. Shortly after completion of Fowler's memorial, the *Architectural Forum* praised it for its "fine spirit."[25] Beaux-Arts alumnus that he was, Fowler ensured that his temple contained the obligatory allegorical mural, in this case Baltimore artist R. McGill Mackall's depiction of Victory standing over

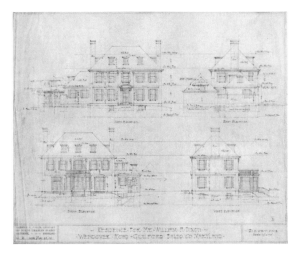

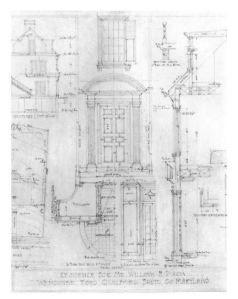

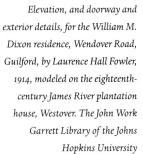

Elevation, and doorway and exterior details, for the William M. Dixon residence, Wendover Road, Guilford, by Laurence Hall Fowler, 1914, modeled on the eighteenth-century James River plantation house, Westover. The John Work Garrett Library of the Johns Hopkins University

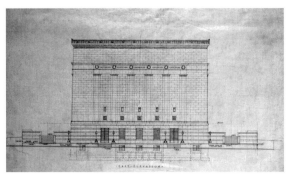

TOP:

West façade of the War Memorial, Laurence Hall Fowler's winning competition design, 1921. Peale Collection, Maryland Historical Society

BOTTOM:

War Memorial, as photographed ca. 1925. Maryland Historical Society

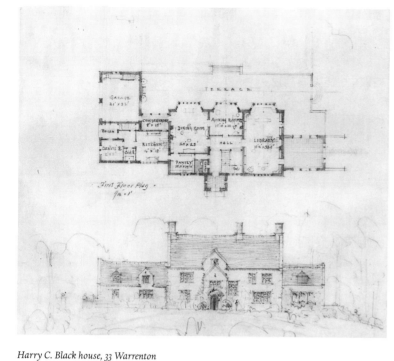

Harry C. Black house, 33 Warrenton Road, designed by Laurence Hall Fowler, 1919. Fowler's sketch of the exterior and first-floor plan. The John Work Garrett Library of the Johns Hopkins University

RIGHT:

Black house, interiors of the dining and drawing rooms, as photographed in 1923 for Architectural Forum. *The John Work Garrett Library of the Johns Hopkins University*

the Tomb of the Unknown Soldier at Arlington National Cemetery. Fowler also designed the plaza that stretched between the memorial and, immediately to the west, City Hall.

Fowler demonstrated the depth of his stylistic repertoire in houses he designed after the war. For Sunpapers publisher Harry C. Black, he completed a Tudor-style brick and timber house in Guilford in 1919. It received much national attention—no fewer than eight photographs and two plans—in the October 1923 issue of the *Architectural Forum.* The dwelling included small-paned casement windows, decorated brick chimneys, gable-end parapets, and a romantic, irregular roof line. Notwithstanding the Elizabethan touches Fowler gave the exterior of the house, its interior, at least the main block, followed a symmetrical, three-bay plan. Designing a house for himself, which was built on a lot on West Highfield Road in 1925, Fowler chose a restrained Mediterranean-style stuccoed design for the exterior while making the interior a minimuseum of period buildings. He enriched the living room with the entablature and fireplace from a demolished Gay Street dwelling dating from the 1780s; the dining room contained a wooden mantel from a Ridgely family farmhouse, dating to about 1800, salvaged when the house went under water with the creation of Loch Raven Reservoir. In the garden Fowler eventually placed granite columns and capitals from the original Enoch Pratt Free Library on Mulberry Street.

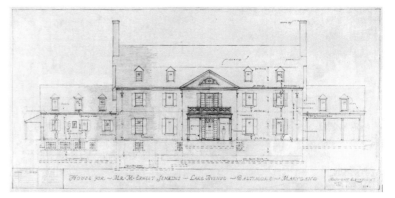

TOP:

*Laurence Hall Fowler residence,
West Highfield Road, 1925. The John
Work Garrett Library of the Johns
Hopkins University*

RIGHT AND BOTTOM:

*Fowler's design for the house of
M. Ernest Jenkins on Lake Avenue,
1926; entrance hall, Jenkins house.
The John Work Garrett Library
of the Johns Hopkins University*

Today the Jenkins house fills administrative needs at the Boys'
Latin School of Maryland.

A house in 1925 for Laurence Miller offered, Fowler wrote, a "cubical composition adapted from Federal precedents."[26] If not the Dixon house, the signature American colonial–inspired Fowler design may have been the five-part Palladian residence he created in 1926 for M. Ernest Jenkins, a prominent attorney, at 907 West Lake Avenue, near the city's northern boundary. Perhaps no building in Baltimore better illustrated Fowler's attempts to re-create the Chesapeake past.

While still a student, Fowler found the perfect hobby for a historically minded architect, namely, collecting antique architectural treatises and pattern books. He made his first purchases on his 1903 trip to Europe—a 1565 edition of Alberti's *De Re Aedificatoria*, a copy of Vignola's *Perspective* (1644), and Serlio's *Tutte l'Opere d'Architettura* (1619)—and he continued to buy throughout his life (he bequeathed his library of roughly four hundred fifty titles to the Johns Hopkins University). Old books confirmed and built upon Fowler's studies at Columbia and Paris and no doubt salved any pain he may have felt for having failed to complete his work at the Ecole; these sources had practical application, too, for the roots of many of his projects lay in those venerable texts. In the late 1930s the noted scientist and sanitary engineer Abel Wolman asked Fowler to design a residence for himself and his wife, Anne, at 3213 North Charles Street. Fowler turned for inspiration to London town house designs, such as those detailed in his copy of William Halfpenny, R. Morris, and T. Lightoler, *The Modern Builder's Assistant* (1742), and smoothly adapted them to suit the needs of a narrow lot. Turning the house so that its length ran the long side of the property and the entrance faced south, Fowler placed the dining room and kitchen on the ground floor; the living room, master bedroom, and secondary spaces were located on the principal floor above. Guest rooms filled the third floor. Faced in well-laid brick, the Wolman house featured a structural steel skeleton, something rarely found in private houses.

The difficult-to-define word *taste* circles around the work of Fowler and other revivalists of this period. In 1922 Keefe peppered the introduction to *The American House* with references to "taste"; the Roland Park Company stipulated that all its houses be designed "reasonably in accordance with the canons of good taste."[27] Without doubt, those canons governed one of Fowler's most important commissions, his decades-spanning involvement with the owners of Evergreen House, career diplomat John Work Garrett and his wife, Alice Warder Garrett. At Evergreen House, Fowler's work demonstrated the quest for a distinctly American revival style to replace the fussy eclecticism of earlier decades.

Not surprisingly, since Alice Garrett and Edith Wharton were friends, "good taste" at Evergreen meant what Wharton referred to in her *Decoration of Houses* (1897). The Garretts had fallen heir to the forty-eight-room mansion and its fifty acres of gardens in 1920. They were emphatically modern creatures, for they borrowed from Wharton in dismissing their architectural inheritance as "superficially ornate,"[28] and they felt obliged to remodel the building to reflect the aesthetics of their own time. Fowler's first task, in 1922, was to turn the second story of a north wing into a theater and convert what had been a billiard room and bowling alley into museum space suitable for John Garrett's superb collection of Chinese porcelain and Japanese netsuke.

Five years later, the Garretts hired Fowler to add a library to the house and redesign the garden behind the house, where he replaced a Victorian hodgepodge of plantings and greenhouses with a central axis punctuated by a few well-placed urns and vases. This horticultural simplification reflected the architectural simplicity Fowler sought in the library, a room whose exterior walls are marked by three large French windows and a chaste cornice. The library's clean, unadorned façades contrast sharply with the decorative elements of the original building. Inside the library, a square room that measures thirty-three feet on each side with an eighteen-foot-high, slightly domed ceiling, Fowler lined the walls with walnut paneling of restrained design. For this distinguished library Fowler designed arched, grilled bookcases of a shape and scale that echo the French windows.

Fowler and the Garretts knew that a room as important as the library demanded an appropriate series of anterooms to ensure that as one walked toward it, one would be preparing for something special (Wharton urged "a carefully graded scale of ornamentation

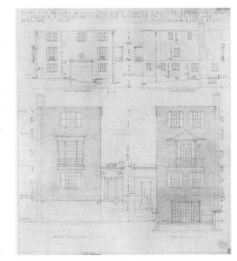

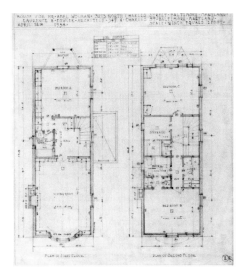

House for Abel Wolman, 3213 North Charles Street, designed by Laurence Hall Fowler, 1938; elevations and first- and second-floor plans. The John Work Garrett Library of the Johns Hopkins University

The Johns Hopkins University acquired the Wolman house in 1993.

culminating in the most important room of the house"). Thus, in 1932, he remodeled the former dining room into a reading room by eliminating the Victorian-era decoration and reorienting the space so that it became part of one great ceremonial axis, which runs through the library and out to the garden beyond. Fowler made the dining room smaller, designed an oblong room that led to the library, and in this anteroom anticipated some of the library details, among them alternating open and closed book shelving: "While similarities were intended and can be observed," wrote a student of Fowler's work, "no doubt is left that the small room's function is to prepare for the ornateness of the library."[29] Finally, when the Garretts asked Fowler to redesign the house's old double parlors in 1941, Fowler fused the two fussy rooms into a single majestic seventeen-by-forty-seven-foot neo-Georgian expanse. He replaced the highly ornamental pilasters and Victorian-era plasterwork that Garrett's mother had installed with dignified butternut wainscoting and restrained cornice, all in the finest "modern" taste.

Besides the houses he executed in Guilford, Fowler secured many commissions on Blythewood Road, served as architectural consultant to the Blythewood board, and sat on

TOP:
Evergreen House, watercolored drawing by Laurence Hall Fowler, 1927. The John Work Garrett Library of the Johns Hopkins University
LEFT:
Evergreen House from the rear, showing Fowler's library addition and formal gardens. Enoch Pratt Free Library
RIGHT:
Evergreen library, interior. The John Work Garrett Library of the Johns Hopkins University

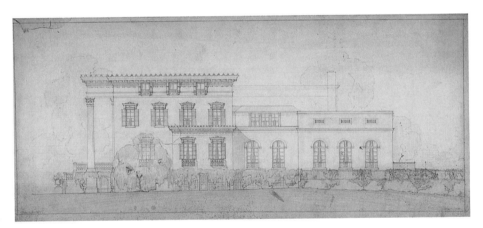

the review boards for Roland Park and Guilford. He thus exercised considerable aesthetic influence over these neighborhoods, applying and enforcing design guidelines and restrictive covenants. The architect Henry Hyde observed with satisfaction that these boards had to approve all plans before even a shovelful of soil could be excavated.[30] Yet in other ways, too—working with typewriter and film—Fowler furthered the local neocolonial revival. He planned an inventory of Maryland antiquities and published research articles on important houses like Montpelier in Prince George's County and Montebello in Baltimore. His camera documented surviving historic architecture, especially those buildings soon to come down. Most sources credit him with saving Latrobe's springhouse and having it moved to the grounds of the Baltimore Museum of Art, which launched its own American Wing in 1925. At about the same time New York architect William Lawrence Bottomley, while decrying buildings that were "Italian, French, Japanese, anything!" heartily applauded the effort Fowler led in Baltimore. Revival architecture, Bottomley declared, "should fit its setting," and "its character should reflect the best cultural traditions of its locality."[31]

Such advice helps to explain the development of the Johns Hopkins University's Homewood campus. In its early years the university occupied undistinguished Romanesque-style buildings near Howard and West Monument Streets, where it remained until, after the turn of the century, president Daniel Coit Gilman (member of the Sons of the American Revolution and biographer of James Monroe) began to lobby for a more rural location and more traditional architecture. In 1902 the financier and university trustee William Keyser donated the 120-acre site of the Carroll mansion at Homewood to the university, and two years later Gilman's successor, Ira Remsen, held a competition for a new main building. John Russell Pope prepared a predictably elaborate classical design for the structure and suggested a campus layout in the same style. Instead, the trustees chose Georgian revival, the submission of Parker & Thomas. This selection would have pleased Bottomley, for the design aimed to emulate the features of Homewood House, the shining architectural light already occupying the ground.

The greatest Baltimore commission of the first decade of the century, perhaps of the century itself, the Homewood campus went up more or less according to plan and laid down a neocolonial course for the future of the university. Gilman Hall, a reinterpretation and enlargement of Independence Hall in Philadelphia, allowed the still-new university to strike a harmonious chord with the colonial American past and also conform with the many other

American institutions of higher learning that had adopted the Georgian aesthetic. Joseph Evans Sperry made notable contributions to the campus—a mechanical engineering laboratory in 1913 and a civil engineering building two years later—all in accordance with the original Parker & Thomas plans. Charles Adams Platt, serving on the university's Homewood Advisory Board from 1919 until his death in 1933, closely guarded the neo-Georgian motif. He approved designs for chemical laboratories (Remsen Hall) in 1923, new dormitories and a general landscaping plan the year following, and in 1928 the partial restoration of the Homewood mansion. During Platt's tenure he persuaded the trustees to decline another Pope proposal, this one for a classical domed auditorium to face Gilman Hall and close the main quadrangle. In 1925 Pope applied a similar concept to a structure Platt could not object to, University Baptist Church, across Charles Street from Homewood. Its smooth stone walls, solemn Greek-cross plan, and low dome provided classical dignity to the university's surroundings.

TOP:

Gilman Hall, The Johns Hopkins University, designed by Parker, Thomas & Rice, 1914. Ferdinand Hamburger Archives, Milton S. Eisenhower Library, The Johns Hopkins University

RIGHT:

View of Latrobe Hall, looking south through the pillars of Gilman Hall. Ferdinand Hamburger Archives, Milton S. Eisenhower Library, The Johns Hopkins University

BOTTOM:

Maryland Casualty Company, West Fortieth Street, near Roland Avenue, designed by Simonson & Pietsch, 1920. Enoch Pratt Free Library

Institutional neocolonialism flourished in Baltimore and in Maryland. In 1921 Otto G. Simonson, a Baltimore architect who had practiced briefly with Theodore Wells Pietsch and had worked mostly on row houses, provided a Georgian structure for the Maryland Casualty Company, a sprawling three-story complex crowned with a clearly Georgian clock tower. Four years later, in Annapolis, Fowler designed a colonial (though flat-roofed) brick home for the state Hall of Records. After fire destroyed Wyatt's shingled masterpiece at the Baltimore Country Club, Sperry designed a new clubhouse, a somewhat banal colonial-revival brick building completed in 1931. At about the time of the 1934 tercentenary celebration, Maryland officially adopted neocolonial as the preferred style for all state buildings.

Apartments, Row Houses, and "Architectural Democracy"

Early in the twentieth century architects from Baltimore and beyond designed the city's first large apartment buildings, innovations that sprang from the same technological developments that permitted commercial skyscrapers. They followed a variety of historical styles, and the first of them not surprisingly went up in fashionable neighborhoods. The Beaux-Arts-inspired Marlborough Apartments opened on Eutaw Place in 1906. Sperry designed Isaac Emerson's Emersonian apartment complex overlooking Druid Hill Park in 1915. Leaving no doubt about the cachet of the nearby Riviera Apartments, which opened in May 1915, the *Sun* described them as "among Baltimore's handsomest and most costly."[32] Standing on the southwest corner of Lake Drive and Linden Avenue, the building featured spectacular views of the park, ten-foot-high ceilings, enclosed porches, and separate servants' entrances.

The stately, six-story Washington Apartments, immediately northwest of the Washington Monument, derived its classical features from Edward H. Glidden, a Cleveland native who trained at the Ecole des Beaux-Arts before settling in Baltimore about 1900. Glidden's structure resembled many a period piece in the socially acceptable neighborhoods of Paris and New York. By the 1920s North Baltimore claimed another set of luxurious apartment buildings. Friz designed the Italian villa–like Garden Apartments at 230 Stony Run Lane in 1923. Three years later Palmer and his partner William D. Lamdin completed the Roland Park Apartments, at 6 Upland Road. Wyatt & Nolting's Warrington Apartments, at 3908 North Charles Street, went up in 1928. All these structures demonstrated the influence of various romantic European styles.

Still, for most Baltimoreans, home meant a row house. So, while Fowler and his clients wrestled with the niceties of Federal sconces, building developers built vast stretches, literally miles, of row houses, more or less by the block. Changes in building materials, for example, increased use of "iron-spot" brick, led to further variation in these vernacular buildings. Iron-spot brick, highly fired and therefore extremely durable, featured a surface

speckled with iron dots darker than the prevailing orange color of the clay, and after about 1890 it became immensely popular with the house-buying public because it did not need to be painted. In the early 1900s developers began offering what they called marble houses, whose flat-fronted Renaissance Revival façade design used white Beaver Dam marble to accent the basement level, window lintels and sills, and, of course, to create Baltimore's signature white marble steps. The marble trim, as well as stained-glass window transoms, aimed to remind buyers of the opulence of the three-story Italianate town houses of Mount Vernon and other popular squares.[33]

One large-scale developer, Walter Westphal, built marble houses of iron-spot brick in 1912 in the 2600 block of Wilkens Avenue, in southwest Baltimore. There fifty-four buildings (with Beaver Dam marble steps and trim) marched along to form the longest row in the city: 1,180 feet, nearly three times the length of the typical downtown block. Within the fourteen-foot-wide houses, Westphal employed stylish middle-class features like pressed-tin ceilings, stained-glass windows, skylights, mantel pieces with columns, and pine floors stained and grained to resemble oak. Crowning a hill that leads down to the Gywnns Falls, the row went up to house garment-industry workers and employees of the nearby William Wilkens upholstery factory. When new, the golden-hued row houses sparked the ire of Mencken, who likened their tones to "the more uremic colors of the rainbow."[34]

TOP, RIGHT:
Washington Apartments, Mount
Vernon Place, designed by Edward
H. Glidden, 1905. Maryland
Historical Society
BOTTOM, RIGHT:
Clyde N. Friz's Garden Apartments,
Stoney Run Lane, as they appeared
in the 1920s. Courtesy of
Christopher Weeks
LEFT:
The Warrington Apartments.
"Typical Floor Plan." Drawing by
Wyatt & Nolting, 1928. Courtesy of
Frank R. Shivers, Jr.

Row of marble houses with corner storefront, Saratoga Street west of Pulaski Highway. Photograph by John Dubas, 1922. Peale Collection, Maryland Historical Society

RIGHT:

The longest row of houses in Baltimore, the 2600 block of Wilkens Avenue, built by Walter Westphal in 1912. Photograph by A. Aubrey Bodine, Peale Collection, Maryland Historical Society

The 2600 block of Wilkens Avenue is now a registered historic district.

Rarely did a builder follow a community plan, but in 1917–18 the Roland Park Company architect Edward L. Palmer Jr. designed a shopping center and some five hundred houses in Dundalk for Bethlehem Steel Company workers. Elsewhere, builders followed streets or natural features or filled in between existing neighborhoods. The most active building developers began on a small scale in the 1880s and 1890s, but by the early 1900s they were putting up rows by the block. Frank Novak, the "two-story king," dominated East Baltimore, from Patterson Park north to Clifton Park and Lake Montebello. Edward J. Gallagher began in East Baltimore, built houses west of Wyman Park, and then developed the southern portion of the Montebello estate on land he purchased in increments from Mary Elizabeth Garrett. His son, Edward J. Gallagher Jr., carried on the family tradition until the 1950s. Irish-born James Keelty grew up in an Irish ward in East Baltimore and trained as a stonemason; he constructed thousands of row houses on the west side of the city, including the area along Edmondson Avenue; Wildwood, south of Gwynns Falls Park in the 1920s; and then, in the 1930s, Rodgers Forge, west of York Road and just north of the city line. The Jewish real-estate broker and building developer Ephraim Macht built his Welsh Construction Company business by using the name of one of his clerks to avoid the prevailing antisemitism; he focused his efforts to the west and northwest. Edward Storck continued the development of Peabody Heights (later Charles Village); along St. Paul and Calvert Streets he built block after block of stately, highly decorated row houses, each with a prominent second-story bay window, front porch, and small front yard.

After 1915, with Gallagher in the lead, builders offered their many customers a new design approach they called the daylight house, which again aimed to make features of high-style architecture accessible to every wage earner. In this case, the developers mimicked the new aesthetic of the detached suburban house, with its front lawn and spacious porches. Two stories high, about twenty feet wide and thirty-six feet deep, red-brick daylight row houses—two rooms wide and two rooms deep—had the advantage of allowing more natural light and fresh air to reach every room ("Do you want to live in a tunnel?" queried newspaper ads).[35] Red brick walls, white wooden trim, and green tile roofs bespoke colonial-revival influences; front yards and deep porches offered some of the amenities of the suburbs. By the late 1920s, stylish row houses being built throughout the city featured neo-

Tudor and neo-Norman designs, imitative of the contemporary houses being built in fashionable Homeland and other suburban developments. At Ednor Gardens, north of Thirty-sixth Street and the municipal stadium, the Gallaghers created a harmoniously designed community of Tudor and Norman-style houses set high above terraced front gardens; in the automobile age, each house also boasted a rear garage. By the mid-1930s, with the popularity of the newly opened Colonial Williamsburg, red-brick, neocolonial row houses filled large-scale row-house communities being developed on the city's fringe. Keelty adopted the style for Edmondson Village, and the Gallaghers expanded Ednor Gardens with row houses sporting red-brick façades with white trim, gable roofs, pedimented doorways, and neoclassical interior wood trim.

That's Entertainment

If *modern* means "up to date," there has rarely been anything more modern in Baltimore than the so-called Russian theater at Evergreen. Until John Work Garrett inherited Evergreen and began reworking it in the 1920s, the diplomat and his wife had lived abroad for extended periods. In addition to being an earnest student of modern music and dance, Alice Garrett was an early patron of Picasso and Modigliani, Bonnard and Dufy, Cocteau and Satie—and Serge Diaghilev, whose Ballet Russe had fascinated her since its Paris debut in 1909. She grew particularly close to Diaghilev's designer of sets and costumes, Leon Bakst, whom she met in 1915. Seven years later, learning that Bakst had fallen on hard times, she invited him to come to Evergreen. Soon afterward she commissioned him to design the interior of Fowler's new theater.

Most observers later agreed that Bakst's designs—more than the music of Stravinsky, more than the innovative choreography of Massine, more even than the sensational dancing of Nijinsky and Pavlova—accounted for the Ballets Russes's total effect. A gifted stage designer who forever changed the worlds of theater and dance, Bakst spent months on the Evergreen project. He devised stylized roosters and other peasant motifs, which he stenciled in blazing colors onto the theater's whitewashed walls and proscenium arch. He believed that his electrifying color combinations—azure and orange, for example—were "rich, magnificent, and blinding."[36] Not content with mere wall decoration, he created scores of costumes for his patroness and even constructed three colorful stage sets. One can only imagine the reaction of the Baltimoreans who convened at Evergreen in May of 1923: They entered the theater and took their seats; as the lights dimmed, a spotlight illuminated the stage and out danced Alice Garrett in her Bakst-designed peasant costume, the sensational first performer at her sensational new theater. Insofar as *modern* means something never before experienced, then this room—"one of the finest pieces of modern theater decoration in America," commented the critic Charles Spencer, something "both à la mode and a vin-

Interior of Bakst's theater at Evergreen House, 1923. Laurence Hall Fowler Collection, John Work Garrett Library, The Johns Hopkins University

dication of the mode"—must be reckoned among Baltimore's greatest three-dimensional modern masterpieces.[37]

Those same words—"both à la mode and a vindication of the mode"—describe Alice Garrett, as well. In the twenty-odd years she reigned as chatelaine of Evergreen, one of the few houses in town where the arts were patronized and the artists were not, she organized hundreds of recitals and concerts on the estate and built a series of cottages on the grounds in which she let "geniuses," as she said, live unmolested by outside cares. With Mildred Bliss of Dumbarton Oaks, in Georgetown, she underwrote the Musical Arts Quartet and provided Stradivarius violins for the musicians. "There are few places in the world that are very dear to me, where I have known something of the poignancy of life," the columnist Walter Lippmann wrote to Alice Garrett in 1925. "One is a garden near Florence, one a hill in Surrey, one an old lane in Cambridge where I used to walk with William James, and one your Evergreen."[38]

Meanwhile Art Deco, the period style that eventually came close to being a universal modern style, appeared in Baltimore. The Austrian decorator Josef Hoffmann, who in 1903 had founded a Wiener Werkstatte studio to produce high-quality handmade household goods, became its primary progenitor. The style's curious combinations of exotic motifs— drawn from ancient Egyptian and Aztec forms and designs for the Russian ballet—and its fascination with machinery and the machinelike was very appealing during the first three decades of the twentieth century. Hoffmann adopted shapes, themes, materials, textures, and colors—chrome and stainless steel, colored mirrors, and glass blocks—that harmonized with the jazz music of the time and complemented Cubist painting.

Americans gained firsthand familiarity with this new style in 1919, when the Werkstatte opened a showroom in New York; in 1928, through Bullock's Department Store in Los Angeles, it arrived in California, where it attracted Hollywood set designers, especially those working with Fred Astaire and Ginger Rogers. In 1929 architect Eliel Saarinen curated an exhibition on the Werkstatte manner, or Art Deco, at New York's Metropolitan Museum of

Art. Popular with graphic artists and with interior and fabric designers, Art Deco soon found its way into the decoration of buildings, for example, Rockefeller Center and the Chrysler Building in New York.

As Europeans envisioned and practiced Art Deco, it found expression in Cartier bracelets, Lalique's etched-glass panels for the ocean liner *Ile de France*, and various conspicuously expensive objects. Few Baltimoreans wished (or could afford) to live amidst such open luxury, and there were few private Art Deco building projects in the city. The twelfth-story apartment that Lawrence and Mary Tyler Cheek created in the Warrington in 1939, however, provided one example. A Yale-trained architect, Cheek came to Baltimore to serve as director of the Baltimore Museum of Art. He and his wife chose the traditional Warrington ("a building smelling of old furniture and old money," Mary Cheek recalled) but decided to make over their own living quarters "in the then-popular Art Deco style." The Cheeks's modernity did not find universal favor among the Warrington's older residents. At one of their dinner parties the Johns Hopkins anthropology professor George Boas sat next to a matronly sort who expressed horror at the Cheeks's "modern daring." "You know, my dear," she told Boas, " they even have indirect lighting."[39]

Art Deco–style interior of the Lawrence and Mary Cheek apartment in the Warrington, 1939. Courtesy of Christopher Weeks

It was different at the office, however, and Baltimore merchants and businessmen commissioned several fine examples of Art Deco design. In 1924 the Baltimore Trust Company broke ground for a new office building on the southwest corner of Light and Baltimore Streets. Taylor & Fisher and Smith & May designed the thirty-four-story, 509-foot structure, which opened five years later. Of traditional spirelike composition, its soaring main shaft of

LEFT:
The Baltimore Trust Building, an early Art Deco–influenced Baltimore building. Photograph by Holmes I. Mettee, 1950. Maryland Historical Society
RIGHT:
Interior details of the Baltimore Trust Building. Bank of America

Later the property of banks that merged with ever-larger firms, the Baltimore Trust building received a regilded roof in the 1990s and new exterior lighting. Today it stands as one of the city's best preserved and most distinctive downtown landmarks.

red brick rested on a five-story Indiana limestone base and, after a series of dramatic set-backs, climaxed in an exuberant copper-sheathed mansard roof accented with gold leaf. Stylized decorative ironwork around windows and doors portrayed local favorites like oysters and crabs; street-level embellishments, especially around the main doors, included bronze, marble, and glass panels, all decorated with zig-zags, sunbursts, and other popular Art Deco motifs.

The equally lavish interior featured a main banking room, rising two full stories from a mosaic floor (designed by Hildreth Meire, who contributed to the design of Radio City Music Hall in New York City) to an ornately painted ceiling. Murals on the surrounding walls, the work of R. McGill Mackall, offered homage to the subjects that made Baltimore famous, including medicine, shipping, railroads, horse racing, and *The Star-Spangled Banner*. Nationally known metal worker Samuel Yellin crafted the elegant wroughtironwork

With Art Deco ornamentation and a dazzling all-white finish on its concrete exterior surface, Montgomery Ward's enormous Monroe Street warehouse, opened in 1925, helped to mark the rise if not the peak of mail-order retailing. Designed by W. H. McCaully, this enormous eight-story structure went up on eleven acres bounded by Monroe Street, Washington Boulevard, and a B&O Railroad branch in southwest Baltimore. Its 700,000 square feet of storage space met the needs of the company's entire eastern United States mail-order operations. Although it came a generation later than Camden Warehouse and incorporated modern exterior features, reinforced-concrete construction, and large windows, it basically followed the layout of its turn-of-the-century predecessor. Further following well-established precedent by being built as close as possible to existing transportation routes, the Montgomery Ward building shipped and received goods via the B&O rail line or by trucks using U.S. 1, the nearby East Coast's main north-south highway.

A few blocks to the northwest of the Baltimore Trust Building, Hutzler's department store in 1931 opened its new "Tower," the work of James R. Edmunds Jr., a Baltimore native who had studied architecture in the office of Joseph Evans Sperry. The façade of the five-story tower was designed to give vertical thrust to the building, thus emphasizing its importance and monumentality, an impression heightened by the changing colors of the pink bricks, which lighten as they move up the façade. (Hutzler's built a stylistically similar five-

Aerial view of the Montgomery Ward mail-order warehouse, designed by W. H. McCaully and opened in 1925. Photograph ca.1960. Baltimore Museum of Industry

Hutzler's Tower Building, 234 North Howard Street, designed by James R. Edmunds, 1931, was planned literally to "tower" over the old Palace building, to the left. Maryland Historical Society

Hutzler's closed in 1989, and today the Hutzler Tower serves as office space.

RIGHT:
Senator Theatre, 5904 York Road, designed by John Zink and photographed in 1948. Courtesy of Tom Kiefaber

The Senator, a stylistic treasure, is still used as a movie theater.

story addition in 1941.) The corners of the tower proclaimed the name of the store, spelled out in period lettering placed in bands of concrete, as if to reassure shoppers that they had come to the right place. Eye-catching black granite, polished to a high sheen, sheathed the entire building at street level, while the inviting entrance doors, revolving masterpieces in bronze and glass topped by beautiful urn-shaped lights, filled the two end bays.

Splendid as these designs were, Art Deco's almost frivolous theatricality clashed with the popular notion of the time that "the business of America is business." The style seemed to reach its zenith when employed in the design of buildings whose whole purpose was to induce enjoyable flights of fancy: movie theaters. In Baltimore, the Senator Theatre, designed by John Zink in 1939, eloquently makes that point. The Senator's façade showcases the favorite materials of Art Deco design: glass block, neon, Bakelite (hard plastic), and stainless steel. Its circular lobby, floor mosaics, veneered walls, sunburst panels beneath a lounge balcony, and mural depicting the progress of visual entertainment all made it a star of its period.

Despite the date of the Senator's construction, the Great Depression rendered the expensive Art Deco style impractical, thus encouraging designers to devise the simplified, cheaper alternative that came to be known as Art Moderne, or "streamline modern." In 1938, at 1020 St. Paul Street, Charles Nes designed a two-story, stucco-clad building to house the architectural firm of Palmer & Lamdin (Nes was then an associate in the firm). The office nicely illustrated Baltimore Art Moderne, as did Emile Jehle's Kresge's department store (completed in 1937) on West Lexington Street, where the interplay of horizontal and vertical elements and flashy color scheme of cream (walls), red (first-story metal cornice), yellow (signage), and green (second-story window trim and stone panels) made the small structure a shining example of Art Moderne store design.

Most Americans probably found the style appealing because it gave three-dimensional representation to the concept of speed, so its use in the design of the Howard Street Greyhound Bus Station (1941), whose stepped, buff-colored concrete walls suggest sleekness and fluidity, was highly appropriate. Greyhound architects created a national prototype, mak-

Howard Street Greyhound Bus Station, built 1941. Enoch Pratt Free Library

In the late 1990s the Maryland Historical Society acquired the Baltimore Greyhound station and bus barn, converting the station to offices and the barn to dramatic exhibition spaces.

ing all their stations instantly recognizable. Fortunately, their small size and flowing, open plan make them ideal candidates for restoration and adaptive reuse projects.

The Bauhaus Style and Alexander Cochran

As spectacular and novel as the Garrett/Bakst theater or the Senator must have seemed when new, most people today would hesitate to class them as modern architecture. For the majority, *modern* meant skyscrapers and the Bauhaus style.

"Truth was so much more easily perceived then," wrote the longtime *New York Times* critic Ada Louise Huxtable, discussing the impetus behind the Bauhaus movement. "Right was so clearly distinguished from wrong. The angels were an identifiable band." Here, she said, was "the kind of history that changed the world."[40] The movement dated from 1919, when Walter Gropius, a daring German architect then in his mid thirties and living in Weimar, opened what he called his Bauhaus school. Six years later he moved the school to the industrial city of Dessau and designed a workshop whose form and plan suggested an airplane, the very symbol of the new age. Gropius envisioned the Bauhaus as a place where architecture, the fine arts, and industrial design would be taught in pursuit of an ideal machine-age environment; he called for new cultural effort and concepts that moved "away from the static space established unchangeably by enclosing walls toward a flowing space sequence, corresponding to the dynamic tendency of our time and seeking to combine the dimensions of space and time in architecture." The purpose of the Bauhaus, he later explained, "was not to propagate any style, system, or dogma, but to exert a revitalizing influence on design, We sought an approach to education which would promote a creative state of mind and thus help to reestablish contemporary architecture and design as a social art."[41]

For all his effort to find an architecture appropriate to the machine age, Gropius infused Bauhaus modernism with humanistic values. He and his followers—fellow German Ludwig Mies van der Rohe; an early French student, Charles-Edouard Jenneret, known as Le Corbusier; and the Hungarian-born faculty member, Marcel Breuer—aimed to raise the human condition itself. Far from being anarchists, faculty and students of the Bauhaus valued continuity and sought to achieve a successful coexistence of the old and the new. Le Corbusier made loving sketches of old buildings and celebrated the proportion and character of places as diverse (and "unmodern") as Venice, Greece, and North Africa. Modernists criticized "urban sprawl"—the haphazard way cities seemed to be growing—and advocated revolutionary design solutions; even so, they looked with nostalgia to urban life in the past. The Congrès Internationaux d'Architecture Moderne, which formed in 1929 to advance modernist principles, published not only Gropius and Le Corbusier but also works that celebrated the beauty of the Italian piazza and the urban life it expressed and engendered.

Bauhaus innovators did not—indeed, refused to—repeat historic styles. Their buildings were carefully groomed, sophisticated, legible iterations of the relationship between building materials and methods of construction, both of which were new. Bauhaus structures were often white, their walls sheer. These architects eschewed ornament. Drawing attention to the beauty of vernacular architecture and the instructive value of indigenous forms, the creators of this sophisticated new architecture simultaneously—and interestingly—alerted the world to the value of "architecture without architects." Structure itself became the style, a rule that applied in the decorative arts as well as in the design of buildings. In 1925 Breuer designed a tubular steel chair that was widely used for generations. Bauhaus modernism confirmed the belief that architecture was an art to be used, to be lived in, and that its design could mirror and influence the quality of life.

European critics, historians Nikolaus Pevsner and Sigfried Giedion among them, and American students of architecture, chiefly Philip Johnson and Henry-Russell Hitchcock, helped to popularize the new movement. Hitchcock and Johnson (along with Alfred Barr) in fact coined the term *International Style* for a show they organized in 1932 at the Museum of Modern Art in New York.[42] Meanwhile, political oppression in Europe forced many modernist leaders to flee to the United States, where the New Deal, open to ideas about the connection between architectural design and social reform, provided a sympathetic environment. Gropius went to Harvard in 1936, and Breuer joined him there a year later. Mies and László Moholy-Nagy, a Hungarian modernist, settled into the Illinois Institute of Technology in Chicago.

Frank Lloyd Wright, an American stylistic innovator who, in retrospect, appears to have been one of the greatest among the reformers, did not design in this new manner, but his rebellion against traditional eclecticism and his creation of a personal style based on Japanese and American traditions and his own instincts earned him membership in the insurgency. In the 1930s, determined that good contemporary design not be the exclusive property of the rich, Wright experimented with what he called Usonian houses, practical dwellings that used fine architecture to achieve both privacy and affordability. He created one such house on Baltimore's Cross Country Boulevard in 1940. Wright's only local commission, the small residence achieved the charm of perfect simplicity. Of

Frank Lloyd Wright's 1940 floor plan for the Joseph Euchtman house, and the living-room interior after restoration and renovation in the late twentieth century.
Private collection

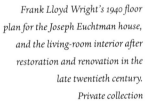

Patterson Park High School, designed by the firm of Wyatt & Nolting, not long after its completion in 1933. Maryland Historical Society

Patterson Park High School is now the Hampstead Hill Elementary School.

RIGHT:

Western Electric Plant at Point Breeze, as photographed in 1979. Baltimore Museum of Industry

frame construction, the cypress-sheathed, flat-roofed structure offered a model of compact planning. Wright gave the house no parlor as such; he separated major rooms by slight changes in roof lines and floor plans and by partial screening walls. A concrete floor contained radiant heating pipes. Wright provided for indirect lighting (similar to that which so impressed the Cheeks' neighbors) and bookcases and furniture of his own design.

Mencken and others grumbled about "the new architecture" and took satisfaction that it enjoyed far less success in the United States than in Germany or Scandinavia. "We live in a Machine Age," Mencken fumed in one essay, "but there are still plenty of us who have but little to do with machines, and find in that little or no answer to our aspirations. Why should a man who hates automobiles build a house designed upon the principles which went into the Model T Ford?"[43] Nonetheless, Bauhaus modernism eventually reached conservative Baltimore. Gropius might have been pleased at the clean lines of the Patterson Park High School, at East Pratt Street and Ellwood Avenue, which the city built in 1933 after a design by the old firm of Wyatt & Nolting (Wyatt died in 1926; his partner survived until 1940). The boxy, purposeful brick building had horizontal lines and square, factory-like windows; it represented Baltimore's first break from history-laden eclecticism in school design.

The Bauhaus founder would surely have approved of the functional discipline of a sprawling, low-rise factory complex built by the Western Electric Company in Baltimore at about the same time. By then industrial location and design had begun pointing in a new direction, away from multistory factories and warehouses and from cramped, costly urban locations where property was expensive and expansion difficult. Moving to outlying areas, where land was open and cheap, and relying more on automobiles and trucks and less on railroad lines, manufacturers could build plants in which mechanized production flowed across a single floor. In search of a site for the manufacture of communications cable, the Bell System subsidiary settled on a 125-acre tract on the harbor at Colgate Creek, southeast of Canton. Such large clear areas were scarce within the city; this one came available with the closing of Riverside Park, earlier a popular streetcar-spawned amusement park. The site allowed space for parking and easy access to railroad, streetcar, and highway. On it Western Electric built two immense two-story brick buildings, a power house, and other support facilities. Designers placed the integrated complex in a parklike setting following the Bauhaus model. For all his effort to find an architecture appropriate to the machine age, Gropius and his followers still wished to integrate the natural and the artificial, blend old and new, and improve the human condition.

This philosophy greatly appealed to Alexander Smith Cochran, a Baltimorean who, like Alice and John Garrett a generation earlier, found himself perfectly and uniquely positioned to introduce his fellow citizens to new perspectives on old issues. His father, a New Yorker, had married Annie Lorraine Gill, whose family had deep Maryland roots, and the couple settled just north of the Baltimore City line, on Woodbrook Lane. After Gilman School and Princeton University, young Cochran studied architecture for one year at Yale, where he heard Wright, Breuer, Le Corbusier, and other leading modernists deliver lectures. In 1937 he transferred to Harvard's Graduate School of Design, where he developed into one of Gropius's firmest disciples. Cochran graduated and then, a bit uncertain as to where he

James W. Rouse house, designed by Alexander S. Cochran, 1947. Maryland Historical Society

James Rouse House: Main façade

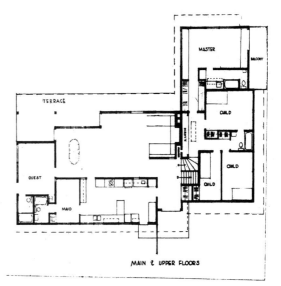

James W. Rouse house, main- and upper-floor plans. Maryland Historical Society

James Rouse House: Plan

MAIN & UPPER FLOORS

should practice, met Frank Lloyd Wright at a party and asked him what to do; should he go back to Baltimore? Wright "put an arm about me," Cochran wrote later, "and said, 'Go to that benighted city, young man.'"[44]

Cochran did return to Baltimore, after wartime service in the navy and a brief tour of California "to see the new architecture," and in 1947 he opened Alexander Cochran & Associates, Architects, at 411 North Charles Street (James Stephenson and Richard C. Donkervoet later joined him, giving the firm its initials CS&D). "We all thought he was going to pick up Mr. Fowler's baton," recalled an observer of the scene. "We all got surprised."[45] Cochran refused to design revivalist houses and churches; "we should not be surprised that Baltimore's memorial to the dead of 1917 took its form from a Greek temple," he wrote of Fowler's work, given the city's predilection for architecture "unconcerned with industrialism." Instead, the *Evening Sun* later noted, Cochran set out alone "to fight the lonely battle for modern architecture in Baltimore." According to one friend, "Alex always told prospective clients that he simply wouldn't do a building unless it was modern; I suppose he lost a lot of commissions that way, but he certainly maintained his integrity."[46]

Cochran's early work introduced his hometown to modernist residential design. For his fellow navy veteran James W. Rouse, an investment banker who shared Cochran's penchant for experiment, the architect in 1947 designed a house that marked a true beginning for "contemporary architecture" (a phrase Rouse preferred to "modern architecture") in Baltimore. Its unusual features, for Baltimore, included clean lines, a flat roof, and an open floor plan that recalled Wright's Euchtman house. Cochran's own 901 West Lake Avenue residence, completed in the spring of 1950, drew praise—"Mr. Cochran's vision-come-true," announced the *Sun*, "a marvel"; "as modern as today's sun," proclaimed the *Washington Post*— and won the AIA National Honor Award for 1951. Cochran's innovative features included a thirty-five-foot-long Plexiglas skylight; floors of flagstone, cork, and asphalt tile; walls of plywood and of stone quarried on site; untreated cypress exterior siding; and floor-to-ceiling plate-glass windows. Perhaps mindful of fears that embracing modernism meant jettisoning local architectural traditions, Cochran stated that he viewed his new residence as "a Maryland house, married to the soil" and designed "for Maryland weather and scenes and living."[47]

Cochran continued to design residences, a few of them landmarks. In one case Harrison Garrett, a Princeton friend of Cochran and nephew of the owner of Evergreen House, asked Cochran to design something for him that would be completely new. The resulting large house in Brooklandville synthesized the Bauhaus approach in its exterior horizontality, open plan of rooms, exposed brick interior walls, and simple fireplace openings. Cochran called for cork floors in the service areas and heated slate in the more public spaces. The following year Cochran completed work on two more signature designs. The Dr. Milton Sacks house in Pikesville had the look of a Le Corbusier structure—sharp, tight massing, a smoothly functioning "machine for living," as the modernist had prescribed. Inside details further illustrated the Cochran approach: a crisply cut fireplace and a two-part bookcase that visually divided living and dining areas. The Charles E. Smith house, balancing compact closed spaces with open areas, admitted much light, encouraging the impression that *indoors* and *outdoors* were words with little meaning. Its reflecting pool demonstrated another Cochran touch.

In 1996 the original Cochran house was demolished to make way for new buildings at the Boys' Latin School of Maryland.

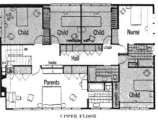

Alexander Smith Cochran house, 901 West Lake Avenue, 1950: Garden façade and floor plan as it appeared in House and Garden, *January 1951, 51.*

Harrison Garrett house, 1952.
Maryland Historical Society

Dr. Milton Sacks house, 1953.
Maryland Historical Society

In the 1920s, Edward L. Palmer had helped to plan single-family housing in the industrial area of Dundalk. In quite different fashion, Cochran in the 1950s became involved in several large-scale urban renewal programs in Baltimore. As a member of the Citizens' Planning and Housing Association (CPHA)—an advisory group to city government with special interest in the related issues of substandard housing and traffic congestion—and also as a disciple of the Bauhaus, Cochran had many ideas for the attack on "blight." Collaborating financially with Rouse, he designed one of the first privately financed low-income housing projects in the nation, the Freedom Apartment and Shopping Center complex, which opened on Erdman Avenue in east-central Baltimore in 1951. The name of the two-story, court-grouped apartments (308 units in fifteen buildings) stemmed from Rouse's suggestion that residents there would enjoy "freedom from care." As part of the rent-controlled complex, Cochran designed an eleven-store shopping center with ample parking. European architects, touring the complex in its first year, praised its "tapering fascia" and "strong horizontal line."[48] The design represented vintage Bauhaus modernism, especially the belief that the key to urban happiness lay in proper planning and attention to infrastructure.

The following year another Cochran-designed affordable-housing complex opened, this one, Flag House Courts, standing on East Pratt Street between the Jones Falls and the Johns Hopkins Hospital. Working under contract with the city, Cochran adopted the Le Cor-

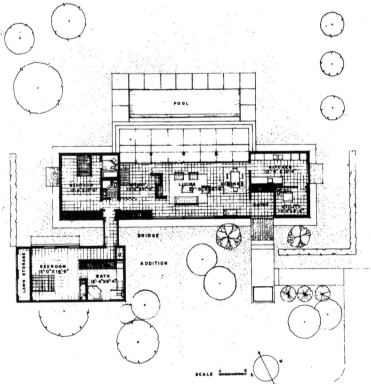

Charles E. Smith house, 1953. Main façade showing the reflecting pool, which became a Cochran signature, and floor plan. Maryland Historical Society

Freedom Apartments and Shopping Center, Erdman Avenue, completed in 1951. Maryland Historical Society

Flag House Courts, East Pratt Street, finished in 1952, as seen from the air, looking northwest. Maryland Historical Society

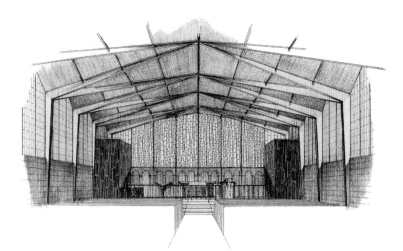

*Church of Our Saviour, Broadway
and McElderry Streets, interior
view. Maryland Historical Society*

busier idea that in the future people would live happily in massive high-rise blocks, which he described as vertical garden cities. Land around such buildings would be left free for schools, parks, and other community needs. Following Le Corbusier in spirit (and in cooperation with the Baltimore firm Wrenn, Lewis & Jencks), Cochran called for three twelve-story apartment towers of plain brick and simple windows. Though each floor had some open space in the service area dividing the two halves of each tower, Cochran avoided balconies. He planned the apartments so that families with small children would occupy the lower floors and rely less heavily on the elevators. Among the towers, he intermingled fourteen three-story garden-apartment blocks. The complex provided 352 residential units for poor families.

Cochran's work did not win unanimous praise, and a house he designed for a lot on Blythewood Road, where the historic-minded Laurence Hall Fowler had done so much work, had to undergo modification (a pitched rather than flat roof) to quiet critics in the neighborhood. Yet in the early-to-mid-1950s, while serving as president of the Peale Museum Board of Trustees and in that role supporting publication of Richard H. Howland and Eleanor P. Spencer's history of Baltimore architecture, Cochran carried on the modernist crusade. In 1957, when he designed the little Church of Our Saviour at Broadway and McElderry Streets, he built it of steel, which he left exposed, within and without. The *Sun* noted with pleasure "that architects no longer see any need for hiding steel."[49]

Gradually, a few other Baltimoreans enlisted in the modernist movement. Gaudreau & Gaudreau (successors to Lucien Gaudreau's firm) designed the striking Carl Murphy Auditorium and Fine Arts Building at Morgan State College in 1960. Charles Richter and Walter Ramberg both designed innovative modernist houses in the region. But in the early 1950s the most important contribution of the modernist sensibility may have been its impulse to reform and to think in large terms. Not accidentally did Cochran belong to the CPHA, and the impulse to fight blight from many angles eventually led to larger coalitions—the Committee for Downtown in 1954 and the Greater Baltimore Committee in 1955 were made up of business and corporate leaders who could envision tearing down much of the city and rebuilding it.

8

BUILDING A RENAISSANCE, 1955–2000

"When a man is tired of London, he is tired of life; for there is in London all that life can afford," Dr. Samuel Johnson wrote of eighteenth-century-London. All city lovers treasure the phrase, which Baltimore writer Gerald W. Johnson quoted when he moved into a new Bolton Hill town house in 1965. Substituting "Baltimore" for "London" in the famous sentence, Baltimore's Johnson remarked that deciding to live in the city was not as simple as it had been for his eighteenth-century counterpart. Together with air pollution and noise, he observed, "the physical giantism that afflicts our cities" makes urban life difficult.[1]

Anxiety about those difficulties—about the future, as well as surviving the present—preyed heavily on the minds of Baltimoreans in the second half of the twentieth century. Fleeing the old city for the suburbs offered one solution, and thousands embraced it, producing a sharp decline in population, which, from an all-time high of 949,708 in 1950, dropped to 905,787 in 1970, to 736,014 in 1990, and to 651,154 in 2000. During a time when Baltimore professional sports teams won enviable football (1958, 1959, 1971) and baseball (1966, 1970) championships, which enabled Baltimoreans to refer proudly to their city as "Flagtown, USA," community leaders and business people worked hard to stem the outflowing tide and resurrect the city's center. In the late 1950s business leaders cooperated with elected officials, Gov. Theodore R. McKeldin chief among them, in planning and building Charles Center, a highly successful downtown development project. In 1964 city fathers created the Commission for Historical and Architectural Preservation and charged it with evaluating and saving architectural treasures in the city. William Donald Schaefer, a former city council president who won election to the mayor's office in 1971,

The landmark McCormick spice building as it appeared before demolition of the last of the steamboat piers on lower Light Street. Maryland Historical Society

Two views of downtown Baltimore at mid-century, when the city embarked on the Charles Center redevelopment project. Hired by the planning department to document the changes soon to be under way, the photographer Marion E. Warren captured the continuing importance of inner-harbor shipping, the level of industrial activity along the lower waterfront, and the comparative emptiness along Light Street. Photographs by Marion E. Warren

thereafter became Baltimore's leading cheerleader. In 1977 he and other officials broke ground for a spacious new convention center, and in 1980 the Rouse Company opened Harborplace, a festival market that soon drew millions to the Inner Harbor. In the 1970s and 1980s the national media and Baltimoreans themselves spoke of a "renaissance." Many public figures and personalities championed the redevelopment of downtown. Besides McKeldin and Schaefer, mayors D'Alesandro (father and son), J. Harold Grady, Clarence "Du" Burns, Kurt L. Schmoke, and Martin O'Malley presided over the rebuilding, but the city owed much to the agency administrators who directed the task, including J. Jefferson Miller, Walter Sondheim Jr., Martin Millspaugh, Robert C. Embry Jr., M. Jay Brodie, and Larry Reich.

The success stories were the result of self-help and a heavy influx of federal funds, not all of which benefitted the downtown or the city proper. Millions of dollars from Washington gave the region a beltway, encouraging sprawl beyond the city limits; a north-south commuter highway following the bed of the Jones Falls and ending near City Hall; a bridge over the Patapsco River east of Fort McHenry and two tunnels under the harbor, one in the 1950s and another in the 1970s. Federal money produced a partial subway system, which carries commuters to and from the northwestern suburbs to downtown and east to the Johns Hopkins medical campus. More money gave riders a light rail line from points well north of the city, through it, to stops that include Baltimore-Washington International Airport. More federal money went into housing under the rubric of "urban renewal." Some funds built high-rise, subsidized apartments, structures later derided and replaced; some money—not enough—went into recycling old housing stock.

The plight of the city prompted creative local solutions, often copied elsewhere. Charles Lamb, an architect heavily involved in downtown renewal efforts, recalled one Baltimore twist: the latitude the city granted private developers. "We had private parking garages under public streets and private buildings over public plazas"; he added that it is very complicated to build that way, but it got results. "In its time, the plan was unheard of—eons ahead of what other cities were doing."[2] As city housing commissioner between 1968 and 1977, Embry strongly encouraged urban homesteading, a program that relied on federal funds and financed the sale of old houses to people who pledged to renovate them. Preservationists nationwide applauded Baltimore's dollar-house lottery, which became one of the most successful programs of its kind in the country. Creative mixes of private, city, and federal monies helped to revive old theaters or open new ones, including Center Stage, the Morris A. Mechanic Theatre, Lyric Opera House, the Hippodrome, and homes for the Arena Players and Theatre Project.

The innovative City Fair focused attention on the key role of neighborhoods in revitalizing Baltimore. Bolton Hill residents lobbied for a city tax code that encouraged restoration and created their own revolving fund to buy and renovate substandard houses. Such achievements lay behind Baltimore's designation in 1978 as "the American city with the best urban revitalization program." "It is a place that simply feels good to walk around in, where every prospect pleases," reported one visitor to Bolton Hill. Young renovators of those Victorian row houses were happy, as an observer wrote, "just to collapse into exhausted sleep with plaster dust in their hair."[3]

Other patterns could only leave a lover of the city anxious for its future—racial divisions, the discovery of dangerous industrial-pollution sites, street crime, turmoil in the public schools, and the flight of a stable middle class. The erosion of family-supporting skilled and unskilled jobs in an international economy hurt many old American cities in the late twentieth century; Baltimoreans, too, deplored the shift from a manufacturing to a service economy. Older city residents could point to the loss of downtown department stores and of Pennsylvania Avenue's shopping and entertainment blocks. Local in-

The Charles Street corridor, with its architectural treasures, looking north-northwest from Mulberry Street ca. 1970. A new apartment building just north of the Unitarian Church obscures the Walters Art Gallery and the Thomas-Jencks-Gladding mansion; on the right, the Peabody Institute and Mount Vernon Place Methodist Church lead the eye upward to the Belvedere Hotel. From this perspective the Washington Monument points to the Johns Hopkins Homewood campus and, almost directly, to the Gilman Hall clock tower. Baltimore City Planning Department

terests no longer controlled most of the banks. At the start of the twenty-first century, no Fortune 500 companies were headquartered in Baltimore, an absence that deprived it of civic leadership as well as dollars. If they could afford to do so, families of all races moved beyond city boundaries, leaving houses in old neighborhoods vacant. Continued loss of population fueled a "vacant housing crisis" in the later 1990s and focused national attention on Baltimore's plight.

Amidst such change and all of its harsh realities, one may well have asked how to preserve the character of Baltimore. "The problem of how to keep traditional towns alive, without destroying what makes life worth living in them, remains," the architectural historian Mark Girouard has observed. "There is no easy answer, no grand, sweeping solution. But to love one's own town, and to learn everything one can about its history and what gives it its individuality, is at least a step in the right direction."[4]

AT THE END OF WORLD WAR II, Baltimore had a handsome traditional urban architecture of its own, one characterized by a practical sense of the possible—by taste rather than originality—and its citizens were devoted to it. Baltimore, an old city with inherited patterns of urban living, found expression in neighborhoods characteristic of its life, public transport (even as late as 1950 Baltimore was still a streetcar and bus city), and architecture.

Beginning in the 1950s and 1960s, however, because of growing acceptance of Bauhaus principles of design and urban planning and the optimism that went with them, Baltimore began building in earnest what, for this conservative city, were fairly daring International-Style structures. The impetus owed a great deal to public funding and public agencies. Before World War II, many American cities established departments of planning, often led by directors whose education and training had exposed them to the new, imported design ideas. The full impact of this change was not felt until after the war. Then, along the lines that Alexander Cochran and members of the Citizens' Planning and Housing Association had established in Baltimore, leading public officials addressed large social problems by means of urban planning—so much so that planning seemed to drive architecture. After 1950, efforts at purposeful planning—decisions about land use, street patterns, and building heights and volumes—rather than the style of individual buildings told the central architectural story. Yet the excitement of the modern dream was one thing; its translation into the language of Baltimore quite another.

Inventing Charles Center

Like other American cities in these years, Baltimore tore down whole neighborhoods of old row houses and built public-housing towers in their place. In 1956, when the newly established Baltimore Urban Renewal and Housing Authority eliminated some twenty thousand houses with privies that had survived the installation of a sewerage system half a century earlier, the city erected a series of high-rise public housing complexes east of downtown. More towers went up west of downtown in the 1960s, so the central business district was eventually surrounded by public housing. The availability of federal funds fueled the construction of these high-density apartment blocks. They were in keeping with the wipe-the-slate-clean planning models that had gained attention in Europe, such as Le Corbusier's Villa Radieuse plan for Paris. But as building forms they were foreign to Baltimore, with its strong tradition of row-house neighborhoods. In the end, there was little money for the design details, amenities, and constant maintenance that might have made the high rise a successful solution to the housing crisis. Just keeping all the elevators in working order proved to be a financial nightmare.

Theories advanced by leaders of the modern design movement were also influential in the construction of highways, streets, and roads. Elevated superhighways swirled around the high rises in Le Corbusier's beautiful drawings; in his fantasy for the redesign of Algiers he laid expressways across the roofs of his skyscraper dwellings. He was convinced that separation of the automobile would free the ground for undisturbed use by people. Spaghetti-like roads on concrete platforms had a strange beauty and equated with technological achievement; they figured prominently in portrayals of the "city of the future" at the New York World's Fair of 1939. Highways and expressways proved a mixed blessing in practice. They made travel by car easy, and they protected certain residential areas from heavy traffic. But they also generated more traffic than before and consumed inner-city land, sometimes tearing neighborhoods apart. From the 1950s to the 1970s, Baltimore gained several such highways: a depressed roadway that brought U.S. 40 into the center of the city from the west; the Jones Falls Expressway, which split the city along the course of the falls that once had powered its mills; and the circumferential Baltimore Beltway.

So necessary to the accessibility and speed of the Bauhaus ideal, these ribbons of concrete also met a powerful and growing popular need, for the automobile had become as indispensable in Baltimore and its environs as anywhere else in America. As business, industry, and dwelling patterns changed, Baltimore was increasingly surrounded by growing communities that depended on the city but were not responsible to or for it. The de facto city—the residential area dependent on commercial and industrial activity within the urban core—spread far beyond the political limits of Baltimore. Chicago had faced the same problem in the early twentieth century, and Philadelphia debated it in the 1950s. But these examples made Baltimore no less afflicted when it faced the issue.

So, like most postwar cities, Baltimore grew outward at a rate governed by the speed at which one could travel, to some extent by public transport but mostly by car. Its radial road network, which spread from the heart of the city like spokes from the hub of a wheel, enabled drivers to move quickly and easily from downtown to practically any point on the outskirts. By the mid-1950s one could detect an exodus from central and eastern Baltimore to places such as Northwood, Loch Raven Village, and Parkville. The G.I. Bill made it possible for veterans to get mortgages for new homes, and developers naturally encouraged the pattern. The consequent reliance on cars forced reconsideration of street usage. In 1953 the city retained Henry A. Barnes, a traffic specialist who set about turning two-way streets into one-way streets, increasing the speed and volume of traffic that moved through town, and otherwise altering how people perceived the city. His changes were particularly damaging to the older parts of town, and they stayed in place, despite construction of the Jones Falls Expressway, which might have eased the use of older streets. As outlying communities such as Towson, Pikesville, and Catonsville rapidly became housing-construction hot spots, developers built large suburban shopping centers to cater to consumers, filling the role formerly served by the downtown shopping district. Completion of the beltway eventually generated more traffic, encouraging travel between communities on the city's periphery. One could live in "Baltimore" without ever visiting its original center.

Concern about the survival of Baltimore's downtown grew deeper. Groups as diverse as the Citizens' Planning and Housing Association and the Municipal Art Society, along with outspoken and insightful individuals, sounded the alarm. The most severe warning came in a report from a commission formed to study the preservation of real estate tax values in Baltimore. The group analyzed the decline in the assessable tax base of properties in the central business district and showed conclusively that the city would soon reach the point at which the loss in property value from deterioration of older buildings would outstrip any gains from new construction. It concluded that Baltimore's once-robust center was not only in trouble but about to hit bottom. "Aggressive and positive action is needed to arrest and counteract depreciating influences, to correct adverse tendencies and to stimulate the preservation and improvement of real estate values throughout Baltimore," it said. "Upon such action, effectively guided and applied, well may depend the continued solvency of the Municipal Corporation and the future well-being of the community."[5] That dire assessment led in January 1955 to the formation of the Greater Baltimore Committee, a private, nonprofit group of civic leaders who decided to put the power of the business community to work on projects that would help rebuild the inner-city tax base and thus help turn the city

Redwood and Hanover Streets, a prime target of Charles Center renewal, as it appeared in the mid-1950s. Photograph by Marion E. Warren

around. Composed exclusively of the top executives of local corporations, the fledgling organization did what Baltimore leaders had often done before—it looked to other cities for ideas, which it sought to implement in ways that would work for Baltimore.

The Greater Baltimore Committee first focused its attention on what it considered a dilapidated commercial district in the heart of downtown: the blocks between Charles Street on the east and Hopkins Place and Liberty Street on the west, and from Lombard Street on the south to Saratoga Street on the north. This district separated the eastern part of downtown, with its banks, newspaper offices, and City Hall, from the stores and theaters along Howard Street. The committee named the project to redevelop this area Charles Center and hired an architect, David A. Wallace, and staff to create a master plan to guide construction—not merely a mapped out receptacle of all that had been built before but a comprehensive plan that set priorities for growth and averted the wheel-spinning of piecemeal development. Wallace arrived from Philadelphia in 1957. The following year, at a meeting with Mayor Thomas J. D'Alesandro Jr. and Greater Baltimore Committee leaders, Wallace presented a redevelopment plan that had been informed by visits to other cities that faced similar problems, notably Philadelphia and Pittsburgh, and was respectful of the character of old Baltimore. The plan encompassed approximately thirty-three acres and, unlike other large-scale projects under way at the time, did not call for total demolition of the area. Instead, it built around and incorporated some distinguished older structures that stood within its boundaries; survivors included the B&O, Baltimore Gas & Electric, and Fidelity buildings and the Lord Baltimore Hotel. The plan also left alone the east side of Charles Street and the buildings to the west of Charles Center; they were to be redeveloped separately, in response to the presence of the new center.

Wallace's plan for Charles Center called for a mixture of uses, another characteristic that set it apart from projects in other cities. Besides private and government offices, there would be housing, shops, restaurants, and a theater to help keep the area alive after the close of the business day. It was designed around two plazas, which reduced the density and offered open space for recreation. A network of overhead walkways connected the area while ensuring that pedestrians could move about without encountering automobile traffic. New parking went out of sight, beneath the buildings and plazas. The center's various levels protected its buildings without isolating them from streets and traffic.

Millions of dollars from combined federal and city sources paid for the acquisition of properties and the rearrangement of utilities and streets to make way for the new buildings and

An early depiction of the plan for Charles Center, superimposing a model of major new buildings onto an aerial photograph by Marion E. Warren.

amenities. The city recouped money through the sale of land to developers and taxes on the new structures. Ultimately, private sources contributed $200 million for land acquisition and construction. Over time, Charles Center gained more than a dozen major buildings. Terms governing the sale of parcels for new buildings specified how they should be designed to fit into the master plan: how they would address streets and where street-level retail stores, loading docks, and parking entrances should be. All buildings had to receive design approval from an architectural review board appointed by the administration of Charles Center.

Planning and urban-design considerations weighed heavily in the deliberations. While the city gained plenty of serviceable, even handsome, buildings during this period, few stood alone as world-class works of architecture. The effectiveness of Baltimore's rebuilt environment came not so much from the sculptural qualities of individual structures as from the efforts of planners striving to create a whole greater than the sum of its parts. In hindsight, one might argue that the Charles Center plan led to the destruction of too many historic buildings and the appearance of uninviting plazas and dubious overhead walkways. But in its time, Charles Center represented an improvement over civic centers that did not have as many different uses or show as much sensitivity to their surroundings. As *Fortune* magazine put it in 1958, "it looks as if it were designed by people who like the city."[6]

During this period, when in many respects the International Style still reigned, Baltimore

One Charles Center, a Mies van der Rohe design. Praising Mies's contribution to the overall Charles Center plan on January 6, 1967, the Sun quoted Philip Johnson, who characterized Mies as "the greatest living architect. In the twentieth century only Frank Lloyd Wright and Le Corbusier equaled him in stature. In influence on world design standards, even they could not compare." Photograph by Marion E. Warren

could hardly be said to have embraced expensive or avant-garde works of modern architecture. And yet in 1960, when city officials held a design competition to select a developer for Charles Center's first major project, an office tower known as One Charles Center, they chose from among five entries the design offered by Metropolitan Structures, Inc., of Chicago. Thus, the commission for the premier building in the renewal district went to one of the masters of the International Style, Ludwig Mies van der Rohe (another, Marcel Breuer, also entered a design). Mies's twenty-four-story glass and aluminum tower at the northwest corner of Charles and Fayette Streets, which opened in 1962, amounted to a Baltimore version of his acclaimed Seagram Building in New York. The tower portion, T-shaped in plan, responded to a volumetric requirement the city set, and it was somewhat uncharacteristic of Mies. Timeless in its design and exquisitely detailed, the building provided an appropriate symbol of the pride and optimism that civic leaders brought to the task of rejuvenating downtown. It set a high standard for other buildings in Charles Center and proved that Baltimore could indeed be a setting for world-class modern architecture.

The One Charles Center design competition produced rivalries among developers that no one had predicted and that ultimately showed the power of the Charles Center plan to stimulate investment. Baltimore businessman Jacob Blaustein had sponsored the Breuer design, and he took umbrage at its rejection. In 1961 he purchased and demolished a department store on the southeast corner of Fayette and Charles Streets (a site just outside Charles Center's boundaries) and built a competing office tower designed by Philadelphia architect Vincent Kling. The Blaustein Building was dedicated in 1964. Since the success of Charles Center depended heavily on control over the marketing of new office space, planners watched carefully to see what effect this unexpected infusion of new office space would have on leasing in the area. In the end it seemed to do the program little harm, and perhaps good: Planners had hoped that Charles Center would encourage private investment nearby, and the Blaustein Building was just that.

Of the other new buildings in or near Charles Center, six were undistinguished or service structures, such as parking garages, which made no pretense of design. The Fallon Federal Office Building (1967, designed by Nes, Campbell & Partners, Fenton & Lichtig, and James R. Edmunds Jr.) and the Baltimore Arena (1962, designed by A. G. Odell Jr.), cumbersome and unattractive, enclosed Charles Center to the south and the west. The Hilton (later the Wyndham Baltimore Inner Harbor) Hotel, built between 1967 and 1972 (William Tabler and Idea Associates, both of New York), and the twenty-story addition to the Baltimore Gas & Electric Company Building (1966, Fisher, Nes, Campbell & Partners, a local firm) were inoffensive and neutral. The Vermont (later Harbor) Federal Building on Fayette Street, completed in 1964 (Edward Q. Rogers, architect), replicated the former Olivetti Building in New York City.

Besides One Charles Center, six projects added significantly to the renewal area—the Sun Life Building, the Morris A. Mechanic Theatre, the Two Charles Center and Park Charles apartment towers, the Mercantile Bank & Trust Building, and the Charles Center

Helmud Jacobi's rendering of the Sun Life Building (Peterson & Brickbauer, in association with Emery Roth & Sons), completed in 1966 on Hopkins Plaza. Martin Millspaugh chose the drawing for the cover of the Urban Land Institute's Technical Bulletin 51, *which appeared in November 1964 and focused on the Charles Center project, "A Case Study in Urban Renewal." Courtesy of Martin Millspaugh*

RIGHT:

Mercantile Bank & Trust Building (Peterson & Brickbauer, in association with Emery Roth & Sons), finished in 1969, viewed from the southeast on Hopkins Plaza. Photograph by Marion E. Warren

South office tower. These buildings, three by local architects, do not resemble one another. All are polished performances. Each addressed not only its place and role in Charles Center but the architectural environment in which the center rose. Charles Center was notable, in part, because its open spaces, plazas, and pedestrian walkways permitted the new buildings to stand away from one other, to relate both to each other and also to older buildings nearby. The Sun Life and Mercantile Bank & Trust buildings (1970, both by Peterson & Brickbauer, in association with Emery Roth & Sons) were distinguished for their rich materials, subtle exterior and interior proportions, and straightforward structural systems.

The Charles Center plan led to the destruction of one old theater, Ford's. The genesis of the design for a new one, the Morris A. Mechanic Theatre (1967, John M. Johansen), reflected a change in Baltimore's approach to modern design. During the years when most of Charles Center's buildings went up, architects (despite their homage to urban planning in the Bauhaus manner) began to question the authority of the masters of the International Style. The understatement and purity of design that its advocates in Europe preferred often translated in urban America to a conservative, stultified modernism, leaving architects and clients without means for personal expression and the pleasures and comfort of ornament. The trouble with the first-generation moderns and their battle to get rid of decorative details, observed historian and critic Nikolaus Pevsner, was that buildings lacking ornament could be boring.

The modern master Le Corbusier had been invited to consider the Mechanic commission. Too busy, he recommended Philip Johnson, who also felt he could not undertake it but suggested Johansen, who accepted the assignment. He responded with a building whose exterior form reflects the shape of the theater inside—an approach the architect called functional expressionism. The mass and weight, the harshness of its material, the way openings are treated as apertures in the wall, and the studied omission of fastidious details usual in

Morris A. Mechanic Theatre, as John M. Johansen envisioned it in the mid-1960s and as completed in 1967. Baltimore City Planning Department. Photographs by Marion E. Warren

Charles Center South, completed in 1975, as RTKL Associates rendered it. Baltimore City Planning Department

theater exteriors and interiors define it as a work of Brutalism, one of a series of "isms" that challenged the International Style. Because of the exposed concrete on its interior and exterior and because it was heavily used, the theater soon began to show its age. But among its staid neighbors it remains an original, one of the few Baltimore representatives of a particular point on the road away from the smooth, stripped-down International Style.

Two Charles Center (1968, by Conklin & Rossant of New York), a pair of high-rise apartment towers at the north end of the renewal area, employed brown brick, which contrasted with the glass and metal of One Charles Center and the grey stone and terra cotta of the old Fidelity Building on Charles Street. Because of their materials,

The University of Maryland's growth later encouraged private adaptive reuse of old brick loft buildings that stood between its campus and downtown. Another conversion, involving the low-rise Hamburger's clothing store, at the southwest corner of Charles and Fayette Streets, for houses and offices, illustrated Charles Center's ability to evolve over time. By the late 1990s, the store had closed and a new owner, Peter Angelos, converted it to become part of the Johns Hopkins University's Downtown Center. Working with Angelos, who also restored One Charles Center with Jonathan Fishman, of RCG, Inc., the city took down the section of the Hamburger's building that spanned Fayette Street, opening up a vista from City Hall to the west side of downtown. The Baltimore firm of Ziger/Snead Architects redesigned and reclad the remaining portion of the Hamburger building so that it provides a counterpart to its Miesian neighbor, its light glass and metal skin playing off the dark glass of One Charles Center to the north. In this case a succeeding generation of architects improved upon the original master plan.

Two Charles Center as RTKL Associates planned the ensemble— an artist's depiction at ground level and a model of the two towers and attached commercial buildings— and, upon its completion, the view from one of the top floors of the southwestern tower, showing the walkway patterns of Charles Plaza. Three notable nineteenth-century structures stand across Saratoga and Charles Streets: (clockwise), the original YMCA, St. Paul's Church, and the old Masonic Hall.
Baltimore City Planning Department

The housing component of Charles Center grew in 1986, when another architect and developer placed a third residential tower, the Park Charles (designed by Winsor/Faricy, Inc. of St. Paul, Minnesota), next to Two Charles Center. Its materials and forms related to, rather than replicated, those of the earlier buildings.

---

window patterns, and the way the roofs are terminated at various heights, these towers manage to suggest that they are residential buildings. The irregular tops also speak to the mansard roof of the original YMCA building across Saratoga Street.

Charles Center South (1975, designed by RTKL Associates of Baltimore, with George Kostritsky and Mario Schack as the lead architects) rivaled One Charles Center in its refinement and quality. A beautifully proportioned hexagonal tower of black granite, glass, and other reflective materials, it rose from a plaza as somber as itself—addressing One Charles Center to the north, the Sun Life Building beside it, and the toughness of the Mechanic Theatre and newer buildings across Lombard Street. In its color it echoed and concluded the composition that began with Mies's tower.

The Charles Center experiment was widely discussed and praised in architectural and planning circles; in 1964 the plans of Charles Center and One Charles Center won national awards, and such success encouraged further rebuilding. As Charles Center took shape, the city undertook to link it with the older commercial area of downtown. The bed of Lexington Street between Charles Center and Lexington Market became a pedestrian mall. The mall also connected Charles Center and the campus of the University of Maryland, Baltimore, which then awaited new buildings for its medical, dental, pharmacy, nursing, and law schools.

Renovating the Inner Harbor

Emboldened by the success of the Charles Center effort, Mayor Theodore R. McKeldin in 1963 announced plans to redevelop the Inner Harbor shoreline, an effort that eventually produced more than three times as many structures over several hundred acres. McKeldin intended not only to turn a corner in rebuilding the city tax base but also to capitalize on a valuable natural asset: Baltimore's waterfront. That shoreline had become a sorry scene of rotting piers, parking lots, and derelict industrial buildings, which detracted from the revival of downtown. Two years later the city adopted a David Wallace plan establishing as the limits of the Inner Harbor project the Jones Falls on the east and the old B&O Railroad line and Camden Yards on the west. On the north it was bounded by Lombard Street, on the south by Federal Hill. This land ultimately produced three projects. The first, Inner Harbor I, addressed the area bounded by Lombard, Charles, and Hanover Streets and Key Highway. Inner Harbor West included land from Hanover Street to Camden Yards. Inner Harbor East included Market Place, Piers 4, 5, and 6, and the old lumber yards east of the lower Jones Falls.

To coordinate these efforts, the city in 1965 created a new agency, Charles Center–Inner Harbor Management, Inc., and gave it responsibility for assembling land for redevelopment, selecting developers, and maintaining a high quality of architectural design. For this area city officials wisely adopted a comprehensive planning approach similar to the one that had produced Charles Center. Combined city and federal investment set the project on its way. The money was used, as it had been in Charles Center, to acquire and prepare land for redevelopment. The city maintained considerable control over what could be built because it assembled the land and awarded it to developers willing to follow its design and construction guidelines. Before building on the cleared lots, developers had to agree to specifications laid down for the replacement structures, such as their uses and the ways they addressed the street. Architectural style was left an open question, but a panel of architectural advisors reviewed designs repeatedly, in general and in detail. The same group oversaw architectural and planning proposals for both Charles Center and the Inner Harbor, to ensure a consistently high level of quality and coherence between the two areas.

As with Charles Center, the strength of the Inner Harbor plan lay in urban design principles that subordinated individual buildings to the total composition. Structures did not fight with one another for attention. In general, the forms of new buildings reflected greater concern for siting, mass, proportion, and scale than for stylistic trends. That way, planners could create a pleasing and cohesive environment without needing every building to be a masterpiece.

Relatively low buildings along Pratt and Light Streets provided the urban frame for the Inner Harbor, making essentially recessive statements punctuated by towers at strategic locations. Along Pratt Street, the horizontal office buildings, constructed at a consistent height and distinguished primarily by façade details, formed a quiet outline, like a picture frame. These background buildings provided a counterpoint to the more sculptural foreground buildings, which generally contained public attractions and helped to define and enliven the water's edge. They also gave the lakelike harbor a sense of containment without making it seem too walled in. By keeping the frame low and the occasional towers slim and far apart, planners attempted to give the taller and more massive buildings, located several blocks from the water, views of the harbor they otherwise would not have had.

For many years city planners rigorously enforced the Inner Harbor plan and its design principles, which included a consistent height limit for buildings along Pratt and Light Streets of 145 feet above mean low tide, or about ten stories (the limit was derived from the height of the old McCormick & Company spice factory, which was torn down in 1988). A wide, planted promenade was created on the north side of Pratt Street, to separate pedestrians from traffic. The result was an environment of considerable architectural control. "I am convinced that this frame is a primary cause of the feeling of well-being that everyone

enjoys along the shoreline," Martin Millspaugh, former chief executive of Charles Center–Inner Harbor Management, Inc., later commented. "The massing of structures created by the Inner Harbor plan has produced a priceless asset for all of the owners and occupants and, therefore, for the city itself." Adherence to the plan was crucial to the success of the renewal effort, according to George Pillorge, a former principal of RTKL. "It is no wonder that the harbor skyline is photographed from a distance," he said. "It is a very attractive composition and one that is growing more attractive as these principles are followed."[7]

The Inner Harbor's key early structures included the United States Fidelity & Guaranty Life Insurance Company (USF&G, later Legg Mason) building (1970–73, Vlastimil Koubek); 100 East Pratt Street, originally the IBM building (1973–75, Pietro Belluschi and Emery Roth & Sons, with a twenty-eight story addition by Craig Hartman of Skidmore, Owings & Merrill, in 1991); and the World Trade Center, Baltimore (1973–77, I. M. Pei & Partners, with Richter, Cornbrooks, Matthai, Hopkins, Inc.). Standing foursquare on its own raised plaza bounded by Pratt, Lombard, Charles, and Light Streets, the thirty-six-story USF&G structure

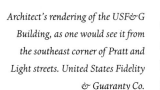

Architect's rendering of the USF&G Building, as one would see it from the southeast corner of Pratt and Light streets. United States Fidelity & Guaranty Co.

proved as critical to the success of the Inner Harbor redevelopment effort as Mies's tower had been to Charles Center. It was the first high-rise corporate headquarters built in the Inner Harbor renewal area, and its rapid construction in the early 1970s provided tangible evidence that the city's grand plans for the waterfront could be realized. Its boldness and high-quality finishes helped set the tone for other buildings that followed.

Koubek designed the tall, slender building to be a linchpin for the Inner Harbor—an exclamation point that broke the low urban frame and signified where the central business district met the rejuvenated waterfront. His client, USF&G, spared no expense, cladding the entire exterior with Spanish pink granite and, inside, making extensive use of rosewood and English brown oak. A Henry Moore sculpture graced the plaza, which concealed four levels of underground parking. "We want a signature building that will be recognized around the world as our home offices in Baltimore," Koubek recalled USF&G executives as saying at the time, "so magnificent that even our agencies in Australia will know it when they see it."[8] USF&G leaders originally wanted to locate their tower one block closer to the waterfront, but city planners insisted that it rise at the point where buildings framing the west shore and north shore come together. They had the clout to do so because the city con-

Baltimore World Trade Center (I. M. Pei & Partners), as rendered at the planning stage. Baltimore City Planning Department

RIGHT:

The Inner Harbor project under construction ca. 1978, the World Trade Center having risen in the right center. The IBM Building stands to the west on Pratt Street, the USF&G Building and the C&P Telephone Building on the southwest corner of Pratt and Light Streets, and, lower left, the Christ Church Harbor Apartments on Light Street. Photograph by Marion E. Warren

The Deaton Center later became part of the University of Maryland health system and was renamed University Specialty Hospital. In 1989 the complex grew in size when a courtyard plaza and building with shops on Barre Street went up between it and the west side of the apartments. Ten years later, it grew again with completion of the Lutheran Center, headquarters of Lutheran World Relief and Lutheran Immigration and Refugee Services. As designed by Gwathmey Siegel & Associates of New York, with Marks, Thomas & Associates of Baltimore, the Lutheran Center terminated the long block like a caboose at the end of a train. Marking a strategic point where the Inner Harbor West renewal area met the tightly knit south Baltimore historic district, it provided an example of contextual modernism, with each side of the collagelike building designed to respond to the scale and materials of the area it faced.

trolled the land. While dozens of additional structures have risen around the Inner Harbor, Koubek's tower remains a pivotal building in the composition.

The twenty-eight-story Baltimore World Trade Center, completed in 1977 at 401 East Pratt Street, provided another punctuation-point tower, one whose design brought the world-famous firm of I. M. Pei & Partners to Baltimore, with Henry Cobb and Pershing Wong as the lead architects. Billed as the world's tallest pentagon, the $20 million tower became home to the Maryland Port Administration. Elegant in its simplicity, it gracefully addressed the harbor to its south and its own plaza to the north. Its exterior honestly expressed its structure of reinforced concrete; sixty-five-foot-long windows on each face provided sweeping harbor views, as did a public observation deck on the twenty-seventh floor. The pentagonal shape, novelty aside, enabled the architects to provide more usable office space in less visible mass.

Since 1887, Christ Lutheran Church has had a building at the southwest corner of the harbor; its current sanctuary dates from 1955. Although many of its members had moved away from the immediate area, they remained loyal to the church and viewed harbor redevelop-

Maryland Science Center, as architects and planners first conceived of it—as an anchor to the southwest corner of the Inner Harbor—and as built. Baltimore City Planning Department; Cochran, Stephenson & Donkervoet

Since the Science Center opened, administrators have worked to correct its flaws. In 1988 a new entrance lobby and IMAX theater (designed by Cochran, Stephenson & Donkervoet) improved the building's demeanor and usefulness by reorienting it to the harbor and setting the stage for the addition, in 2004, of a wing designed by Design Collective, Inc., that will contain an Earth Sciences and Dinosaur Hall.

ment as an opportunity rather than a threat. In these precincts, the church in 1972 built the John F. Deaton Medical Nursing Center (Cochran, Stephenson & Donkervoet). Two years later it added a nine-story building that fronted on Light Street and contained 288 subsidized apartments for the elderly. The Christ Church Harbor Apartments (architect Donald M. Hisaka) featured some of the best views available of the city and the harbor. The lowest structure in this sequence along Light Street, the apartment building nevertheless offered an accomplished evocation of Le Corbusier's refined manner.

Across Light Street from the Christ Church Harbor Apartments, the Maryland Science Center ushered in a new architectural manner, departing from the influence of the International Style as abruptly as the Mechanic Theatre had done in Charles Center. The British rebellion that led to Brutalism had begun to produce other experiments. The Science Center (begun in 1971 and occupied in 1975, architect Edward Durell Stone) rejected in many and fundamental ways the manner of the International Style. Stone often designed buildings that resembled pavilions, including the U.S. Embassy in New Delhi, a hospital in Palo Alto, California, and, after the Inner Harbor commission, dormitories for the Peabody Institute in Baltimore.

This work represented personal and romantic improvisations on the principles of the International Style and the forms of tropical architecture. Stone practiced in a conventional, refined modern idiom; he had designed the Museum of Modern Art in New York. In Baltimore, tempted by the dramatic site on the Inner Harbor, where open land invited monuments, Stone made the Science Center a freestanding brick structure that looked inward rather than outward and supplied exotic interior spaces. For all his worldly travels and exposure to high-style design, however, Stone never fully understood the city's plan for transforming the harbor, and he ended up creating a fortresslike building that turned its back on the very waterfront it was meant to help revive.

Another design, roughly contemporary with the Science Center but on the north side of the Inner Harbor basin, also heralded the arrival of stylistic revisionism. In 1969 the city approved plans for a harbor campus of the Community College of Baltimore (architect An-

Daniel, Mann, Johnson, and Mendenhall's rendering of the Harbor Campus of the Community College of Baltimore. News-American *Collection, Marylandia and Rare Books Department, University of Maryland Libraries, University of Maryland, College Park*

In 2000, the Lockwood Building was demolished to clear the way for new development, making the remaining campus building an even greater curiosity.

thony Lumsden of Daniel, Mann, Johnson & Mendenhall) on a Market Place site in the Inner Harbor East renewal area. Before construction began in 1973, the English architect James Stirling, a warrior in the revisionist cause, had designed the history faculty building in Cambridge. With brick and red-tile skin, much glass and sloping walls, Stirling's building was promptly dubbed "Big Red." In materials, color, and shape, the community college's Bard and Lockwood Buildings owed much to Stirling's design. A gargantuan staircase on the Market Place side of the Bard Building did not improve on the Stirling inspiration, however, and after its red tiles began to leak, portions of it received new roofing in the form of mauve-colored sheathing.

While the Inner Harbor master plan controlled many aspects of waterfront development, it was also flexible enough to accept ideas for buildings and land uses the original design had not contemplated. Indeed, Baltimore's redevelopment effort was strengthened because its leaders were constantly looking to other cities for economic development concepts that worked in an urban setting and then thinking about how to adapt them in ways that would work even better back in Baltimore.

One of the city's largest buildings when it opened in 1979, the Baltimore Convention Center (Naramore, Bain, Brady & Johansen, with local architects Cochran, Stephenson & Donkervoet) offered 115,000 square feet of column-free exhibition space. But while other urban convention centers were big and boxy, Baltimore's was low-slung and glassy. Its orientation on the south side of Pratt Street, facing north, helped to relate it to the city, as did the way the center's three levels stepped back in tiers from the street. The decision to put the bulk of its exhibition space below ground, with a graceful catenary truss structural system to support the roof, made it much less intimidating than it might have been.

In 1996, the city and state completed an addition (designed by the Chicago firm Loschky, Marquardt & Nesholm, with Cochran, Stephenson & Donkervoet) that resembled but did not replicate the earlier building. The low profile and column-free spaces were again impressive, though the trusses did not turn out to be as pleasingly slender as those of the first phase.

Addition to the Baltimore Convention Center (1979), partly a work of the Baltimore firm of Cochran, Stephenson & Donkervoet. Cochran, Stephenson & Donkervoet

The nature of the Inner Harbor shoreline changed forever in 1980, when the Rouse Company opened two shopping and dining pavilions, one on the north shore and the other on the west (Benjamin Thompson & Associates). Original harbor plans, which called for most of the shoreline to remain open, had never contemplated a shopping center; Baltimore did not think about attracting tourists when first developing the plan. But city officials were so impressed by the instant success of Boston's Faneuil Hall–Quincy Market redevelopment, created by Thompson and Rouse, that they asked the same team to undertake a similar project in Baltimore.

As Thompson and Rouse conceived it, the urban market differed from suburban malls in that it had no department store anchors, no acres of parking, and few chain stores or franchises. The idea was to have a wide array of specialty shops, including merchants featuring fresh produce and other foods found in the city's municipal markets, with restaurants as the larger attractions. It would be in the heart of the city, so it could draw both office workers and tourists. Baltimore planners at first wanted Rouse to recycle the Pier 4 Power Plant, thus combining historic preservation and retailing as did the Faneuil Hall complex. But Rouse believed that for a collection of shops and restaurants to succeed in Baltimore, it had to be as close as possible to what he considered the center of the Inner Harbor, the intersection of Pratt and Light Streets, and that idea meant building anew.

Following this approach, Thompson created an exuberant waterfront marketplace that in the 1980s became synonymous with Baltimore's renaissance. Evoking market sheds of old, the two buildings provided a setting where people could enjoy the color and pageantry of crowds and goods—all the sights and sounds and smells of the traditional marketplace. Before construction began, many people feared that the pavilions would ruin the public's ability to enjoy the harbor. But in many ways they ended up heightening the experience, providing terraces and balconies that encouraged visitors to focus their attention on the water. The area between the two pavilions remained open, as an amphitheater, to provide a symbolic connection between the water and the central business district, and in recognition of the importance of providing public access to the shoreline.

The Harborplace pavilions became templates for a new type of "festival market" that later won acceptance around the globe. Thompson's ability to create buildings that fit in with their surroundings, rather than sticking out, had much to do with their ability to adapt

Planners' blueprint rendering of the Inner Harbor project as it would appear following completion of the Harborplace Pavilions and National Aquarium. News-American Collection, Marylandia and Rare Books Department, University of Maryland Libraries, University of Maryland, College Park

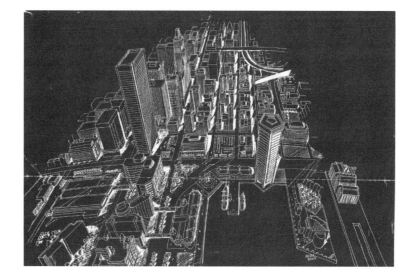

Harborplace according to the planners' vision: specialty-shop and food-gallery pavilions, snapping pennants, and large peaceful crowds. The Rouse Company, with Benjamin Thompson Associates, architects, and Carlos Diniz, artist/renderer

RIGHT:

The vision achieved. A view from the Light Street food pavilion, looking to the northeast and the Pratt Street Pavilion. Photograph by Marion E. Warren

to different settings. He believed that buildings should be regarded as backdrops for human activity, not held up as objects unto themselves. That philosophy was entirely consistent with David Wallace's approach to the Inner Harbor plan, and it was a large part of the reason Thompson's festival market made such a good fit for Baltimore. Designers and developers have since moved on to explore more elaborate combinations of urban retailing and entertainment. Many of the most successful ventures have their roots in the prototypes that Thompson & Rouse pioneered— designs based not on changing styles or fashions but on the immutable laws of human nature.

The National Aquarium represented another idea that Boston first explored but that planners developed more fully in Baltimore. Baltimore housing commissioner Robert C. Embry Jr. had visited Boston's New England Aquarium shortly after it opened in 1969 and envisioned a similar attraction for Baltimore's Inner Harbor. To design it, he turned to the same architect who had led the team responsible for the New England Aquarium, Peter Chermayeff of Cambridge Seven Associates, an interdisciplinary firm that combined architecture, urban design, graphic design, exhibit design, industrial design, landscape design, and even film making. The New England Aquarium had been the team's first project. As a structural type, aquariums dated to the nineteenth century, but the Cambridge designers set out to break the mold. They made the exterior of the aquarium a relatively subdued concrete box that fit in with other warehouses on Boston's waterfront. Inside was a burst of color and activity—an aquatic show world. It supplied just what the sponsors wanted: a building that took aquarium design in a new direction, artfully combining entertainment and education.

For Baltimore, Chermayeff and his colleagues created a seven-story aquatic museum that became the sculptural centerpiece of the Inner Harbor. When it opened in 1981 it instantly became the most successful aquarium in the United States, drawing an average of 1.6 million visitors a year and setting off a wave of aquarium construction around the world.

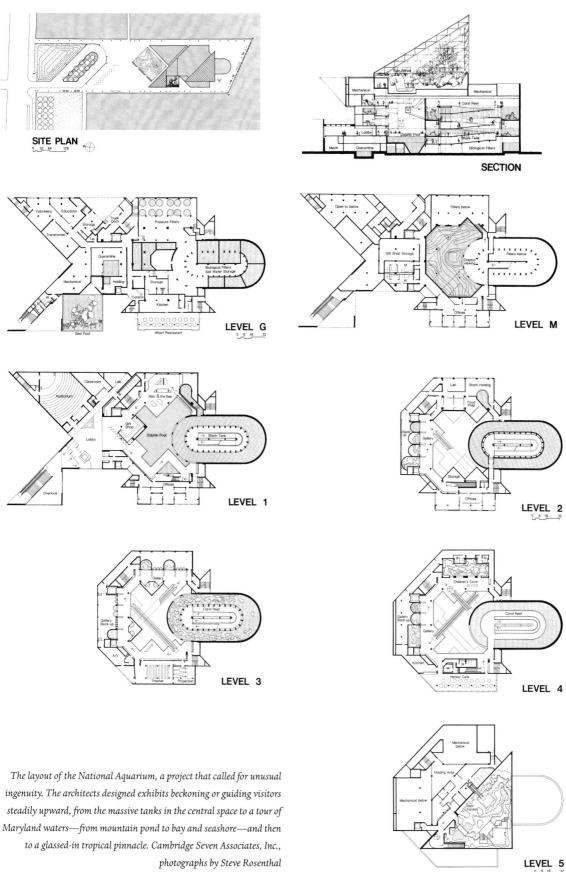

SITE PLAN

0 32 64 128

SECTION

LEVEL G

0 8 16 32

LEVEL M

LEVEL 1

LEVEL 2

0 8 16 32

LEVEL 3

LEVEL 4

LEVEL 5

0 8 16 32

The layout of the National Aquarium, a project that called for unusual ingenuity. The architects designed exhibits beckoning or guiding visitors steadily upward, from the massive tanks in the central space to a tour of Maryland waters—from mountain pond to bay and seashore—and then to a glassed-in tropical pinnacle. Cambridge Seven Associates, Inc., photographs by Steve Rosenthal

Baltimore's aquarium went beyond New England's because its exhibits were more advanced technologically and its exterior was as dramatic as its interior. Although both the Boston and Baltimore buildings were set on the end of a pier, Baltimore's aquarium had offered the potential for far greater architectural drama than New England's, which, as Chermayeff explained, was designed to conform to "the reticent simplicity of Boston's old waterfront. We decided that in Baltimore, we should be more boldly expressive of what we were doing."[9]

The strategy worked. The interior took visitors on a simulated journey from the bottom of the Atlantic Ocean to the top of an Amazon Rain Forest. It featured Cambridge Seven's trademark mixture of architecture and exhibit design, with a one-way circulation sequence, backlit graphics, and dark, Piranesian spaces. The concrete exterior, a work of expressionist sculpture, encased the tanks, around and through which visitors move in a passage that leads to a striking glass pyramid, which formed the roof. Peter's brother, Ivan Chermayeff, created art that relieved the exterior form, including signal-flag graphics, an orange pipe sculpture, and a blue neon wave. The designers were especially proud that Baltimore's aquarium was the first in the country to include a terrestrial exhibit—the rooftop rain forest—that received equal weight with aquatic exhibits. "It's not just a token exhibit stuck in the corner," Peter Chermayeff said. "It makes the point that all life is dependent on water, and, in fact, unified by water."[10]

The Harborplace ensemble, complete with the clipper schooner Pride of Baltimore, *once the aquarium had opened. Photograph by Marion E. Warren*

Even before it opened, the building won a national award for its design, which recalled the Sydney Opera House in the way it jutted into the harbor. Baltimore's aquarium was to its industry what Harborplace was to festival markets: a project whose success spawned copies all over the country. Although not the first to be completed, it seemed the best for its time and the one that got the most attention as a result. The combination of festival marketplace and aquarium found sincere flattery as far away as Osaka, Japan.

Other new buildings appeared as sites became available, but by the mid-1970s expedience and practicality often determined how they would look. Several buildings went up along the west side of Light Street, with uneven results. At the southwest corner of Pratt and Light—where plans once called for a hotel by Louis Kahn, a remarkable and original designer who could have set high artistic standards for further development—the first building in the Light Street sequence (1977, designed by RTKL Associates) housed offices of the Chesapeake & Potomac Telephone Company (later Bell Atlantic and Verizon). To the south the Hyatt Regency Baltimore hotel (1981, by A. Epstein & Sons and RTKL Associates) offered an accumulation of forms unified by a continuous surface of reflective glass. The emphasis on that mirrored material, as much a Hyatt trademark as glass elevators, transparently aimed for glamour and commercial appeal. The hotel's garage stood directly beside it—arguably a waste of valuable harbor frontage.

Beyond Downtown

Although there was never a rush among Baltimoreans to embrace the International Style, in the late twentieth century some architects and builders did explore modern-design concepts outside the deliberate plans of the Charles Center and Inner Harbor projects. The aesthetic and social principles associated with modernism thus made appearances beyond the center city, representing a pluralistic approach to design.

As a leading Baltimore modernist, Alexander Cochran continued to influence select Baltimore designs, sometimes indirectly. In the mid-1950s the congregation of the Episcopal Church of the Redeemer approached him about designing a large sanctuary to supplement its small Gothic chapel on Charles Street near Melrose Avenue, a lovely if modest structure Richard Snowden Andrews had designed and completed in 1856. As a member of the vestry, Cochran declined, recommending Pietro Belluschi, who accepted the commission. Working with Rogers, Taliaferro & Lamb, the predecessor of RTKL, Belluschi devised a structure with exposed wooden arches that supported the roof and allowed the walls to rise to a clerestory that stopped just short of the vaulting roof. Belluschi believed that separating framework and rooftop symbolized the spiritual; it expressed the building's function as the link between heaven and earth. When the sanctuary was completed, in 1958, the dominant form of its roof and the use of stained glass suggested Gothic architecture; indeed, the church was a subtle composition uniting the modern with a longing for the riches of the past.

Pietro Belluschi's and RTKL's artful addition to the original Church of the Redeemer. RTKL Associates

RIGHT:
Architect Charles H. Richter Jr.'s spare design for a house built into steep, wooded terrain. Courtesy of owner

BOTTOM:
Marcel Breuer's Hooper house, a bucolic retreat that maximized interior exposure to the exterior. Reprinted with permission from Architectural Record, *a McGraw-Hill Construction publication. Copyright 1960. All rights reserved*

UPPER LEVEL   LOWER LEVEL

Architect's rendering of Temple Oheb Shalom, an architectural statement from Walter Gropius, which opened in September 1960. News-American Collection, Marylandia and Rare Books Department, University of Maryland Libraries, University of Maryland, College Park

Levin/Brown & Associates extensively renovated the sanctuary in 2000 and reversed the direction of the seats in the main sanctuary so that they face north instead of south and slope downward instead of upward. The signature Park Heights Avenue façade was not changed.

Once again through Cochran's connections, Marcel Breuer in the late 1950s designed two superlative Baltimore residences, the Blum house and the Hooper house. The latter was a deceptively simple glass and stone structure, which nestled into a deep stand of woods overlooking Lake Roland. Other noteworthy modern houses were designed in the 1960s by Charles H. Richter Jr. and Walter D. Ramberg.

Walter Gropius, collaborating with Sheldon I. Leavitt, designed Temple Oheb Shalom, completed in 1960 at 7310 Park Heights Avenue. The building's most distinctive feature was a series of four large concrete vaults, which gave the Park Heights Avenue façade and the interior of the main sanctuary their character. These vaults evoked the outlines of stone tablets while supporting the roof over a sanctuary large enough to accommodate more than a thousand worshipers. According to historian Avrum Kampf, Gropius believed that he had created the ideal twentieth-century synagogue at Oheb Shalom, by merging "the turbine with the Torah" in the tablet forms of the façade.[11] The design included an entrance hall and auditorium with a brick exterior; an enclosed passageway led to bright classrooms of concrete and glass construction.

After completing One Charles Center, Mies van der Rohe began work on a second building in Baltimore. Highfield House, an elegantly proportioned fifteen-story apartment tower of reinforced concrete, opened in 1964 at 4000 North Charles Street. It displayed the massing, open-ground-story arrangement and sleek, curtain-wall façades, made of repetitive grids of glass and metal, that typified Mies's residential work. Its proportions, assurance, and calm simplicity, as well as the understated contrast in its materials, made other apartment houses in the vicinity seem heavy-handed.

Artist's drawing of the projected Highfield House, a design by Mies van der Rohe, completed in 1964. Highfield House Committee on Archives and History

Two planned communities appeared in Baltimore in the late twentieth century, each in its own way adhering to modernist design principles. The Village of Cross Keys was created in the early 1960s as a Rouse Company development on a seventy-two-acre site between Falls Road and the Jones Falls. Adjacent to Roland Park to the east, the land had earlier served as the grounds of the Baltimore Country Club. Developer James Rouse and architect

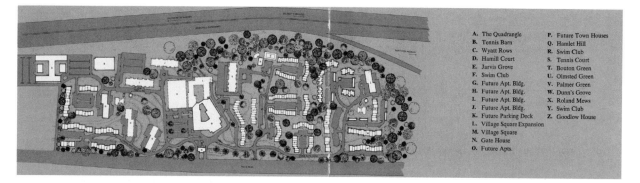

A.	The Quadrangle	P.	Future Town Houses
B.	Tennis Barn	Q.	Hamlet Hill
C.	Wyatt Rows	R.	Swim Club
D.	Hamill Court	S.	Tennis Court
E.	Jarvis Grove	T.	Bouton Green
F.	Swim Club	U.	Olmsted Green
G.	Future Apt. Bldg.	V.	Palmer Green
H.	Future Apt. Bldg.	W.	Dunn's Grove
I.	Future Apt. Bldg.	X.	Roland Mews
J.	Future Apt. Bldg.	Y.	Swim Club
K.	Future Parking Deck	Z.	Goodlow House
L.	Village Square Expansion		
M.	Village Square		
N.	Gate House		
O.	Future Apts.		

Original Cross Keys site plan, the concerted work of architect Richard Stauffer and developer James Rouse, unbuilt structures represented by crenelated outlines. From a promotional brochure the Rouse Company produced in about 1965. Enoch Pratt Free Library

LEFT:

Roland Mews, built on high ground to the north of Cross Keys Village Square, as viewed from the town houses of Palmer Green in the early 1970s. News-American Collection, Marylandia and Rare Books Department, University of Maryland Libraries, University of Maryland, College Park

RIGHT:

An artist's rendering of the Rouse Company's planned expansion of the west side of Village Square, October 1971. The addition included new shops, second-level offices, and a 150-room inn. News-American Collection, Marylandia and Rare Books Department, University of Maryland Libraries, University of Maryland, College Park

BOTTOM:

Harper House, by Frank O. Gehry, as it appeared well after its completion in 1976. The Rouse Company

Richard C. Stauffer deliberately worked the self-contained community into the natural setting, preserving as much as possible of its charm and quietude.

Opening in phases starting in 1964, Cross Keys housed some twenty-five hundred residents (the Silver Spring firm of Collins-Kronstadt & Associates designed the original town houses), grouped shops around a version of a traditional village square, provided office space over the shops, featured a comfortable inn, and included such amenities as tennis courts, swimming pools, pedestrian walkways, and careful landscaping. Cross Keys in many respects provided a practice run for Rouse's much larger development of Columbia, begun in the late 1960s.

In 1976 the village acquired a fifteen-story condominium building, Harper House, the work of the West Coast architect Frank O. Gehry, who later won fame for his titanium-clad Guggenheim Museum in Bilbao, Spain. Setbacks, balconies, terraces, and two-story penthouses at the top create an irregular roofscape, which echoes shapes of the low-rise town houses and other buildings near its base. To residents' chagrin, the tower's brick skin leaked and eventually had to be rebuilt—making the building an unintended early example of "deconstructivist" architecture. While merchants in the retail center struggle to compete with upscale retailers in the suburbs, Cross Keys has for the most part been highly successful as a planned community within the city limits.

Moshe Safdie's ambitious Coldspring New Town—a model for public viewing and a later street scene—a dream never quite fulfilled. Moshe Safdie & Associates

The Joseph Meyerhoff Symphony Hall, Pietro Belluschi with Jung/Brannen Associates, completed in 1979. Baltimore Symphony Orchestra. Photograph by J. Brough Schamp

Coldspring New Town, texturally quite different and perhaps even more ambitious than Cross Keys, owed much to an innovative master plan developed by an adventurous young Israeli architect/planner, Moshe Safdie, in the late 1960s. As part of the attempt to bring modern design to Baltimore, the city gave a Boston firm rights to develop one of the largest virgin tracts in the city, nearly four hundred acres of high ground west of the Jones Falls Expressway (west of Cross Keys), south of Cylburn mansion (a massive, Second Empire, local-stone structure that George A. Frederick had seen to completion in 1889), and straddling West Cold Spring Lane. In 1972 the firm hired Safdie, who had produced the sensationally successful "Habitat" for the Montreal Exposition of 1967, to prepare a design. Safdie found the work of Le Corbusier inspiring, shared his vision of "architecture without architects," and admired Le Corbusier's Near Eastern villages, such as Maalula, in Syria. Working with the principles he extracted from such models, Safdie devised a new kind of urban plan and architecture along lines he later explained in his book, *For Everyone a Garden* (1974).

Safdie's was a sophisticated scheme, one that featured groups of houses, some piled above each other, garages hidden beneath the clusters, common pedestrian walkways, landscaped open spaces, and buildings that were irregular in form. Safdie envisioned a community of some eleven hundred residents. The first housing units—the architect expected to build 3,800—went on the market in 1977, but sales proved as slow as costs were high. Despite heavy public subsidy, Coldspring New Town never developed as Safdie had hoped, and in the late 1970s the project fell on hard times. Its developer floundered, nonetheless leaving behind enough construction, along with less experimental houses added to its edges in the 1980s, to make the community a Baltimore landmark.

Also in the 1970s, a precinct devoted to the arts gradually developed along Mount Royal Avenue between Charles Street and North Avenue. The University of Baltimore and the old Lyric Opera House anchored the district on the southeast, and the Maryland Institute, College of Art campus and Corpus Christi Church occupied much of the land to the north and west. The Joseph Meyerhoff Symphony Hall, home of the Baltimore Symphony Orchestra (1979, Pietro Belluschi, with Jung/Brannen Associates), supplied a centerpiece of the cultural district. To make room, the builders purchased the old Bryn Mawr School buildings (once the historic Deutsches Haus) and several apartments that stood where Mount Royal Avenue turned north; these old buildings, some interesting in design, were not in the best of shape, but their demolition represented a serious loss. Nor did the symphony hall break new ground stylistically. Its curvilinear brick exterior reflected the shape of the hall within. Belluschi placed the entrance on the north, causing the hall to turn its back on the downtown and Mount Vernon areas, to which it presented an unattractive view of its sloping roof. From certain angles, the building resembles a French foreign legionnaire's cap. The interior, with its scalloped balconies and warm wood finishes, offers its most attractive features. Subsequent fine-tunings by RTKL Associates made already-good acoustics even better.

TOP:

The Carnegie Institute Embryology Building, perched comfortably in its wooded corner. Ferdinand Hamburger Archives, Milton S. Eisenhower Library, The Johns Hopkins University

BOTTOM:

The Johns Hopkins University Glass Pavilion. Ferdinand Hamburger Archives, Milton S. Eisenhower Library, The Johns Hopkins University

While all this was going on, the Lyric Opera House received several facelifts—it had never been quite completed—in the form of a new lobby and several wings along Mount Royal Avenue, the latter enabling it to accommodate opera and traveling Broadway shows (Richter, Cornbrooks, Gribble and successors, beginning in 1985). As a result of these changes, it is practically impossible to see any sign of the 1896 theater shed beneath the new exterior, although the building now functions better for large productions. The auditorium retains much of its historic character.

Some of the most sophisticated modern design work in the Baltimore area is to be found on Baltimore's college and university campuses. In 1958, on a far-flung corner of the Johns Hopkins Homewood campus where San Martin Drive joins University Parkway, William E. Haible of Anderson, Beckwith & Haible designed one of the most effective modern buildings in the city, the Carnegie Institute Embryology Building. Perfectly suited to its setting, it provides a model of sensitive scale. Haible called for first-class materials, demonstrating the durability of this style in cases of attentive design and construction. In the 1970s, Donald Sickler, who had worked with Mies van der Rohe on One Charles Center and Highfield House, designed a glass pavilion adjoining the neo-Georgian Levering Hall, the Johns Hopkins Homewood campus student union. Sickler's open, economical structure supplied a bright spot, a lantern in the trees, for an otherwise conservative environment and may be said to pay tribute to the Mies spirit.

Baltimore's two medical schools, each with its own hospital and complement of research facilities, faithfully patronized late-twentieth-century architecture. They expanded regularly, and their buildings seemed to age rapidly, as emerging technology made older facilities obsolete. In the 1990s the University of Maryland Medical Center, besides improving the entrance to its original hospital, added to its compound large buildings, including the Homer Gudelsky Building (Zeidler Roberts Partnership). An atrium structure without the depressing institutional atmosphere that had for too long characterized hospitals, the tower changed the character of the whole. Using techniques associated with shopping centers,

The Johns Hopkins Hospital Outpatient Building (Payette Associates), completed in 1992. Alan Mason Chesney Medical Archives, The Johns Hopkins Medical Institutions

After the turn of the new century Hopkins unveiled a master plan by Cooper, Robertson & Partners for a rebuilding program to replace or upgrade many existing Hopkins facilities and expand the complex south of Orleans Street.

Zeidler designed a "hospitable hospital" that uses architecture as part of the therapy, including green plants and fresh air.

Another of the better modern buildings is the outpatient facility and garage (Payette Associates) added to the Johns Hopkins medical campus in 1992. The structure established a respectful relationship with the landmark domed building across Broadway; an underground pedestrian passage connects it to both the subway station and the original hospital. Its interior offers quality and spaciousness, fine materials, suitable furniture, and gradual shifts in scale, from large public spaces, to the smaller corridors leading to the clinics, and finally to the waiting spaces that adjoin the consulting rooms.

Equally bold as a modern design, a green-glass office building in Mount Washington, completed in 1990 (Peterson & Brickbauer, with Emery Roth & Sons), provided new quarters for the United States Fidelity & Guaranty Life Insurance Company. Charles Brickbauer designed the building to be an essay in glass and steel recalling the early-modern stone buildings of Paul Cret. The grounds were designed as a salute to the European landscapes of Vaux-le-Vicomte. The composition represented a breakthrough effort to reinvigorate the ubiquitous modern glass box by infusing it with historic meaning and giving every employee a view of the outdoors.

The Walters Art Gallery (now Museum) and the Baltimore Museum of Art both acquired mid- and late-twentieth-century additions in the International Style. In 1974 the Walters nearly doubled its exhibition space by opening a wing (Shepley, Bulfinch, Richardson & Abbott) to the west of its original building, extending along Centre Street. Striving for compatibility, the Centre Street building followed roughly the scale of the Beaux-Arts structure it adjoined, and employed a concrete exterior that continued the color and solidity of the

older building. The irregular interior spaces enabled the staff to surprise, if not confuse, visitors with rooms, nooks, and crannies, as well as larger exhibit areas.

In like manner the Philadelphia firm of Bower, Lewis & Thrower designed a new east wing for the Baltimore Museum of Art, which opened in 1982. With its glass-roofed lobby, abstract exterior lines, and new materials, it departed from the neoclassicism of John Russell Pope's central building of 1929 and yet complemented it as well, respectfully continuing the horizontal line of Pope's cornice. The wing included a new main entrance, gift shop, upstairs auditorium, and restaurant, which, in pleasant weather, offers outdoor dining on a patio with pools of water and running fountains—an inviting space mediating between the interior and the museum's outdoor sculpture garden.

In 1994 the BMA opened another wing, this one on its west side. Again the work of Bower, Lewis & Thrower, this three-story structure was more of a departure from the Pope building than the 1982 wing. It had as its express purpose the display of the museum's modern art collection. From the burnished aluminum skin outside to the large, luminous galleries inside, the building broke with the past both physically and intellectually, and with mixed results. Inside, the new wing is a model of organization and clarity, with spaces that provide entirely new ways to view art. Interior-design breakthroughs include clustered galleries, whose corners are cut away so that one space flows into another, and a fluorescent lighting system that turns exhibit areas into veritable light boxes. The designers' search for just the right materials and finishes further helped create distinctive settings. The white ash floor, for example, is not only handsome but effective in reflecting light from above. The delicate truss work that supports the roof in the tallest galleries has a vaguely industrial feel, re-

Bower, Lewis & Thrower's design for the Baltimore Museum of Art's east wing, 1982. Bower, Lewis & Thrower, Philadelphia

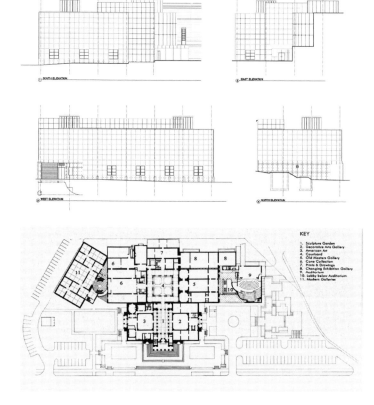

Bower, Lewis & Thrower's design for the Baltimore Museum of Art's west wing, 1994, and second-floor plan upon completion of both wings. Bower, Lewis & Thrower, Philadelphia

calling the loft spaces in which artists may have worked. Outside, the addition strove to pique visitors' interest about what might be going on inside. But mostly it falls flat, lacking the weight and dignity of the rest of the museum or any affinity to it.

Persistent Conservatism

Modern experiments notwithstanding, many Baltimoreans, in an expression of persistent conservatism, continued to prefer structures that perpetuated established styles. Maginnis & Walsh, architects of the Roman Catholic Cathedral of Mary Our Queen (1959), on North Charles Street, set out to reconcile contemporary design with Gothic allure. "By its straightforward lines and structural honesty, that is, by the absence of purely ornamental forms," declared a commissioned account of the structure, "it is credibly modern. At the same time, it easefully achieves many hallowing Gothic effects by means of its nervous vitality, its generous window areas, the pronounced slimness of its form, its softly pointed arches, and by buttresses."[12]

Baltimore's penchant for clinging to the past, or for attempting to fuse past and present, led to truly impressive contributions to a fairly new movement—historic preservation—and its various efforts at restoration, adaptive reuse (restoring but also redesigning an old building to give it a new function), and "contextual infill" (designing new buildings not as

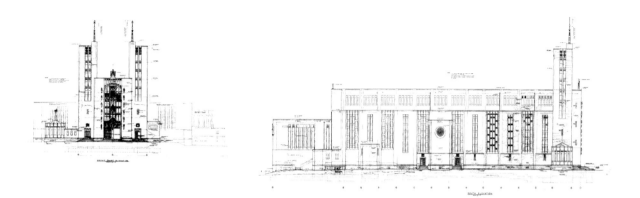

Front and side elevations for Maginnis & Walsh's Cathedral of Mary Our Queen (1959). Associated Archives at St. Mary's Seminary and University

BOTTOM:

The Milton S. Eisenhower Library, closing the Keyser Quadrangle in a modern manner but in keeping with the Georgian surroundings. Architect's model and a view from ground level to the A-level reference area. Ferdinand Hamburger Archives, Milton S. Eisenhower Library, The Johns Hopkins University

isolated statements but as pieces of a larger, pre-existing context). "Our new buildings," Cochran wrote in 1963, "must live alongside of, and therefore become a visual part of, our old," and he stated his disapproval of architects who chose "to ignore older architecture," which he described as a form of rudeness. Yet simple copying was not so much the answer as finding "subtle and ingenious ways" to make references to the past, often within the modernist idiom.[13]

On the Johns Hopkins Homewood campus, for example, the neocolonial style had remained dominant through 1957, when Buckler & Fenhagen completed Shriver Hall. Several years later, Wrenn, Lewis & Jencks—Robert Erskine Lewis, collaborating with Richard W. Ayers of Ayers/Saint and Henry Powell Hopkins—designed quite a different building, the Milton S. Eisenhower Library. The new structure combined neocolonial stateliness with modern central-block plate windows and five below-ground levels for offices, stacks, and carrels. This strategy of countersinking space prevented the library from overwhelming nearby Homewood House. Even with its "modern" lines, the library, finished in 1964, complemented its early-nineteenth-century neighbor.

Cochran demonstrated the importance of historic context when, in 1964, he and his associate Richard C. Donkervoet designed the Bolton Place Townhouses off the 1200 block of Park Avenue in Bolton Hill. The architects grouped seventeen new row houses around a landscaped pedestrian "street" in a manner suggestive of the surrounding neighborhood.

Unadorned, rosy-hued brick façades, regularly placed window openings, arched doors, side-hall plans, and varied heights all blended peacefully with the hundred-year-old houses of Bolton Hill. The landscaped "street" called to mind the 1600 and 1700 blocks of Park Avenue. Above all, the decision to construct row houses, not freestanding dwellings, demonstrated the developer's harmonious intentions; they plucked Baltimore's architectural heartstrings. The success of the Bolton Place Townhouses encouraged others to make knowing use of local building traditions. In 1968 Hugh Newell Jacobsen's nearby Bolton Commons drew praise specifically for creating modern homes in harmony with the area's nineteenth-century row houses.

In 1965, renovating the old B&O Railroad station on Mount Royal Avenue for the Maryland Institute, College of Art, Cochran and Donkervoet provided the city and the country with a landmark example of adaptive reuse. The railroad had closed the building in 1961 and sold it to the institute. Cochran urged his fellow modernists to remember that "the individual can never disassociate architecture from his experiences in life," that "the old could be beautiful, relevant, and still useful."[14]

Cochran and Donkervoet set out to find a way to preserve the exterior and respect the character of the interior while subdividing it for a variety of uses. They altered the exterior only by enclosing open roof areas; most of the interior architectural decoration they "pre-

Donkervoet's Bolton Place Townhouses, soon after their completion in 1964, with the dome of Temple Oheb Shalom in the distance. Photograph by Marion E. Warren

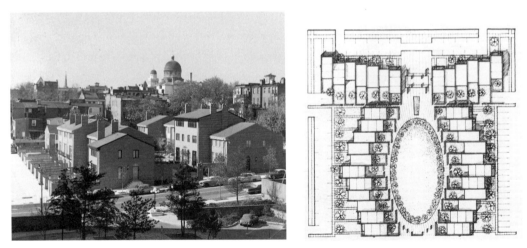

RIGHT AND BOTTOM: Bolton Commons, in conception and as completed by Hugh Newell Jacobsen in 1968. Hugh Newell Jacobsen, A.I.A., photographs by Robert C. Loutman

served in toto" while nonetheless transforming the large open space of the waiting room into studios, galleries, classrooms, office space, and a library. They preserved the iron train shed behind the station—typical of large, late-nineteenth-century railroad architecture—leaving Baltimore with one of the last surviving examples. Cochran and Donkervoet increased the building's usable space from 22,500 to 47,000 square feet. At a cost of $18 per square foot, the renovation was a financial success, but in 1967, when the station reopened, its beauty brought forth the loudest acclaim. The editors of *Architectural Forum* described the venture splendid enough "to strike joy in the hearts of preservationists and art lovers alike." The renowned anthropologist Margaret Mead declared Mount Royal to be "perhaps the most magnificent example in the Western World of something being made into something else." Paul Goldberger, architecture critic of the *New York Times*, called it "the keystone of a new urban movement."[15] Baltimore had placed itself at the forefront in architecture, but it did so by bowing to its ingrained fondness for the past.

Improvements made in the course of the Inner Harbor Project I redevelopment raised the hope that, if carefully managed, they would lead to the revival, rehabilitation, and rebuilding of adjacent residential neighborhoods. By the late 1960s and 1970s evidence mounted that investment in the commercial downtown encouraged investment in nearby neighborhoods, notably in Federal Hill, with its resplendent views of the harbor, and the Otterbein neighborhood, south of Pratt Street and west of Light Street.

In 1972, in a continuing effort to have major modern architects design buildings for the Inner Harbor—the Louis Kahn proposal for the southwest corners of Charles and Pratt Streets was one such attempt—planners considered commissioning Japanese architect Kenzo Tange to redesign and rebuild the entire Otterbein area. In the end the city elected to keep the old houses, some of which were remarkable survivals, and let them go by lottery for a dollar each to people who had the means and commitment to repair them to standards the city established. City officials actually got the idea of selling "dollar houses" from a similar lottery in Wilmington, Delaware, and, like many of the ideas they imported over the years, it worked better in Baltimore.

Old and new Otterbein carefully wove themselves into a whole. The old houses were beautiful; the new ones filled the spaces between the old, accepting the idioms of the old without replicating them. The city repaved the tree-lined streets and routed traffic to the interstate highway, away from the residential area. On the west side of Sharp Street, the Federal Reserve Bank of Richmond built large but not over-

The 100 block of East Montgomery Street, Federal Hill, 1980, showing restored Federal-period houses, including a frame house from the 1780s. Courtesy of Mary Ellen Hayward

TOP, RIGHT:
A renovated Italianate house in the 200 block of Montgomery Street, one of many with a splendid view of the Inner Harbor, in August 1979. News-American *Collection, Marylandia and Rare Books Department, University of Maryland Libraries, University of Maryland, College Park*

BOTTOM, LEFT:
East side of Stirling Street in the Old Town neighborhood, an example of downtown dwellings restored through the "dollar house" program created by the Baltimore City Housing Authority in the 1970s. Courtesy of Mary Ellen Hayward

BOTTOM, RIGHT:
Preserved and partially renovated buildings facing the water on Thames Street, Fells Point, in the 1970s. Photograph by Marion E. Warren

bearing offices (1979, by Hellmuth, Obata + Kassabaum), more horizontal than vertical in design. The remarkable Baltimore & Ohio Railroad warehouse, one of Baltimore's major artifacts from its industrial past, formed a wall that helped to define Otterbein as part of the waterfront district.

Some of the most extensive contextual infill development followed upon a reversal in public policy and the decision, in the mid-1990s, to replace mid-century, International-Style high-rise public housing. By the summer of 1995 Baltimore had its complement of these "hulking towers, ghettoized within dangerous, barren parks," as the *New York Times* styled them, in four public housing projects, and decided to demolish them, thus becoming the first city to eliminate all its vertical federal public housing.[16] Like other cities in the United States and abroad, Baltimore replaced the high rises with carefully designed communities of row houses and low-rise apartment buildings, which, in both scale and form, resembled those torn down decades earlier. Besides favoring their lower density, city officials planned these new communities—Pleasant View Gardens and Flag House Courts to the east, Heritage Crossing and Lexington Terrace to the west—with a mixture of subsidized and nonsubsidized homes, for sale and for rent. Two of the top "new urbanist" design teams in the country, Torti Gallas & Partners / CHK of Silver Spring and Urban Design Associates in Pittsburgh, headed by Ray Gindroz, prepared the master plans. These communities, made possible by federal Hope VI funding and each more sophisticated than the one before, promised to reverse much of the damage caused by the earlier concentration of subsidized housing around the downtown business district and may have been one of Mayor Kurt Schmoke's greatest contributions to Baltimore's urban landscape.

Instrumental in the rejuvenation of residential areas, adaptive reuse suggested itself when city planners dealt with aging business districts, as well. Market Place, running north from Pratt Street to Baltimore Street, had long been associated with light industry and marketing. Its redevelopment and rehabilitation proved somewhat erratic, particularly as the alien Community College buildings made it difficult to integrate with the blocks immediately to the west. The leading candidates for adaptive reuse, the old Wholesale Fish Market and the Candler Building, boasted character and history but were large structures and thus challenging to overhaul.

Designed by Otto Simonson and Theodore Wells Pietsch in 1906, the fish market at 35 Market Place thrived for nearly a century, closing in the early 1980s, when the fishmongers moved to Jessup. Its conversion in 1985 to a Country and Western–themed entertainment center failed financially, and then a string of night spots forming an entertainment mall failed in 1989. In 1997, a nonprofit group working with the Rouse Company and a subsidiary of the Walt Disney Corporation combined to use the structure to house one of the nation's largest children's museums, Port Discovery. It was the only children's museum in the country designed by Disney. Developer David Cordish ultimately restored the plaza and buildings on the west, north of the Community College, as a collection of restaurants and nightspots. A pavilion that resembled a market shed filled the north end of the street, and a parking garage completed the east side.

The Candler Building, a noble structure that visually terminated the north side of the Inner Harbor, also received a thorough renovation and survives as office space. Its preservation was one of the benefits associated with the rebuilding of the Inner Harbor.

On Pier 4 the Power Plant (Design Collective and others, 1996–98) represented an adaptation from the United Railways & Electric Company power generating station, actually three interconnected buildings dating from the early 1900s and one of the Inner Harbor's most imposing landmarks. Design Collective, the master planner, treated the building as a

LEFT:

The old Fish Market, later Port Discovery. Port Discovery, the Kid-Powered Museum, photograph by Dan Beigel

RIGHT:

The renovated city-streetcar Power Plant, festooned with signs that had more to do with commercial utility than aesthetics. The Cordish Company

three-dimensional jigsaw puzzle, creating retail spaces on the lower floors and offices above. The developer, Cordish Company, at one point contemplated removing the four huge smokestacks in the center building but wisely decided not to do so; besides retaining the buildings' brooding silhouette, the stacks have supplied some remarkable interior spaces. Like the Inner Harbor itself, the building has shown an ability to absorb change without losing its character.

Enough time had passed by the end of the twentieth century to make the city aware of the quality of some of its older buildings and conscious that their aura could be imparted to new neighbors. The old Mercantile-Safe Deposit & Trust Company building at Calvert and Redwood Streets, reborn as a nightclub, made this point. The longer such buildings survived unscathed, the likelier they would be to find protection as redevelopment progressed around them. In the meantime, Baltimore redevelopers avidly invested in the old structures. Their renovation proved profitable, both financially, to the investors, but also culturally, to the public—which, one hoped, would benefit from having physical links to the city's historical experience.

Efforts to rebuild without tearing down centered on many older parts of the city. They were not limited to areas near the water—the Howard Street corridor and near west side generated much debate as the century closed—but waterfront or near-waterfront places, such as Brown's Wharf in Fells Point and Tindeco Wharf and the American Can Company

LEFT:
Rendering of the Tindeco Wharf project, 1988, and view from the interior after its opening. Struever Bros., Eccles & Rouse
RIGHT:
The original American Can Company building, as Struever Bros., Eccles & Rouse envisioned its reuse in 1996–97, and interior view during construction, 1989. Struever Bros., Eccles & Rouse

Two projects of the period well illustrated the movement to build to context and adapt to new uses, even on a modest scale. In the early 1990s, Schamu, Machowski, Doo & Associates designed a dormitory complex for the Maryland Institute, College of Art—the first living quarters the college had built—to meet the needs of the school's growing student body and fit within the historic context of the Bolton Hill neighborhood. Built by Roy Kirby & Sons and completed in 1992, the buildings house 350 students in 103 apartment-style living units with 17 studio spaces. All apartments in the three- and four-story building complex open onto exterior corridors encircling an open courtyard and green space. SMG Architects

In the fall of 2000, the Maryland Historical Trust, which then held an easement on the properties, considered a proposal by David H. Gleason Associates for the restoration of the London Coffee House and adjacent George Wells house in Fells Point, at the northwest corner of Bond and Thames Streets. The project would have included compatible new construction and provided 17,000 square feet of office and retail space. The firm planned much of the new construction as infill along Thames Street and in the rear of the historic buildings—creating traditional courtyard space while retaining the historical integrity of the façades of the buildings, both dating to 1772. Later, Struever Bros., Eccles & Rouse opened a new retail office complex, the Bond Street Wharf, on the waterside just opposite the London Coffee House. David H. Gleason Associates, Inc., Architects

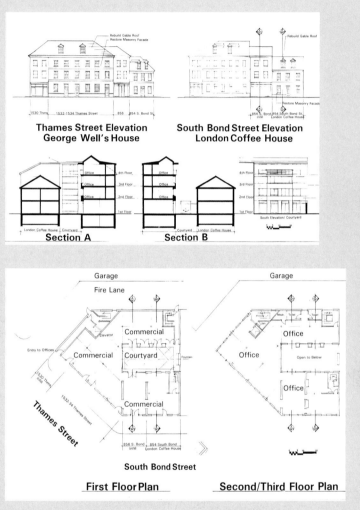

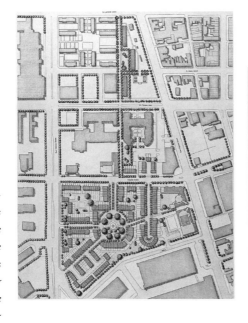

Pleasant View Gardens public-assistance housing, as Torti Gallas & Partners envisioned the site layout at the former Lafayette Courts in the mid-1990s, and as built, the Gothic fire station tower on Gay Street visible in the background. Torti Gallas & Partners, photograph by Alain Jaramillo

in Canton, exemplified adaptive reuse. Toward the end of the century Struever Bros., Eccles & Rouse, one of the city's leading redevelopers, turned the massive Procter & Gamble soap factory on Locust Point into Tide Point, a business campus with dramatic views back toward the Inner Harbor, all of the buildings being named after soap products once manufactured there. Design Collective's master plan for the project was so appealing because it juxtaposed contemporary touches with the 1930s-industrial character of the buildings (which argued for retaining elements such as the old Procter & Gamble logo) and connected them to the waterfront with a magnificent promenade. Almost magically, these projects helped transform and reclaim areas of the city that many considered frontiers; once they had been completed, intrepid developers went off in search of new challenges, and housing in the old neighborhoods was suddenly in demand.

At the dawn of the twenty-first century, the Basilica of the Assumption Historic Trust asked John G. Waite Associates and Beyer Blinder Belle to undertake a nearly complete restoration of Latrobe's cathedral. The plan includes restoring the dome to its original purpose—to admit overhead light—and replacing mid-twentieth-century stained-glass with clear windows.

By the late 1990s, many of Baltimore's best historic buildings—City Hall, the U.S. Customs House, the Washington Monument—had been renovated and restored. Others underwent recycling, some by design firms having formed specifically to specialize in restoration and adaptive reuse and many by private owners taking advantage of federal and state tax credits for historic preservation. A partial list of reused venerable buildings included the Atrium (earlier a Hecht Company building), Bagby Building, Charles Theatre, Cecil Apartments, Congress Apartments, Greyhound Bus Terminal and Garage, Eastern Avenue Pumping Station, Hackerman House, Hansa Haus, Hippodrome Theatre, Marikle Chapel at the College of Notre Dame of Maryland, Montgomery Park (the old Montgomery Ward warehouse), Munsey Building, Orchard Street Church, Peabody Conservatory, President Street Station, St. Ignatius Church, Senator Theatre, and Standard (Oil Building) Apartments. One of the most unusual restorations involved the Fava Building, whose cast-iron front was taken down from its original location near the Inner Harbor in the 1970s, shipped to Salt Lake City for repairs, and twenty years later reassembled near the Carroll Mansion as the frontispiece to a new museum complex for the Baltimore City Life Museums. In the reassembly, Peterson & Brickbauer and Ziger Snead Architects folded the five bays of the façade like an accordion to fit onto the site. The city museum later dissolved because of budgetary cuts, but the building remains visible on President Street, a gateway to East Baltimore.

Two inheritances from the modern era of rebuilding thus survive and remain highly influential in Baltimore. First, respect for the past and appreciation of the riches of tradition came through these changes, not unscathed, but alive. Historic preservation suits the native preferences of Baltimore, a city with so much worthy of preservation. Second, the modern ideal of architecture in service to society—the view that good design can improve life—also remains in evidence, as was made clear by the plan to rebuild, where high-rise projects once stood, in the low-rise pattern native to the city.

Beyond the Plan

The resounding success of Harborplace brought with it fruits of different colors. The Inner Harbor plan had called for continuous public access to the water's edge, with a brick-paved promenade free of fences or railings. After Harborplace opened, drawing millions to the Inner Harbor, city officials launched plans to create a seven-mile stretch of public promenade, from Fort McHenry in Locust Point, along Key Highway to the Inner Harbor, and then eastward to Fells Point and Canton. Those public walkways, extending one of the simplest yet boldest aspects of the Inner Harbor plan, turned out to be an excellent way to make the refurbished waterfront accessible and inviting to the greatest number of people.

Success also spurred demand for space in the "front row" of the Inner Harbor and applied pressure on planners to make adjustments to accommodate private visions. As long as the city controlled the land, planners and the architectural review board could insist that developers adhere to their guidelines. For a time, new construction followed the master plan rather closely. For example, 400 E. Pratt Street (RTKL Associates, 1977) strengthened the frame around the harbor.

If, however, the original plan had been to create a whole greater than the sum of its parts, it sometimes seemed, after the opening of Harborplace, that parts were being added at the expense of the whole. The quality of new buildings varied significantly. Departures from the city's master plan for the waterfront, besides responding to growing demand, also reflected the realities of the times. During the Reagan administration and afterward, the city did not receive as much federal funding to stimulate urban development as it did during the Carter years and before. Without federal funding to buy land and attach strings to development, the city was not in a position to demand as much from developers. Because the Inner Harbor had become so attractive and successful as a people magnet, more companies wanted to be there and were willing to pay for the opportunity. Once in control of a prime site, they wanted to capitalize on what they had by building as much as possible, and that translated into requests to waive height and other limits.

Architecture in the 1980s thus became—or ran the risk of becoming—a corporate marketing tool, a way for a company to create a signature on the skyline. From the 1980s on, buildings stood more and more as individual expressions of their builders and less as contributors to the whole. "Trophy" buildings in cities such as Dallas and Houston showed that architecture could be used for promotion, a company's visual calling card. In Baltimore, too, some companies were no longer content to lease space in an understated tan cereal box. They wanted buildings with more pizzazz, designs that were instantly recognizable to their clients. Developers saw attention-getting architecture as a way to give speculative buildings an edge over the competition.

250 West Pratt Street. Photograph by Mark B. Miller

A thirty-story tower erected in 1985 at 250 West Pratt Street (David Childs of Skidmore, Owings & Merrill, for Cabot, Cabot & Forbes) supplied one of the best tall downtown buildings of the post-Harborplace era. It both recalls the restraint and refinement of the International Style and also reflects the relaxation of its stern standards. Its blue stone surface changes with the light and the sky, and its form steps down to address the lower skyline of the old city while providing terraces with sweeping harbor views. The result is a timeless work of architecture, which shows how much modern buildings can enhance the city.

Other efforts were not as impressive. At the northwest corner of Baltimore and St. Paul Streets, developer Gerald Klein worked with the Hillier Group to create a tower with a six-story "needle" designed to make it the tallest building in the city, with room for a hot tub at the top. Hillier originally proposed that the skin be green glass, but the design panel had the architect tone it down to bronze. For Baltimore Federal president Robert Hecht, Donald Coupard Associates designed a curving glass and brick tower at 301 E. Lombard Street; one critic likened it to a stack of sardine cans. On St. Paul Place, developer David Kornblatt built a tower above a Coupard-designed parking garage that looked like an oversized chicken coop. All of these buildings were constructed during the 1980s on land that was assembled and cleared by private developers, not the city.

A rendering of the Towers at Harbor Court, which the architects described as adhering to "a Splendid Tradition of Graceful Elegance." David H. Murdock Development Company; architects: Arnold Savrann/Leo Daly Associates

City planners, Larry Reich among them, feared that design controls were no longer working, and Baltimore was in danger of becoming Dallas on the Chesapeake. Their fears were well founded. For developer David Murdock, Arnold Savrann and Leo Daly Associates in 1983 designed a Light Street hotel and condominium complex, Harbor Court, and un-veiled plans for it at the Baltimore Museum of Art as if it were a work of art itself. Although the hotel interior is tasteful in its design, the exterior may represent one of the Inner Har-bor's biggest missed opportunities. The tall red-brick building exhibits few design graces and makes no apologies, either to the street it fronts or to the Otterbein neighborhood be-hind it. The condominium windows are oddly shaped, and the Charles Street side is a cliff of bricks—a poor neighbor to its surroundings. In this case city officials allowed a head-strong developer to build what he wanted, despite the objections of the city's review board, showing what can happen when a city lowers its standards in the hope of pleasing a power-ful builder.

Scarlett Place (Meyers & D'Aleo) rose in 1988 as a large condominium and office build-ing incorporating the former Scarlett Seed Company building at the southwest corner of Pratt and President Streets and again ignoring the Inner Harbor master plan. By the time of Scarlett Place's design, postmodern architects were drawing on historical references in an effort to impart meaning to new buildings. Since Scarlett Place would stand near Little Italy, architect Leo D'Aleo had the idea of creating a building that evoked a Mediterranean hill-side. Key to the design were what appear to be little ranch houses—penthouse apart-ments—piled up along the building's southern crest, with the roof of one becoming a ter-race for the one above. In the end, Scarlett Place offered a period piece rather than notable design. More troubling than the kitschy details, the sheer bulk of the building put a full stop to the Inner Harbor and formed a wall between it and Little Italy.

The tower at 100 E. Pratt Street, formerly known as the IBM Building, registered another aberration. In 1992 new owners wanted to take advantage of the building's position in the front row of the harbor by adding more leaseable office space with water views. The only way was to go up, with a twenty-eight-story addition, rising above the eleven-story base, de-signed by Pietro Belluschi with Emery Roth. The architect, Craig Hartman of Skidmore, Owings & Merrill, set the tower back from Pratt Street half a block and tried to be respect-ful of Belluschi's modern vocabulary while adding some touches of his own. He also de-signed a garage on the north side of the block to replace one originally constructed to ac-company Belluschi's building. Unfortunately, because of its aggressive design (with something resembling a hairnet at the top) and the way it defied the height limitation set down in the Inner Harbor plan, the tower upstaged the original building and, in the manner of Scarlett Place to the east, acted as a barrier between the harbor and the business district, which stands farther from the water. The master plan called for buildings either to be long and low or tall and slender. The tower, a hybrid, weakened the original concept and proved to be a precedent for other variations.

Although the Inner Harbor master plan prevented construction of any more retail space on the shoreline, the rise of Harborplace led to more commercial development nearby. In the 1980s, encouraged by the response to the shopping pavilions, city leaders sought a de-veloper for one of downtown Baltimore's most valuable real estate parcels, the city-owned "magic corner" at the northeast corner of Pratt and Light Streets. After reviewing thirteen proposals, they awarded development rights to the Rouse Company, which proposed "The Gallery at Harborplace," with elements reflecting both the business and leisure sides of the Inner Harbor. The plan called for several levels of shops, an office tower, and a luxury hotel with parking below grade.

Rouse held its own limited design competition and selected Eberhard Zeidler of the Zeidler Roberts Partnership in Toronto to be the project architect. Zeidler designed a building

The Gallery at Harborplace. Zeidler Grinnell Partnership/Architects

whose exterior clearly expressed the different uses inside—a glassy entrance to mark the retail center at Pratt and Light Streets, human-scaled windows for the hotel, reflective glass for the office tower. When it opened in 1986, the Gallery was by far the most complex building on the north side of Pratt Street, representing a new effort to put more than one use on a block and spread the vitality around the water's edge northward, toward the central business district. The combination of uses was handled well from a functional standpoint, but the tower rose above the eleven-story cornice line suggested by the Wallace plan for buildings on the Inner Harbor frame.

For city planners, the biggest challenge in this new economic climate was to strike an appropriate balance—to find ways to keep the revitalization momentum going without diminishing or negating what had already been achieved. Whereas once the main job had been to stimulate development, now they also had to be prepared to rein it in—and to know when to do one or the other. It continued to be a constant struggle.

In some respects the original Inner Harbor plan had to respond to changes in certain fields, such as aquarium design. By the year 2000 professionals placed less emphasis on creating settings in which dolphins jump through hoops and more on conveying a message about the need to conserve the world's natural resources. Architects planning additions to the National Aquarium in Baltimore responded by reducing the written information visitors had to digest, freeing them to concentrate on the living creatures. Designers struggled to create more naturalistic habitats, even if that meant downplaying or eliminating architectural infrastructure. Many of the country's newest aquariums, enclosed by glass rather than concrete, attempted to make exhibits more visible and accessible. "It's not just about architecture," Peter Chermayeff said at the time. "It's about places. We're choosing less complex subject matter but getting more into it so we can go deeper. We don't just want to show dolphins. We want to find ways to show how intelligent they are and make the point that they have complex social lives. If we can pull it off, it's a richer experience for people."[17]

Two additions responded to the original aquarium in different ways. The aquarium's marine mammal pavilion (by James R. Grieves Associates, which later became Grieves, Worrall, Wright & O'Hatnick) opened in 1990 on the south end of Pier 4, with an enclosed pedestrian bridge linking it to Pier 3. It contained a 1,200-seat amphitheater where patrons

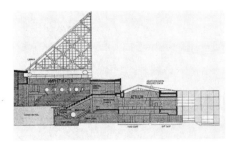

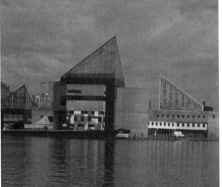

The Marine Mammal Pavilion, an eastern addition to the National Aquarium on Pier 4. A sectional drawing of the northern side made clear its economies of space. Enoch Pratt Free Library

LEFT:

The expanded Aquarium as built, viewed from the harbor, the original building to the left. Copyright National Aquarium in Baltimore, used by permission. Photograph by Ron Haisfield

RIGHT:

Architects' model of the north addition to the National Aquarium. Copyright National Aquarium in Baltimore, used by permission

could watch thirty-minute behavorial presentations by Atlantic bottlenose dolphins, which are among the aquarium's biggest stars. The pavilion posed a dilemma. Should the architects resist the urge to imitate Cambridge Seven's landmark on Pier 3 or give in and make their building similar? In the end, they played to something of a stalemate.

Inside, Grieves did not try to replicate the first building at all; the architects came up with an impressive new space that complements the original. They envisioned it as a bright, airy building that would let the outside in—a deliberate contrast to the dark "world of water" on Pier 3. They wanted visitors to be free to move in many directions, as opposed to the one-way sequence on Pier 3. Above all, they wanted to create a healthy habitat for dolphins. At the heart of the building, the amphitheater provides a cross between a stadium and a theater, the water being the stage. In the center the architects placed four interconnected pools, separated by lily-pad-like formations where trainers stand and framed by semicircular rows of seating. Acrylic windows enable spectators to view the mammals underwater either from their seats or from a special "splash zone"; two giant "vidiwalls" show close-ups of the mammals and help convey such concepts as the adverse effects of tuna nets on dolphins. The amphitheater has proven to be a valuable educational resource for the region, a hit for Baltimore's tourism industry, and a must-see attraction for self-respecting Baltimoreans.

Establishing a visual link with Pier 3, Grieves ensured that the exterior of the pavilion incorporated forms and motifs from the parent building, but he did not wish to copy it. Instead of pointing toward Federal Hill, as the peaks on the first building do, the pyramid atop the marine mammal pavilion has its highest point facing back toward Charles Center. Its trim is white instead of black—an allusion to the bright-dark contrast—and its roof is opaque rather than clear. Grieves believed the design well suited to interior use, given sun angles and other factors. While Cambridge Seven concentrated on making strong volumetric forms, Grieves and his partners seemingly paid more attention to surface details, such as window patterns and paint colors. Cambridge Seven used bright colors sparingly and with dramatic effect; the Grieves team used them throughout the building. The pavilion, on the south side particularly, does not exhibit the sculptural strength or simple lines of the building on Pier 3. Even so, on Pier 4, the dolphins and marine mammals that live there, not the building, supply the true center of attention. Close to the action, thanks to the Grieves design, visitors see dolphins in a new way and perhaps identify with them more closely as a result.

To design an expansion just north of the original building on Pier 3, featuring an exhibit on Australia's river canyons, directors of the National Aquarium in 2000 went back to Chermayeff and his colleagues. They had left Cambridge Seven in the 1990s and formed their own company, CSP (Chermayeff, Sollogub & Poole), to focus on aquarium design. Instead of continuing the same sort of building that stood on Pier 3, the architects came up with a design that in many ways represents the exact opposite: a glass cube that allows visitors to look in and see a fifty-foot waterfall and related habitats they can explore inside. While the original building is relatively dark and introverted, the addition would be bright and extroverted. While the old one relied on striking architecture to catch the eye, the design for the addition featured striking exhibitions, some spilling right onto the plaza. This daring approach succeeded in preserving the original building's appearance while adding a new dimension to attract visitors. The glass front provides a bold new face for the aquarium and makes a gesture of openness to the city. It also mirrors the way the aquarium has blossomed from a civic institution of limited means to one with great impact and a widespread community outreach. "We thought, if we don't try to replicate it, the other way is to treat it as an extrovert, in comparison with the introverted building" already on Pier 3, Bobby Poole later explained. Twenty years ago, "we had to design a building that was an experience on a pier. We were creating an architectural expression when there was no institution. Now that

Columbus Center, 1995, interior and exterior, designed by Zeidler Roberts Partnership, an exhibition space that was truly distinctive in concept and execution. Zeidler Grinnell Partnership/Architects

it's a very, very rich institution, with a lot of breadth and depth, we think it's appropriate to express the institution more than the architecture."[18]

The design for Columbus Center, which opened in 1995, blurred the line between business and pleasure. For the northern half of Piers 5 and 6, Zeidler of the Zeidler Roberts Partnership, architects of the Gallery at Harborplace, proposed a plan to combine laboratories for marine biotechnology with exhibit space, where visitors could see scientists at work. The original idea was for the scientists to come out of their labs during breaks and greet the public in the exhibit hall under a fabric canopy (the concept did not last, and the University of Maryland subsequently leased out the exhibit area to a private company, leaving the architectural expression unchanged). For Columbus Center, even more than the Gallery at Harborplace, Zeidler attempted to sum up everything about the Inner Harbor—work and play, public and private, imagination and reality—under one roof. Rather than being an either/or building, he designed a both/and building. He then went even further and proposed that the public half assume a kind of zoomorphic imagery, intended to reflect the activities inside. Its chief feature was a white ribbed Teflon skin, giving the impression that a giant sea serpent had taken up residence on the Inner Harbor; Mayor Schmoke described it as "science on the half shell." Like a giant shell or a mollusk, the architect said, "the sculptured white roof form will stand out during the day and glow like a beacon in the night."[19]

This organic roof covers a 33,300-square-foot exhibition area on the west side of the pier, with entrances on the north and south. It adjoins a five-level laboratory building on the east, a metal and glass structure with subdued high-tech detailing. Under the canopy, visitors can see through a glass wall into the research area. The idea of splitting the pier down the middle offered several organizational advantages. It resulted in a plan that was simple to follow and promoted activity along Pratt Street as well as the water's edge. It worked well with the idea of putting cars out of sight below wharf level. Most intriguing was the opportunity to explore dualities: serious/whimsical, hard/soft, organic/inorganic.

On an urban-design level, however, the building created more problems than it solved. While the design had the potential to generate activity along Pratt Street, it did little to pull together the hodgepodge of buildings already positioned around the Inner Harbor. A large part of the problem was that the two major forms were too close in size. There was no tension, no play, no fun side bouncing off the serious side, because one could not see the serious side from many angles. The clamshell top was an alien shape that only added to the cacophony of pyramids, canopies, and ranch-burger roofs in the area. Such a mix of geometries traveled a great distance from the unity and cohesion of the early Inner Harbor development.

The design for Columbus Center illustrated a tendency, perhaps a flaw, in the Inner Harbor's master plan, which placed pressure on buildings along Pratt and Light Streets to be "background" structures and practically forced all pier structures to be eye-catching, "foreground" buildings. Zeidler swallowed the bait, trying to make his building a prima ballerina when it might have worked better as part of the *corps de ballet*.

As sculptural expression, few if any late-century Baltimore structures surpassed the American Visionary Art Museum at the eastern foot of Federal Hill (Rebecca Swanston, Alex Castro and Davis, Bowen & Friedel), which opened in 1995. The project originated when city officials agreed to sell a curving brick building once used for trolley buses at the

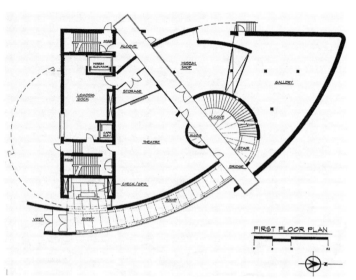

FIRST FLOOR PLAN

The eastern exterior and first-floor plan of the American Visionary Art Museum, showing how it adapted to the existing brick structure. Natural light brightens the stairway as it reaches the third floor. Photograph by Bill Lyons; Swanston & Associates

intersection of Key Highway and Covington Street to a group that wanted to build a museum that would showcase works by "visionary" or "outsider" artists, self-taught individuals not influenced by mainstream art. Swanston and Castro developed a plan not only for recycling the Trolley Works but also for enlarging it with an addition that echoed the curves of the original building and appeared to be in a constant state of motion. Its swirling exterior hints at the whirlwind of artistic ideas that confront visitors who go inside. Not since the National Aquarium had an Inner Harbor project displayed such architectural verve and energy.

At first glance, the design seemed to be one of the first local examples of deconstructivism—the architectural style in which walls or floors form unconventional, often unsettling, angles, frequently as commentary on the chaos and confusion of society. Signs of deconstructivism include the way the new building wraps around and pops through the shell of the existing structure. More than striving for the unconventional, however, this composition succeeds in an expressionistic purpose, sensitively following the bend of Key Highway and nestling into its setting between the harbor and Federal Hill. Its design gives the museum a nonthreatening mien and fits in well with the collection of attractions already around the harbor. In a sense, this sculptural assemblage symbolizes the creative process of the visionary artists whose work is displayed inside. Many of them took "found objects," such as toothpicks, matchsticks, or eggshells, and transformed them into works of art that reflect an intensely personal vision. On a larger scale, Swanston and Castro did the same, transforming their found object, the brick warehouse, into a work of art as intriguing and eccentric as any of the works inside—and every bit as spirited.

By the mid-1990s property owners, who of course had the most both to gain and to lose in the building-approval process, complained that the master plan that had guided development for so long was not being followed and that the city's development process lacked the certainty and predictability it once had. Some of them warned that developers would refuse to do business in Baltimore if the process were fluid, if rules that guided construction could be changed to suit one developer. They noted that no plan or a weak one would make Baltimore simply like other cities, with few design controls and no special character. City officials, eager to promote development, nonetheless continued to permit alterations to the master plan.

One of the most egregious examples involved the thirty-two-story Marriott hotel, which in 2000 opened in the Inner Harbor East renewal area. The city had commissioned Cooper, Eckstut & Associates to design a plan to guide development of thirty acres east of the central business district. Architect Stanton Eckstut recommended a mixed-use community similar to Battery Park City in lower Manhattan. Buildings were to step up in height as they stepped back from the water, just as they did around the Inner Harbor. His well-received plan, which had support from neighboring communities and elected officials, recommended a hotel rising no more than eleven stories at the water's edge. But the administration of Mayor Schmoke recommended that the Eckstut plan be amended to permit a high-rise hotel proposed by a politically connected developer, John Paterakis. Schmoke believed a larger hotel would bring more jobs and conventioneers to Baltimore and wanted to assist the developer with tax incentives. Citizen groups saw a larger building as a violation of the lengthy planning process and feared that it would cast Little Italy in shadows and bring more traffic congestion to the area. At meetings of the planning commission and city council they protested with placards that read, "Why Plan?" But the developer got his way and the tower went up— a symbol of the new, ad hoc approach to planning in Baltimore. It shows the damage that can occur when planners let down their guard and put greater value on launching new projects than on protecting what is already in place.

Camden Yards

For proof of the benefits of sound planning and creative design, one need look no farther than Camden Yards, where, in building two downtown stadiums, Baltimore played the roles of both follower and leader. By century's end, modern design had generally taken much of the life out of America's ball parks. Fans had become accustomed to watching baseball games in structures that resembled concrete donuts or flying saucers. Many stadiums had artificial turf and covered domes; they typically sat outside of town on an interstate highway and were built for more than one sport.

Since the 1970s, William Donald Schaefer had advocated building a downtown sports complex, and yet the original Inner Harbor plan had made no such provisions. Then, in the 1980s, team owner Eli Jacobs, a serious patron of architecture, and club president Larry Lucchino announced plans to move the Baltimore Orioles from venerable Memorial Stadium, on Thirty-third Street, to downtown Baltimore. The agency with oversight responsibility for any new ball park (and for enticing a professional football team to Baltimore), the Maryland Stadium Authority, working with RTKL as master plan coordinator and urban design consultant, hired HOK (Hellmuth, Obata + Kassabaum, Inc.), Sports Facilities Group of

Oriole Park at Camden Yards. Architects Hellmuth, Obata + Kassabaum produced this watercolor drawing for the Maryland Stadium Authority in March 1990. HOK Sport

Oriole Park upon completion, in April 1996, crowds thronging Eutaw Street, and a view of the old Bromo-Seltzer tower, showing the compatibility of the old railroad terminal, venerable warehouse, and new ball park. RTKL Associates; photograph by Mark B. Miller

Kansas City, to design it. Jacobs and Lucchino hired Janet Marie Smith, an architect and baseball buff, to serve as the Orioles' liaison with the stadium authority and HOK. The result of their collaboration was Oriole Park at Camden Yards, which opened in April 1992. It combined the character and quirkiness of classic baseball stadiums from the past with amenities fans had come to expect in the 1990s, while celebrating Baltimore as much as baseball.

Throughout the design and construction process, the team leadership, members of the stadium authority, and architects stayed true to the idea of creating "an ideal place in which to enjoy America's national pastime." As HOK senior vice president Joseph Spear put it, "They don't play the World Series in a bank. This is a place where memories are made."[20] The important decisions came early on—to put the ball park downtown, make it for baseball only, leave it open to the sky, and plant natural grass. Aligning the third-base line so that it ran due north meant that many of the 48,000 seats faced the downtown skyline, as a dramatic backdrop to the game. Saving the 1,116-foot-long B&O Warehouse yielded a one-of-a-kind right-field backdrop, one that rivaled Fenway Park's left-field wall, the "Green Monster," as one of baseball's most distinctive architectural features.

So many stadiums from the 1960s and 1970s looked like cold, alien objects because they were essentially feats of modern engineering, with little embellishment to add warmth or character. At Oriole Park, the architects took components that had typically been left to engineers, such as exit ramps and elevator towers, and turned them into architecture, cladding them in a red brick and precast stone veneer along with the rest of the façade. The brick treatment and arched openings represent a response to the brick warehouse and other buildings nearby, while giving the ball park a more human scale. Each façade looks different, reflecting the area it faces. The architects marked entries with street names as well as gate numbers, making it easy for fans to remember where they came in. Everything visible from the seats reinforces the theme of traditional baseball, from the color and shape of the slatted seats to the design of the steel sun screen. Although none of the construction budget had been set aside for public art, graphic designer David Ashton & Associates devoted attention to signs and banners, using the Camden Green logo of the 1890s Baltimore Baseball Club and an old-fashioned scoreboard with a vintage Oriole weather vane. The planting of hundreds of shrubs and trees helped to transform the area into a true park. Architects thus interwove the ball park with the character of the city.

This respectful treatment of the cityscape grew out of a master plan for the eighty-five-acre site that prescribed a way to knit the ball park into the area, rather than dropping it from the sky. Developed by RTKL Associates and Wallace Roberts & Todd, with help from the city planning department and others, the plan called for radical thinking about stadium design; saving the warehouse, it also reopened Eutaw Street as part of the lower concourse. Besides making good urban-design sense, the recommendations coincided with the old-time spirit the Orioles wanted to cultivate. Designers broke down the ball park's apparent scale by setting the upper deck back from the street, so passers-by saw what amounted to a five-story rather than a nine-story façade. Their decision to use steel trusses rather than concrete to support the upper deck made the building light and transparent, like many older ball parks. Setting the top deck back also resulted in the creation of a semicircular viewing platform five stories off the ground. Fans in search of refreshments enjoy splendid views of nearby Ridgely's Delight, the University of Maryland professional schools, and the central business district. Baltimore's "retro" park owes much to the spirit of its time and to postmodern preferences in American architecture.

Part of the innovation of Camden Yards was the idea of putting two major league stadiums side by side within the city, one for baseball and one for football. It was an urban variation of the suburban Harry S Truman sports complex outside of Kansas City—another HOK project. Although a football stadium was always part of the vision, planning for it intensified in 1994, when the Cleveland professional football franchise moved to Baltimore and became the Ravens. Once again the stadium authority turned to HOK to design the building, working within the master plan established by RTKL and Wallace Roberts & Todd. Six years after having designed Oriole Park, HOK could not overlook the differences in the two projects. To the north, Oriole Park nestled next to two historic buildings that set the tone for its architecture: the B&O Warehouse and the 1857 Camden train station. On the south, the Ravens' stadium was to occupy a former parking lot. While the baseball field was sunk eighteen and a half feet, the football stadium could not be buried so deep

The stadium HOK Sport designed for the Baltimore Ravens.
HOK Sport

because of a high watertable. The southern end of Camden Yards was more industrial than the north, and no adjacent buildings provided a transition in scale between the stadium and the rest of the city, as the right-field warehouse did for Oriole Park. The strongest architectural influence may have been a tangle of elevated highways.

When it opened in 1998, the stadium for the Ravens spoke with an honesty that befitted Baltimore and its working-class heritage. A bird of a different feather, it supplies no nostalgic references to the 1890s, no ornate scrollwork, no ornithologically correct weather vanes atop a vintage scoreboard. If Oriole Park is a graceful stroll into the past, the football sta-

The north lounge of the Ravens' stadium, an example of its striking interior details. Cho Benn Holback + Associates, photograph by Erik Kvalsvik

dium resembles a rocket blast into the future—bigger, bolder, and brawnier than its intimate, old-fashioned neighbor.

With 20,000 more seats and a 100-yard grid requiring a different approach to seating angles and sight lines, the Ravens project could not be a carbon copy of Oriole Park. For it, HOK developed a different vocabulary, one that started with the traditional brick feel of the baseball part but went on to reflect the grit of south Baltimore. The composition succeeds in being as modern as Oriole Park is traditional. Clad in brick and precast stone, with arched openings all around, the base of the stadium yields to a middle layer consisting largely of alternating sections of glass and exposed ramps, punctuated by brick towers. With green-tinted windows and pewter-colored steelwork, the exterior evokes a factory from the 1940s or 1950s. Vibrant purple seating further illustrated the Ravens' decision to create a stadium suited to their sport and personality rather than imitating their neighbor's. In between the purple seats on the upper and lower decks, the Ravens opted for a pewter-colored club level, which echoes the industrial materials used elsewhere in the building. Behind the glass walls of the club level, in the lounges and bars designed by the local firm of Cho, Wilks & Benn, one finds pleasant interior surprises. The local architects used an unconventional but pleasing palette of materials and colors—such as dark polished concrete for the bar surfaces—that play off the industrial feel of the exterior. One particularly impressive space, the north lounge, features high ceilings and a dramatic view of the downtown skyline. The graphics, again by David Ashton & Associates, include handsome, sans-serif lettering for the gates and suites and colorful banners that mark restrooms and concession stands. Intentionally understated, they pick up on the spare, Bauhaus-like quality of the architecture.

Above the midsection of the stadium its most prominent element—four upper decks—soar like the outstretched wings of a bird. This configuration departed from that of other stadiums, in which the upper deck forms one continuous oval. Here the architects eliminated the four corners, typically considered the worst seats, to create notches that permit views into and out of the seating bowl; they also lowered the upper decks at the ends, putting the seats closer to the playing field. On the north side, Wallace Roberts & Todd of Philadelphia designed a playful plaza, which helps bring the Eutaw Street experience from Oriole Park into the Ravens' domain. On the southwest corner, the same firm designed the landscape to suggest a grand piano—a sly reference to the Knabe piano factory, which once occupied the site. To the east, a light-rail pedestrian bridge takes passengers directly to the game without the need to cross any streets or train tracks. These touches show that the design team was serious about tailoring the stadium to its setting and creating a building that could only be right for Baltimore.

The *New York Times* architecture critic Paul Goldberger praised Oriole Park as "the best design for a major league baseball park in more than a generation," "a building capable of wiping out in a single gesture fifty years of wretched stadium design."[21] *Time* magazine included it on its annual list of best designs. The football stadium did not break new ground in the same way, but it does have its signature elements, and it fulfills the vision of making Baltimore the first city to create a dual-stadium sports complex in an urban setting.

Epilogue

If Charles Center, the Inner Harbor, and the two stadiums at Camden Yards provide any lessons for Baltimore and Maryland, it is the value of having a big idea, sticking with it, and executing it well. A two-stadium sports complex was not part of the original master plan for the Inner Harbor, but it gave the west side a strong anchor and an ideal way to attract visitors year round.

Harborplace and Camden Yards supplied bookends to a period of growth—not since the early part of the nineteenth century has the face of the city changed so dramatically—that would have been difficult to predict before the rebuilding occurred and that continue to shape the way the city grows and changes. From several perspectives, there are strong parallels between the two projects, including the energy that William Donald Schaefer took to one as mayor and to the other as governor. In urban-planning terms, the stadiums were capstones to the renaissance that Harborplace put in high gear, the culmination of city revitalization efforts throughout the 1970s and 1980s. The stadiums share with Harborplace the power to make an uplifting psychological impact on the city, over and above any direct physical or economic returns. Both serve as people magnets. Just as Harborplace uses shopping and dining as an excuse to bring people together, the stadiums use sports as an excuse to do the same. Each attraction draws people to the heart of the city. Yet they are not merely gathering places; each helps generate excitement about Baltimore, excitement that can be fueled by media coverage. Each shows that cities can be fun, addressing the basic yearning of people to come together and share time and space with each other.

Harborplace from Federal Hill in the late 1990s, in a view of the modern city that approximates the perspective of John Moale's mid-eighteenth-century sketch. Photograph by Marion E. Warren

The marketplace and the stadiums also put Baltimore on the cutting edge of national development trends, for the first time since the era of Latrobe, Godefroy, and Mills. In 1981 the Boston architect and critic Robert Campbell observed that festival marketplaces captured the spirit of the present age more than any other type of building. "Perhaps each generation creates a kind of mythic building type for itself," he wrote. "What the skyscrapers were to New York in the 1930s, the market is today: . . . the place where the god of the city has taken up residence for the moment; the place where you take the visiting cousins, the place, where, mysteriously, for a time, the Delphic air vibrates."[22] Seven years later, New York architect John Burgee made a similar observation, culturally accurate if also a bit worrisome, about sports arenas. Stadiums, he said, are "the most monumental structure that cities are building these days. They're not building City Halls. They're not building cathedrals. The sports palace is the new national meeting place." In terms of design and development, Harborplace and the stadiums were critical to what the noted planner Kevin Lynch called "the imageability" of the city.[23] They are well-designed, image-making buildings that became an integral part of Baltimore's identity—and of the collective consciousness of its residents. One might even say that if the glass and brass of Harborplace's pavilions could be seen as a feminine kind of place, the brick and steel of the stadiums make a perfect masculine counterpart. Both were places where locals could take out-of-towners when they wanted to show them a good time and put the city in a glowing light.

The modest or at least well-defined proportions of Charles Center, the original Inner Harbor, the Ravens' roost, and the avowedly old-fashioned approach to Oriole Park are perfectly appropriate for Baltimore, a city steeped in tradition and blessed with historic buildings that set the tone for the city. Architects demonstrated that Baltimore works well when it taps into what is authentic. Designers took these projects beyond the level of an engineering exercise and made them works of an architecture that responded to needs while capturing the city spirit. The lesson was not to make nostalgia the new cookie cutter; the lesson was that the best solutions come out of the place itself.

Before his death in 1996, former city planning director Larry Reich frequently voiced concerns at planning commission meetings and elsewhere about the danger of growth for growth's sake. A city or institution sets out to build and build, he warned, and before long it has managed to wipe out all the good things that made people want to be there in the first place. In the end, civic leaders are left with the same fundamental challenges they have always faced: How to bring in new ideas and solutions that will keep the city alive without destroying the scale and character that makes it worth saving and cherishing. How to grow in a way that is authentic and true to the place—not just grow for growth's sake. If they find a way to meet these ends, they will have discovered the secret to what makes Baltimore Baltimore.

GALLERY

GEORGIAN BALTIMORE, 1752–1790

Adam Boss house, Bond Street,
near Eastern Avenue, Fells Point.
Photograph ca.1880. Enoch Pratt
Free Library.

St Paul's Rectory, captured in a
detail of a painting by Thomas
Ruckle, ca. 1801. Maryland
Historical Society

FEDERAL DESIGNS, TOWN AND COUNTRY, 1789–1819

Willow Brook oval room, ca. 1799, as reconstructed in the Baltimore Museum of Art after demolition of the original house. The Baltimore Museum of Art: Gift of the City of Baltimore. Installation and renovation made possible by contributors to the Willow Brook Fund BMA 1965.8

Perspective view of Montibello, the Seat of Genl. S. Smith, Maryland, *colored engraving by William R. Birch, published in his* Country Seats, *1808. Maryland Historical Society*

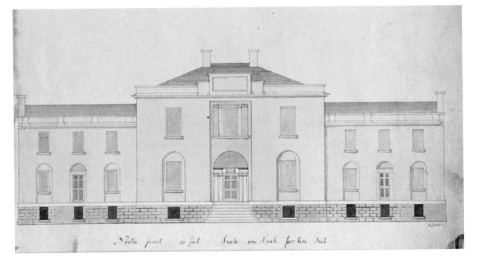

Oakland, north front, watercolored presentation drawing by Abraham Lerew, ca. 1810. Maryland Historical Society

"Baltimore Room." The second-floor front parlor from the house at 913 East Pratt Street, built ca. 1810 for merchant Henry Craig. The Metropolitan Museum of Art, Rogers Fund, 1918 (18.101–4). Photograph by Richard Cheek. Copyright The Metropolitan Museum of Art

Bentalou (later Dugan-Hollins house), on Water Street, in a late-nineteenth-century photograph. Maryland Historical Society

*Caton-Carroll house exterior. Enoch
Pratt Free Library*

MONUMENTAL BALTIMORE, 1806–1831

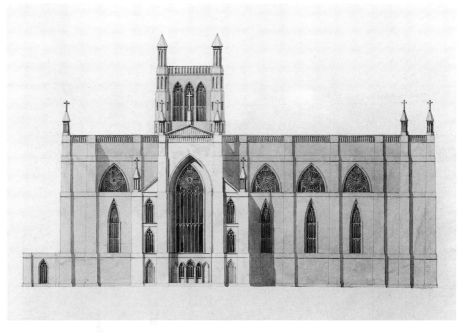

Benjamin Henry Latrobe's Gothic design for the Baltimore Cathedral. Watercolor on paper, 1805. Maryland Historical Society

Latrobe's perspectival watercolor of the Roman Catholic cathedral, ca. 1818. Maryland Historical Society

Interior of St. Mary's Chapel, mid-twentieth century. Peale Collection, Maryland Historical Society

Detail from View of the center of the Baltimore Exchange on Gay Street, as proposed to be built in 1816. *Watercolor on paper by Benjamin Henry Latrobe and Maximilien Godefroy. Maryland Historical Society*

Maximilien Godefroy's adopted plan for the Battle Monument, 1815, engraved by B. Tanner, Philadelphia. Maryland Historical Society

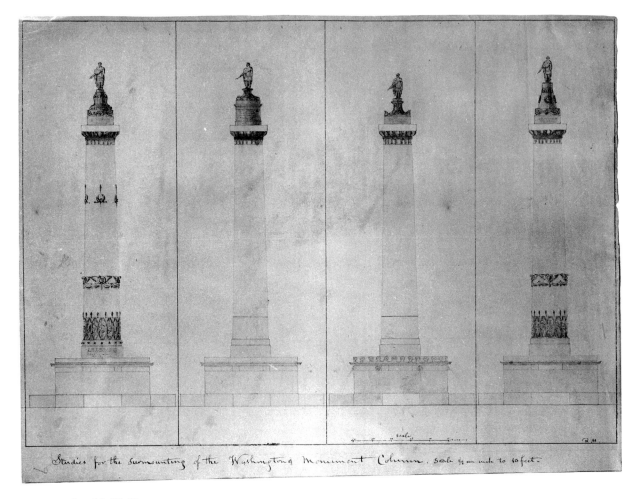

Studies for the surmounting of the Washington Monument Column. scale ½ an inch to 10 feet

Four studies of the Washington Monument, by Robert Mills, ca. 1815. Maryland Historical Society

Maximilien Godefroy's cross-sectional plan for the First Unitarian Church, showing dome and interior details. Peale Collection, Maryland Historical Society

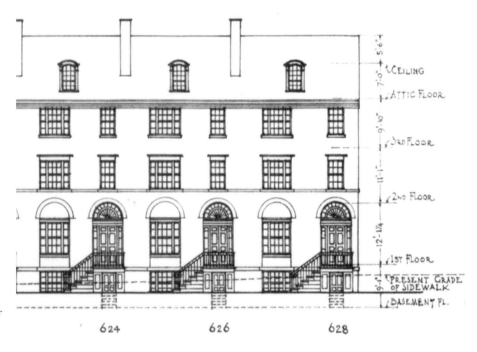

Detail from Waterloo Row, east elevation. Historic American Buildings Survey, Library of Congress

Waterloo Row, front parlor, as reconstructed at the Baltimore Museum of Art. Baltimore Museum of Art

Apostel St. Pauls, *St. Paul's Protestant Episcopal Church*, as designed by Robert Cary Long Sr. and built 1814–17. The engraving also depicts, below and right, the two predecessor buildings. Peale Collection, Maryland Historical Society

William Gwynn house, the Tusculum, built ca. 1820, as it appeared not long before demolition in 1891. Maryland Historical Society

THE REIGN OF THE ROMANTICS, 1829–1878

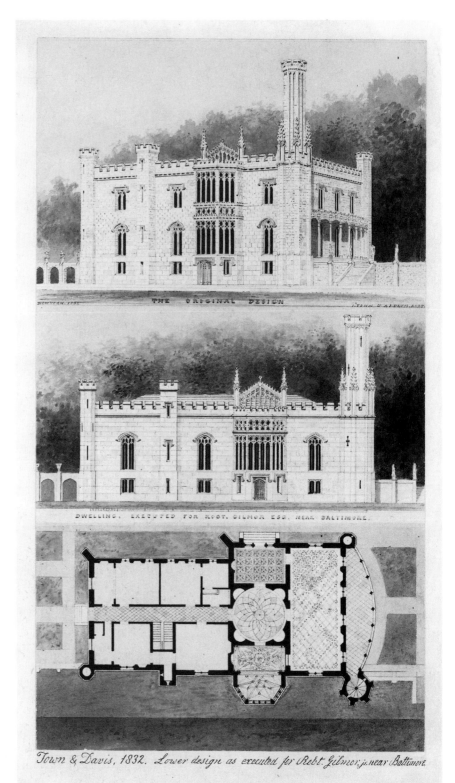

Designs for Glen Ellen, the Robert Gilmor house, north of Baltimore, by Ithiel Town and Alexander Jackson Davis, 1832. Gilmor's original, vaulting ambitions called for a two-story structure (top); the house as built was revised to just one story (center). Metropolitan Museum of Art, Harris Brisbane Dick Fund, 1924 (24.66.17)

German Catholic Church, Balto., *the design for St. Alphonsus drawn and etched by Robert Cary Long Jr., 1843. Maryland Historical Society*

The Athenaeum, front elevation, on St. Paul Street, drawn by Robert Cary Long, Jr., 1845. Maryland Historical Society

The north side of Franklin Street, west of Cathedral Street, showing the Gustav W. Lurman house in the center of the block, with its fourth story raised, and the W. F. Frick house to the left. Laurence Hall Fowler photograph, ca. 1910. The John Work Garrett Library of the Johns Hopkins University

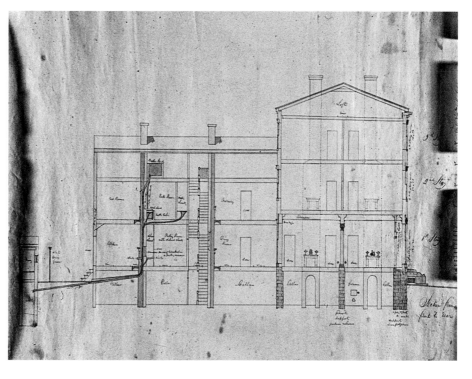

Section of a three-story Greek Revival–style Baltimore town house and back building, architect unknown. Baltimore Museum of Art

William McDonald's Italianate villa, Guilford, watercolor by Edmund G. Lind and William T. Murdoch, 1857–58. Maryland Historical Society

Interior of the First Presbyterian Church, the nave and altar viewed from the choir balcony. Photograph by Lanny Miyamota, September 1958. Historic American Buildings Survey, Library of Congress

Perspectival view of St. Paul's Episcopal Church, watercolor drawing by Richard M. Upjohn, 1854. Avery Architectural and Fine Arts Library, Columbia University in the City of New York

INDUSTRIAL DESIGNS, 1840–1917

Detail from The Union Manufactories of Maryland on Patapsco Falls Baltimore County. *Maximilien Godefroy sketched this model mill complex, which included housing for managers and workers as well as laundry and brick kiln, ca. 1810. Maryland Historical Society*

Poole & Hunt Union Works. Lithographed and published by A. Hoen & Co., Baltimore, ca. 1870. Maryland Historical Society

*Calvert Station, Baltimore &
Susquehanna Railroad, 1850.
Peale Collection, Maryland
Historical Society*

*Sun Iron Building as it appeared on
the sheet music for the "Sun Quick
Step," colored lithograph by A.
Hoen & Co., 1854. Maryland
Historical Society*

*Cutaway view, Baltimore Traction
Company railway cable power
house, this one placed in a former
Methodist church in 1892. From
Street Railway Journal,
March 1894, 160.*

ECLECTIC CITY, 1865–1904

*Brown Memorial Presbyterian
Church. From George W. Howard,*
The Monumental City: Its Past
History and Present Resources
(Baltimore, 1873), 436.

Baltimore American Building, designed by Dixon & Carson, built 1873–75. From A History of the City of Baltimore, Its Men and Institutions *(Baltimore: Baltimore American, 1902), frontispiece. Enoch Pratt Free Library*

*Mount Vernon Place Methodist
Church, designed by Dixon &
Carson, 1872. Peale Collection,
Maryland Historical Society*

Abell Building, designed by George A. Frederick and completed in the late 1870s. From Howard, Monumental City, 832.

The Johns Hopkins Hospital and School of Medicine upon completion, from the northwest, ca. 1900. Maryland Historical Society

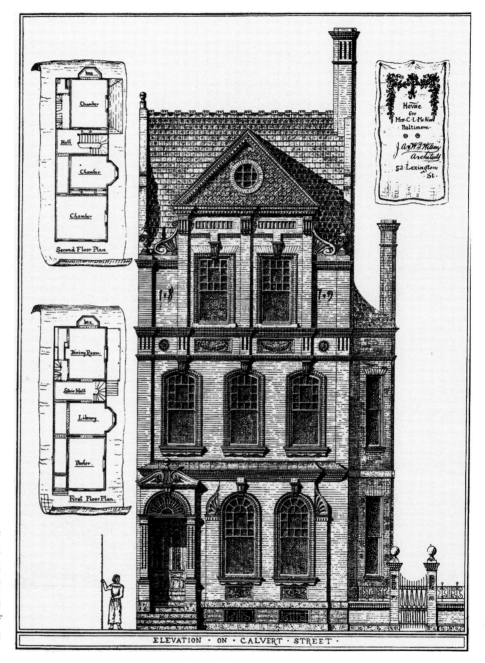

McKim house, 1035 North Calvert Street, designed by J. Appleton Wilson and completed in 1879, when this elevation and plan appeared in American Architect and Building News. *Courtesy of Mary Ellen Hayward*

Detail from Hutzler Bros Store,
212–218 North Howard Street,
designed by Baldwin &
Pennington, 1886. From Frank
Leslie's Illustrated Weekly,
Supplement, *October 27, 1888.*
Courtesy of Arthur J. Gutman

Goucher Hall of the Women's College of Baltimore, with Lovely Lane Church in the background, west side of St. Paul Street, north of Twenty-second Street, designed by Charles L. Carson and completed in 1887. Maryland Historical Society

Associate Reformed Church, northwest corner of Maryland Avenue and Preston Street, designed by Charles Cassell, 1889. Enoch Pratt Free Library

Oheb Shalom Synagogue, northeast corner Eutaw Place and Lanvale Street, designed by Joseph E. Sperry, 1891. The Jewish Museum of Maryland Institutional Archives

*House of Ross Winans, east side
1200 block of St. Paul Street,
designed by McKim, Mead &
White, 1882, as it appeared in
American Architect and Building
News, April 30, 1887. Maryland
Historical Society*

Detail of West Mount Vernon Place showing the Robert Garrett house as designed by Stanford White in 1884. Lithograph from "In and About Baltimore," Harper's Weekly, *September 7, 1889, 716.*

Continental Trust Building, southeast corner of Baltimore and Calvert Streets, designed by Daniel H. Burnham, 1899. Maryland Historical Society

Alexander Brown & Sons building, southwest corner of Baltimore and Calvert Streets, designed by Parker & Thomas, 1901. Maryland Historical Society

MODERNISMS, MODERNISTS, AND MODERNITY, 1904–1955

Walters Art Gallery, begun in 1905, completed in 1909. Maryland Historical Society

Baltimore Museum of Art, designed by John Russell Pope, as completed in 1929. Maryland Historical Society

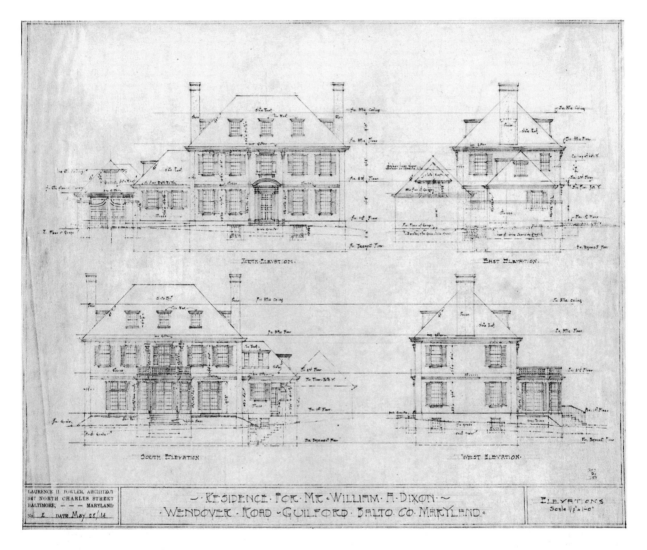

Elevations for the residence of William M. Dixon, Wendover Road, Guilford, by Laurence Hall Fowler, 1914, modeled on the eighteenth-century James River plantation house, Westover. The John Work Garrett Library of the Johns Hopkins University

Washington Apartments, Mount Vernon Place, designed by Edward H. Glidden, 1905. Maryland Historical Society
BOTTOM:
Alexander Smith Cochran house, 901 West Lake Avenue, 1950. Garden façade as it appeared in House and Garden, *January 1951, 51.*

BUIILDING A RENAISSANCE, 1955–2000

Detail from Helmud Jacobi's rendering of the Sun Life Building (Peterson & Brickbauer, in association with Emery Roth & Sons), completed in 1966 on Hopkins Plaza. Martin Millspaugh chose the drawing for the cover of the Urban Land Institute's Technical Bulletin 51, *which appeared in November 1964 and focused on the Charles Center project, "A Case Study in Urban Renewal." Courtesy of Martin Millspaugh*

Harborplace according to the planners' vision: specialty-shop and food-gallery pavilions, snapping pennants, and large peaceful crowds. The Rouse Company, with Benjamin Thompson Associates, architects, and Carlos Diniz, artist/renderer

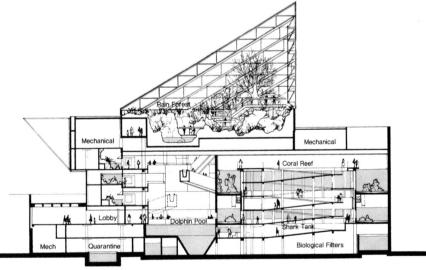

SECTION

A sectional view of the National Aquarium. Cambridge Seven Associates, Inc., photograph by Steve Rosenthal

Lobby interior of the renovated and restored Mount Royal Station, a Cochran, Stephenson & Donkervoet project, which opened in 1967. Cochran, noted his biographer, "took pride in having saved the marble floors and columns and most of the ceiling when he transformed this 1896 train station into the Maryland Institute, College of Art."
From Christopher Weeks, Alexander Smith Cochran: Modernist Architect in Traditional Baltimore *(Baltimore: Maryland Historical Society, 1995), 150. Maryland Institute, College of Art*

Detail from Oriole Park at Camden Yards. Architects Hellmuth, Obata + Kassabaum produced this watercolor drawing for the Maryland Stadium Authority in March 1990. HOK Sport

The Maryland Institute, College of Art, opened the Brown Center—the first new building at the college in nearly a century—in the fall of 2003, to house the school's digital arts program. The building encloses 61,000 square feet in a crystalline form that grew out of the constricted site, which suggested creativity, innovation, and an aesthetic of contrast to the architects. Exposed concrete supports an unusual several-sided silicone-glazed curtain wall system. Its translucent geometry contrasts strikingly with, and provides dramatic counterpoint to, the white marble of the Renaissance Revival main building across the street. Courtesy of Zigler/Snead and Charles Brickbauer

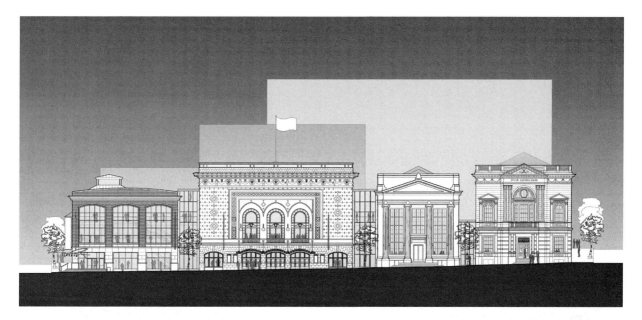

The restored Hippodrome Theatre at the France-Merrick Performing Arts Center, an anchor in plans to redevelop the city's west side, including North Eutaw and Howard Streets, as it appeared in an artist's rendering of about 1999. Designed by the Scottish architect Thomas W. Lamb, the Hippodrome, at 12 North Eutaw Street, opened in 1914 as a richly appointed vaudeville establishment, became a motion-picture theater in 1949, and closed in 1990. After the turn of the new century, the France-Merrick Foundation led efforts to renovate the building (then owned by the state of Maryland) and make it part of an almost full-city-block theater complex that would overcome the limitations of the original, shallow Hippodrome—incorporating the shells of two former bank buildings to the north; creating reception, backstage, and restaurant spaces; and providing ample parking. A New York firm specializing in theater restoration, Hardy Holzman Pfeiffer Associates, with Murphy & Dittenhafer, of Baltimore, headed the design team; Schamu Machowski Greco, another local firm, handled construction administration. The Hippodrome Theatre reopened in February 2004. Courtesy of the Hippodrome Foundation, Inc.

NOTES

1 | GEORGIAN BALTIMORE, 1752–1790

1. For petition see William Hand Browne, ed., *The Archives of Maryland*, 72 vols. to date (Baltimore: Maryland Historical Society, 1883–), 36: 464. Quoted in Garrett Power, "Parceling Out Land in Baltimore, 1632–1796," pt. 1, *Maryland Historical Magazine* 87, no. 4 (1992): 460.

2. See Power, "Parceling Out Land," 460, for a reference to the survey by Richard Gist.

3. Thomas W. Griffith, *Annals of Baltimore* (Baltimore, 1833), 32.

4. Lease to Robert Long from Edward Fell, August 16, 1765. Liber AL, no. D, folio 206, Maryland State Archives, Annapolis, Md.

5. In this period, the limits of glass-blowing technology restricted the size of clear-glass panes; as methods improved later in the century, larger panes became available. By the 1790s, six-over-six windows were common; by the 1850s, four over four; and by the 1870s, two over two. One-over-one windows, seen in most late-nineteenth-century houses, were not available until the introduction of plate-glass technology.

6. In a manuscript given to the Maryland Historical Society in 1851, John H. Naff described houses "painted red" or green; see "Recollections of Baltimore," *Maryland Historical Magazine* 5 (Mar. 1910): 104–23. Robert Gilmor Jr., in a paper read before the society on May 9, 1844, remembered yellow-painted houses; see "Recollections of Baltimore," *Maryland Historical Magazine* 7 (Sept. 1912): 233–42.

7. Gilmor, "Recollections of Baltimore," 233–42. For the interested student of early Baltimore houses, both Gilmor and Naff give almost block-by-block descriptions of the houses and businesses of the revolutionary era. See also Claire Wittler Eckels, "Baltimore's Earliest Architects" (Ph.D. diss., The Johns Hopkins University, 1950).

8. John Pendleton Kennedy, "Baltimore Long Ago," in *At Home and Abroad* (New York, 1872), 180.

9. John Adams, *The Diary and Autobiography of John Adams*, 2 vols. (Cambridge, Mass: Harvard Uni-

versity Press, Belknap Press, 1961), 2:257–58, quoted in Barbara Wells Sarudy, *Gardens and Gardening in the Chesapeake, 1700–1805* (Baltimore: Johns Hopkins University Press, 1998), 20.

10. Gilmor, "Recollections of Baltimore," 241.

11. Sarudy, *Gardens and Gardening in the Chesapeake,* 130, 134–35.

12. Gilmor, "Recollections of Baltimore," 241.

13. Count Gallatin, ed., *The Diary of James Gallatin: Secretary to Albert Gallatin, A Great Peacemaker, 1813–1827* (New York: Charles Scribner's Sons, 1930), 246.

14. Mary Ambler and Adams quoted in Sarudy, *Gardens and Gardening in the Chesapeake,* 48.

15. See Lance Humphries, "Provenance, Patronage, and Perception: The Morris Suite of Baltimore Painted Furniture," in *American Furniture, 2003,* ed. Luke Beckerdite (Milwaukee: Chipstone Foundation, distributed by the University Press of New England, 2003), 152–53, 197. Lance Humphries, William Voss Elder, and Peter Pearre assisted in the drafting of this passage.

16. *Federal Intelligencer and Baltimore Daily Gazette,* Apr. 15, 1795, quoted in Matthew Page Andrews, *The Fountain Inn Diary* (New York: Richard R. Smith, 1948), 62–63.

17. Charles E. Peterson, FAIA, *Notes on Hampton Mansion,* with an Introduction by Lynne Deakin Hastings, Glossary by Gregory R. Weidman, References updated and expanded by R. Kent Lancaster and Lynne Deakin Hastings; Sally Sims Stokes, ed., and Jennifer J. Snyder, technical ed., 2d ed., rev. (College Park, Md.: National Trust for Historic Preservation, Library Collection of the University of Maryland Libraries, 2000).

2 | FEDERAL DESIGNS, TOWN AND COUNTRY, 1789–1819

1. François-René de Chateaubriand, *Mémoires d'Outre-Tombe,* 2 vols. (Paris: Quarto, Gallimard, 1997), 1:407.

2. *Maryland Journal,* Aug. 10, 1792, quoted in Mills Lane, *Architecture of the Old South: Maryland* (New York: Abbeville Press, 1991), 84.

3. Baltimore *Federal Gazette,* Oct. 24, 1803, quoted in Stiles T. Colwill, *Francis Guy, 1760–1820* (Baltimore: Maryland Historical Society, 1981), 4.

4. Médéric Louis Elie Moreau de Saint-Méry, *Moreau de St. Méry's American Journey, 1793–1798,* ed. and trans. Kenneth Roberts and Anna M. Roberts (Garden City, N.Y.: Doubleday & Co., 1947), 79; *Niles' Weekly Register,* Sept. 19, 1812.

5. Robert Adam, *Works in Architecture of Robert and James Adam* (1773), quoted in John Summerson, *Architecture in Britain, 1530–1830* (Harmondsworth, Eng.: Penguin Books, 1970), 425–26.

6. *Maryland Journal,* Oct. 6, 1789. Quotations from artisanal newspaper advertisements in this chapter derive from Rodris Roth, "Interior Decoration of City Houses in Baltimore: The Federal Period," *Winterthur Portfolio* 5 (1969): 62–63, and, ultimately, from Alfred Coxe Prime, *The Arts and Crafts in Philadelphia, Maryland, and South Carolina, 1721–1785: Gleanings from Newspapers* (Topsfield, Mass.: Walpole Society, 1929), and Prime, *The Arts and Crafts in Philadelphia, Maryland, and South Carolina, 1786–1800: Gleanings from Newspapers* (Topsfield, Mass.: Walpole Society, 1932).

7. *Maryland Journal,* Apr. 1, 1788.

8. *Federal Gazette,* Apr. 22, 1797.

9. Robert L. Alexander, "The Riddell-Carroll House in Baltimore," *Winterthur Portfolio* 28 (1993): 122.

10. *Maryland Journal,* July 2, 1795.

11. Ibid., Apr. 13, 1792, Apr. 20, 1784.

12. *Federal Gazette,* Jan. 20, 1808.

13. *Federal Intelligencer,* Aug. 18, 1795.

14. Thomas Twining, *Travels in America 100 Years Ago: Being Notes and Reminiscences of Thomas Twining* (New York: Harper & Bros., 1894), 82.

15. Ibid.

16. Officials levying the federal direct tax of 1798 assessed the value of both Bolton and Belvidere at $4,000, a princely sum for the period.

17. Robert Gilmor Jr., "Memoir or Sketch of the History of Robert Gilmor of Baltimore," MS 30, Maryland Historical Society.

18. Twining, *Travels in America,* 118.

19. Carroll of Carrollton to Carroll Jr., Jan. 30, 1801, and July 31, 1803, Carroll Family Letters, Maryland Historical Society.

20. *Federal Intelligencer and Baltimore Daily Advertiser,* October 3, 1795, quoted in Lane, *Architecture of the Old South: Maryland,* 84, 90.

21. Baltimore *American and Commercial Advertiser,* March 11, 1820, cited in Lane, *Architecture of the Old South: Maryland,* 237, no.81. Lane mentions French publication of the plans but offers no specifics (125).

22. Ferdinand Marie Bayard, *Travels of a Frenchman in Maryland and Virginia, with a Description of Philadelphia and Baltimore in 1791,* ed. and trans. Ben C. McCary (Williamsburg, Va.: The Editor, 1956), 160; American Commentator James Kent, quoted in Fred Shelley et al., eds., "A New Yorker in Maryland, 1793 and 1821," *Maryland Historical Magazine* 47 (summer 1952): 193; Twining, *Travels in America,* 85.

23. Twining, *Travels in America,* 82.

24. Smith to P. and U. Filliccki, Sept. 21, 1796, vol. 3, Smith Letterbooks, 1774–1818, Ms. 1152, Maryland Historical Society.

25. *Federal Gazette and Baltimore Daily Advertiser,* Feb. 25, 1800.

26. These and the following descriptions of the Riddell-Carroll House come from Alexander, "Riddell-Carroll House," 113–39.

27. John H. Scarff, Notes on Allender House, 4 Baltimore 23, Historic American Buildings Survey, Maryland, Library of Congress.

28. Robert Gilmor Jr., "Family Record," 52, Gilmor Papers, Ms. 2682, Maryland Historical Society.

29. *Baltimore Gazette and Daily Advertiser,* Oct. 23, 1832.

30. John H. B. Latrobe, *Picture of Baltimore, Containing a Description of All Objects of Interest in the City; and Embellished with Views of the Principal Public Buildings* (Baltimore, 1832).

31. "Recollections of George A. Frederick," a paper presented to the Baltimore Chapter of the AIA, October 1912. Maryland Historical Society.

32. This passage and those following rely heavily on the research published in Mary Ellen Hayward and Charles Belfoure, *The Baltimore Rowhouse* (New York: Princeton Architectural Press, 1999).

33. For further information on rows of this type, see Mary Ellen Hayward, "Urban Vernacular Architecture of Nineteenth-Century Baltimore," *Winterthur Portfolio* 16, no. 1 (1981): 33–63.

34. Robert L. Alexander, "Baltimore Row Houses of the Early Nineteenth Century," *American Studies* 16 (fall 1975): 74.

35. Thomas W. Griffith, *Annals of Baltimore* (Baltimore, 1833), 250–51.

36. Isaac Weld, *Travels through the States of North America,* 3d ed. (London, 1800), 45.

37. James Kent, quoted in Shelley et al., "A New Yorker in Maryland, 1793 and 1821," *Maryland Historical Magazine* 47 (summer 1952): 139; James S. Buckingham, *America, Historical, Statistic, and Descriptive,* 3 vols. (London, 1842), 1:426.

38. Latrobe, *Picture of Baltimore,* 81.

3 | MONUMENTAL BALTIMORE, 1806–1831

1. *Newport* (Rhode Island) *Mercury,* June 28, 1790, quoted in *Maryland Historical Magazine* 19 (summer 1924): 196–97.

2. John Pendleton Kennedy, "Baltimore Long Ago," in *At Home and Abroad* (New York, 1872), 181.

3. Baltimore *Federal Gazette,* Mar. 30, 1822.

4. Médéric Louis Elie Moreau de Saint-Méry, *Moreau de St.-Méry's American Journey, 1793–1798*, ed. and trans. Kenneth Roberts and Anna M. Roberts (Garden City, N.Y.: Doubleday & Co., 1947), 79.

5. Adlard Welby, *A Visit to North America and the English Settlements in Illinois, with a Winter Residence at Philadelphia* (London, 1821), 290.

6. Henry Russell Cleveland, "American Architecture," *North American Review* 43 (Oct. 1836): 372 and passim, quoted in Phoebe B. Stanton, *The Gothic Revival and American Church Architecture: An Episode in Taste* (1968; Baltimore: Johns Hopkins University Press, 1997), 164.

7. Latrobe to Godefroy, July 19, 1815, in *The Correspondence and Miscellaneous Papers of Benjamin Henry Latrobe*, ed. John C. Van Horne et al., 3 vols. (New Haven: Yale University Press, 1964–88), 3:674.

8. Robert Mills to Board of Commissioners, Jan. 14, 1814, and Oct. 30, 1820, and to Robert Gilmor Jr., Dec. 14, 1820, July 6, 1827, and June 30, 1830, Washington Monument Papers, Ms. 876, Maryland Historical Society. Thanks to Robert L. Alexander and Frank R. Shivers Jr.

9. *Memoirs of John Quincy Adams, comprising Portions of His Diary from 1795 to 1848*, ed. Charles Francis Adams, 12 vols. (Philadelphia: J. B. Lippincott, 1847–77), 7: 338.

10. Talbot Hamlin, *Benjamin Henry Latrobe* (New York: Oxford University Press, 1955), 219.

11. A description of the interior and furnishings appeared at the time of Oliver's death in the *American and Commercial Daily Advertiser,* Oct. 2, 1835. See Mills Lane, *Architecture of the Old South: Maryland* (New York: Abbeville Press, 1991), 103, 236.

12. Library Company records, Maryland Historical Society, cited in Lane, *Architecture of the Old South: Maryland,* 107.

13. Rogers to the Rev. James Kemp, Feb. 2, 1814, Archives of the Episcopal Diocese of Baltimore, cited in Lane, *Architecture of the Old South: Maryland,* 108.

14. Museum-opening announcement quoted in Charles Coleman Sellers, *Charles Willson Peale,* 2 pts. (1947; New York: Scribner's, 1969), 2: 278.

4 | THE REIGN OF THE ROMANTICS, 1829–1878

1. Frances Trollope, *The Domestic Manners of the Americans* (London, 1839), 171; Frances Wright, *Views of Society and Manners in America . . .* (New York: E. Bliss and E. White, 1821), 361.

2. John C. Gobright, *The Monumental City; or, Baltimore Guide Book* (Baltimore, 1858), 59.

3. John E. Semmes, *John H. B. Latrobe, 1803–1891* (Baltimore: Norman Remington Co., 1917), 557–58.

4. [Sir Francis Palgrave], "Normandy–The Architecture of the Middle Ages," *Quarterly Review* (London) 25 (Apr./July 1821): 116–17.

5. *Baltimore Sun,* May 8, 1843.

6. Ibid., Sept. 1, 1843.

7. Ibid., May 4, 1843.

8. Robert Cary Long Jr., "Gothic Architecture: A New Church," *United States Catholic Magazine* 2 (May 1843): 302, quoted in Phoebe B. Stanton, *The Gothic Revival and American Church Architecture: An Episode in Taste* (1968; Baltimore: Johns Hopkins University Press, 1997), 229.

9. Robert Cary Long Jr., "On the Development of the Semi-Arch with the Future Advancement of Architectural Art," *Civil Engineer and Architect's Journal* 5 (Nov. 1842): 370.

10. Inscription on original drawing, Maryland Historical Society.

11. *Baltimore Sun,* Oct. 1, 1846.

12. *Literary World* 3 (Oct. 14, 1848): 759.

13. R. Cary Long, *The Ancient Architecture of America . . .* (New York: Bartlett & Welford, 1849), 5.

14. See original drawings in the Washington Monument Papers, MS 876, Maryland Historical Society.

15. *Catalogue of the Splendid Library and Philosophical, Chemical and Astronomical Apparatus of the late Dr. William Howard* (Baltimore, 1843), as discussed and cited in Mills Lane, *Architecture of the Old South: Maryland* (New York: Abbeville Press, 1991), 146, 237.

16. *Republican and Argus*, Sept. 6, 1842; with thanks to John McGrain.

17. *Baltimore Sun*, Apr. 3, 1846.

18. Ibid., Feb. 27, 1846.

19. Ibid., Aug. 1 and Nov. 9, 1848.

20. Ibid, Dec. 1, 1848.

21. Ibid., Jan. 24, 1851.

22. Ibid., Sept. 30, 1851.

23. Ibid., Feb. 10, 1853.

24. Ibid., Jan. 24, 1855.

25. Gobright, *The Monumental City*, 93

26. Ibid., 65.

27. *Baltimore Sun*, Mar. 28, 1851. The Maryland Institute, an association of inventors, scientists, and manufacturers based loosely on the Franklin Institute in Philadelphia, was founded in 1826 but disbanded in 1837 after a terrible fire had destroyed its headquarters. In 1847 the group reorganized and began plans for its imposing new building.

28. Gobright, *The Monumental City*, 85–90.

29. *Baltimore Sun*, June 4, 1850, June 21, 1852.

30. Ibid., Dec. 14, 1859.

31. Ibid.

32. Nathaniel H. Morison, "Eleventh Annual Report of the Provost to the Trustees of the Peabody Institute of the City of Baltimore, June 1, 1878," 27, Peabody Institute Library.

5 | INDUSTRIAL DESIGNS, 1840–1917

1. Charles R. Weld, *A Vacation Tour in the United States and Canada* (London, 1855), quoted in Raphael Semmes, *Baltimore As Seen by Visitors, 1783–1860* (Baltimore: Maryland Historical Society, 1953), 162–63.

2. Gilman quoted in "Baltimore," *St. Nicholas* 20 (Aug.1893): 732–33.

3. *The Monumental City, the Liverpool of America: A Souvenir of the 121st Anniversary of the Baltimore American* (Baltimore, 1894), 24.

4. *Municipal Journal*, Apr. 11, 1913, quoted in Sherry H. Olson, *Baltimore: The Building of an American City*, rev. and expanded ed. (Baltimore: Johns Hopkins University Press, 1997), 245.

5. This paragraph and those following draw heavily from John W. McGrain, *Gristmills in Baltimore County, Maryland* (Towson, Md.: Baltimore County Public Library, 1980), 2–7 and passim. See also Dennis M. Zembala, ed., *Baltimore: Industrial Gateway on the Chesapeake* (Baltimore: Baltimore Museum of Industry, 1995), and various Maryland Historical Trust–Baltimore Museum of Industry site surveys, Maryland Historical Trust, Crownsville, Md., and Baltimore Museum of Industry, Baltimore.

6. See Robert M. Vogel, ed., *Some Industrial Archeology of the Monumental City and Environs* (Washington, D.C.: Society for Industrial Archeology, 1975).

7. *Baltimore Sun*, May 2, 1856. Reference supplied by John McGrain.

8. Vogel, *Monumental City and Environs*, 8. Carlos P. Avery, *E. Francis Baldwin, Architect: The B&O, Baltimore, and Beyond* (Baltimore: Baltimore Architecture Foundation, 2003), 54, and Zembala, *Baltimore: Industrial Gateway*, 137–38, also comment on the structure.

9. *Western Brewer*, May 15, 1887, 1012.

6 | ECLECTIC CITY, 1865–1904

1. Stephen Bonsal, "The New Baltimore," *Harper's New Monthly Magazine* 92 (1896): 331.

2. George W. Howard, *The Monumental City: Its Past History and Present Resources* (Baltimore, 1873), 67.

3. Ibid.

4. *The City Hall, Baltimore: History of Construction and Dedication* (Baltimore: By Authority of the Mayor and City Council, 1877), 106.

5. Howard, *Monumental City,* 252.

6. *Baltimore Sun,* Jan. 31, 1876.

7. AIA constitution, quoted in Henry H. Saylor, *The A.I.A.'s First Hundred Years* (Washington, D.C.: Octagon, 1957), 11.

8. *American Architect and Building News* 1 (Jan. 1, 1876): 9.

9. *Baltimore Sun,* Nov. 21, 1877.

10. Howard, *Monumental City,* 64.

11. Ibid., 339.

12. Ibid., 333.

13. McGhee Harvey and Susan L. Abrams, "John Shaw Billings: Unsung Hero of Medicine at Johns Hopkins," *Maryland Historical Magazine* 84 (summer 1989): 127–29.

14. *American Architect and Building News* 3 (May 11, 1878): 165–66.

15. *Baltimore Sun,* Oct. 7, 1884.

16. Ibid.

17. *American Architect and Building News* 8 (Aug. 14, 1880): 73, illustrated the original design.

18. Ibid. 22 (Oct. 14, 1882): 182.

19. *Baltimore Sun,* Aug. 20, 1883.

20. Henry Hudson Holly, "Modern Dwellings: Their Construction, Decoration, and Furniture," *Harper's New Monthly Magazine* 52 (1875–76): 855–67, quoted in Mary Ellen Hayward and Charles Belfoure, *The Baltimore Rowhouse* (New York: Princeton Architectural Press, 1999), 91. The following three quotations derive from this same source.

21. *Baltimore Sun,* Nov. 21, 1877.

22. *American Architect and Building News* 6 (Sept. 27, 1879): 102.

23. Ibid. 12 (Oct. 14, 1882): 183.

24. Although Lovely Lane was Stanford White's first church, it was not Baltimore's first ecclesiastical building in the Richardsonian mode, having been preceded by the 1878 Church of St. Michael and All Angels at St. Paul and Twentieth Streets, the result of a winning competition entry by local architects James Bosley Noel Wyatt and Joseph Evans Sperry.

25. Lewis Mumford, *The Brown Decades: A Study of the Arts in America, 1865–1895* (1931; New York: Dover Publications, 1971), 58.

26. The buildings were donated by Benjamin F. Bennett, a trustee of the college and the contractor responsible for Lovely Lane Church and Goucher Hall, as memorials to his wife.

27. *American Architect and Building News* 17 (May 1885): 491.

28. *Baltimore Sun,* Sept. 18, 1888.

29. The building closely resembles Yale University's Osborn Hall in New Haven, designed by Bruce Price and published in *American Architect and Building News* in March 1890.

30. *Baltimore Sun,* May 19, 1890, Sept. 25, 1891.

31. Ibid., May 2, 1881.

32. Ibid., Sept. 20, 1888.

33. Henry Pratt Janes, quoted in John Dorsey and James D. Dilts, *A Guide to Baltimore Architecture,* 3d. ed. (Centreville, Md.: Tidewater Press, 1997), 135; see also Dorsey, *Mount Vernon Place: An Anecdotal Essay with Sixty-six Illustrations* (Baltimore: Maclay & Assoc., 1983), 15.

34. *Baltimore Sun,* Nov. 17, 1891.

35. Ibid., 1894, and quoted in Frederick N. Rasmussen, "The Stafford: A Grand Old Dame Falls on Hard Times," in ibid., Sept. 30, 2000.

36. Frank R. Shivers Jr. interview with spokesman for COUNT, Baltimore, Aug. 8, 1995.

37. William J. Fryer Jr., "Skeleton Construction: A New Method of Constructing Tall Buildings,"

Architectural Record 1 (1891–92), quoted in Sara E. Wermiel, *The Fireproof Building: Technology and Public Safety in the Nineteenth-Century American City* (Baltimore: Johns Hopkins University Press, 2000), 147.

38. *Baltimore Sunday Herald*, June 11, 1893, quoted in Peter E. Kurtz, "Benjamin Buck Owens (1848–1918)," *Historic Architects' Roundtable Newsletter* (Baltimore), May 20, 1992.

39. See Phoebe B. Stanton, "Baltimore in the Twentieth Century," in Dorsey and Dilts, *Guide to Baltimore Architecture*, 36.

40. Henry James, *The American Scene* (1907; New York: St. Martin's Press, 1987), 220.

7 | MODERNISMS, MODERNISTS, AND MODERNITY, 1904–1955

1. Henry James, *The American Scene* (1907; New York: St. Martin's Press, 1987), 223, 225.

2. Sherry H. Olson, *Baltimore: The Building of an American City,* rev. and expanded ed. (Baltimore: Johns Hopkins University Press, 1997), 302.

3. City Plan Commission, *Municipal Journal*, May 19, 1919: 1.

4. Olson, *Baltimore*, 320–21.

5. W. W. Emmart, "Report on Housing and Commercial Conditions in Baltimore," unpublished manuscript, 1. Maryland Department, Enoch Pratt Free Library.

6. Palazzo Ducale, Sala dello Scrutinio, *Il Campanile de San Marco: Il Crollo e la Ricostruzione* (Venice: Silvana Editoriale, 1992), 48.

7. "The Bank Buildings of Baltimore," *Architectural Record,* Aug. 1907, 89.

8. Alexander S. Cochran, "Baltimore Architecture Today," in John Dorsey and James D. Dilts, *A Guide to Baltimore Architecture* (Centreville, Md.: Tidewater Press, 1973), xlv-l.

9. Quoted in Charles A. Platt, *Italian Gardens* (Portland, Ore.: Sagapress/Timber Press, 1993), 15.

10. Wright quoted in Keith N. Morgan, *Charles A. Platt* (New York: Architectural History Foundation, 1985), 69.

11. Delano (Feb. 1950) quoted in William R. Johnston, *William and Henry Walters, the Reticent Collectors* (Baltimore: Johns Hopkins University Press, 1999), 166.

12. "Baltimore's Changing Skyline," *Sunday Sun,* Nov. 29, 1908; *Evening Sun,* Sept. 10, 1923, Feb. 7, 1927, and June 11, 1934.

13. Report, 1933, Maryland Department, Enoch Pratt Free Library, quoted in full in Dorsey and Dilts, *A Guide to Baltimore Architecture,* 105.

14. James, *The American Scene,* 227.

15. Baltimore Municipal Art Society, *Report upon the Development of Public Grounds for Greater Baltimore* (1904; Baltimore: Friends of Maryland's Olmsted Parks and Landscapes, 1987), 30, 62, 67.

16. See *American Architect,* Mar. 5, 1927, 313.

17. Charles Keefe, *The American House* (New York: U.P.C. Book Co., 1922), 17. See also *Architectural Record,* Oct. 1919, 238.

18. *A Book of Pictures in Roland Park* (Baltimore: Norman T. A. Munder & Co., 1912) includes several photographs of houses in Goodwood Gardens but credits all houses illustrated in the book to such local architects as Wyatt & Nolting, Ellicott & Emmart, and Edward L. Palmer Jr., with no mention of Platt. Perhaps Platt roughed out some ideas for the block and left Wyatt to oversee actual construction.

19. Edith Wharton, *The Age of Innocence,* ed. Michael Nowlin (Peterborough, Ont.: Broadview Literary Texts, 2002), 327.

20. *Billy Baldwin: An Autobiography*, with Michael Gardine (Boston: Little, Brown, 1985), 29–30.

21. *Evening Sun,* Nov. 28, 1911.

22. Commissions, 1913/11, Fowler Collection, John Work Garrett Library, The Johns Hopkins University.

23. *Architectural Forum* 41, no. 4 (Oct. 1924): 203.

24. Commissions, 1914/06, Fowler Collection, John Work Garrett Library, The Johns Hopkins University; Keefe, *The American House*, 18 and pl. 118–20.

25. John H. Scarff, "The Maryland War Memorial, Baltimore. Lawrence Hall Fowler, Architect," *Architectural Forum* 43 (1925): 68.

26. Commissions, 1925/08, Fowler Collection, John Work Garrett Library, The Johns Hopkins University.

27. Roland Park covenant, quoted in Egon Verheyen et al., eds., *Laurence Hall Fowler, Architect (1876–1971)* (Baltimore: Johns Hopkins University, 1984), 40.

28. Wharton, quoted in ibid., 49.

29. For Wharton quote and Verheyen comment, see ibid., 51.i

30. Henry Hyde, "Roland Park and Guilford: An Appreciation," *Gardens, Houses, and People* 6, no. 7 (1931): 7.

31. Bottomley, quoted in John Taylor Boyd, "The Country House and the Developed Landscape: William Lawrence Bottomley Expresses His Point of View," *Arts and Decoration* 31 (Nov. 1929): 98.

32. *Baltimore Sun,* May 1, 1915.

33. See Mary Ellen Hayward and Charles Belfoure, *The Baltimore Rowhouse* (New York: Princeton Architectural Press, 1999), 130 ff.

34. "Aesthetic Diatribe," *Evening Sun,* Feb. 7, 1927.

35. *Baltimore Sun,* May 25, 1909.

36. Quoted in Henry McBride, "A Private Theater by Bakst," unidentified clipping, Evergreen House files.

37. See Charles Spencer, *Leon Bakst* (New York: Rizzoli International Publications, 1973), 214–15.

38. Walter Lippmann to Alice Garrett, June 25, 1925, Garrett Collection, John Work Garrett Library, The Johns Hopkins University.

39. Mary Tyler Cheek to Christopher Weeks, Mar. 12, 1992.

40. Ada Louise Huxtable, *Have You Kicked a Building Lately?* (New York: Quadrangle/New York Times Book Co., 1976), 227.

41. Walter Gropius, *Apollo in the Democracy: The Cultural Obligation of the Architect* (New York: McGraw-Hill, 1968), 9, 29.

42. "Modern Architecture—International Style" opened in February 1932. Brendan Gill called the exhibition a "turning point in the history of American architecture . . . after which the then prevalent douce tyrannies of the Beaux-Arts tradition could no longer be unthinkingly accepted" (*New Yorker,* Apr. 27, 1932, 93).

43. Mencken, "The New Architecture," *American Mercury* 22 (Feb. 1931): 164.

44. Cochran on Wright quoted in Jeff Kosnet, "Cochran Plans to Move Over So Others Can Rise in Design Firm," *Sunday Sun,* Oct. 15, 1978, quoted in Christopher Weeks, *Alexander Smith Cochran: Modernist Architect in Traditional Baltimore* (Baltimore: Maryland Historical Society, 1995), 34. Cochran-related citations below also draw upon this second work.

45. Mrs. George Constable (nee Elizabeth Whedbee) in conversation with Christopher Weeks, Mar. 19, 1994.

46. Cochran, "Baltimore Architecture Today," xlix-l; *Evening Sun,* May 20, 1971. In a conversation with Weeks, May 17, 1992, Esta Maril commented on Cochran's commissions; see also Phoebe Stanton, "Architecture: The Art of Public Purpose," *Sunday Sun,* Jan. 21, 1974.

47. James H. Bready, "Architect's New Home Embodies Ideas That Make Housing News, *Baltimore Sun,* Apr. 14, 1950; *Washington Post,* May 27, 1951.

48. "Shopping Strip," *House and Home,* May 1953, 148–49.

49. *Baltimore Sun,* 1959, quoted in Weeks, *Alexander Smith Cochran,* 129.

8 | BUILDING A RENAISSANCE, 1955–2000

1. Gerald Johnson's reference to James Boswell, *The Life of Samuel Johnson, LLD,* 3d ed. (1799; 2 vol. repr., New York, 1933), 2:137, quoted in Frank R. Shivers Jr., *Bolton Hill: Baltimore Classic* (Baltimore: John Maclay Assoc., 1978), 42.

2. Lamb, quoted in *Baltimore: A Living Renaissance,* ed. Lenora Heilig Nast, Laurence N. Krause, and R. C. Monk (Baltimore: Historic Baltimore, 1982), 204.

3. See Shivers, *Bolton Hill,* 42.

4. Mark Girouard, *The English Town* (New Haven: Yale University Press, 1990), 313.

5. "The Conservation of Taxable Real Estate Values in Baltimore"(1952), 26. Maryland Department, Enoch Pratt Free Library.

6. *Fortune* magazine quoted in *Traditions for the Future* (Baltimore: Mercantile-Safe Deposit & Trust Co., 1997), 15.

7. Millspaugh and Pillorge quoted in Edward Gunts, "What's Wrong with This Picture?" *Baltimore Sun,* Apr. 8, 2001.

8. Koubek quoted in Edward Gunts, "USF&G Building: A Giant That Told of Wonders to Come," *Baltimore Sun,* Jan. 1, 1995.

9. Chermayeff quoted in Edward Gunts, "High-Water Mark: A Cube of Glass and Water," *Baltimore Sun,* Aug. 12, 2001.

10. Ibid.

11. Avrum Kampf, quoted in Edward Gunts, "Temple's Future Set in Stone," *Baltimore Sun,* Oct. 9, 1999.

12. *A Merchant in Search of Pearls: The Story of Baltimore's New Cathedral, the Cathedral of Mary Our Queen* (Baltimore: Archdiocese of Baltimore, 1958), 13.

13. Alexander S. Cochran, "Rethinking American Architecture Today," in John Dorsey and James D. Dilts, *A Guide to Baltimore Architecture* (Centreville, Md.: Tidewater Press, 1973), 4–5.

14. Ibid.

15. *Architectural Forum,* Mead, and Goldberger quoted in Christopher Weeks, *Alexander Smith Cochran: Modernist Architect in Traditional Baltimore* (Baltimore: Maryland Historical Society, 1995), 62, 151; *New York Times,* June 2, 1996.

16. *New York Times,* Aug. 21, 1995.

17. Chermayeff quoted in Gunts, "High-Water Mark."

18. Poole quoted in ibid.

19. Schmoke and Zeidler quoted in Edward Gunts, "The World's First Mer-Building: Columbus Center Plan Neither Fish nor Fowl," *Baltimore Sun,* Mar. 22, 1992.

20. Spear quoted in Edward Gunts, "This Diamond Is a Cut Above: Oriole Park at Camden Yards Celebrates Baltimore, Baseball," *Baltimore Sun,* Mar. 22, 1992.

21. Paul Goldberger, "A Radical Idea: Baseball as It Used to Be," *New York Times,* Nov. 19, 1989.

22. Robert Campbell, "Evaluation: Boston's 'Upper of Urbanity' Faneuil Marketplace after Five Years," *AIA Journal,* June, 1981, 31.

23. Burgee, and Lynch, quoted in Edward Gunts, "Stadium and Marketplace: Milestones in Development," *Baltimore Sun,* Apr. 5, 1992.

GLOSSARY

Anthemion	Decorative floral or leaf pattern modeled on ancient Greek forms.
Architrave	The lowest part of a classical entablature; the horizontal beam resting directly on the columns.
Balustrade	A low railing, often hiding the roof.
Bay	The portion of a façade equivalent to the width of a door or window unit.
Belt course	Projecting- or molded-brick line along the exterior of a building, usually at the level of a floor; a stringcourse.
Bluestone	A bluish-grey sandstone.
Bow room	A polygonal or an oval room, one end of which projects out from the exterior wall so as to overlook or open onto the grounds of a house.
Classical orders	Tuscan, Doric, Ionic, Corinthian, and Composite column, base, and capital designs from ancient Greece and Rome.
Clerestory	A structure running the length of a building above the main roof line, its windowed walls providing light to the space below.
Corbel	A block (typically stone or timber) projecting from a wall to support the beams or eave of a roof, floor, vault, or similar feature; often elaborately carved.
Cornice	The crowning, or upper, part of a wall or entablature.
Dado	The lower part of a wall when decorated.
Dentils	The small, toothlike elements decorating friezes, usually set directly beneath the cornice, often in conjunction with modillions.
Dependency	In Palladian or Georgian design, an outlying building connected to the central block by a hyphen.

Dormers	Windows, usually with triangular pediments, set into gable roofs to light the attic story.
Engaged column	A half-round column.
English basement	The ground-floor, entry level of a Palladian-style building, often scored or rusticated, which supports the floor above.
Entablature	The upper part of a classical order, consisting of the horizontal architrave, which rests on the columns or pilasters, the decorative frieze above, and the crowning cornice.
Façade	The front, or face, of a building.
Finial	The upper part of a decorative element, including those features marking the corner or apex of a roof, gable, or pediment.
Flemish bond	A method of laying brick so that, for added strength, stretchers (long sides of bricks) and headers (ends) alternate in each row.
Frieze	The portion of the entablature set between the architrave and the cornice, usually decorated; a decorative band running around a room beneath the cornice; the decorated portion of a mantel.
Gable roof	A steeply pitched roof, usually with its ridgepole running parallel to the street.
Gambrel roof	A roof with a broken pitch, an obtuse angle making the lower slope steeper than the upper.
Glazed brick	Kiln-treated brick with a glossy surface.
Hipped roof	A roof whose four sloping sides meet to form a ridge or center.
Hyphen	The smaller structure that provides an indoor passageway between—or structurally connects—the central block and outlying buildings in Palladian or Georgian design.
Jack arch	A stone or brick lintel with projecting keystone.
Lintel	The horizontal top piece of a window or door opening.
Loggia	In a building façade, a recessed space open to the air on one side; an open-air room or entrance arcade.
Lunette	An arched or rounded window, usually semicircular.
Metope	Sets of vertical markings decorating friezes, representing the ends of the wooden roof joists used in ancient frame temple construction.
Modillion	Blocklike, often carved forms that decorate the frieze on classical buildings and help support the cornice; often used in association with dentils.
Molded	Decorative shapes or designs given to projecting members or pieces of a design.
Muntins	The horizontal and vertical moldings used to create multipaned windows.
Oculus	An eyelike circular opening in the pediment of a building.
Ogee	A form made up of convex and concave curves used for moldings, arches, and small roofs.
Oriel window	A large bay window, sometimes extending the height of two floors, and usually supported by a corbel or bracket.
Palladian window	A three-part window, often used to mark the center bay of façades, consisting of a large, central, arched window flanked by smaller panes; also known as a Venetian window.
Pavilion	An element projecting from a façade to create architectural emphasis.
Pediment	A crowning decorative element, usually a triangular form.
Pendentive	The triangular part of a groined vault that springs from the corners of a room or from a column to support a dome above.
Pent roof	A short shed roof marking a façade at the top of the first-floor level.

Piano nobili	The main floor of an Italian palace, one story above ground level.
Piazza	A covered porch, veranda.
Pilaster	A slightly projecting, flattened column decorating a façade or interior wall.
Portico	A colonnaded space—detached, attached, or recessed—with columns supporting the roof on at least one side.
Quoins	Cut stone pieces (or other building materials), flat and butt sides alternating, which add strength and decoration to the corners of a building.
Reveal	A flat, shallowly recessed plane, particularly under a façade arch.
Rusticated	Cut, marked, or beveled, usually said of stone, so as to appear irregular or "rustic."
Sallyport	The arched passageway running back between early-nineteenth-century row houses, leading to the rear yard.
Sash	The upper and lower portions of a double-hung window.
Soffit	The underside of a structural beam or arch.
Stringcourse	*See* belt course.
Stucco	Plaster or cement coating used to cover façades.
Terra cotta	Fired or baked molded clay used for exterior decorative elements in the later nineteenth century.
Vault	Stone or brick arched covering.
Venetian window	*See* Palladian Window.
Wainscot(ing)	Wooden lining or paneling on a wall, usually the lower part; any decorative element on the lower part of a wall.
Water table	A projection of the lower masonry or brickwork on the exterior of a wall, at or near the first-floor level, typically marking the break between basement and first floor.
Weatherboarding	Overlapping horizontal wooden boards that form the exterior of early frame buildings.

ACKNOWLEDGMENTS

It may help to shape these acknowledgments of valuable assistance if one recalls a Welsh proverb: "Three things for which thanks are due: an invitation, a gift, and a warning."

GIFTS that arrived at this book's birth and during its development greatly assisted us. We express thanks for them all—whether ideas, funding, time, advice, information, or encouragement. At the outset of the project in the early 1990s, Walter Schamu, FAIA, approached a major Baltimore benefactor, H. Furlong Baldwin, who, as president of Mercantile-Safe Deposit & Trust Co., quickly showed generous interest in our progress. We hope that this volume both pleases him and rewards his considerable patience. How fitting that this architectural record of nearly three centuries enjoys the major sponsorship of a venerable hometown bank.

Mr. Baldwin's challenge grant helped to generate monetary support as well as services from multiple Baltimore organizations. The list of them includes Schamu Machowski Greco Architects, Inc.; Cho Benn Holbach & Associates, Inc.; Marshall Craft Associates, Inc.; RTKL Associates, Inc.; Cochran, Stevenson & Donkervoet, Inc.; Ayers/Saint/Gross, Inc.; Heery, Inc.; Kann & Associates, Inc.; Rubeling & Associates, Inc.; Alex. Brown & Sons Charitable Foundation; AIA Baltimore; Baltimore Heritage; Municipal Art Society of Baltimore City; Baltimore Building Congress and Exchange; and the Larry Reich Memorial Fund.

We would also like to thank Mr. and Mrs. Roger Redden, Mrs. John W. McNair, Mrs. Ann Delsheimer, Mr. and Mrs. Mike Craft, Ms. Sherrie L. Kormann, and Dr. Phoebe B. Stanton for their generous contributions.

We gratefully acknowledge yet another generous gift toward this book's unusually high design and production expenses, a major grant from Furthermore, a program of the J. M. Kaplan Fund, in New York City. We count Mr. Peter W. Davidson, chair of the fund, and Joan K. Davidson, trustee and chair emeritus, among the staunchest friends of architectural scholarship in America.

This book should also please the extensive membership of COUNT (Contractors and Unions Together), who gave money and provided fresh insights into our architecture. Led by Bernard Vondersmith and William Amelia, COUNT's representatives introduced us to the hidden interior workings of buildings and the talented men who put in such things as plumbing, elevators, electrical systems, and air conditioning. Making their mastery of old and new technology available to us, they can boast of playing a major part in the building of this book.

Early on, we received a different kind of gift, the blessing of Richard Hubbard Howland, co-author, with the late Goucher College professor Eleanor P. Spencer, of *The Architecture of Baltimore* (Johns Hopkins Press, 1953). When published, their book (and the accompanying exhibit created by Wilbur Hunter, director of the Peale Museum) first brought attention to the importance of the city's architecture, and their clear prose and well-chosen illustrations provided many lasting insights.

Since illustrations expand our text so richly, we are glad to thank contemporary Baltimore-based architectural firms for gifts of drawings and photographs (we mention those individuals who were our contact persons): Tim Elliott of CSD; Cathy Fialkowski of Cho Benn Holback & Associates; Thomas S. Brudzinski and Candy D. Wood, the Rouse Company; Marigan H. O'Malley of RTKL Associates, Inc.; Mabel F. Smith of Swanston & Associates, Inc.; W. Peter Pearre of Trostel & Pearre; Charles Brickbauer of Ziger, Snead & Brickbauer. These firms belong in the long parade of talented local architects, beginning with the Robert Cary Longs, father and son.

Thanks also are due to contemporary out-of-town architectural firms: Dagmar von Schwerin, Cambridge Seven Associates, Inc.; Helen J. Maib and Carrie Plummer, Hellmuth, Obata & Kassabaum, Inc.; Rosalind Yang, Zeidler Grinnell Partnership/Architects; and Julie Eakin, Moshe Safdie & Associates. Firms from outside Baltimore have been adding to this city's architectural heritage since the great days of Godefroy, Latrobe, and Mills.

For the past two decades perhaps the most talked-about recycler of the city's landmark industrial architecture has been Struever Bros., Eccles & Rouse. Fortunately, the company allowed us to go through their photographs and choose what we needed. As another major force in changing old Baltimore into new, Martin L. Millspaugh, of Enterprise Development Corp., shared some of his experiences with us, drawing on his work at Charles Center–Inner Harbor Management. His first-hand knowledge stretches back to "urban renewal" days, when he wrote an influential small book about Baltimore's old housing stock in the neighborhood that is now the parlor district called Bolton Hill but was then the rather neglected area called Mount Royal. Developer Stanley Paritz lent us images of Bolton Common.

For assistance with obtaining original images, photographs, or high-resolution scans of architectural landmarks, we thank the legendary photographer Marion Warren, press author, and his assistant, Joanie Surette; Edward C. Papenfuse Jr., Maryland state archivist and press author; the Baltimore-area photographers Bill Lyons, Mark B. Miller, Wayne Nield,

Edwin Remsberg. and J. Brough Schamp; Barbara Wells Sarudy, press author; Prof. Frances Ferguson, Highfield House; Dr. Amy Macht, whose family owns Frank Lloyd Wright's Euchtman house; Richard B. North, M.D., owner of the Marcel Breuer house; Allison Parker of the Cordish Company; Arthur J. Gutman, Lance Humphreys, and Garrett Power, Baltimore; Tricia Pyne, the Associated Archives at St. Mary's Seminary and University, Baltimore; Douglas P. McElrath and Joanne Archer, Marylandia and Rare Books Department, University of Maryland Libraries, College Park; Ruth Henderson, Maryland State Law Library, Annapolis; Gwen Doak, Lovely Lane Church Archives; Kim Carlin, Maryland Institute, College of Art; Jim Hall and his staff, Baltimore City Planning Department; Mark Dawson, Baltimore Streetcar Museum; Michelle Winner of Port Discovery; Tom Kiefaber, Senator Theatre; Lou di Gennaro and Angela Giral, Avery Architectural and Fine Arts Library, Columbia University in the City of New York; Rebecca Akan of the Metropolitan Museum of Art; Kia Campbell, the Library of Congress; and Jeanne Solensky, librarian of the Downs Collection of Manuscripts and Printed Ephemera, the Winterthur Museum.

Beginning with Walter Schamu—who among others founded the Baltimore Architecture Foundation and who served as its first president—leaders of the BAF, notably Jillian Storms, Jarrod S. Walpert, and Charles B. Duff Jr., helped in any way they could with the book project. They, including Archibald Rogers, founder of RTKL, gathered financial and offered moral support; when we faced the task of collecting illustrations for the final chapters, the BAF assigned its knowledgeable and capable acting director, Adam Blumenthal, to tackle it. As the project neared completion, Walter happily permitted a member of his own firm, Rosalie Fenwick, to come to our aid by producing computer-assisted drawings of rowhouse types. We thank Adam and Rosalie for their cheerful and steadfast help over the past year.

INVITATIONS are the second reason for giving thanks, according to the Welsh proverb. We employ the word as meaning a cheerful willingness to open one's door and reply to requests. Many archivists, curators, librarians, and other professional workers were thus inviting as we came knocking. We were particularly fortunate to have the broad support of the Maryland Historical Society staff—from specialists to the director, Dennis A. Fiori—and its resources. We have particularly burdened Robert I. Cottom, Nancy Davis, Barbara Weeks, Mary Markey, Francis O'Neill, and especially the staff photographer, David Principe.

If we had space we could cite hundreds of times we received help from other professionals in various stations. What follows is grateful acknowledgment of assistance from a magic circle of friends. Sometimes it was in the form of a short answer to a phoned question. Sometimes librarians faxed needed pages. But most importantly, colleagues shared photographic resources and their own specialized knowledge. Beginning with university library staff, thanks therefore go to Cynthia H. Requardt and Amy Kimball, Special Collections, and James K. Stimpert, Ferdinand Hamburger Archives, both at the Milton S. Eisenhower Library, the Johns Hopkins University; Nancy McCall, Heidi Herr, and Gerard Shorb, the Alan Mason Chesney Medical Archives, the Johns Hopkins Medical Institutions; Anne Garside of the Peabody Institute of the Johns Hopkins University, Elizabeth Schaaf, Peabody Institute archivist, and Robert Follett, head librarian, the Arthur Friedheim Library, Peabody Institute of the Johns Hopkins University.

We owe one of our largest debts to Jeff Korman and his staff—Don Bonsteel, Nancy Derevjanik, Mendy Gunter, Lee Lears, Kristen Romano, Eva Slezak—in the Maryland Department of the Central Branch, Enoch Pratt Free Library, Baltimore. They always served well beyond the librarian's call of duty and offered generous access to all of the library's visual collections.

Invitations to come and explore came from professional colleagues at various museums and landmark buildings. For their unstinting help we thank James A. Abbott, Jay Fisher, and Sona Johnston of the Baltimore Museum of Art; William R. Johnston of the Walters Art Museum; Tyler Gearhart, director, and Kathleen F. Kreul, outreach coordinator, Preservation Maryland; Nancy Perlman, long-time archivist at the Baltimore Museum of Industry, and her successor, Carrie A. Albert; Robert J. Lancelotta Jr. of the Basilica of the Assumption Historic Trust, Inc.; Avi Y. Decter, director, and Erin Titter, archivist, of the Jewish Museum of Maryland; Courtney B. Wilson, director, and Anne Calhoun, archivist, of the B&O Railroad Museum; Chris Wilson of Civic Works at Clifton Mansion; and Lynne Dakin Hastings, Hampton National Historic Site.

Special thanks go to two steadfast friends of the project. John McGrain of the Baltimore County Planning Department, who—while tending to regular duties—for years has recorded, nurtured, and preserved much of Baltimore's past, both in the city and county. He painstakingly answered our every question and shared much original research. So did preservation architect James T. Wollon Jr., FAIA, driving force behind the Baltimore Architecture Foundation's Historic Architects' Round Table (also known informally as the "Dead Architects' Society"). He reviewed various drafts of the manuscript and helped answer many specific queries. Thanks also go to the many long-time members of the Roundtable, whose multiyear investigations into the careers of Baltimore's architects served as a critical basis of information for this volume. William Voss Elder and Lance Humphries aided us with last-minute corrections.

Another dedicated student of Baltimore's architectural history, the late preservation architect Michael F. Trostel, helped immeasurably with work on the early chapters. Mike had the Baltimore past on the tip of his tongue and shared it with us, usually punctuated with humor.

WARNINGS supply a final reason for offering thanks, says Welsh wisdom. The definitions of "warning" that fit into this paean of thanks include (1) admonishing as to action; (2) cautioning or calling for the use of prudence, as in avoiding unpleasant consequences; (3) and apprising in advance. These meanings fittingly describe the help we have enjoyed from a number of people:

Jim Wollon, who, besides being a wealth of information, was one of the great admonishers. W. Peter Pearre, another contributing architect, preservationist, and warner, shared his deep understanding of local architecture and also his scholarly rigor, which he credits in part to the standards of his late partner, Michael F. Trostel.

Also by way of warning we had in front of us earlier books on Baltimore architecture.

Following Howland and Spencer's groundbreaking 1953 text, two local scholars, John Dorsey and James D. Dilts, have kept alive an interest in the city's architectural heritage through three updated editions of *A Guide to Baltimore Architecture,* first published in 1973. It has remained a favorite on area bookshelves. In 1991, in the Maryland volume of his series on architecture of the Old South, Mills Lane gave us a detailed and heavily illustrated look at Baltimore's classic antebellum buildings. Other work has focused on Baltimore's indigenous row houses—Natalie W. Shivers' *Those Old Placid Rows: The Aesthetic and Development of the Baltimore Rowhouse* (1981) and Mary Ellen Hayward and Charles Belfoure's *The Baltimore Rowhouse* (1999). The many other books of value to us appear in the chapter notes.

At the Johns Hopkins University Press we owe debts that mere listing cannot repay. Barbara Lamb, as copy editor, served as the quintessential "warner" and "admonisher," carefully shaping the final text and making sure that *all* queries were answered. Melody Herr, as assistant to Bob Brugger, history and regional books editor, deserves our thanks for cheerful attention to many requests and details. Bob, himself, always acted as the chief advisor, cheerleader, cautioner, admonisher, and appriser. For more than a decade he shepherded this challenging project through to completion. He generously gave attention to every line, footnote, and illustration, making sure that this book was the very best that it could be.

Finally, we must end with sadness. Over the course of preparing this volume, we lost two of our major contributors. The first, Dr. Robert Alexander, long-time professor at the University of Iowa, was a nationally recognized scholar of America's pre-eminent classical revival architects—Latrobe, Godefroy, and Mills, and was largely responsible for the chapter entitled "Monumental Baltimore." And only recently, as we received the designer's sample pages, we learned of the death of one of our major contributors, Dr. Phoebe B. Stanton, former professor of architectural history at the Johns Hopkins University, local design advocate, and active preservationist. Phoebe always demanded that we create a book worthy of Baltimore and its underappreciated treasures. We hope the sum of all our efforts will live as a memorial to her and to her scholarly dedication to her adopted city.

INDEX

Note: Page numbers in *italics* indicate illustrations; entries in SMALL CAPS denote buildings that the city has lost.

THE ARCHITECTURE OF BALTIMORE

AN ILLUSTRATED HISTORY

EDITED BY *Mary Ellen Hayward and
Frank R. Shivers, Jr.*

Designed by Kathleen Szawiola

*Typeset in Monotype Dante and Adobe Syntax
by Graphic Composition*

Printed in the United States by Maple Vail